The Awakening Of Death

DAVID E. JONES

SOCCIONES

Copyright © David E. Jones 2020

All rights reserved.

David E. Jones has asserted his right under the Copyright, Designs and Patents Act 1988 to be identified as the author of this book.

No part of this publication may be reproduced, distributed, or transmitted in any form or by any means, without the prior written permission of the author, except in the case of brief quotations embodied in critical reviews and certain other non-commercial uses permitted by copyright law.

For permission requests, contact the author.

ISBN: 9798588964470

Typesetting and cover design by Socciones Editoria Digitale
www.socciones.co.uk

This book is dedicated to my biggest teachers:
my nan, my mum, my dad, Deano, Louise and Bella.

Contents

Introduction i

1. First Memories 1

2. Dad 4

3. My Light 6

4. Primary School 8

5. More Than A Friend 14

6. Secondary School 16

7. A Cheeky Chappy 19

8. Secondary School: The Later Years 21

9. College 31

10. The Party Years 34

11. Enough of All This! 44

12. Working in the Pub and Drinking in the Pub 49

13. The Final Straw 51

14. That Special Someone Who Helps You to See Things Differently 55

15. Something Still Lacking 61

16. Unconditional Love 64

17. A Beautiful Teacher 71

18. A Fresh Start 77

19. LoubyLou 84

20. The New Job 90

21. A Unique Opportunity 92

22. The Wedding.. 93

23. Stars in Their Eyes... 98

24. Life Goes On.. 105

25. When the Student is Ready, the Teacher Appears 109

26. The Fortune Teller 113

27. A New Path 119

28. Is Every Meeting Just a Coincidence? 123

29. Choosing Your Life Path and Lessons 130

30. Soul Mates, Karma and Reincarnation.................................... 138

31. The Ego 147

32. The Ego and Others 156

33. Your Body Is Not Who You Think You Are............................... 165

34. Possessions and Pack Mentality 169

35. Taming the Ego and Unconscious Behaviour with Observation.................... 175

36. Meditation and Awareness 181

37. Lessons of life 189

38. Living in the Moment; The Here and Now 203

39. Religion 210

40. S&S... 226

41. Media and Sugar... 238

42. Time to Exit the Ego Express 247

43. Law of Attraction 252

44. The Power of the Subconscious Mind, Science and Healing 266

45. Ailments and Dis-ease 284

46. Nutrition and Exercise 297

47. Our Brief Holiday on Planet Earth: What Souvenirs Will You Take Back with You? 310

48. Heaven, Hell, Dying, Souls & Spirit 319

49. The Power of Perception 333

50. Teachers 340

51. Identifying Fear and Substituting It for Love 350

52. What Is God? 359

53. Telling Others What to Do 376

54. Enlightenment 380

55. Dean's Description of The Divine 386

56. Conclusion 393

57. My Book in 30 Points! 407

58. Signing Off 418

Poems 422

Suggested reading 424

Suicide Helplines 425

INTRODUCTION

I will never forget watching *Danny Dyer's Deadliest Men* when I was younger. At that time in my life, he was a person who I mimicked and aspired to be like. In my eyes he was funny, cocky and had charm, a real character that I thought women were attracted to. My friends also thought he was funny, so in my insecure mind, I thought that I would adopt some of his carefree, laddish traits. Danny's rogue persona, in my eyes, was pure gold and by incorporating some of Danny's cheeky ways into my own personality, it would be the perfect way to hide who I truly was!

Danny's documentary series, *Deadliest Men*, is where Danny spent time in the criminal underground with some of the most feared gangsters and found out what made them tick.

I recall a gentleman that Danny was interviewing called Stephen French. French was known as 'the devil' in the criminal underworld. He had found himself in that dark environment since his youth and spoke openly about some of the unthinkable things he had done and encountered.

At the time of filming, French was a reformed man who dedicated his life to minimising gun crime in any way he could. His life's mission was to now help and inspire troubled youths to stay away from the gang culture. One particular thing that he said all those years ago resonated with me on a profound level. He said that if he could change just one person's life, then his work here was done. He would be happy in the knowledge that he played a role in changing an individual's path for the better.

I speak of this story as it's how I feel about writing this book. If my book can change just one person's life for the better, then I'm content.

Obviously, I would like it to help more than one person, millions ideally, but that's only my ego talking, which we will address much later in the book.

I have always felt an urge to help others for as long as I can remember. Some of the topics which I will cover in this book are what I have experienced first-hand. Some topics are common, others, not so common. Maybe by reading this, I can help you to understand depression or anxiety? Maybe I can help you to realise that you are already perfect and don't actually need anything in order to feel fulfilled in life. You are perfect simply because you exist. Maybe you will be able to relate to my story and findings? This book is about self-love and remembering who you are. I hope it will leave you with a greater understanding of what life is about. Life is about love and I see no harm in promoting that message in our short time together on this planet. There are parts of the book that your mind will dismiss but your heart will recognise.

I am going to state on the record that I am not a professional book writer, although I did dabble in A-level English literature on the rare occasions that I did actually attend college. I, by no means have had extensive lessons in book writing or had any previous aspirations to write. I have never felt the urge to write a book and the prospect of embarking on this whole project is exciting, while at the same time daunting. I am writing this book on a whim, fuelled by a spontaneous message that popped into my head while meditating.

If the book appears incohesive, repetitive, jumbled or not entirely linear, I can only apologise for my novice skills. I want you to have the best possible experience while reading this. I have simply done my best at this current point in time.

Now, this sounds like I'm defending myself and setting you up for a fall in the whole reading experience of this book. I only highlight my deliberate choice of words for you as I am speaking from the ego. You will become very familiar with what the ego is throughout this book and will no doubt be sick of it by the end.

This is not an autobiography as such, although the earlier portions of the book are about my life, so that you can understand what I have been through to arrive at this point. I will address the causes of my behaviour later on in the book and why I behaved in the way I did. So, you could say that you are getting two books in one, you lucky so and so!

If I were being asked to summarise this book and to categorise its content, then I would describe it as a 'spiritual' book but a simplified version for beginners. Our human minds like to label things so we know what to expect, we will examine why this is throughout the book. Don't be scared by the label 'spiritual', I'm not going to trick you in to joining a cult or doing a naked dance in the woods at midnight, it's more about who we are as humans and why we are here. We've all asked that question at some stage of our lives, haven't we? What's the point of it all, eh?

Cast your mind back to when you were at school. For some, that will be easy, for others it may seem an eternity ago! Imagine you are to take an exam that everyone is studying for, but you have absolutely no idea as to what is going to be on the paper, not a single clue. Wouldn't you like some sort of reference point to begin with so that you knew what to study for your exam? If you knew what you were studying for, then surely the exam would be easier? Otherwise you would just be going in blind. What I've found is that we are all studying the same curriculum, we just choose to study for it in different, unique ways. I aim to clarify what it is we are all studying for using my experiences of life.

I am aware that there are people all around the globe that are having to endure far more challenging and harrowing events than I ever will experience. Everyone has their own individual challenges and unique path to walk. We are all simply doing the best we can with the knowledge that we have in the present moment.

You may think nothing of my journey and that I've made a song and a dance about nothing. I sometimes compare my life to the journey of others and think that my life has been a walk in the park in some respects, but it is my path. At the end of the day, I was just playing the cards that were dealt to me, which were perfect for my journey. A journey that I had, indeed, chosen for myself...

I believe that all we can do is send love to everyone in life and respect each individual journey, past and present. There are 7.53 billion people in the world, so that is 7.53 billion different perceptions of the world and 7.53 billion different paths. Each path ultimately leads to the same destination though, some just take longer than others. This is the story of just one of those paths and I'd like to share it with you. Whatever you take from this book, know that I love you. Know that the energy that animates me as I write these words, is the same energy that animates you as you read them, and for that, I love you.

So, I think that's everything, shall we commence?

1

First Memories

My earliest memories as a child were pain, violence and arguing. The violence was not so much aimed towards myself; it was more so what I was witnessing between my parents. Hostile and aggressive behaviour seemed the everyday norm. I was in the middle of it all as a two-year-old child thinking, *why is this happening?*

I vividly recall my mum and dad pulling me between each other like a rag doll. They would argue over who was going to have me, as if I were an inanimate object or a possession. I felt like I was being used as a weapon in the middle of their own personal war. My mother and father each gripped an arm from my tiny body and pulled it towards one another, as if they were having their own human tug of war match. This was all done in the living room of my house as my dad attempted to eat fish and chips.

They often say that children are extremely perceptive and even then, as a two-year-old, I had a feeling something wasn't quite right. After all, I hadn't long arrived on the planet! My parents met in a mental institution for which they were both patients, not staff! With this in mind, it should give you a brief glimpse as to some of the turbulent affairs that they both encountered in their relationship.

From those early memories, I can recall that my parent's fragile and volatile relationship was only worsening as time progressed. Children are susceptible little creatures and can pick up on anything. I can remember how I would feed off my parents' arguments and emotions still to this day. The toxic atmosphere that would linger around after each heated exchange soon became the norm for me. Knots would form in my stomach and I would often have sharp pains rushing through my tiny belly. I could literally feel the pain in the air to the point where if it wasn't there, I would become confused. In a strange way, it became comforting and made me miserable at the same time. This was my egoic pain body developing which over time would shape my behaviour into my adult life. I couldn't help but think, even as a child, that I was responsible for all this pain and commotion.

At the tender age of three, my mum left. I guess she couldn't deal with the turmoil anymore and decided to regain control of her life. I remember the day she left vividly; she sat me down at the bottom of the stairs and told me that she was leaving. *Where was she going?* I wondered. I didn't know or understand, why this was happening to me. She gave me a 'Dusty Bin' toy just before she departed. For those of you old enough, you will know who this is, for those who don't, Google it!

The thing was though, I didn't even like 'Dusty Bin'!? The idea that my mother didn't know what I truly loved hurt me; more than the prospect of her leaving. With that said, she presented me with the lacklustre gift, gave me a kiss and exited via the front door. I didn't fully understand what was going on or what she was saying, *she will probably be back soon*, I thought to myself, although I was still unsure as to where she'd gone. Days turned into weeks then months. As time passed, it dawned on me that my mother wasn't going to be returning to my father and I. My dad would remain positive and loving but it was too much for my young, developing mind to comprehend.

Life after Mum left was surreal for my dad and I. The atmosphere in the house just felt flat and even though the toxicity in the air, which I was so familiar with, had dissipated, it made me feel even more pain. My dad and I went along with our lives like true Brits; pretending everything was fine even though it wasn't. I could sense my dad's broken composition in all that he did, and he had to put a brave face on for me. We were both in the same boat and were pining for the woman that was once in our house.

This affected me more than I would realise growing up. It all really came to light when I started to socialise with other children at nursery and Sunday school. I still had that resilient, childish vigour that children have but as I grew older, this vanished, and life began to become a struggle. I was dragged to Sunday school by my dad; I hated it from an early age. I guess in hindsight, I hated seeing what was in my eyes, normality in other people's lives. The children I met there appeared happy and they all had a mum and dad. This was the first major inkling that there was something not right about my life and that I may be different to others. The Church really didn't feel right to me and felt wrong even in my early years. Those stupid bible stories and contrived songs really irritated me, what was it all about!? Something about it all just didn't sit well with me, it felt almost seedy, but I went along with it all and accepted it nevertheless.

2

DAD

In my dad's words, it took him twelve years to get over my mum leaving, although the way he has lived his life to this very day suggests otherwise. My dad has chosen never to have another relationship, which is so upsetting as he would have made someone a lovely husband. My father would tell me that he loved my mum despite all of her actions and no matter what she did, he took her back every time. I cannot imagine what it must have been like for my dad raising a little boy while being heartbroken. He always hid his pain from me, although I would hear him crying at night when he thought I was asleep.

Even throughout all the pain that my father was experiencing, he would make Christmases so special for me. I will always have fond memories of them despite not having my mum there. Despite my dad having a volatile temper towards life, I loved him. I now understand that when an issue is not resolved deep within yourself, it will be projected onto other people or life in general through anger or fear.

My dad's sporadic outbursts of rage were only a cry of hurt and pain, a cry for help. He was trying to deal with what my mum had done and raising a young boy on his own. Remember this the next time someone is angry at you, what's the real reason that they are mad? Nine times out of ten, they are hurting deeply within themselves or merely angry that your viewpoint doesn't match theirs. When two egos meet and deem each other to be wrong, there is no winning, only frustration! There it is again: the ego!

My dad had strict beliefs about God and Christian principles. The Bible was considered gospel by him and that was that. My father was raised this way, so he was only teaching what he knew. I grew up with rigid rules about what was acceptable behaviour in the eyes of the Lord. I never questioned any of this and accepted everything that I was told, even though not all felt completely right to me. My dad knew everything, he had to, right? He was my father and I loved him; he wouldn't lie to me.

I suppose Dad's strict rules about my attendance of Sunday school and church, were a way of him trying to restore some normality to the whole situation for both of us. His parents dragged him to church, so he would continue the tradition that he knew and worked for him. Either way, he was trying to do what he thought was best and for that, I love him and thank him. People will carry on traditions and behaviour that they have learnt blindly, sometimes without ever seeking if there is another way. I will talk more about this later on.

My dad would do little things for me that mattered in my eyes. I will always remember that it is the little things that count in life and that they help to make the bigger picture. My dad dealt so well with my traumatised behaviour and he always made me feel loved as a child. As I grew older, our relationship dwindled due to my selfish and delusional behaviour. I will discuss this in more detail as the story progresses.

3

MY LIGHT

This woman was my sanctuary, my light, love personified. She was my mother's mum, but to me, she was my mum. She showed me a level of love that was simply impossible for any other being to ever match. I just can't describe how beautiful, perfect and loved she made me feel. Of course, we are all perfect, but we never really see it until someone makes you feel it.

I would live for Friday evenings after the school week had finished, when all the weeks' woes would fade away and I could spend the night around my nan and grandad's. They would both spoil me rotten and I milked it! All of the inferior feelings that I would feel when comparing myself to the other children at school would vanish, swept away with waves of love. I love my nan with every fibre of my being and still talk to her every day. My nan always said that she had a son and that I was him. To me, she will always be my second mum.

Grandad would give me lifts everywhere and he always came across as a stern, rigid man but I knew there was a softness deep down in there! Grandad would guard his emotions around people, but he would always find time to play with me and make me giggle! I will never forget his big red van that delivered me anywhere that I requested; they were happy times. However, it was Nan who pulled the strings here and really had the keys to my heart. It's normal to have favourites, isn't it?

Nan and Grandad would take me on holidays to Sidmouth and Cornwall. They tried to provide an element of the family unit that I so craved and wanted in my everyday life. I have countless wonderful memories of these times.

I recall one holiday where we were walking down a country path a mile or so from our campsite. We came across a field that had multiple donkeys in. One donkey in particular had an injured foot and had it bandaged up. This upset me at the time, but Nan and Grandad turned it into a joke and cheered me up. We beckoned the donkey over to the fence where we all stood and it hobbled over. We stroked him and made a wish for him to get better.

A few weeks later when we were back home at Nan's, I cuddled next to her in her chair, as I always would. She held a pencil and paper in her hand and suggested that we draw. She asked me what I would like her to draw and I said the injured donkey that we had seen from our holiday! Nan then proceeded to sketch the donkey. It was one of the funniest illustrations that I had ever seen! The donkey had accentuated features and such a confused expression on its face, to the point where it looked lost! She even drew a little bow on the shoe of his wounded foot, which was satirically oversized and looked simply hilarious. It had me in absolute hysterics and Nan, Grandad and I could not stop laughing.

I tell this story to you because those evenings around my grandparents' house were magical. They helped to alleviate my worries and anxieties. They helped me to enjoy my life. I will hold the tale of the donkey and all it encompassed in my heart forever, for whenever I think of that tale, I am transported back to those warm and loving moments.

4

Primary School

My mother called me one day out of the blue and began to explain to me what had happened. I still didn't understand but she said she would be visiting me each weekend. I couldn't believe it; I was so happy! My mum wanted to see me. Even if she didn't want to live with me, at least she wanted to see me. I would live for the weekends even more for the fact that I got to spend it with my mum and my nan.

My relationship with my mother had progressed to telephone calls and weekly visits; for me this was a relief, *maybe I wasn't evil after all?* I learnt that my mum had a new partner called Jim and she lived in London with him. This was difficult to comprehend as a child and made her visits and conversations on the phone clumsy and contrived. Over the phone, I would just make airplane and crashing noises to mask the fact I had no idea what was going on, it just seemed easier!

My dad would scribble down sentences on paper for me to read to my mum while I was on the phone to her. They were generally guilt-tripping sentences about how lonely I was and how we longed for her return, but I knew deep down that this was not going to happen. Those little notes that my dad wrote were his way of conversing with Mum and he delivered his messages via my tiny childish voice. My parents would not speak to one another, so that was as close as my father could get with my mum.

I now understand that my dad just wanted our family back together and that he still loved my mother dearly, even after everything. His messages that were communicated via me were hopeful, yet futile at the same time. She was never going to return to us, despite what my dad hoped.

My mum was true to her word though and started to visit me on weekends. She brought Jim with her too which was difficult for me. When I first met Jim, I guarded my emotions around him, I just felt awkward. It did get easier as time progressed, and he was a cool guy to give him credit. Mum and Jim would take me shopping, swimming and even to the safari park; it was so much fun, even though I tried to resist it. I was scared to enjoy myself too much for I felt like I was betraying my father. Part of me deep down resented Jim for stealing my mother off me. I suppose I viewed him as competition. As time passed though, I warmed greatly to him. He was nothing but good to me, although I thought there was always an air of awkwardness between the two of us when we were left alone together; maybe that was just me.

Jim was a straight talking, firm man and I admired this about him. He was the complete opposite to my dad; my father was very gentle in comparison. I sometimes wanted to be horrible to Jim, due to the jealousy bubbling deep within me, but it simply wasn't in my nature. In hindsight I was blessed to have two dads and grew to love Jim very much. I loved spending time with Mum and Jim, but those weekends went so damn quickly! Before I knew it, Monday mornings would arrive and I would be back at primary school, which I hated.

Starting primary school only exacerbated my underlying issues that I was a freak with the fact that every fellow pupil I met had a mum and a dad. My thoughts as a young child then proceeded like this: *Hold on a minute, am I the only one without a mum!? Maybe I'm the one who's in the wrong? Maybe I deserve this because I am a bad child? This is my punishment for being bad!* That's what I told myself.

My mother didn't want to live with me, so there must be something wrong with me. Perhaps I was an evil child? This is how my young mind thought and my thoughts only consisted of how evil I must be for my mum to pack up and leave me. Those thoughts of self-persecution only perpetuated and I began to self-harm at the naive age of five; a way of punishing myself.

I started to hit myself at night-time when I was on my own. I would punch myself as hard as I could in the face. I would use a shoe sometimes. I would bite my hands and arms too. I would do this privately, although it would soon progress to public displays. It gave me the attention from people that I craved so much, due to my loneliness and pain. I was a problem child in my eyes, and I had already forgotten who I truly was. Physical punishment towards my young body was something that my developing mind deemed necessary, in order to make myself feel better.

I recall being in church one Sunday morning and I started putting my entire hand in my mouth; as if to choke myself. I actually couldn't breathe! My dad did his best to play down the incident in the middle of Mass, but in the end, he had to physically pull my hand away, as I would have choked myself. This gave me all the attention I needed, and I felt a strange sense of satisfaction that was also coupled with sadness.

Although I was at primary school, I would wet the bed until the age of eight. I just couldn't cope with events or life and it just added more disarray to an already confused situation. I asked my friends at school if they still wet the bed to which they all replied, "No" and laughed. It appeared that I was a freak in that sense as well.

My dad finally helped me to stop this distressing habit by bribing me with Batman stickers; it worked. For every night that I agreed to get up and go to the toilet when he asked me to, I received a pack of Batman stickers. It's amazing what Batman can get you to do, and I'll let you in on a little secret: I still love that caped crusader to this day! My bed wetting episodes ceased, but my self-loathing behaviour continued to grow and consume my innocent mind.

One holiday, while I was in Wales with my father and his parents, I hid under the settee of the house we were staying in for amusement. The adults started talking amongst themselves and began asking where I had gone? I thought it was a game and hid longer. The game soon turned sour and my paternal grandparents were frantically searching for me.

Their sentences were curt and of a pensive nature. It soon became clear to me that if I revealed my hiding location, I was going to be in trouble, big trouble. I decided to style it out and watch the situation unfold from the safety of my new-found cavern. About an hour had passed and half the sleepy little seaside town had been informed of my disappearance. I began to enjoy the scenario that was unfolding before me, because it gave me that feeling of being missed and wanted, something which I craved so much.

Eventually my grandad looked under the settee in an act of desperation and found my hiding hole. Embarrassment, fear and anxiety consumed my body. What was going to happen to me? Initially I got told off, due to the fact that all these local people, and even the police, were out looking for me. This quickly subsided and there was just sheer relief and gratitude that I was okay. In fact, the amusement arcade let me have a free hour in there as they were just as relieved as anybody that I was alright, this did soften the blow of being told off somewhat! I still feel guilty about the whole episode to this day, but I am sure all is forgiven! I was a confused child to say the least!

As my dad worked a full-time job, I would go to a childminder after school. She was called Christine. Her husband was Tony and they had two sons called Mark and Kieron. These beautiful people showed me a glimpse of the family unit and were nothing but good to me. Christine would pick me up from school and cook beautiful meals, similar to what my nan would cook for me, it was perfect. My dad would pick me up and take me home after he had completed his day's work, it must have taken such a toll on him.

Christine would also take me to school in the mornings and walk with me and other children. She would then wave bye to me as I began my day at school. During my time at primary school, I would latch on to my female teachers and develop unhealthy crushes on them, craving that motherly figure and wishing they would come home with me. I would always try my hardest in the female taught classes in order to gain acceptance and merit from them.

Now I haven't mentioned my paternal nan and grandad much other than when I hid under the settee! This isn't because they didn't mean much to me, it was because I had such a beautiful bond with my maternal grandparents. They were my favourites honestly, and I felt at peace with them. My paternal grandad was fantastic to me though and we would always play football together and he built goalposts for me. He was a very creative man and would always manage to build something out of nothing for me. I would play with the toys that he made for me for weeks, especially the Thunderbird ones!

My paternal nan was a gentle lady and would always be cooking or cleaning. She would whistle while going about her business in a chirpy manor. Her fresh meals were beautiful, and we would all sit around the table together. She would help me to build things out of cardboard and was a very creative woman, just like my grandad. She was a fairly active woman who had a few problems with her legs but always managed to get around the house, nevertheless. Her whistling will always stick with me to this very day.

One day when school had finished, my maternal nan was waiting at the school gates for me. It was strange as it was usually my childminder who was there. My nan explained to me that as a treat I would go to her house that night. "Amazing," I thought, "what a bonus, it wasn't even Friday!" Nan and I made our way back to hers where she cooked me a beautiful meal. As the night wore on, it would soon be time for my dad to come and pick me up. Nan stated to me that he may be late tonight due to work. I was fine with this as it gave me more time to play.

Eventually my dad arrived and came in, but to my surprise his dad was with him too. They both walked into the front room and stared at me for a second before my dad said quietly, "David, Nanny has gone to be with Jesus." I kind of knew what they meant but couldn't grasp the magnitude of the situation. My dad and grandad both burst into tears while my other grandparents sat in silence. My nan's passing all happened unexpectedly; it was a shock to everyone. It happened in the daytime and just like that, she was gone, no health issues, she just went. I find it hard to recall most of it to be honest, probably because of my young age. My young mind did not want to process it properly, as it was just mixed in with all the other thoughts that were swirling around in my developing mind. I just went about my life as normal, whereas Grandad and Dad were distraught.

I tried to bury myself in my schoolwork as a way to distract myself from my nan's passing and what I was already dealing with. I was good at hiding things from others, especially at school. I felt like a full time actor sometimes just to appear normal at school. If I appeared engrossed in my schoolwork, I could pass for a normal child!

I made good friends at school and I wasn't completely socially inept, I just kept all the dark stuff hidden. When children did persist with their questions about my family I would panic and change the subject. It got to the point where, if other children continued to ask about my life, I would just tell them that my mum was dead! It was just easier and it avoided the embarrassment of telling people that she had left me; it would literally kill the conversation. Of course, I never told her this though, as it would have probably added to what must have been a difficult situation for her already.

Most of the time my fellow pupils were cool with me and we had great fun. I would play football, join in the games and just avoid questions about my family. I met one young man who was very open with his questions; his name was Lee and I began to form a very close bond with him. For some reason, his questions didn't seem so invasive as others would, and I felt a real sense of warmth from him.

5

MORE THAN A FRIEND

Lee was an unathletic kid and he won't mind me saying this! I wanted to play football, but he just wasn't interested! His life was the total opposite to mine, and I was curious as to what a 'normal' life was like. I remember the first time that I went to his house and we had microchips; this was all new to me and I loved them! My Dad didn't possess a microwave and we lived mainly off tinned food, so these tasty chips were a godsend.

Lee's parents were lovely, and they had just had a little girl. I remember the day she came home from the hospital; she was perfect, and her name was Charlotte. Lee had this beautiful, perfect family that I was very jealous of, but at the same time, I felt happy to be a part of it. Emotions are strange things!

Lee and I would play Rambo. I would always get the crap gun and he would play the masculine hero! But I didn't care, I just loved having interaction with someone who I considered to be normal. Lee slowly became like a brother to me and I would do anything for him. His mum, Mandy and dad, Robert (Bobby) were so considerate and I would eagerly look forward to Monday evenings after school, as that's when I would visit. Going to Lee's would also help prepare me for the weekly phone call that I would receive from my mum when I returned home, which always upset me and unsettled me.

Lee would have all the latest gadgets and clothes. He would also have the state-of-the-art games consoles! I never had a games console due to them being so expensive, so I really enjoyed playing all the different games; it was like a new world to me. Lee had a bike and would give me lifts on the back of it. He would ask me if I wanted to ride it to which I would always play it down and say I was tired. The fact was that I couldn't ride a bike because I had never owned one, but I didn't want to appear even more of an oddball and lose my true best friend. Lee was my only link to the outside world of normality, and everything was so casual for him, whereas I was far more sensitive.

Lee helped me more than he will ever know growing up and he was the only one who knew the truth about my mum, eventually. He never even passed a remark or made a big deal out of it. He was so blasé and acceptant about things, that he made me feel no different to any of the other children. He always treated me the same as anyone else, normal. I loved him for that, and will for eternity.

At the same time that Lee and I had grown particularly close, I had a court case going on. He was my rock and supported me so much throughout it all. The court case involved my mother, and she was pushing for custody of me over the weekends. This was eventually thrown out due to the fact I would have to travel to London every weekend, which was about a three-hour drive. This would have left me exhausted for school and interfered with my schoolwork.

I had to attend a few private court sessions where I had to testify against my parents, but I really didn't want to take sides for fear of upsetting either of them. Even at that young age, I felt that I had a huge responsibility in trying to keep both of my parents happy. You could say that I had the weight of the world on my little shoulders. At least that's how it felt. I even had to write a letter to the judge explaining how I felt. I was trapped in the middle of it all. I was so happy when the whole ordeal was over to be honest, it just seemed to screw my brain up even more. My mum would have to just see me in the holidays. If Lee had not been there to play Rambo with me in between the whole ordeal, who knows where I would have been?

6

SECONDARY SCHOOL

I will never forget the long, hot six weeks in the summer of 1996; it seemed to go on forever and I would be embarking on a new chapter of my life, by moving to secondary school! I spent the entire time down in London with my mum and her new husband, Jim. My mum had recently married Jim which I was a part of. I warmed to the idea over time, but it was tough to digest initially. I was the best man at their wedding and looked after the rings. It was a small ceremony and I felt quite honoured and privileged to be the best man.

The wedding made me crave the family unit even more and added to my desires. My relationship with my mum via the phone and her periodic visits on the weekends just weren't enough. She wanted to spend more time with me, which was clear from the whole custody battle that I had endured a few years prior, so the six weeks holiday together was perfect.

I was so happy that she wanted to see me, and I met Jim's family who were beautiful and welcomed me with open arms. My new stepbrother and sisters were all so full of life. Lynne, Karen, Kevin and Sara were much older than me and had children of their own. Rhianon, Naomi and Jób were Lynne's children. Liam and Darren were Karen's children and Sara had Jade and Kiri. When all the children were together, it felt fantastic and we would play in the huge garden out the back of the house until the sun set. They treated me as if I had known them forever and I will never forget that feeling, I thank them for it! We would have barbecues, play sports and computer games, it was brilliant. I was so used to my own company and being on my own, it was a welcome change. I formed close bonds with all of them and for once, I didn't feel like the outsider, I felt part of something.

My mum, Jim, and I also went on a holiday to Portugal that summer. It was the first time I had been abroad, and I loved it. It felt like a proper family holiday with Mum and Jim. I felt for Dad back home on his own, but I loved being with my mum. We went on so many happy trips together during that holiday, including scuba diving. I never wanted it to end, but with all good things, it did. I didn't want this to be temporary, I wanted it to be a permanent state of affairs. This only added to my hurt when time with Mum and Jim did end. It was always going to be temporary, much to my frustration.

I'd had a brief glimpse into what life could have been for me. Mum asked me one day to hypothetically choose who I wanted to be with, her or Dad? I wanted to be with her, but I couldn't just abandon my dad could I, after all he had done? I felt so guilty for feeling like this though, especially after the whole court case scenario, Dad had fought so hard to protect my welfare, to the point where he actually became ill with nerves at the thought of losing me. I was truly bamboozled with everything, my emotions, parents, everything! I felt my dad's happiness was my sole responsibility. If I left, who would he have?

I decided to leave things as they were as I didn't want to rock the boat too much. My relationship with my mum improved greatly after that holiday and we would speak more often over the phone. I would go down to London a lot more to see my new, extended family. I would become so excited at the prospect of seeing my step siblings in the approach to the holidays. I would savour every moment with them but when it drew to a close, I would often become moody and upset. My mother would also become withdrawn and erratic. We would argue over petty things, usually on the last day of the holiday; it happened every time like clockwork!

It is sad looking back upon these situations but in hindsight, it was just our defense mechanisms both operating to hide the pain and hurt that we were both experiencing. Anyway, the time with my mother and Jim had come to an end over the summer of 1996 and the dreaded dawn of secondary school was fast approaching. The anxiety set in!

The six weeks came and went and I began life at secondary school. My primary school teachers had advised that Lee and I were to be separated in our new school, as in their eyes, we were just disturbing one another's learning. I overheard this being discussed with my childminder one afternoon, just as school was finishing. I didn't think my new school would pay any attention, so it didn't worry me. It soon dawned upon me that my primary school's advice had been heeded. I soon discovered that Lee and I were in totally different parts of the school. This caused more pain and confusion for me; *how dare they take away my best friend! I didn't want any new friends; I had a perfectly good one here!*

This new transition was tough for me and I would be physically sick for about a month every morning before arriving at school; my nerves were all over the place. Oh, and guess what, every fellow pupil that I came into contact with there had a mum and a dad, great! Everything was definitely my fault in my eyes, and I deserved everything that I received, including Lee being taken away from me. That was it, it was me and I was on my own, I felt sorry for myself. I started to feel like a victim, why was everything against me? Life was cruel, I didn't like it. Lee would surely make new friends because he was so popular, and I would be left as an outcast, truly alienated from everyone else.

Needless to say, I made friends, lots of friends, friends that I still keep in touch with now. I am truly thankful to have had such beautiful people in my life. I had the gift of being a social chameleon and could mix with anyone, which was quite amazing really coming from the boy who would harm himself with a shoe and had such a unique past!

After a few months of being at secondary school, when the initial novelty of it all had worn off, I began to hang around with Lee again in break times. Lee met some of my new friends and we all mixed well. Lee had a new best friend now though; his name was Dean.

7

A Cheeky Chappy

I didn't like Dean initially, he spent more time with my best friend than I did, why would I like him? I've never been one to wish harm upon people, it just isn't in my nature, but my ego saw Dean as a threat and apparently, he had it all according to Lee. Dean was small, like five feet, 3 inches small. I was much taller than him, in my mind this mattered as this was what made a man! Also, I thought that Dean had a crap haircut that made him look like Toad from Super Mario. This was of course painfully ironic, as I probably had the most generic, boring haircut going. It was brushed forward and flicked up at the front.

My view on the whole situation was that I was a superior person because I was taller and had a better haircut! Dean had a PlayStation, all the new games and a big family to boot as well. So from Lee's perspective, what wasn't to like? To be honest, I was jealous of what Dean had. I tried to tell myself that what Dean had meant nothing because he was still little and had a bowl head haircut!

After a few months of hanging out with Dean, I actually began to see his charisma and realised why Lee liked him; he was a fun, cheeky little guy. The more I got to know him, the more I realised he was just a normal, happy kid who had a laugh with everyone. The pair of us would even take the piss out of Lee for being the most unathletic guy that you have ever met, but that's what kids do, right!? The three of us built an equal love for one another and I grew to love Dean just as much as Lee.

One day Lee told me that Dean had something called Cystic Fibrosis. I had no idea what this was and didn't see it as a big deal as Dean was a healthy, normal guy who hadn't said anything to me. Apparently, Dean's life expectancy was not very long, early 20's to be precise. Rubbish, I thought to myself! This guy was ace, and he was so positive with his outlook on life, there is nothing wrong with him. Dean would play football with me, which was brilliant as Lee was one of the most anti-sporting people that you could ever wish to meet! I really have painted Lee as though he did nothing, haven't I!? But he did like skate boarding and was very talented at it. Just to tarnish Lee's sporting image a tiny bit more, he had no clue whatsoever about football and Dean knew everything. With this, Dean and I forged a bond over our love for football and the fact that Lee knew nothing. Soon it was Dean and I who were becoming best friends! We would hang out after school together and get up to general mischief, as kids do. They were glorious times that I cherish. The three of us certainly had a special bond together and I feel that we were all meant to meet by divine intervention.

8

Secondary School: The Later Years

I have always had the ability to mix with anyone and hung out with most peer groups during my school years. As I reached the later stages, I began to fall in with the 'bad boys' crowd. We'd be labelled as this by teachers or outsiders but these lads I hung around with all had good hearts and we just wanted to have a laugh.

Lee and Dean were in this group too, so wherever they went, I went. This is when I tried my first cigarette and started smoking just to fit in with all the crew! I wanted to be accepted and conform to what 'being cool' was. The majority of the group smoked, and I wanted to be like them, so naturally I copied what they did! I craved acceptance and attention, so I would do anything to be accepted by my new friends. It worked too; smoking enabled me to become one of the 'bad boys,' plus I was the joker of the group. I would do just about anything to raise a laugh from the guys and girls, those brief moments of adulation from others made my heart sing.

If smoking kept me in with the crowd, then I would force myself to like cigarettes. Trouble is, I quickly became addicted to those tempting little cancer sticks, even though I nearly choked to death on my first drag! I graphically recall that horrible sensation of the overpowering, tickly smoke choking me, it's a wonder why I continued? I guess the allure of acceptance and appearing normal eclipsed the issue of health!

Smoking really is a disgusting habit and you truly don't see this until you've quit. However, at that time in my life, I really didn't care about my health or anything really, I just wanted to be acknowledged as being 'normal'.

Smoking cigarettes soon progressed to cannabis. Personally, I didn't see cannabis as a drug or a problem. To me, smoking weed just propelled me up the ladder of acceptance even further, plus it had a very calming effect on my angry body. My friends and I would skip class to smoke weed and I loved the idea of all the other kids in class complying to the school rules and being 'losers' while I was getting stoned.

I even started to sell cannabis resin at school. I would cut what I had in half and sell it. This gave me a reputation and one that I was proud of. I gained more popularity and credibility within my peer group by doing this. My confidence levels were sky-high because of this.

Friday night was party time and we would venture over the park and spark up joint after joint. These party nights were a blast, and this is when I was first introduced to the wondrous effects of alcohol. My first experience of alcohol was through cider and alcopops. We would down the bottles like they were nothing and drink until we were sick! It was great! Hold on a minute, what was this alcohol substance that I had discovered? It made me feel invincible. The combination of alcohol and weed seemed to make my problems of insecurity and self-loathing simply drift away into obscurity.

I began participating in these 'sessions' more frequently and these substances were changing my life for the better, (or so it seemed) despite me throwing up half the time! In my eyes, I started to become even 'cooler', plus when I was under the influence, it would alleviate the weight of self-hate that I permanently carried around with me. I was a 'legend' according to my peers due to the dizzy heights of intoxication that I could reach. I can't lie, I loved it, finally, actual acceptance.

I kept all this hidden from my dad, who would have gone spare at me if he had found out. My nan and grandad however knew about my drinking and did not have a problem with it, as long as it was in moderation. When it came to the weed though, I did keep that to myself, as telling Nan and Grandad would really land me in the crap!

I would sleep at my grandparents on a Friday night so my dad would never find out about my drinking. Grandad said it was fine to drink but in moderation. Of course, I assured them that it was all under control but the moment their backs were turned, I would always take things to the extreme.

My grandad would give me two cans of beer to take out with me and I would promise him that they would be all I would consume. It turns out though that when the peer pressure was gently applied, I immediately folded and the wise words of my grandparents were thrown out the window. It's a funny thing isn't it, peer pressure and what it can make you do? I would do anything when in the company of my peers, from downing bottles of cider to smoking water bongs, anything! Those two cans that my grandad so kindly gave me were just to get me started; I abused his trust. I would then consume vodka and cider until it was all a foggy haze!

I met my first girlfriend Nicky, who was a year younger than me, around this time. She was a beautiful soul, but I treated her like a trophy and just something to brag about to my friends. She too had a mum and dad and again, I felt the odd one out when I had to explain my situation to her. Her parents were good as gold to me as well and they would invite me round for tea. Nicky had such a beautiful family, but I felt like the black sheep due to my background. Her family were fairly well off and I used to get so embarrassed about being dropped back at my house in the 'rough' part of town. Of course, all of this was probably in my head but nevertheless, this is how I felt.

Nicky and I had happy times together and I'd like to think that I wasn't a complete dick to her. We shared so many beautiful moments together that young love can create and I recall them fondly. We would walk home after school in the summer sun and talk about our childish fantasies. I often skipped the topics of my life and tried to focus on her life as much as I could.

It was only when my friends were around us that I would change to impress them and belittle her; a classic trait of the ego. The ego will often belittle others in order to make their fragile self feel better. We broke up a few times, simply because I couldn't handle the genuine affection that she was showing me and so the self-destruct phase began, again. It's crazy isn't it? I craved female love and attention so when I finally caught a glimpse of genuine sincerity and affection, I ran a mile! I was punishing my young self by denying myself happiness - something that I had always done. I would create issues out of nothing and become sporadic with my emotions. Nicky and I would always get back together but the novelty was wearing thin for her.

One day, I broke up with Nicky, not really expecting any major repercussions. I thought I would wait a few days and make her sweat; I loved the drama! I expected to click my fingers and she would return, but this time it was the straw that broke the camel's back. I pleaded with her to get back with me and she flat out said, "No!" I couldn't believe it! I had let her go umpteen times before, but this time, the ship had sailed and you know what, I couldn't blame her. My drinking got in the way of us and I told myself that I was better off without her. She always wanted to spend time with me after school, but I was always too busy. I would happily choose a smoke and a drink with the lads over her. She was a stable influence in my life, one to which I discarded. I wonder what she is up to these days? I hope she's happy.

Now I imagine you are wondering as to where all this money came from that funded my nasty little marijuana and alcohol habits? My mother would give me weekly money as a way of trying to stay in my favour, which again I abused and would guilt trip her. The way my selfish mind saw it was that she left me, so it was the least she could do.

My other means of finance was to steal. I would steal off my dad's dad. I loved my grandad and we had a loving relationship where he was always there for me, but it was nothing compared to my relationship with my mum's parents; they spoiled me. With this being said, it gave me no right to abuse my grandad's trust and unconditional love for me by stealing from him.

Towards the end of my grandad's life, I would spend a lot of time around at his house as it was close to my school. I would often be alone in his house while he was in the garden. I found myself in his room one day exploring his cupboards until I came across a safe. To my astonishment, the safe was unlocked, I couldn't believe it. I slowly opened it to see what treasures were tucked inside. As I searched, my mouth dropped, it was full of notes. I quickly scooped them up and counted them. There was about £400 altogether. At first, I felt compelled to take the money but then a little voice inside of me said, "No." I decided to listen to that little voice and I placed the money back where I had found it and closed the safe.

That night, I fantasized as to what I could do with that money: all the drugs I could buy, the CDs and clothes. Lee and Dean would be impressed too. So the next time I was at my grandad's, I checked that the coast was clear and made my way back to the safe. I took about £300 and scattered the remaining notes around a little just so it looked like it was untouched to the naked eye.

When I ask myself why I took the money that day, I did it to be accepted by Lee and Dean. In my mind, I hoped that they would view me as a 'bad man' like on the rap records that we listened to. I also treated them to games with the money that I had stolen and lived the dream for a short amount of time. Lee and Dean weren't overly impressed with my thieving antics though and I didn't get the reaction that I expected.

Nothing ever came about from the missing money until Grandad mentioned it to my dad one day. My dad asked me if I knew anything about it, to which I said no. Dad thought that the early stages of dementia were setting in for Grandad, so I went along with his theory and reiterated his suspicions with my own make believe stories. I said that I had witnessed Grandad becoming forgetful in order to clear my name. I was in the clear, but I felt guilty about my actions.

What my friends thought about me was far more important than my family's perception of me, that's just the way I saw it. The whole moral repercussions of the theft mattered little to me, for my street credibility was my main priority. The irony of it all was that Lee and Dean had already accepted me, regardless of what I did. It was I who could not accept that they loved me for who I was. If anything, my little attempt to obtain more validation from my peers had the opposite effect and Lee and Dean were slightly put off by what I had done.

The taste of theft had given me a real appetite for it. I could no longer steal from my grandfather, as all of his money that I knew about had gone, plus Dean and Lee hadn't given me the reaction I thought I would receive. I decided to go elsewhere for my thrills.

Dean, Lee and I would venture out each Saturday to a huge shopping mall called *Merry Hill* and just get up to general mischief. I would literally walk into shops, pick things up for the sake of it and walk out the door while pretending to be on my brick of a mobile phone. Of course, I was only doing this to impress Lee and Dean and didn't actually need the stuff that I was stealing. You know what though, my little trick of talking on my phone and acting oblivious to the world always worked. If anyone were to ever stop me, my plan was to act confused and apologise profusely, but I never needed to, as no one ever stopped me. This went on for a while, plundering useless gadgets and frivolous possessions, all for the thrill of it and to impress my mates at the same time. I can't lie, it gave me a buzz on many fronts.

One holiday, Lee's parents took me away to Cornwall with them and Charlotte. Lee and I would go out together in the town and I would continue my stealing sprees in this new part of the world. I kept using the same tactics that I had played before. The act of a simple youth on his phone bewildered with the world whilst carrying something in plain sight under his arm never failed, I never once got caught.

At the end of that particular holiday, Lee and I had befriended one woman in a clothes shop all week and had our eyes on an expensive shirt in there. Looking back, the shirt was hideous with Japanese writing on it and the image of a dragon, but hey, that was the 90's fashion back then!

We arrived late to the shop on the last day of our holiday and the woman was just about to close. She told us to hurry up if we wanted anything and continued with the closing down of her shop. While the shop owner was distracted, I saw my opportunity and seized it. I grabbed the shirt we had been longing for all week and casually walked out of the store. Lee followed closely, sweating profusely and looking like he had seen a ghost; obviously his adrenaline was pumping, as was mine.

We quickly went to a nearby shop to regain our composure. The assistant in the shop asked if Lee was okay, as he looked really ill. I told her that he was fine and we both blamed Lee's dad's cooking from the night before. Lee continued to talk to the shop assistant while I browsed through the shelves as to what this shop had to offer.

We exited the shop to which Lee professed his disbelief for what I had done in the previous shop by stealing the shirt. I told him he was overreacting and pulled out a little trophy that I had stolen from the shop we were just in! Lee couldn't believe it, "How the hell did you get that?" he said. "I nabbed it from the shelf, while you were talking to the woman about how pale you looked," I replied. I felt a real buzz; proper Billy big balls and with that, we returned home.

At home Lee told me that I had gone too far and that I needed to calm down. This wasn't what I wanted to hear at all! I only wanted recognition! At the same time though, I didn't want to upset my best friend. With that, I promised him that I would never steal again and that was that, I never actually did. I kind of missed the buzz that theft gave me, but alcohol and weed continued to do a sturdy job in helping me to escape from the grim realities of the world.

Shortly after I had stopped my thieving ways, my grandad, who I had once stolen off, had a severe stroke. I returned one day after school to discover him slumped in a chair unable to speak or move. I immediately called my nan on my mum's side and she came round to help. Grandad was rushed to hospital, but it was the beginning of the end for him. After a few painful months of him being totally incapable of caring for himself, he passed away.

I felt particularly guilty for the way I had treated him regarding the money I had stolen, and his passing was something I didn't want to address. I pretended in a way that it hadn't happened and just swept in under the rug. I ignored it all and told myself that the money didn't matter now that he had gone. I would keep that secret to myself forever.

His funeral was tough for my dad to take and hit him hard. I did my best to support him but felt useless. I guess my apathetic approach to the whole situation helped me to cope, but it numbed me to my own emotions. The weed also helped to calm my mind and keep things in perspective.

I was due to finish school and had taken a lot of time off over the period of my grandfather's passing. I guess it had hit me on a subconscious level, but one which I was not willing to acknowledge. Deep down I kept thinking, "What would he have thought if he knew I had stolen off him?" Guilt consumed me in a very important time of my life when exams were imminent.

Exam time soon rolled around and I had developed a niggly little habit of smoking weed every night, in order to help me sleep. Weed was a great antidote for me as it helped to clear my mind of all the shit and I would wake up relatively fresh too. All the rap CDs that I would listen to told me that weed was normal.

Rappers like Dr. Dre and Snoop Dogg were my idols, they were cool, so I was just like them in a way! I actually wanted to be like the rappers who I had grown to love. Alcohol, weed and womanising was apparently the way forward in my choice of music. I, of course, took all of their lyrics literally and missed the fact that it was just entertainment.

As I stated earlier, cannabis and rap were all jumbled and interwoven between my exams. I did little revision, instead, all I did was party and hang out with my friends drinking cider. I remember my three-hour maths GCSE exam; we had a twenty-minute break in between it, as it was so long. So, what did we decide to do in this precious time? We went and smoked a spliff, of course. My friends and I then spent the entire second half of this very important exam laughing and giggling to ourselves like demented mad men. Needless to say, I failed most of my exams. Not all of them, but most. I still got four grades; enough to get me into college, so I wasn't a complete failure. I was a bright kid but just didn't apply myself when it truly mattered!

I didn't really have a plan as to what I actually wanted to do in life, but I had it drilled into me by staff and fellow pupils that if I didn't progress into further education, my life would be a waste. Of course, nothing is further from the truth, but in this westernised system that we find ourselves part of, I had little option. I would conform and play my part in the world just to 'fit' in. My inability to think for myself meant that I went to college, even though I didn't want to. Fitting in with everything and everyone is all that I ever wanted, so by doing this I kept the wheels of society turning. I did not want to be a social outcast, or rather my ego didn't want to, but I was all too young to realise this.

After our exams, my friends and I all made our way to the woods and got steaming drunk. We smoked copious amounts of cannabis and made complete fools of ourselves; it was a sensational time! Hindsight shows me that this was all mindless, but we all have to make our own mistakes in this world in order to learn. I loved the feeling of being drunk as it numbed everything for me. As I saw it, it was part of what our friendship group did. With this mentality, it wasn't a problem for me.

After school had finished, all of our group still hung around together, even though we did our separate things. Lee and I still spent plenty of time together and planned a holiday to celebrate being released into the real world! Lee, myself, and a mutual friend, Claire went away to Crete for our first holiday. Lord knows how three 16-year-olds were allowed to travel to another country, but somehow, we did!

Claire got a job as a travel agent as soon as she finished school and got us a cheap deal! Travelling this young is at the discretion of the airline and travel operator, but we convinced our parents to let us go away and give us written statements. I lied to my dad and told him that Claire's parents were going, but told him that I still needed a letter as it was my first time away without a guardian. He said that I could go on the condition that I would be responsible and well behaved. Yeah, whatever!

We all had our letters from our parents declaring us responsible young adults and away we went. The three of us went to Crete and partied every night. We were so carefree, it was magical. It was exciting to be entering the big bad world alone. It felt liberating and I thought that I knew it all! Dean couldn't come unfortunately due to his health and money situation, but we made sure that we made him jealous with all the pictures that we took! It was all polaroids back then though, how times have changed...

9

College

I somehow managed to scrape into college choosing to study sociology and English Literature. I hated English so God only knows why I chose it, but I loved sociology, so I guess I went along for that. Oddly enough now, I suppose that studying English helped contribute to the writing of this book; however, my spelling and grammar is still atrocious, so thank goodness for the spell checker!

College was a doss really; I didn't go that much as I had just met my second serious girlfriend. I didn't care about my grades, so I just hung out with her. Stacey was fun, attractive and liked drinking and smoking! Right up my street back then!

I moved in with Stacey and her parents very soon after we had started dating to escape my dad. This was mainly because of the ridiculous curfews that he had administered upon me. Stacey and I grew close very quickly and we were quick to go on holidays together at any chance we got. We did everything as a couple and were constantly by each other's side. We had a couple of very happy years together.

Her family accepted me, which I found hard to believe. My own mother had shunned me, but there must be good in the world for these kind people to accept me as the problem child I was. It began to make me think I hadn't been so bad and that it may have been my mother who had the problem, but my silly mind told me to stop thinking like this and knocked me straight back down to earth. A voice in my head said, *Dave, your mum left you for a reason, you were the problem, deal with it.*

Exams were looming and I was being threatened by the college to have my placement for the course terminated, as I never attended. I was too busy smoking weed and skipping sessions to spend time with Stacey. I pulled my socks up for the final part of my college life and attended classes. I mean my body was attending the classes but my head was a million miles away.

Exams came and went and I came out with a D grade in sociology and an E grade in English. These were still classified as passes, so I was happy and amazed that I had produced such a miracle. Considering that I was stoned for most of my college life, it truly was amazing. Exams and I didn't always have the best relationship! Maybe if I would have attended college and taken it seriously, I could have achieved superior grades but it was what it was. All that mattered at that time were the loves of my life, which were Stacey, weed and alcohol!

Stacey and I were partying most of the time, going to concerts and getting smashed, this was paramount to me. All my friends liked Stacey too, which was a plus. We had a beautiful little group going and we were just having fun.

Whilst I was at college, I got a job with Stacey's mum in a care home. Remember that song 'Stacey's Mom'? I loved that song and used to sing it all the time to her, but anyway, I'm off on a tangent again. I continued to work in the care home after my college years and I slowly got into cooking there, as I worked in the care home kitchen.

Stacey and I split up after about six months of me starting this job, which made it awkward as her mum was there. Her mother was cool to be fair and handled it all very professionally. Stacey would have a lot of male friends due to the army work that she did at weekends. I couldn't cope with it and I always suspected her of cheating on me with these real men. I saw these men in the army as real men as I didn't have it in me to physically hurt anyone. These men defended us and were fearless, I wanted to be like that but couldn't, so I became consumed with envy. Eventually, this would drive a wedge between Stacey and I and we grew apart.

My self-sabotaging behaviour really started to manifest my reality again and splitting up with Stacey would hit me harder than I thought. My ego saw this whole break up as another form of rejection, and that I was not good enough to be with someone. The pain body of my childhood had been triggered again. I loved Stacey and had truly screwed things up. How was I going to deal with this new level of pain? Alcohol. Drugs. Party...

10

The Party Years

I kept my job at the care home and began to develop my cooking skills. The chef there, Carole, helped me to grow in confidence as I had never even cooked beans on toast before! The job helped me to fund my *party* lifestyle, that was what I referred to it as anyway. I would justify the harsh reality of what it actually was by calling it a party lifestyle, but the fact was that these issues of rejection and pain were only growing inside me and I was just blotting them out with various substances. I don't really think drinking a bottle of vodka alone on your bed, when nobody was available to go out, can really be considered a party lifestyle!

I moved back to my dad's after my split with Stacey and he was great with me. I was heartbroken and he knew that feeling all too well. His curfews were so unrealistic in my eyes though; ten o'clock for an eighteen-year-old was not cool! My other friends could stay out until whenever, so why wasn't I allowed to!? This, of course, was the catalyst of my rebellious stage against my father. Also, I wasn't permitted to drink by him; he didn't agree with it, as it was evil!

Errrr, hello, I thought to myself, *what do you think I have been doing around Stacey's!? Playing snakes and ladders? No, we were drinking, smoking weed, having sex before marriage and using the Lord's name in vain!* My dad would have erupted had he known the full truth! I had kept my secret little life well under wraps from my dad up until that point. That was who I was though, and he would just have to accept it.

A lads' holiday would surely help me forget about Stacey, so twenty of us went to Kos in Greece. Fourteen nights of drunken adventures were absolutely perfect for me. Dean and Lee were amongst the guys that were there too. I loved these guys and they were my family as far as I was concerned. It was wonderful to have two uninterrupted weeks of carnage with everybody.

Three nights into the holiday, I greeted a couple of my mates who flew out later than everyone else, Tom and Adam. I was exceedingly inebriated when I initially saw them and ran to greet them with my trousers around my ankles, as you do.

I thought in my infinite wisdom that this would be a grand idea, unfortunately, it wasn't. I attempted to jump, got my legs tangled in mid-air and somehow landed on my ankle. I had torn my ligaments. This was only discovered after three days of walking on it. I was numbing the ever-growing pain with alcohol and achieving legendary status with my friends, so every cloud and all that.

Dean and Lee helped me to walk for many of the nights, but my ankle was like a balloon. My friend big Tommy G gave me a dirty football sock to support my ankle, which did the trick for a while but my condition was only worsening. It was time to seek professional medical attention and I booked a trip to the main part of town for the next day. That night, all of my friends agreed to come with me the next morning to keep me company.

The morning arrived and everyone was dead, not literally, but they were all far too hungover to travel with me. I, myself, felt equally awful and I'd had about two hours of sleep altogether. I met the rep who was part of the doctor's clinic and we got a small bus into town. I will never forget the humidity on that tiny bus and I vividly recall the alcohol literally seeping out of my pores, I felt a mess.

We arrived in town and made our way to the surgery. I will always remember the doctor's words after he examined me. He showed me the x-ray that he had taken and said, "David, you have been a very silly boy!" If only I had remembered these words as I grew older, maybe it would have helped me to avoid further dramas in my life! I left with my ankle in a cast and a pair of crutches to assist me with my manoeuvring around, not exactly what I had in mind for my perfect trip away.

I arrived back at the hotel where my friends were just awakening! I had been out for nearly half a day and it was mid-afternoon! They were all great to me and chipped in some money to help with the medical bills. This touched me more than they realised, they were always there for me. I was so thankful for their generosity and I always had a hard time accepting gifts. Pride is a stubborn thing and that I was so used to doing things on my own, accepting generosity was difficult for me. I speak of this story because the whole ordeal could have so easily been avoided if I had not allowed my drinking to reach such extreme limits.

I stayed out in Kos for the remaining eleven nights and had the time of my life, despite my plaster cast ankle. Casual sex and an abundance of free-flowing alcohol were still readily available to me, even while my leg was in plaster! Girls would approach me and ask what had happened to my foot? I would tell them that I had saved a kitten from drowning who was stuck in shoreside rocks and twisted my ankle in the process. They loved the story, although I feel most women saw through my heart-wrenching tale of heroics, but nevertheless, it helped me to form a connection with them. I was getting smashed 'til six every morning with my friends and beautiful women. I finally felt accepted by everybody, life was blissful, so I thought. We returned home and that holiday will live with me forever as a purely happy time despite my accident.

I think the holiday had given me a new sense of confidence and the ability to talk to anyone, or was it the alcohol that was in my system most days? Either way, I was now able to talk to strangers and meet many people in pubs and clubs this way. I met fascinating, interesting characters doing the thing I loved: getting wasted. This is where I also encountered a new substance, called cocaine.

I loved gangster movies like Scarface, Goodfellas, Pulp Fiction and Casino. I watched these films nearly every day and knew most of the scripts. When I was drunk, I would put on one of my favourite films and let them embed into my subconsciousness as I drifted off into a drunken slumber. These films would all glamourise cocaine use and I thought that by taking cocaine, it would provide me with extra recognition amongst my friends.

I loved the mystery of going to the toilets to snort a line off the top of a dirty toilet seat, through a worn, grubby bank note. I mean, if this doesn't scream glamour to you, I don't know what else does!? I felt like a movie star for those brief, fleeting moments when the bitter white powder was hoovered up by my willing nostrils.

Cocaine soon took a firm hold of my life; I would obsess over coke. I needed it in clubs to complete my *Tony Montana* persona, this is who I was, and it was cool, right!? I started snorting at work too. I would sniff my nose to appear cool. I loved the edgy, wired look that I had perfected also. A classic trait of the ego is role playing. The ego is a brilliant actor and will adapt your character traits to suit the situation. Depending on what group you are entertaining, the ego will become a chameleon in order to gain acceptance!

Observe how your own behaviour can alter around certain people. You may not even be aware that you act differently, but this is all the work of the ego. At work we demonstrate a certain type of behaviour that is expected by an employer. We all play our roles in the imaginary hierarchical structure, and the way we behave reflects this. When we are with our friends, our egos play a totally different role compared to the role we play when we are at work; this is role playing.

I kept the severity of my cocaine use to myself as I could see my old friends were worrying about me. Again, my behaviour was getting the opposite reaction to that which I wanted. In my eyes though I was fine and they were the ones being so damn soft, what was wrong with them? Maybe they need to loosen up a little and have a line themselves? The fact was though, that all my money was going on cocaine and alcohol. I recall pawning my gold chain that my own mother had bought me for my eighteenth birthday, just so I could have a night out. It's so sad when I think back to that boy and where his priorities lay.

I began snorting cocaine at work to get me through the boring shifts and it made me feel powerful. The majority of the staff were female and it gave me that extra bit of confidence to be flirtatious with them. The instant buzz it provided, the drip down the back of my throat, I loved it all! I was simply fascinated by chopping up each line with a bank card and trying to get it as straight as I could, it was like a game! I would create little devices to enhance the sniffing process that were made from food dating labels at work. They worked a treat and were far more hygienic than a back note; after all, health is paramount.

Cocaine and alcohol would now go hand in hand as it enabled me to drink more and remain focused; or so I thought. A standard night out would start by sinking a few pints and then making my way to the toilet to snort a line. This would then enable me to drink all night.

One day I walked into a wall through being so intoxicated. I looked like I had been in a brawl and half my face was torn open. I have zero recollection of how I managed this glorious feat of self-abuse, but it was bad. Dean helped me back to my dad's that night and, as you can imagine, fireworks erupted!

I couldn't remember a thing the next day about the night before. All I did remember was how scared I felt when I woke up with my face stuck to the blood-stained pillow. What the hell had happened? Dean had to fill me in via an anxious phone call that morning. I hated those feelings of dread, angst and guilt in the pit of my stomach. I often experienced these feelings the next day when drawing a blank about the night before.

I went to work and people were quizzing me about what I had done. It looked unprofessional to say the least, and I was so concerned about what the old people would think of me, as I was cooking for them. I cared for them and didn't want to be this person.

When work finally finished that day, I went to visit my nan and grandad. I knocked on their front door and my nan was the one who opened it. She took one look at my face and flung her arms around me immediately. She ushered me into the house as she cried. Nan was sobbing and said, "Why are you doing this to yourself? Can't you see that we love you and worry about you?" I sat there in silence; ashamed of what I had done and the worry that I had caused my nan and grandad.

I agreed with Nan and Grandad that, from that day forth, I would limit my drinking. Deep down I remember thinking, *How the hell am I going to cut down on my drinking and drugs and still have fun?* The prospect of a sober life, one of self-discipline, scared me. I agreed to limit my drinking but I knew that I was just telling Nan and Grandad what they wanted to hear. This was my lifestyle and this was who I was now. *They are overreacting*, I thought, after the initial shame and guilt had passed. Plus, they didn't even know about my drug use, I kept this to myself. I genuinely thought that there was no problem and truly believed that this was what all kids aged nineteen did, wasn't it!? Needleless to say, I didn't heed their advice and soon after I did a U-turn on our little agreement. It is funny how emotions can change so quickly. I went out to the pub that very same night.

I would always crash at Lee's house to avoid confrontation with my dad when I was late or smashed again. His parents were wonderful to me and in hindsight, I feel I abused their generosity. They assured me I didn't and that I was always funny but still, it was unacceptable to get in the states that I did under their roof. I never went out of my way to be horrible to anyone, apparently, I was a funny drunk who just wanted to love everyone. Still, this was no excuse for my frequent debauchery and being a lairy burden to people was such selfish behaviour.

My drinking was getting way out of hand and I would often drink half a bottle of Southern Comfort on the bus journey home on a Saturday night after work. This was in preparation for going out, just to get me warmed up, if you like! What can I say? All the heavy drinking gave me a high tolerance.

One Saturday evening though, I drank an entire one litre bottle of Southern Comfort while I was on the bus travelling home. I did this as there were some girls on the bus who I was trying to impress. Like I said, I would usually drink only half the bottle but I was on a mission to impress these lucky ladies who were sitting next to me and also drinking.

I mean what's not impressive about someone who can drink as much legal poison as humanly possible in a short amount of time? As I did this, I remember looking at the units of alcohol on the bottle. I was drinking more than a week's recommendation for an adult in less than half an hour - and you know what? I was proud of myself.

After much drunken flirtation with those lucky ladies, I stumbled off the bus. I arrived home that evening already steaming drunk, to which my father was infuriated. I just put my headphones on and turned my music up to ignore him. There were so many occasions that I pushed my dad to the edge and I loved the response he would give me: sheer rage. Part of me fed off his anger. I secretly enjoyed seeing him lose his mind at his precious little boy who was wasted!

Although this time my dad saw the red mist due to the state I had inflicted upon myself on the bus. It turns out that one litre of strong spirits consumed in less than an hour can seriously knock you about. I had drunk way more than I anticipated on that bus journey home, and I had been sniffing coke at work to get me through the shift. I was in a mess and I hadn't really experienced a state like this before. I couldn't function properly, and even I was worried.

Lee and Dean arrived at the door to take me out partying with them but Dad was refusing to let me leave. He was livid, but worried about me at the same time. I slurred some gibberish nonsense to him, pushed him out of my way and left to go out partying. This was the beginning of the end for our relationship though as I had truly gone past the point of caring. What was my dad's problem? Just let me be and let me live my life, it's not like I had a problem, I was young and having fun. Needless to say, I didn't get accepted into any clubs that night and Lee and Dean sent me back to my Auntie Rachel's, as she was the only one who would have me, bless her! My drinking was affecting the lives of others, I was becoming very selfish.

The next story that I will tell you is something that I could pinpoint as a very low moment in my earthly existence but is also coupled with a beautiful juxtaposition in my opinion, of which, I will explain.

I had been on an all-day drinking session in the pub and a few of us agreed to continue. I was supposed to be at work that day but phoned in sick to go drinking instead. With our agreement in place to continue the party, we made our way back to a girl's house that I was seeing at the time, her name was Becky.

I had met Becky in the pub and seen her around from time to time. The first time that we spoke was at the bar, even though our paths had crossed many times before. As soon as we had our first proper conversation, that was it, we hit it off. We got drunk together there and then. Becky had a strange allure about her that I couldn't quite put my finger on, I was drawn to her. She was eight years older than me so maybe that was the attraction. Whatever it was, I was mesmerised by her.

We arrived back at Becky's place which was the designated party venue. We continued our mammoth drinking session, which accidently turned into an all-night coke binge as well. I proceeded to stay up all night drinking Stella and sniffing line after line of cocaine; this continued until the morning arrived.

The angelic sound of the birds rang out to welcome in a brand new day and the sun's glare got brighter as it rose; all of this natural phenomenon was happening while I was still snorting coke. We had drunk the house dry, so I opted to do the noble thing and volunteered to go up to the shops to buy some more Stella for us all. I left the house full of vigour and as soon as I stepped outside, I felt the warm rays of the early morning summer sun on my blotchy, spotty skin. The air was close as I made my way to the nearest corner shop.

I entered the shop and went straight to the alcohol aisle. I grabbed eight cans of Stella and clutched them closely to my feeble body like a proud parent. I took my place in the queue only to realise that I was surrounded by school children who were buying sweets and drinks in preparation for the day that was ahead of them. At that moment in time, I genuinely thought nothing of the situation and purchased my drinks. I then proceeded to walk home while drinking a fresh, crisp, cold can of Stella. Can I just add that I was due to work at four o'clock the very same afternoon but it was about half past eight at this point, so in my mind, I had loads of time to recover.

It's only now that, through retrospective thought, I see the situation for what it was. What must those children have thought of me? Not that I cared then, I was off my face, but now I care. Not from an egoic point of view either, where we are far too concerned about the opinions of others defining who we are, no. My concern now is, what if a child that day witnessed my actions with close scrutiny and grew up believing that my behaviour that day was an acceptable way to live? What if they thought my actions that day were the norm and that is what adults did?

In that very scenario that I described for you, we have the future of our world queuing up with their hopes and dreams, buying their sweets with their blissful innocence. Then there was me, an adult who was once an innocent child in the very same position, buying alcohol. This was what my life had become and seemed a million miles away from the comparison of the children in the shop that day. I had not dealt with the issues and pain which stemmed from my childhood and look where it had landed me!

I made it to work later that day and I was training a girl who had just started at the care home. She was taking my job as I was leaving to work abroad - to party more in my youthful wisdom. I recall sitting in the pantry and shouting out instructions to her, as that was all I could muster. I had a little bit of coke left which I snorted in the toilet; it gave me a brief buzz but I was exhausted and kept feeling like I was going to pass out. When I returned to the muggy kitchen, I felt even worse and the cold sweats were truly taking a hold of my disorientated body. I somehow completed my shift; it was only four hours long but felt like an eternity! I was still very much under the influence and then went home feeling like the walking dead.

From that moment onwards, I vowed not to drink or to ever touch coke again; I couldn't feel like this and my skin was a complete mess because of my lifestyle; I looked like death. I couldn't even smoke that evening, as I felt like I would vomit if I did. This was it this time; I had an epiphany, a re-birth, I would stop giving the people who cared about me, like my nan, any more cause to worry. I would end this downward spiral of futile self-destruction and halt this cycle of destructive behaviour once and for all. By about nine o'clock the same night, I was back around Becky's house, who I was pretty much living with at that point. Before I knew it, we were halfway down a bottle of vodka and had another gram of coke on the way, courtesy of our considerate dealer. Happy days!

11

Enough of All This!

I left my stable care home job to work abroad in Kos for the summer with Becky. We both thought it would be a great idea to work abroad. I would do anything Becky said; she had a strange hold over me. I was convinced it was love! Becky loved everything I did; basically, she loved to party. We only lasted two weeks out there and soon returned home as the novelty had quickly worn off. Truthfully, I was broke and homesick, so I was relieved when Becky suggested that we return home.

Living with someone constantly for a month can bring to light some glaring issues. When you are under someone's feet all the time, you quickly discover if you are compatible or not; Becky and I were not! We had quite a brief turbulent relationship which came to an abrupt end. It turns out that you cannot have a successful relationship when it is fuelled by drugs, alcohol and sex, our true selves quickly became apparent to one another. We split very shortly after arriving home, with Becky's final words being: "You are emotionally unstable Dave!" *What nerve she had saying that, I was fine, wasn't I!?*

I guess my mind games and creating arguments out of nothing had been unearthed in a very shrewd manner by this bold character. Now I see that Becky had taught me a huge lesson. I was an emotional wreck who liked to play mind games with my partners, I just couldn't see it at that present moment. My pain body loved the drama and that unsettled feeling in a relationship. If things were going well, I would soon put a stop to that!

At that time though, hearing those truths from Becky hurt so much and with that, she disappeared out of my life just as quickly as she had arrived. The passion and emotions in that brief relationship were so intense, why was that? The whole relationship was like a chemical reaction that produced sparks and blinding light, but soon fizzled out. Was it the alcohol? Was it the drugs? Was it the fact she was 8 years older than me and much more experienced? Whatever it was, her departing had left me crippled. I craved for those feelings that I once had with Becky. I was heartbroken.

I had returned home to the realisation that I had no prospects, no income, no girlfriend and I wondered where I would get money from to fuel my debauched lifestyle. I took a loan from the bank; God knows how, but they let me have the money, more fool them! I lived like a king, in my eyes, for a very short time. Alcohol would flow freely and cocaine was readily available. I would drink in the local Wetherspoons all day long, go clubbing whenever possible and take any opportunity I could to get wasted so I could blot out the pain of Becky's absence.

No matter how wasted I got though, those feelings I had with Becky could not be matched. How could someone who I had known for such a short amount of time have such a profound impact on me? Why was this? I hadn't felt like this about anyone before. I would obsess over Becky and walk the streets at night with the slim hope that I would bump into her. I would always have a few cans on me and I would always have cocaine in my pocket so that if we did meet, I could offer her a line; who said romance was dead?

I was becoming obsessed with this girl and was developing stalking tendencies. I mean, walking paths where you knew someone else walked with the hope that you would meet is creepy to say the least. I would phone her multiple times a day with all calls being sent directly to voicemail. I have to say it, I was a wreck. Becky was like a drug and I needed a hit. How could she just cut me off like that? Was I really that much of a freak? I was slowly losing my mind and the pain was overwhelming. I felt like I was drowning. I didn't like who I was becoming, I was like a wild animal pacing the streets in hope of seeing this woman.

Eventually, everything became too much for me. I wasn't sleeping, I wasn't eating, I was just drinking. I looked like an absolute mess. I was staying in parks at night-time just to avoid going back to my dad's, as he had begun to comment on my behaviour. All of this pain was becoming too much. I couldn't speak to anyone about how I truly felt; not Lee, Dean or even Nan, I felt lost. How could I tell anyone that I would walk the streets looking for Becky? That would alienate me even more! I felt ashamed of my neurotic behaviour. I sucked it up and went it alone, I simply swigged more liquor to hide from it all. My money had all but gone and the cocaine that I kept in my pocket, for the off chance that I did bump into Becky, had been hoovered up by my needy nostrils.

I'd had enough of this thing called life; I was a loser. This constant rejection from women was becoming all too much. All it brought was pain, there was no point to it. I decided to end it all. Whatever was on the other side had to be better than all this shit! How could I end this torment in the quickest way possible?

Growing up, my dad had always held a firearms permit and possessed many guns. All were legal and registered with the chief constable. I grew up around guns with the notion that they were all safe and were to be used for sporting pastimes. Dad had always gone shooting down ranges and was a consummate professional when it involved guns. All of his firearms were accounted for and locked away behind several safe doors. The room had an alarm code which only my dad knew; basically, it was like Fort Knox and was impossible to break into.

One day I arrived home intoxicated with pain and alcohol. Dad was out and I sat down in the living room; slumped in the main chair. To my sobering astonishment, there was a handgun next to the chair. What was my dad doing with a handgun? They were supposed to be illegal! No wonder I hadn't seen this one before. Dad must have left it out while cleaning it, this was a miracle! I examined the gun and opened the chamber to discover that it had six rounds in it. This was it! This is what

I was waiting for. I had wanted to end my life but was too scared to slit my wrists as I was afraid of knives; the irony! I wanted something that was quick and easy, it was like this gun had been left as a sign.

Go on, put the gun to your head and pull the trigger. Put an end to all of this hell and your worthless existence. Those were the words that ran through my head at that moment. I acted upon those words and pushed the cold steel of the barrel to the side of my temple. My heart began to race and I felt the adrenaline begin to course through my veins. My fingers began to tingle and I experienced the most aggressive butterflies in my stomach.

It was such a surreal and trippy feeling. The thought of going to a totally foreign place and leaving all that I knew in the blink of an eye was truly nauseating. There was also an extreme level of curiosity at the same time. The drunken haze that I had been in had started to lift and my thoughts became clear. I felt more alive than I ever had. Was this the moment of clarity I had longed for?

A whole host of thoughts ran through my confused cranium and I imagined being gone in a split second. Would my pain stop? Feelings were part of the body, weren't they? Where would I go? Would it be a blank, black space? Would I burn in hell which is what Sunday school had taught me? Would there be pearly gates? Was I evil for what I was about to do? What would the aftermath look like? Would it be messy? Would there be blood and brains scattered everywhere like in the movies? Imagine Dad walking into that mess. My lifeless corpse sat there with a hole in its head. Imagine the trouble he would get into as it was his firearm and illegal! Dad could get locked away for such negligible behaviour. What would Nan say? The light of my life would be heartbroken. She had often warned me about the perils of suicide and made me promise to speak to her if I ever felt like that. Well, I did feel like that, and I had broken my promise to her. That made me feel even worse. I was about to pull the trigger and disregard everything that she had said.

As I cocked back the hammer of the revolver and was about to squeeze the trigger, the thought of my nan, and all she had done for me brought tears to my eyes. I sobbed uncontrollably. She loved me and had shown me how beautiful life could be with the power of love. I froze and gently uncocked the hammer and placed the gun back down to its original resting place. I stood up, walked out of the front room and out of the front door of the house. I walked to the nearby park which provided much solace for me, it had become my new favourite resting place. Tears were in my eyes as I walked down the street but I couldn't end it all, I wasn't that selfish. Nan's love kept me going that day and I believed her teachings saved me.

I never spoke to anyone about that day for a long time. Only recently have I spoken to my father about that moment for the first time. He was shocked and mortified that I couldn't talk to him about how I felt all those years ago. He said he knew better than anyone about pain and love. I told him about the gun and he remembered the gun well. He still owns it, but said that it was deactivated. The bullets in it were just for show and not live rounds. Handguns were illegal to own but Dad wasn't breaking the law, for it was a deactivated one. Dad wasn't getting sloppy in his old age after all.

So, it turns out that if I had pulled the trigger that day, I would still be here to write about it anyway! The fact that I had not seen the gun before and considered it real was ultimately irrelevant. I couldn't have killed myself even though that was my intent. Still, the level of punishment I was subjecting my body to on a daily basis could have been considered a slow death. The intent was still there however, despite the vision of my nan's love saving me that day. I would just have to go about my slow demise in a more socially accepted way.

12

Working in the Pub and Drinking in the Pub

The Wetherspoons pub had become my second home. I actually think I spent more time in the pub than I did at my dad's. I knew all the staff and was friendly with everyone. I had become very good friends with the manager of the pub because of the amount of time I spent there.

I was in a particular stupor one day and the manager came over and sat next to me. We began chatting and she asked if I would be interested in a job in the kitchen. She knew about my previous cooking experience in the care home and offered me the job there and then, after a very informal interview to say the least. Maybe she took pity on me, who knows? *What the hell* I thought, I spent enough time in the place, I may as well work there. My loan hadn't lasted long, so I was in desperate need of income, and with that said, I was soon working in the kitchen, grilling meat and preparing salads. My new job occupied me and I had a lot more shifts than I did at my old place, plus, I now had a regular income again. It's amazing how things come out of nothing.

People would laugh at the amount of time I spent in that building. If I wasn't working, I was drinking there! The Wetherspoons should have just paid me in Stella Artois tokens because as soon as a shift finished, I would make my way to the bar and put all my earnings straight back into the till. Technically, the pub wasn't losing any money because of my wage recycling behaviour.

I was known as 'Stella Dave' or 'drunken Dave' to everyone who knew me, and I loved it. I felt like a bit of a celebrity around all the bars, due to the absurd states that I would inflict upon myself. I would talk to anyone and made lots of friends easily when under the influence. I wasn't doing any harm and people were entertained by me, at least that's what I thought. People liked this drunken guy but if they only knew the real caring soul that I was deep down, maybe they would like him more? Nah, nice guys finish last!

I would still stop at my nan and grandads frequently to avoid friction with my father. My grandparents held liberal views about my late-night shenanigans; they would leave a key for me outside so I could just let myself in undetected. I always hid my states from them and would just sleep downstairs mainly, passed out in *my* chair. My relationship with my dad was still volatile to say the least, so that's why I would shy away from going home at all costs. I would stay at anyone's house who would accept me. My dad was just too suffocating, why did he insist on treating me like a child?

When staying at my nan's, she would feed me and love me. Whenever she asked how much I did drink, I would just tell her that I had a few pints here and there, just like we agreed... I always wonder if she knew the true depth of the pain that I harboured. Either way, whenever I stayed at Nan's, she would make me feel like a child again and smother me with love and care. That special house would help me to forget the woes of the world. I could escape reality for the time being; it was my sanctuary. I felt at peace there and more importantly, loved and secure.

13

THE FINAL STRAW

There were so many times that I pushed my dad to the edge, but this particular time I am about to write about was the breaking point. Christmas used to be a fun time as a child, despite Mum not being there. Dad did his best to make it memorable. However, the Christmas period as an adult was not quite the same between my father and I.

Christmas 2005 came around and there was obvious friction between myself and Dad. My drinking was causing many arguments between us and I was living in a war zone. God only knows what would have happened if he had found out about my cocaine use, I kept that hidden well. Neither of us were going to change our opinions on how I should be living my life, it was growing tiresome. I enjoyed winding him up and loved seeing him hurt. Imagine that, a guy who had looked out for me my entire life and I had this approach to him! I was a sadistic little bastard when I wanted to be.

Christmas day arrived and I was hungover to hell. I didn't want my dinner and told Dad I wasn't hungry as we sat at the table. He said he had worked hard making the meal but I told him where to shove it, I didn't care. His response was that of pure fury and raw pain. He went mad and said how ungrateful I was. This hurt me as I knew he was right, so I hit him where it hurt. Over the years, anger had slowly festered within me towards my dad and I blamed him for Mum leaving. I let go! All of this toxicity came spewing out of my hateful mouth and I accused him of being the reason why Mum had left us, I just let it all out.

A massive argument erupted at the Christmas dinner table and I threw my plate across the table at him with disgust and venom. What was happening wasn't exactly a festive scene to sketch on a Christmas card and display on your mantle, this was hell! Dad said he'd had enough and told me to get out of the house, he couldn't bear to look at me any longer. I couldn't blame him; I had brought so much shame and misery to the house! I just got up and left.

I walked the streets on that cold, damp and grey Christmas afternoon. It was all so quiet. Everyone was enjoying their lunch and family time together, while I was wandering the streets alone. I decided to phone my mum as this was the relationship we had. We had both reached the point where conversations over the phone were the most practical way that we could bond. My visits to London had diminished over the years due to where my priorities lay in life.

I phoned her familiar number and she answered immediately. I explained the situation to her and she told me to be calm and to go back to Dad. I followed her advice and returned. I knocked on the door. Dad answered and let me in, but the damage was done. He gave me one week to leave and that was final.

I left a week later with my life in bin bags, literally. I hated that man. How could he reject me just like my own mother had all those years ago? My dad also banned Nan from getting involved and I wasn't allowed to see her or stay there. My guardian angel had been taken away from me too, but I didn't visit her as I didn't want to inflict any further conflict upon her from my dad. This led to more pain which perpetuated my ongoing problems internally. Obviously, I don't feel like that now towards my dad as I had brought that whole situation upon myself, but at that time in my life, I couldn't see that. I was the victim and my situation only helped to feed my negative perspective on life. My pain body was growing.

So that was it, I was lost! I only spent two nights on the streets which were grim, but I had multiple cans of Stella in my backpack, so it wasn't all bad. I didn't really sleep. I just walked around really, sitting on benches and hiding from people as I was scared and embarrassed of what they would think of me. I still had my job at the Wetherspoons while all of this was going on, so I would just arrive there early, once it opened, and use the staff facilities there to change and wash.

My friends soon offered me sofas to crash on; to which I gratefully accepted. My friends were great to me, especially Tom and Mike. I will never forget their help and how unjudging they were about everything. Deep down though, I was hurt and embarrassed and I hated imposing upon them. I started to worry. How would I cope with all of this? I couldn't sleep on a sofa forever. Time to go full blown party mode, all of the time! The term *party* which I explained earlier just gave the whole situation a very positive and upbeat twist to it all. The fact was that I had a very serious problem that was developing into an uncontrollable addiction. However, in this westernised society, alcohol and recreational drugs are acceptable. I tried to convince myself that I was doing no wrong!

One day while I was over my peaceful little park, that I would frequently visit to get away from it all, I ended up drinking with a tramp. Of course a tramp is a derogatory term but that is what he was to me. In my eyes, he was in more of a mess than me, but in reality, was he? We were both the same. Only now I realise no one is better than anyone in life, but this is to be examined later in the book.

The sofa surfing that I was doing while homeless was wearing thin. I felt bad for taking advantage of my friends' hospitality and wanted to be out of their hair. I will always be eternally grateful for what they did but I was never good at accepting charity. A lady I worked with, called Kay, offered me a place at hers and I could sleep on her futon permanently if I wanted it. I accepted her offer in a jiffy as I was tired of carrying my life around with me in bags. I could finally crash somewhere on a permanent basis.

This lady was beautiful. She had tattoos, piercings and a pink Mohican! A truly unique personality. To the naked, judgemental eye of society, Kay was far from a woman with a conventional appearance. I loved how individual she was and she taught me so much; including that we should never judge a book by its cover. Oddly enough, this book cover was chosen by careful thought and I wanted it to tell a story of its own. The snowy field represents challenges, as snow can often be tricky to walk through yet beautiful at the same time. The sunlight peeking through the branches from behind the woods is symbolic of our ultimate goal. The enlightenment we can obtain through life is only achieved via difficult journeys and challenging terrain. Sometimes, we must walk through snow driven paths and navigate our way through thick, overgrown woodland. Initially this may seem challenging but it is, however, all part of the journey if you want to reach the light at the end of the woods. Always remember as well, underneath all the snow, new life is growing all around us.

Back to the story anyway! I settled into Kay's place well and didn't care that I slept on a futon, it was nice to have somewhere permanent. Kay gave me a little closet for my possessions, bless her. We would smoke, drink red wine and laugh all night. I enjoyed being with her, she was a very warm woman. I will always have tremendous love and respect for what she did for me.

I always had short relationships with girls and hopped from one to another, trying to obtain that female attention which I craved so badly. I often felt empty after those brief encounters and if anything, it only messed my head up even more. One night though, I would meet a lady a couple years younger than me that changed my perception on life.

14

That Special Someone Who Helps You to See Things Differently

I met Laura in a club one night while I was blind drunk. Slurring my words, as usual, I made my way over to Laura, who was a friend of a friend, and I'm pretty sure that I didn't make a good first impression. Somehow, I managed to get her number and we went on a few dates after I had plucked up the courage to text her. Before I knew it, we were an item! She drove, so she would pick me up and take me drinking; this was too good to be true!

After a few months, Laura couldn't bear to see me living out of a closet and sleeping on a futon and offered me a place at her house with her parents. I simply couldn't refuse; I loved this girl! I met her parents for the first time when I was pretty smashed but they didn't judge and they were all so welcoming. In all fairness, I had mastered the art of hiding my intoxications pretty well, or so I thought.

I packed all my possessions from Kay's and bid her farewell. She was upset to see me go but happy at the same time with the fact that I had met Laura. Laura drove me to her parents' house and we unpacked my stuff. I couldn't believe how lucky I was to have met this girl; it was like all my prayers had been answered.

I had applied for a flat through the local council when I was first asked to leave my dad's house, to which I had little success, as I wasn't classed as a high priority. Within months of living at Laura's, she made me re-apply for a flat and told me to be optimistic. I listened to her and applied again. Because I was on the waiting list for so long, my application was sent to the top of the pile and I received a call from the council within a week, they were offering me a place of my own.

Laura and I went to view the flat with anticipation. When we arrived at the council office, they gave me the keys and told us that it was on the 8th floor. We entered the lift of the high-rise building which was covered in graffiti and had a strong stench of urine and vomit. The doors opened at my floor and I turned the key in the lock to my potential new place. I don't know what I was expecting as I opened the door but I was greeted with a surprise. As I looked around at the flat it looked derelict. It had torn, worn wallpaper everywhere and chipped doorways with paint all over the floors. I broke down in front of Laura and sobbed, was this what my life had come to and what I was worth? She picked me up and assured me that this was temporary. We could decorate it and make it beautiful, she assured me. Her optimism that day really showed me that you can see life whichever way you like. Is it a glass half full or half empty? It's down to how you perceive things. We returned to the council office at which, I begrudgingly accepted the flat.

Out of nowhere, the very same week, I received a tax rebate for £700. I used this to clear my loan of £500 and invest the rest into my flat. Laura's parents, Colin and Lynn, helped me to decorate my new place and really helped to get me on my feet. They were so kind to me; I will never forget their generosity, there is so much good in the world.

My flat was in a rough part of town, but I didn't care. When the door was closed, it was mine. I had independence at last and could drink until the cows came home. Each room was perfect and I even put laminate, wooden flooring in the living room over the paint smeared vinyl tiles that were previously there. It was unrecognisable from the initial viewing. Laura's words had come true and we had completed our little project together. I was so proud.

My new flat was ten minutes away from my dad's house. I decided to pay him a little visit (not in a mob way) and make amends for what I had done. So I dropped in on him out of the blue. Bearing in mind that I had not seen or spoken to the man for 9 months, I had no idea what reception I would receive. Nan had also asked me a while back to see my dad and apologise, which I was dubious about and initially refused. Nan and I would only speak on the telephone because I couldn't see her due to the ban Dad had enforced. Eventually I listened to my nan. I wasn't going to dispute what she told me as I worshipped the ground she walked on.

I finally took the step and ventured to the familiar front door of my dad's house. I had spent many a drunken night fumbling with the lock in delirious stupors but here I was again. I knocked on the door and waited… My dad opened the door and was initially surprised to see his son standing there. After a few moments of silence, he greeted me and invited me in. I informed him what had been happening in my life and understood why he did what he did, if anything, what he had done had helped me. We began to build bridges and our relationship has only progressed since that ominous day.

I was also allowed to see my nan again without any furtiveness and with this, I immediately took Laura to my grandparents so I could show her off. I would see my nan every week from that moment forth to make up for the time I'd lost. I hadn't seen her for months because of me living miles away and the awkward circumstances.

My cocaine use had become less and less since I had met Laura, but it was still a problem. It worried Laura and one day we spoke about it. I agreed to quit cocaine for Laura and didn't think it fair to take drugs into her parents' house after what they had done for me. I found it relatively easy to terminate my relationship with cocaine; I just thought of what others had done for me and that inspired me not to go back down that slippery, snowy slope! Considering the huge role it had played in my life, I didn't miss that devil's dandruff one bit!

All I heard were horror stories about people quitting drugs, but cocaine was more of a psychological thing with me. I loved the way it made me feel about myself; as if I were some sort of gangster! Of course, nothing could be further from the truth and it didn't make me cool, despite what I had seen in the movies. It made Laura upset and she would worry about my health, so I packed it in and never looked back. Just like that, I was free! I didn't want to hurt her as she had helped me so much and I loved her. I saw the pain I had caused my nan over the years and didn't want to put Laura through that too.

While we were on the detox trail, I also quit smoking, at the drop of a hat. It is amazing what genuine happiness can do! I learnt from the whole ordeal that when you set your mind to something and actually want to do it, you can achieve it and excuses don't even enter the equation. I didn't have one single relapse with nicotine or cocaine. However, after a while, the novelty wore off and I was left with a huge void which needed to be filled, and quickly! It turned out that despite my earlier optimism, the love of a good woman just wasn't enough.

Shortly after this period of no drugs, I rediscovered my love for Aston Villa and began going to games again. This turned out to be the new drug that I quickly became addicted to as it filled the huge black hole that was the absence of cocaine. My going to the football also had an ulterior motive -drinking. It turns out going to the football and getting completely annihilated was acceptable at any time of day, as long as you wore your team's colours. You can drink Stella at 9 in the morning and it's fine, as you are going to a match! I would go to the games with Dean or my friend Luke and drink in the pubs around Birmingham before the game. I soon made friends in these football pubs and loved my new identity. I was surrounded by like-minded people who were doing exactly the same thing that I was doing. I felt complete solidarity with my new claret and blue brothers.

I got into a few scuffles when walking with our fans as we would clash with away rivals, but I wouldn't describe myself as a football hooligan. I didn't have the heart to hurt anyone physically, I just loved the adrenaline and being surrounded by like-minded people that would protect you simply because you followed the same team. I can see the appeal as to why people join hooligan gangs or firms, it can make you feel invincible. It provides a great buzz when you are in the midst of a giant fracas with opposing fans and the police are everywhere. So, I totally understand why people go to the next level and participate in physical violence. When you're surrounded by your brothers and the adrenaline is flowing, anything is possible. For me though, all I wanted was the liquor and solidarity! That feeling of belonging.

Laura was quickly becoming second best to Villa and we split up a few times because of it; jeez, I'd quit coke and smoking for her, give me a break! It was selfish behaviour to the core on my behalf. Villa quickly consumed my life and I would count down the days until match day, allowing my happiness to be governed by match days and results, I literally lived for it.

Laura and I got back together after I agreed to pay more attention to her but I still thought she was overreacting. After three years together and experiencing a rocky patch, we both thought that getting our own flat together would make us stronger. We went to the estate agents and put down a deposit on the first flat we saw. Laura and I submitted my notice at my current flat and we moved swiftly into our new love nest! It was beautiful and in a posh part of town, next to a giant shopping mall. We were both very proud of our new abode. At the same time as moving, I had just got a job at the Copthorne chain of hotels, as a trainee chef and things were looking up. I was 23 when all this was happening.

I received promotions at my new place of work in quick succession and this meant more money for alcohol and Villa. My dad had installed a strong work ethic into me so I worked consistently, whether I was hungover or not. There was just something very natural about my cooking and I found it very easy and expressive. The food we produced was a million miles away from the Wetherspoons food that I was used to, and I was proud of my talents. I would receive nothing but praise about my food and this helped to raise my confidence.

I met a chef while I was working at the hotel by the name of Ben. Ben and I clicked immediately due to our love for partying and rap music.

We would go out together for pints after each shift and we formed a very close bond. Ben had a rough past, similar to myself, and we both respected each other because of our similar battles. Ben and I are still friends to this day and I am so happy I met him.

I would keep my mum informed of my triumphs via phone calls and my dad was proud of all my hard work, so all was good in my eyes. I had made a lot of effort to get the relationship with my parents back to where it should be.

My role at the hotel just kept growing and I was really seeing the fruits of my labour in full swing. All the non-stop gruelling work and long hours were paying off. I learnt from some great chefs while I was at the Copthorne and I really thrived under the pressure that busy services provided. I suppose food was a way of expressing my buried emotions that lay dormant for so long. My food made people happy, which in turn meant that I was happy. All I ever wanted to do was to make people happy. I just went about it in a very strange way most of the time.

15

SOMETHING STILL LACKING…

So, I had a beautiful girlfriend who loved me, a steady, successful job and a lovely flat too! Dean, Lee, a friend called Matt and I all went on a couples holiday with our lovely partners and had an absolute blast. Two weeks in a private villa with a jacuzzi, pool and unlimited alcohol was just what the doctor ordered.

My life was all good in the eyes of society and I should have been happy, as I was ticking all the boxes. Still, something was missing and I felt unfulfilled, what was it? I lived for the football match days, they helped me to escape from it all and become something that I truly wasn't! I would also happily drink five pints of Stella after a shift at the hotel. I guess it helped me to cope with all the hard work I was putting in. All the time that I spent drinking, I was with friends and I was doing no harm, as this was what everyone did, right? However, I was missing out on time with Laura, who would be left alone in our flat, while I was busy getting sloshed! I would always choose a night out with the lads over Laura, this only invited the inevitable.

One day I arrived home from a split shift which I regularly did due to the life of a chef. Laura was sitting down straightening her hair in front of the mirror and just said, "Dave, I can't do this anymore, it's too much too soon for me and we never go out together." I was truly shocked, as I thought everything was rosy. I told her she was overreacting and waited for her to calm down. She didn't, and she was adamant that this was what she wanted.

Where the hell had this come from? I thought to myself. I couldn't absorb or understand what was being said to me and before I knew it, it was time to return to work for my evening shift. Only a few days earlier, I had borrowed some money off Nan so that I could buy a ring and propose to Laura. We had been planning to book a trip to Venice in the coming weeks and it seemed like a perfect opportunity to pop the question. In my head this was crazy; I was ready to propose and Laura was ready to leave me!? *Laura must have been joking,* I pondered as I walked back to work. My mind was frantically trying to comprehend everything.

I completed a busy shift at work that seemed to just drift by while I was in a haze. I raced back home and returned to an empty flat; Laura had gone. How could two people that lived together be on such a different page?

Well this was a pickle wasn't it! The flat had an eerie feeling of solitude to it with no Laura there; the air felt flat and empty. I dropped to my knees and sobbed, much like the three-year-old child that I once was all those years ago, when my mother decided to leave. Why did all women walk out on me? Was I really that obnoxious? I clearly was still the problem after all this time. All the selfless things Laura and her family had done for me were now gone and in the past. This stung and I couldn't help but think that it had all come about from my selfish behaviour. If I had put Laura first above Stella, my other love, who knows where I would be? I cried for most of that night while in my empty flat, I deserved what I had gotten.

The following Sunday, it was Villa Vs Blues; this was the highlight of the season and needless to say, I got absolutely and truly inebriated. I drank from 7 in the morning, just topping up my alcohol levels from the previous night. The game was a total blur and I hardly recall any of it. All I knew was that Aston Villa won, but deep down it didn't matter; I had to go back to an empty flat. I stayed out all night to avoid the looming loneliness that waited for me when I arrived home. Eventually, after all my friends had gone home, I returned to the soulless flat in the early hours and passed out on the floor. I woke up in the morning with zero recollection of anything and had that dreaded feeling of guilt and hangxiety.

I pushed myself hard at work for the following weeks and could honestly say that I was a fully functioning alcoholic! I would drink in between split shifts and always after work; somehow my work never suffered! I kept progressing with the good chef brigade that I had around me. I was making progress at work, so how was my drinking a problem? How could it be when I was so successful…?

16

UNCONDITIONAL LOVE

I spent most of my time at the Copthorne and worked with great chefs. One chef that I worked with was called Sophie. She was new and we clicked. She helped me with my breakup by listening to me. Sophie was a lovely, sweet, compassionate person. We grew close due to our working patterns and became really good friends. I quickly fell for her and we were quick to announce that we were an item. I was genuinely happy with her but it was way too soon to be with anyone after Laura, I wasn't ready. Nevertheless, I kept justifying my new relationship in my mind, it helped me to move on. Sophie made me feel loved and special; which is what I craved. I had just another example of what love can feel like from Sophie. She knew about my past and my drinking, yet she didn't judge me. Instead she would tell me how special she thought I was every day and didn't try to change who I was.

Sophie and I shared three happy years together, but my pattern of behaviour hadn't changed. I put alcohol and my friends before her and had clearly learnt nothing from the mistakes of my previous relationship. I met Sophie's family and they were so good to me. I was blessed by this factor once again, I just kept meeting such welcoming, genuine people. Sophie and her family showed me nothing but unconditional love.

All of these wonderful, accepting people flowed into my life and always helped me in any way that they could. However, I always had to press the self-destruct button and seemed determined to jeopardise all good things that came my way. Every time, I would always put my need for artificial happiness first, in the shape of alcohol, and continued to drink away everything that was good in my life.

My nan, who had been ill for years, was slowly deteriorating each time that I saw her. This beautiful woman was becoming very frail but she still had that warmth in her eyes which had always been there for me since I was a child. My nan now lived permanently downstairs in her house because she was unable to walk upstairs anymore. My grandad refused to put her in a care home, so he looked after her every moment that he could and private carers would come in to wash and assist Nan. Sophie loved my nan also and would drive me there to see her each week. I would always make sure that each time I left Nan's, I would go back and kiss her again after she thought I had left. One day I knew that my nan wouldn't be there to kiss, so I would make this point of kissing her twice and cherishing the moment.

One day, Sophie and I went to London to see my mum, which was a rare thing. As soon as we arrived, Jim, my stepfather, sat us down and informed me that my nan had passed away while we were travelling. I sat there in silence. I always imagined that death would be on my terms and that I would be informed in a cosy chair in my own home, not after an exhausting journey. All I knew was that I didn't expect to hear this after travelling for three hours to London. In hindsight though, is there really a good time to have death sprung upon you? Like, okay, today seems like a good day to tell me that my nan has passed, hit me with it now! It doesn't really work like that does it? Anyway, I had this bombshell dropped upon me after a tiring trip across sunny London!

I didn't dare cry in front of Jim. I just sat there gazing out of the window hoping that these sickening feelings would pass. I was devastated but I also felt a slight bit of relief as well. The woman who had helped to raise me was out of her misery. I also felt sorry for Jim as he was the one who was burdened with delivering such grim news to us on our arrival. I cried that night in bed while Sophie was asleep. My nan, my light, was gone. It hurt. She was always there for me through thick and thin and now she had gone from this world. What was I going to do? It was a scary thing to process.

As the funeral approached, I wrote a poem called *My Light* dedicated to my nan and read it aloud at her service; I needed the world to know how amazing this woman was to me, she had been my only true love growing up. I have included the poem at the end of the book if you're interested in reading it.

So that was it, Nan was gone. I truly felt that my one guardian angel had gone from this planet. I cannot imagine how Grandad must have felt, the poor man, his life partner gone in the blink of an eye. I made a conscious effort to help him and vowed to see him each week. He looked after me as a child, now it was time to return the favour.

The weeks passed and Nan's death hurt but I adapted to her absence fairly quickly, I guess I had seen it coming for a while and was happy that she was at peace. I just got on with my life but never will forget what she did for me. Sophie, throughout the whole process, was fantastic! All she did was love me and support me, much like Nan did.

Sophie and I would go on holidays together with her huge family. Her family just accepted me as one of their own and they were all so friendly. I was so thankful and realised, once again, that there are always people out there who are ready to help you no matter what.

One holiday, we all went to Florida for two weeks in a private villa. It was a fantastic holiday with unforgettable experiences. Our times away together were always fun and joyful but something was always missing deep down in my soul, what was it? The passing of my nan? My past? Maybe a new job would help things perhaps?

I left the Copthorne after five years of working there as I was ready for my first management job. I moved to a care home to manage my own kitchen, plus the hours were far more sociable. I was so proud to have my own kitchen and I made a conscious effort to treat all of my new staff fairly.

I met some real characters at my new job, residents and staff! Cooking for the elderly really opened my eyes; it was my first time dealing with dementia. These people were on another planet and I loved it! In my kitchen brigade, I met a dear friend called Julie. Julie was a hard worker in all areas of the kitchen and baked some amazing cakes. We forged a beautiful bond and became very good buddies. I still speak to her even now! She was so ditzy but I could talk to her about anything. We just understood each other and we both had a similar sense of humour. It felt like we'd met before.

As I settled into my new job, Sophie and I drifted apart. This was sad but I was to blame. I was going out drinking with new friends and neglecting her. Can you see a firm pattern of behaviour emerging here, because I can!? Unfortunately, I was oblivious to it all back then though!

One day whilst I was at work, all the staff were called into a huge meeting to be told that there were plans to close the home in the coming months. I dismissed it all but still told Sophie that there was a possibility that I was going to lose my job. I didn't truly believe it because I had just literally started there. I had been there for two months, so I tried to brush it under the rug. Sophie was concerned for me, but I assured her it would be fine even though deep down I knew the writing was on the wall. What are the chances eh!? I left a secure job of five years and within months I was to lose my new job!

Over time the prospect of the home shutting down was eating me alive and worry bubbled in my stomach every day. I tried to ignore it but I couldn't. My drinking was getting out of hand again because of this. In my disoriented mind, I thought that destroying the one solid loving aspect of my life would be a good idea. I created dramas out of nothing with Sophie and fed off the turmoil in a sadistic way. Chaos was all I knew when it came to loving relationships, so I behaved how my child-like mind told me to.

Sophie agreed to a trial separation for a week but after that, something had changed within me, what was wrong with me? I called it off with Sophie. The prospect of losing my job and the recent passing of my nan had just messed me up even more. Why was I throwing something that was perfectly good away? I began to worry about my mental health, as I seemed to destroy everything I came across. I was adamant that I had to destroy every bit of good that came my way. My ego simply wouldn't allow me to be. I just couldn't accept all the love that came my way. My own insecurities ruined everything. I completely cut ties with Sophie a week after our trial separation. Months prior to all this, I was thinking that I would like to marry her but now going it alone seemed like my only option. What was wrong with me?

Sophie collected her things from our flat, which in turn was the same flat where I stayed after Laura had left me. We never spoke after that, it was strange to cut all ties from one another, I had never had a relationship end like that before but it made life easier in some respects. Sophie had exited my life in a flash. It was terrible the way I had played with her emotions and to end it so abruptly; she was too sweet to be treated like that. I wish her all the best with her life and hope she has met someone that treats her for the beautiful soul that she is. Once again, I was the one with the problem and didn't love myself. How could I love another if I resented my own existence?

My new, single life began. I brushed aside what had happened with Sophie and told myself that I was happy. I did love my new job and the fact that I could now go out drinking guilt-free with my new friends. I was fitting in nicely at my new place of work and felt so popular; it was great for my self-esteem. I kept pretending that it wouldn't close.

Despite my breakup with Sophie, my mood was good. The residents that I cooked for everyday were loving my food and they would tell me how it would brighten their day. I initially went there to run my own kitchen but that soon became second fiddle to making a difference in the residents' lives. If my cooking could make a small difference to their quality of life, I was happy. Care homes can be quite grim at times and are just businesses when you read between the lines. I've seen so many upsetting events unfold and heard so many heart-breaking tales in care homes, it makes you thankful for what you have.

There is only so much for the residents to do in their limited space. Most of their independence and the freedom of their youth had been stripped away. My eyes were opened to the true beauty and care that was delivered by the staff who worked there. The relationships they forged with the residents were truly unique; it was like one big family. The carers worked for minimum wage and did their best to make the lives of the elderly better. Staff would often go that extra mile, even though it went unrewarded in their pay packets.

After four months of working at my new job, it was announced that the company who owned the home were going to be closing the doors imminently. The reality which I had tried to hide from had come true. *How could they do this?* I thought. All the lives they were about to ruin. This was meant to be caring, loving business? Nevertheless, all the residents that I had grown to love in my short space of time there were being turfed out of their home. This was wrong in my eyes, so wrong. All the staff protested, made banners and we even involved the local newspaper, but all our efforts were in vain. It all fell on deaf ears; the owners were still closing the home.

I had made some terrific friends in my short time there and I was about to lose them all, including the residents. Why did all good things suddenly seem to go in my life? Life was cruel, unfair and I was beginning to get fed up with everything. I became lonely at night times and missed female company, but Sophie was long gone no thanks to my decision.

While working at the care home, I became very close with a girl named Leanne. Leanne had been really supportive and helped me through the breakup with Sophie. She too was about to be taken away from me because of some selfish, corporate decision. I felt robbed and bitter. I told Leanne I would miss her and that we would keep in contact, as you do, but I knew that I would not see her again. I was upset as I felt a strange bond with her.

Time was ticking and plans moved fast to evacuate the home. The residents seemed to be leaving daily and were going to new accommodations that had been found for them in the local area. My position was kept right until the end as I was the cook and people had to be fed. My workload got smaller each day, as more staff and residents were leaving. My clientele was dwindling and I had so much spare time on my hands, I just sat there most days chatting with the remaining residents. Leanne was one of the last staff there and we spent lots of time together as the home was practically empty.

I had nothing to lose now, the home was nearly empty and soon Leanne and I would part company. I was single but Leanne was out of my league, anyway, I plucked up the courage to ask her out for a drink and to my astonishment, she agreed. It was just in the nick of time because everything moved so fast and the doors of the home soon shut for good.

I will never forget walking around that care home with Leanne when it was empty. It was so eerie and horrible, the whole atmosphere just felt off. Its warmth had gone now that it was without the soul of all the staff and residents who were once there. It had been such a special place but now it was desolate and cold. I had got one good thing from my short time there though, Leanne.

17

A Beautiful Teacher

I declared my love for Leanne very early on in our relationship. Was it too soon to be moving on from Sophie? Probably, but this was all I knew, moving from woman to woman, so I didn't really care in my apathetic mind. Leanne told me she felt the same when I told her I loved her and that was that! It was music to my ears. I felt such a connection with her but I was often quick to fall in love or at least, I thought that's what it was. Our relationship was full of passion and love. In our first year, we grew stronger and stronger. She moved in with me within weeks which, again, wasn't unusual for me. I guess I craved that security of having a woman there with me, all stemming back to my childhood issues which were still rooted deep within me.

A new job had been presented to me at another care home as the kitchen manager there. This came out of nowhere and alleviated my worries of the redundancy. Someone was definitely looking out for me after I had taken the gamble to leave a secure job of five years, only to be made redundant. This job came through a link via the care home I had just left. I was so thankful, life was perfect again and had made a total 360-degree turn. Girlfriend - check, new job - check, no one to moan at me about my drinking - check, as Leanne loved drinking too! Leanne and I were like two peas in a pod. She stirred emotions in me that just left me wanting more of her, she was like a drug.

Everything felt magical with this girl, I was infatuated by her and her allure was so strong. Within a year, I had proposed to Leanne; a year to the day we first met, in fact. I did the deed while we were away on holiday together. It was a beautiful night I will never forget. We returned home and began planning our wedding but realised this was going to cost money, a lot of money! As the wedding plans unravelled, it was soon clear that the wedding that we wanted would be out of our budget. We had to have a big wedding so everyone would be impressed, right? We deserved better than a little crummy venue for our declaration of love. We had some serious pondering to do.

We agreed to put the wedding on hold for a while and come up with another plan. Leanne had a ring on her finger, so she was as good as married to me in my opinion. So, on second examination, a wedding wasn't paramount and we decided that we would get our own house together instead.

Lee had just bought a beautiful little house and was looking to sell it on. We were interested and went to view it. It was beautiful and we immediately applied for a mortgage advisor. Things were all going along smoothly but then there were complications with the building society who had initially agreed to give us the mortgage. To cut a long story short, the mortgage attempt fell through and Leanne and I felt disappointed to say the least, but everything happens for a reason as my nan used to say.

Leanne and I decided to take a small loan out instead, as the whole mortgage fiasco had deterred us a little from applying for another. We decided to rent a house instead, this would just be easier. We found a lovely little two-bedroomed house with a pretty, quaint garden. On our first viewing, we knew it was the one for us and wasted no time in submitting a deposit. Within three weeks, we moved into our new house together. Now we had our own place and felt closer than ever.

As our relationship progressed, I have to say, I was happy. My drinking was calming down and I quit my season ticket at the Villa. I was getting bored of travelling up to Birmingham every other weekend and I just didn't get the buzz that I used to from it. Villa's football was becoming really tough to watch at the time; to tell you the truth, it still is! I had more responsibilities and started to feel comfortable with who I was, like I was slowly becoming the true me.

I would travel to see my mum when I had time off from work and I was starting to put the pain of my childhood behind me to focus on the future. I witnessed how my dad was living in the past and how he wasn't happy with life; I did not want to be like that. I wanted to make the most of my life and stop blaming everything on my past.

Leanne and I did many things together and I discovered the gym thanks to her. She dragged me along one day and I loved it. I had always done exercise at home but saw this as taking it to the next step. I immediately saw changes in my body. People would comment on the noticeable change in my physique and my ego loved it. I felt good about myself for once. I was always a lanky, scrawny kid growing up and was just used to being skinny-fat.

As my gym gains increased, my drinking really did start to dwindle. I had finally discovered how important it was to take care of your body and if you look after yourself, your mood improved too! My self-esteem was through the roof and I finally began to accept who I was. All those years of drinking now seemed so futile. I couldn't believe that I had subjected this perfect gift, that was my body, to all that torment and punishment. It seemed crazy that I could actually feel this good naturally and life was far clearer now; I was permanently focused.

Gone were the late nights and waking up with constant hangxiety. I would wake with zero recall about the night before and mull over and over as to who I had offended or how I got home! Hangxiety is when you are hungover and anxious about what has happened, it is actually a term and is a perfect description for what I used to go through on a daily basis at one point.

So my passion for booze had evaporated, but Leanne was starting to go out more. She'd had a tough past, similar to mine, and loved a drink. She would pop out for *one* and wouldn't think anything of coming back at four in the morning on a Monday, a school night! Any night could turn into a party night as far as she was concerned.

Now Leanne was aged just 21 while this was happening and I was 30. When I was 21, I was an animal, as you know all too well, so I didn't want to stop her from having her youth but it all became too much for me to cope with. I would lie awake worrying, watching the clock tick by, unable to sleep at night. Leanne would arrive home in such states and she didn't realise how vulnerable she was. I loved her so much but worry was consuming me at the same time.

Leanne would get into accidental scuffles, be sick and lose days in bed with hangovers. Couldn't she see what she was doing to her perfect self? I began to resent her. How could someone that you would do anything for, treat you like this? It led to many rows, some of which were extremely volatile, which would end in her leaving the house and going to her mother's. Of course, these arguments arose from my ego. I had a concept of what a perfect relationship should be and this wasn't meeting my expectations. The fact that Leanne was not meeting these demands of mine and not conforming to my vision as to what a blissful partnership should be, drove a wedge between us and we could not coincide.

Leanne came home one night extremely sheepish. It wasn't until the next morning that I found out she had lost her engagement ring when she was drunk. I happened to find the ring in the house one day while I was cleaning. I would use it as an emotional weapon, which was wrong, but I was desperate, I needed a way to curb Leanne's drinking. I was losing her and needed to control her. I told her that she could have the ring back if she behaved like a *wife to be* should. Of course, what happens when you place conditions on how love should be? Rebellion! Just as I had rebelled against my dad all those years ago. I handled it all so wrong in retrospect, she was just having fun but I was too concerned for her and always thinking the worst. I didn't want to lose her as I loved her so much. I was desperate to keep our relationship alive.

One beautiful spring eve, I agreed to go to the pub with Leanne, even though I now hated drinking. My healthy lifestyle and gym were paramount to me, even to the point where I was mildly obsessed. The evening was fun down the pub even though I sat there and drank water!

Who would have thought it, Dave Jones in a pub drinking water!? If my 21-year-old self could have seen me, what would he have thought?

As the night wore on, it was approaching twelve O'clock and I suggested to Leanne that we should leave as I had work at seven the next morning. Leanne refused, she said that I was too boring and that she wanted to stay out until one O'clock as that's what time the pub closed. Maybe I was the boring one but I found this so selfish.

I had tried to compromise with her by going out in the first place but it still wasn't good enough for her. The fact was I could have just gone home without her and let her finish her night alone, she was having fun with her friends anyway. But no, my ego simply wouldn't allow that and wanted to assume control over the whole situation, much like our relationship. Leanne should conform to my image of what a loyal partner should be and act like it. That was it; I had an epiphany there and then, I spat my dummy out, so to speak. I didn't deserve to be treated like this, or did I? Either way, we will examine this situation later on in the book.

I told Leanne that if she wanted to put alcohol above me so much, she could have it. It broke my heart to tell this beautiful young woman how I truly felt, but that was it, I knew what was right, or so I thought. I stormed out of the pub and told Leanne not to come home. I was locking the door and she was not welcome in our home, how selfish of me. Leanne slept at her mum's that night and we didn't speak for a day. I contacted Leanne a day later to come around to discuss things.

It was a warm spring Sunday evening and I was nervously waiting in the living room for a knock at the door. I listened keenly for the arrival of Leanne, poised for any sudden sound. Leanne knocked and I jumped up to answer the door. It felt so strange looking at the woman I loved as I answered the door but I knew what I had to say. We sat down in the living room of the house we had once romantically shared together. It was strange, it felt alien and almost that I didn't know the person I was looking at. I still loved her but couldn't continue to live like this; the stress was killing me. We had such different ideas of what a relationship should be. Mine being somewhat manipulative and controlling, it wasn't healthy. I told Leanne it was over and that we both couldn't keep living like this. I expected her to disagree and beg for us to work but she agreed quietly, grabbed a few possessions and left. Why didn't she fight for us? Why didn't she tell me she would change? Deep down, I suppose this is what my ego craved in order to make myself feel special, but Leanne was so wise for her age and just left.

The door closed behind her and I was once again on my own. I dropped to my knees and cried like a child; a situation I was all too familiar with. I loved Leanne so deeply but deep down I knew this was the right decision for both of us. I was so confused though; it didn't seem fair that I had just ended the relationship with the girl of my dreams. I felt like she was a part of me, like we were meant to meet and be forever.

I actually cursed the Universe that night as I sobbed on the floor. What was the point of all this pain? I was all too accustomed with heartbreak and it seemed that it followed me wherever I went. Old thoughts came rushing back into my mind; that I actually deserved all the pain that flowed my way in life. If there was anything out there in control of us, I hated it. This time though, I didn't have my nan to run to and comfort me, no safety blanket. I was lost. Most of my friends were married and I felt like I had alienated myself due to my sober lifestyle. I will never forget how bleak and hopeless everything seemed that horrible night. I had just ended a relationship with the love of my life. I'd done the right thing, hadn't I?

18

A Fresh Start

Leanne cleared her things out of the house within three days and I made the place mine in an instant. I was quite insensitive in hindsight; it was her house too, but I ushered her out as if I had some sort of superior right over her and she were my subordinate. What I did was act out of ego and made a difficult situation even worse through my actions. I did feel like a physical weight had been lifted off my shoulders and I felt free for the first time in years. No more worries about Leanne's wellbeing or what time she'd go out at night, she was free to live the life she deserved as well.

The freedom was good and I could do as I pleased, although I did feel quite lonely in the first few weeks. *What was Leanne doing?* I wondered. *Who was she with? Was she missing me?* These were all thoughts that went through my lonely head.

I spent a lot of time around Dean and Gemma's house in the first few weeks to occupy my mind. Gemma was now Dean's fiancé and I couldn't have been happier for them both. They were both so good to me, and no matter how busy Dean was, he was always there if I needed help. Lee had moved to Dubai to teach, but we still kept in close contact and he was also of great support to me in a painful time.

As I grew accustomed to the loneliness of a night time, I actually began to enjoy my own company. This is ironic as I grew up as an only child but I was really starting to accept who I was and love myself. I really stepped my gym game up and focused on my health and wellbeing. I kept the house clean and kept on top of things. I loved my new environment and while I missed Leanne, I knew that we had both made the right decision to go our separate ways.

It was hard to completely cease contact with Leanne, as she was such a huge part of my life. I still felt that allure towards her. We would text frequently and remained amicable towards one another. I still loved her but knew that our relationship had become so unhealthy for the both of us, that we could never go back.

As the weeks passed, they turned to months, three to be exact, and it dawned on me that this was the longest that I had ever been single for about ten years. What a record! I was now very comfortable with being alone each night and was enjoying my new life. While three months wasn't exactly a long amount of time to be on my own, it may as well have been three years in Dave Jones relationship land, and deep down I longed for someone to share time with again. I guess old habits die hard and I decided to try my luck on a few dating sites to focus my attention elsewhere.

This online dating was all new to me and I created a profile that I thought flattered my greatest attributes. It's all a bit cringey looking back isn't it? Painting a superficial picture of yourself online, to be as an attractive catch as possible to a wanting mate. In this new age of online dating, you can potentially dismiss your perfect match by simply swiping your finger across a screen. This decision is based on a superficial photo that was probably staged anyway. A life partner could show up in a shell that you may not initially find attractive and be disregarded, how sad. With all of this in mind, I made my profile regardless!

I went on a few fun dates with some lovely people, but nothing materialised. I was determined not to go rushing into anything with the first female that showed me any sort of attention, which is what I usually did. With this new mantra of mine, I was actually being sensible from an objective point of view for once in my life. I was however drawing up many blanks with this newfound philosophy of mine; I was beginning to think I may be single forever, (bearing in mind it had been about four months)! I stuck to my guns though as I had now become quite cautious with who I gave myself to, due to the pain of past experiences.

In and amongst my new online dating experiences, I was also getting bored with my current job. I was just as restless in my working life, as I was in my love life. I would often search the web looking for jobs to better myself; much like the dating profiles that I would view. I found a dream job to teach at a college which was for young adults with learning difficulties and challenging behaviour. My heart lit up as I saw the advert. I was going to do this, I was so determined and applied for the position.

I waited patiently as the following weeks passed, and you can imagine my excitement when I received an email offering me an interview for the position that I so desperately wanted. I attended the interview and it went smoothly, I was sure I was going to get the job. I was a pro as far as interviews were concerned, I'd had enough of them! I knew the job was mine and felt it deep within me, in fact, I had never been so sure about anything in all my life, now that's confidence for you!

I waited weeks for a reply about the position and heard nothing. How could I be so wrong? It felt so right for me, it was what I wanted from the bottom of my heart. Life felt a bit drab for those following weeks, as I really thought a new chapter in my life was about to begin. I really considered myself as someone who could inspire young people. To make matters worse, I was still yet to find my dream woman online. Oh well, life goes on.

Towards the end of the month of May, I had been invited to a family birthday party in Brighton. The party was for Darren, my step-nephew, who was turning 30; how could I say no? I was looking forward to seeing my step side of the family again as it had been years since I had seen them all together. Part of me didn't want to travel all the way to Brighton. I was still moping around because of my current state of affairs. I knew, however, that seeing everyone would do me good. I stayed with Mum and Jim in an edgy, contemporary, hippy hotel, or at least that's how I would describe it. There were pictures of Buddhas on the walls, where the hell had they brought me!? Next, they will be lighting up the incense!

It was a beautiful, sunny weekend but walking along Brighton pier made me upset. I was envious of all the happy couples that I was seeing. I still missed Leanne and I wanted her there with me. Even though I had become happy enough with my own company, I craved companionship. Seeing the happiness that others had, made me long for those feelings of a partner again, a person you could tell anything to, joke and laugh with. That night, I foolishly phoned Leanne and told her that I wanted her there with me. I told her that I missed her and that I had changed; all the classic cliches, you know.

Leanne was initially surprised that I would call her out of the blue as our amicable texts to one another had ceased. Leanne explained that she had moved on with her life, my heart sank and I felt deflated. I was angry with myself for calling her as I knew what the answer was going to be deep down. I knew that the ship had sailed. Still my ever-curious ego just had to confirm what my heart already knew.

I cried in front of my mother that night for the first time in my adult life. She could see my pain and just held me without saying anything. I had longed for that sincere moment all my life, just to be held by her when I no longer resented her. I'm glad it happened that weekend, albeit in very bizarre circumstances. We actually bonded even more in that short time away together. The whole experience made me happy and at peace; for the first time in my life, at the age of thirty-one, it felt like I had a real Mum. In the end, I was glad that I travelled all that way to Brighton, it had created a positive experience with my mother in a roundabout way, despite a negative one with Leanne.

We had a fantastic time at the party the following day and it was magical to see my huge, stepfamily! The weather was perfect, food was readily available via the BBQ and everyone was smiling. I caught up on lost time with my beautiful family that had adopted me as their own. The day whizzed by and before I knew it, it was early evening. I said my goodbyes to everyone and made my way back to the hotel.

Mum, Jim and I had agreed to go out for a meal that night after the party. We scouted the streets looking for the best restaurant and settled on a lovely looking Italian; the ambience felt wonderful and promised to be perfect. To cut a long story short, it was one of the worst dining experiences that all of us had ever experienced. It was truly awful, so bad we actually laughed about it. The three of us walked back to our hotel and cackled at the dire experience that we had just been subjected to. This memory is important to me because after this negative experience, a seemingly innocuous conversation led me to a new chapter in my life; I will explain.

We arrived back at the hotel and Mum and Jim suggested a drink in the bar. I had planned on just going to my room, as alcohol would just make me tired and it had been a long day! However, I paused and thought *what the hell, I'm on holiday!* And made my way to the bar for a cocktail! I couldn't have my mum staying up later than me, could I?

We perched ourselves at the end of the bar and Mum got chatting to some women from Essex who were also staying at the hotel. I wasn't feeling very sociable, as I was tired, so I just listened to the women talk amongst themselves. One woman was harping on about how one of their friends had met the love of their life off Match.com. I had tried all the free dating websites, none of which had come to fruition, so kept this Match.com at the back of my mind. I was happy to hear the Essex tales and laughed with the ladies, they were all so full of life!

As the evening drew on I became sleepier, so drank my cocktail and went to bed. It was the first alcoholic drink I'd had in ages and whilst I enjoyed it, it made me realise that I really didn't miss the effects of alcohol at all, not one bit. I just felt lethargic to be honest!

The next day I said my goodbyes to my mum and Jim and set about my journey home. I had always hated saying goodbye to them both, as I was unsure when I would get the opportunity to see them again. I guess it also reminded me of that childhood pain I would experience at the end of every holiday when I had to leave. I had made progress with my mum; this had been a really good weekend. It was lovely seeing a beautiful collection of people who I could call my family.

After arriving back at my house that night, I was feeling lonely after my lovely weekend away. I lay on the sofa and longed for the right companion to enter my life. I remember asking out loud for my nan to help me and to put someone who was right for me into my life. I didn't believe in all that talking to the dead crap but it just felt right speaking aloud at that time. Maybe Nan was there with me that night, who knows? All I knew was that I felt sad and I cried on my own in the front room that I had once shared with Leanne.

As I lay there in my sombre living room, I recalled what those bubbly ladies from the prior night had been talking about. I decided to look into this Match.com to see what all the fuss was about. It turned out that I had to pay for this one though! This was off-putting as I was broke; I mean really broke. Running a house on my own was taking its financial toll on me and I didn't know how much longer I could afford to stay in the house. Every penny was precious.

I was down to my last £40 for the month, but had always struggled for money so thought *sod it!* I took a leap of faith. I signed up for one month on this new app! That would surely be enough time for me to work my magic! I remember thinking to myself that I had better get my money's worth out of this stupid app that had just taken my last £40! My mother had been helping me with money here and there but I couldn't keep asking for her help; I felt ashamed and a burden. Nevertheless, I phoned her that night to see if she could help me until I got paid… of course, she agreed.

The very next day, I woke up feeling optimistic. Mum had provided me with enough money to see me through until I got paid and the sun was shining. I eagerly checked my new dating app that I had just paid for! To my joy, a lady called LoubyLou had winked at me. She was attractive and her profile stated that we had similar interests, plus, she was my age.

I would chat with many women on this new dating app and I even arranged to go on a few dates, but this LoubyLou had something about her that just felt so familiar. LoubyLou eventually gave me her phone number after weeks of persisting on the app and we started talking properly. That was it really, we chatted for a couple of weeks and clicked. I kept pestering her to meet up with me but this LoubyLou was playing it far too cool for my liking. Even to the point where I was tempted to forget the whole thing. She eventually folded and agreed to meet me. I wasn't that bad, what had she got to lose? I had even shown my boy Deano her photo and he approved as well, so it was all systems go.

19

LoubyLou

It was a warm summer's evening and I was waiting tentatively at a pub that Louise and I had agreed to meet at for the first time. I was like a faithful dog waiting for Louise and I even arrived fifteen minutes early. I remember, it felt like I was waiting forever. I was constantly watching the clock and I thought she was never going to show.

Eventually she arrived and walked up to me while I was sipping some red wine. I hadn't drunk alcohol since my family party but I had to appear sophisticated in front of Louise! At that stage of my life, I actually got zero enjoyment from drinking alcohol but didn't want to appear a social outcast, so I forced the wine down, nevertheless. I just told myself it was made from grapes and good for me. Louise was nearly as tall as me, five foot eleven to be precise. I usually went for petite women but thought it was time to be open-minded about things and break the usual mould. Louise was very attractive though, beautiful in fact, so I managed to look past the whole height thing!

We sat down together and didn't stop talking. It was like meeting up with an old friend; a bit spooky to be honest! We laughed all night and would even finish each other's sentences; cheesy but true. I was only planning on staying out a few hours, but time vanished and we stayed out 'til about half past one in the morning, which was way past my bedtime. The manager of the pub had to ask us to leave in the end as they were locking the doors!

Louise and I waited for a taxi to arrive and shared a kiss together. Louise looked so pretty as I gazed into her brown eyes for what seemed like an eternity. She stared back into my eyes as if she had found what she was looking for. I will never forget that look; it made me feel special. We lived near one another so when the taxi arrived, we got in it together. The taxi arrived at my house first and we shared one final kiss and went our separate ways. The whole night was perfect.

Louise and I couldn't wait to see each other again and went out the following night to the cinema; so much for playing it cool! It just all felt very natural and unforced, it was easy. We saw each other again a few days later and I didn't really leave her house after that. Everything just felt so right and it was like hanging out with an old friend. I spent all my waking moments with Louise and couldn't get enough of being with her. She made me laugh so much.

Months passed and it was evident that all of my time had been spent around Louise's house. Louise and I spoke about how we felt towards one another and took a gamble on my house. I was going to get rid of it, which I wasn't afraid to do to be honest. I was paying for something that I didn't use apart from going back there once a week to pick up fresh clothes, I was hardly ever there. Of course, finances played a part in my decision and Louise was aware of my situation, but neither of us cared. I handed my notice in with the landlord and moved in with Louise. It would take a few months to let the house go as I was tied into a contract, but it gave us the time to move things in gradually at a leisurely pace.

Things were just going from good to amazing with this beautiful lady; she was witty and had a dry sense of humour, which I loved. She was also a deputy head teacher which she had kept hidden from me. She told me that men were intimidated by this when they found out but I found it very attractive, I loved a bold woman.

Louise told me that she had attracted me after a year of asking the Universe for me each day. I had no idea what she was on about, but it made me recall the night I lay on my sofa in my old house and had asked Nan to put someone in my life who was perfect for me. Louise certainly did seem to fit the bill but surely it was all just a beautiful coincidence. I'll be honest, I thought it was a sweet sentiment from her when she said she had been asking the Universe every day for me, but to be honest, I thought it was all a load of nonsense!

I introduced Louise to my grandad and my dad and they both approved; why do we need the approval of others so much? Louise and I travelled to London so that Mum could meet her. Needless to say my mother loved her and she was so happy for me. That summer of 2016 really was perfect, not too hot or too warm, just the way I like it. It was perfect for walks, something which I have always loved doing.

Louise also came with baggage; in the shape of a dog named Bella. I was never really a dog person but I pretended to like Bella just for Louise. We would walk Bella in the woods around the back of our house and play with her. This dog had such a warm playful nature, it really was endearing to watch. The more time that I spent with Bella, the more we would play together! I think at one point I was spending more time with the dog than Louise! This creature was just perfect, she became my new best friend. I think Louise was beginning to get jealous!

I challenge anyone who says that animals don't have souls when you witness their traits and the love they give. I had not only fallen in love with Louise but eventually fallen in love with Bella too. Yep, that little teddy bear had won my heart. I say little but nothing could be further from the truth, as Bella was a huge bullmastiff, but she was my little teddy bear. Bella helped me learn so much and I was finally content in my life. Who would have thought a dog could teach a person so much? Bella lived in the moment and loved me unconditionally. She was content with the simple things in life; maybe that was where I had been going wrong?

One day while walking Bella in the sun, I realised all that mattered was the present moment. I finally let go of my painful past once and for all in that very moment. All the lingering hurt that was still with me just drifted away. It was a beautiful moment, just Bella and I walking in the woods as the sun crept through the branches. Louise was sunbathing in the garden back at home, probably wondering why I spent more time with the dog than I did with her?!

Everything felt perfect. It was also the last week of my contract for my house; at the end of the week I would be free of my old house. I decided to spend one last night on my own there for old times' sake and say my goodbyes. I also took the opportunity to do some last minute cleaning in order to make sure that the house was in the same condition as when I found it, in order to receive the deposit back from the landlord. The house was pretty bare to say the least, all that was left was the sofa and bed but I still had wi-fi so not all was lost.

Leanne was going to have the sofa and she would be collecting it the next day so I lay on it for one last time. As I relaxed on the sofa that held many memories for me, my phone began to ring; it was Dean. It was getting late, dangerously late, about 8.45pm to be precise. What a bore I had become! I thought it was unusual as he rarely phoned me, let alone that late. I felt a strange sensation in my stomach as I accepted the call.

I answered the phone and Dean's voice was positive as he greeted me. He informed me that the hospital had found a suitable lung donor for him and that he was on his way to the hospital to consult with the surgeon and doctors. After the consultation, he would decide whether or not to proceed with the operation.

Dean had been on the transplant list for a year or so and I had kind of forgotten about it to be fair. The thing is, if you met Dean, you wouldn't know that there was anything wrong with him. He was always joking, happy, smiling, positive and so warm. You would have no idea of the turmoil that he had to endure on a daily basis because of his cystic fibrosis.

This was all out of the blue; things were going so well and now this!? I knew the risk involved with a procedure this complex. Dean, however, was positive as always and said he would like to see me and meet Louise when he woke up after the operation. I had my concerns, but decided to have faith and take a leaf out of my dear friend's book. Dean hung up and I phoned Louise to tell her the news, I was scared. Even though I had just agreed with myself to be positive, I still felt like crying. I didn't want to cry down the phone to Louise as it was still early doors in the relationship front and real alpha men don't cry! (Silly ego!) Louise was supportive and assured me that Deano would be fine. I slept uneasily that night with a lot of change ahead of me.

I got the call the following morning from Gemma to say that Dean had accepted the risks of the operation and had decided to proceed with the surgery. The operation would happen that very morning as well, *Jesus* I thought, that little guy didn't hang around, did he? He was so brave. The same evening, Gemma called again to say that Dean was out of surgery. Although it was early doors, the operation was considered a success. Gemma kept me constantly informed throughout the entire process, it must have been so tough for her, repeating the same conversation to numerous people. I admire the strength that she demonstrated throughout it all, whilst keeping me up to date and dealing with her own emotions.

About a week passed after the operation and Dean was ready for visitors. Gemma, Dean's friend Matt, and I went to Deano's room. I will never forget seeing Dean for the first time as I entered the room. He was so weak but smiled as we entered. Dean had a top knot haircut, something I was not expecting to see on him, as I knew his opinions on these haircuts! The nurses had tied his hair up to keep it from falling onto his face, so he wouldn't have to keep moving his hands to brush it away. I immediately ridiculed him over his new temporary haircut. He just smiled as that was all he could manage. Dean's hair was so long because he was growing it for charity so he could eventually shave it off for a wig. He was so selfless.

Deano's arms were huge, pumped up from all the steroids! I said he looked like John Cena as we both enjoyed watching the wrestling. It was strange seeing Dean like this; he was always active and vibrant, but here, he was so feeble. To be fair to the man, he had just been cut open and had his lungs removed! I decided I would cut him some slack and give the top knot jokes a rest. Honestly though, he was so brave and tried to joke with us all even in his frail state. That evening in the hospital passed so quickly and was all a bit of a blur. I had never seen Deano like this and it was all one big shock.

I would text Dean every morning with positive words of encouragement and saw him once a week as I didn't drive. The hospital was an hour and a half away on the bus and I hated asking for lifts. Gemma would take me up every Thursday with her. I watched as Dean got stronger each week and he was gradually returning to his former self but with more energy, he appeared rejuvenated.

Six weeks passed and Deano was discharged. He was free! His new life had begun and I was so proud of him. He started coming up the gym with me as he could now walk without being out of breath. It was a miracle! He had always inspired me but this was just something else. I wanted to tell him I loved him but that would have broken the lad code, surely!

You know Dean never once moaned about being in the hospital and showed nothing but gratitude to the staff at the Queen Elizabeth hospital. People often criticise the NHS but the people who work there are only humans trying to do their best, we all make mistakes. I cannot fault them for what they did for Dean in that short time. It is a free service which we are privileged to have; not every country has this luxury. I am so thankful for all the staff there and what they did for my best friend.

20

THE NEW JOB

My current job was getting me down and I applied for a new one on a whim one day. Before I knew it, I was offered an interview, accepting the job and leaving my old job! My new job was a catering manager of three care homes and managing all the kitchen staff in each home. It was a huge responsibility but Dean had shown me that anything is possible with belief. I started my new job full of enthusiasm and I immediately identified problems and sorted issues out in each of the homes. Within three months, I had turned the place around. With all the work done and the systems in place for how the three kitchens should run, I felt bored. What was wrong with me? I had just started this job! I was in the office more than the kitchen and wondered what to do next to take the company forward?

I met a lovely woman while working there, Jennie was her name and we clicked immediately. Jennie had cancer and I had filled her position while she was off work due to her condition. She was initially going to be permanently off work but Jennie decided to come back part time just to occupy herself and stop herself from going mad.

We became very close and I made a real friend in her. She was so happy I had gone there and told me that it helped with her motivation having me around and that she wanted to help me develop the place alongside her. I now had a partner in crime to help me take the kitchens even further. We wrote fancy a la carte menus together; in order to break the mould of what care home food traditionally was. We wanted to make our care homes, that were set in the countryside, stand out from the rest.

Elderly people deserve the best, so we really pushed the menu and focused on seasonal produce. Jennie had helped to reignite my passion for food and I applied all that I had learnt from my previous years at the Copthorne.

I received a call one day on the way home from an unknown number, I answered it apprehensively. It was from the college who gave me an interview 6 months ago, they were now offering me the choice of two positions. I couldn't believe it; I couldn't say no! I accepted the position that I felt I was more suited to and handed in my notice. I knew I was meant to go to that place, better late than never!

I cast my mind back to how I had my heart set on that job and how I was sure it was mine. I guess it just took a bit longer to materialise than I had anticipated. I had only been at my current place four months and I was already leaving. I felt satisfied with the work I had done there though and Jennie could continue with it in her part time role. I was leaving so soon, but it was the right thing to do and I was glad that Jennie had entered my life.

Jennie and I remained friends after I had left and would often meet up for coffees. She was so optimistic and full of life despite her condition; it was inspiring. She reminded me of Dean in some ways, I admired that. She just got on with life in a positive manner and was always smiling. To my surprise, Jennie's condition rapidly deteriorated over the space of a few weeks and she sadly lost her battle with cancer. One week we were texting each other, the next she had passed; it was so bizarre to think that she was here one week and gone the next. I had trouble wrapping my head around that aspect of life; was it all a dream? I don't know. One thing I did know is that the short amount of time that I had spent with Jennie felt much longer than it actually was. It felt as though we had been friends forever and she had left a truly positive and optimistic impression upon me.

21

A Unique Opportunity

I accepted the offer as café and hospitality manager at the college, but I wasn't going there for that, I was going to work with the young adults; that was the real draw. I would be working alongside the students in the café providing them work experience. I would be helping the students to improve their cooking and to also work in a public environment. Many of the students suffered with anxiety and found it difficult to interact with society. The café was a perfect environment to help build and increase their confidence. All the staff that I worked with there were fantastic. It felt as though everyone who came into my life at the college did so for a particular reason. It all felt very homely and familiar, like I belonged there.

The college had a strong ethos on healthy, organic food and they had a farm that provided all the organic produce for each kitchen. The trust itself was based on the theories of Rudolph Steiner, an Austrian philosopher. By conventional terms, this place would be classed as *hippy* but I loved it. Working with the students filled me with such joy and intrinsic satisfaction each day. I felt as though I was making a difference to people's lives. I loved it there and felt honoured to be part of the team.

Louise and I were better than ever; I had truly met my best friend. She was so happy for me that I had the job I dreamed of. Louise bought me driving lessons as a present and I began to learn to drive after 31 years! Money had always hampered me from doing this, plus I had an irrational fear of the roads, but it felt good to be behind the wheel! Life was perfect, and in amongst all of this, there was a very special event approaching.

22

The Wedding

Not my wedding, before you start wondering but for Deano and Gemma. Deano had been engaged to Gemma for about two years and they were still full of jubilance due to the successful transplant; I was so happy for them. Deano really did have a new life and a fresh start ahead of him. Dean and Gemma had been together for about ten years, so it was about time for them to take the plunge!

Dean asked me to be his best man, along with his brother and his good friend Matt. I graciously accepted his offer. I was so proud and humbled that he would consider me to play such a part in his big day. We all chipped in and organised Dean's stag do, for which Matt did most of the work. I thank him for this, as organisation isn't exactly my forte in life!

About twenty of us went on Dean's stag do to Nottingham. Casinos were the order of play for the first night, which was all new to me! It was my first and probably last time in one, but an experience nevertheless. We went axe throwing and clay pigeon shooting the next day, followed by drinks in pubs and clubs at night. I will be honest, at this stage of my life, the idea of clubbing was my idea of hell. I actually loathed alcohol and just didn't see the point in drinking, but I drank just to fit in, peer pressure eh!?

I remember standing in the middle of a packed club and looking at the time, it was about one o'clock in the morning. There I was in a dimly lit room with strobe lights moving in all directions surrounded by drunken youths. All I could think was how lovely it would be to be lying in my own bed next to Louise.

The youths that danced around me appeared to be having fun but to me it was foreign now. There was a point in my life where that was me, jumping up and down blind drunk, but now it all seemed a little sad looking at it objectively. In reality, what I was doing was standing in a dark room with a sticky floor, surrounded by drunken strangers who kept bumping into me. I was buying drinks which were overpriced and watered down whilst listening to awful music that couldn't actually be heard properly because of the distorted bass. I was shouting into the ears of my friends as they couldn't hear one word that I was saying over the music. This was not fun in my eyes. God, had I aged so much!? I just wanted some quiet conversation and to actually spend some quality time with my friends. Shouting over the loud music was really frustrating and off-putting. What sober person would really want to do this?

Maybe I speak for myself, but I saw the whole experience objectively for the first time in my life! Participating in this whole situation sober would be a nauseating experience to say the least. I guess that is why people drink in order to blot out this forced idea of fun, the irony of it all. I can't lie, when I did this in my youth and early twenties, I loved it and lived for it. But why did I feel like that? Because I was lost with who I was and hated my life compared to others; I just wanted to fit in. Either way, I was not judging these people for I was once in their shoes. It was merely an interesting experience to see it from the other side of the coin. I weathered the storm and the night passed. I haven't been out to a club since and I can't say I'm fussed either. It was a fun weekend in retrospect, but I was glad when it was all over and I was home with Louise.

The wedding rolled around shortly after the stag do and it would take place in Ilfracombe overlooking the sea in April. It was a glorious day; the sky was blue with not a cloud to be seen and the sun shone brightly. We all had shorts on as this was what Dean wanted, which I was dubious about at first! I mean it could have rained or been freezing that early in the year. I had visions of torrential downpours and we would all be stood there looking like drowned rats, but this didn't materialise and we all looked the part while the sun blazed down upon us.

I will never forget how happy Dean and Gemma looked as she walked down the aisle to greet him. I cried to myself out of pure joy for them both, not very manly of me but I kept it hidden. They had both been through so much together and this was their chance to start a new life. Dean was now free of cystic fibrosis and nothing could stop them.

I had the task of looking after the rings and eagerly took them up when asked to. The pair of lovebirds said their vows to each other in what was the most beautiful, scenic, picturesque setting you could imagine. The waves rolled in gently on the beach below which was situated next to the rockface where they stood. The sun's warm glow bathed all of the wedding guests, creating what was a postcard-worthy scene. I thought to myself that this was nature's way of blessing Dean and Gemma for being so courageous and such warriors. All the turmoil that they went through over the past year prior to the wedding was harrowing, but in comparison to the beauty of the occasion, it was irrelevant. All that mattered was that moment.

The weather and the food were wonderful, as was the atmosphere. The whole day in general was perfect. All our friends were there, including Lee who flew over from Dubai. It was lovely to all be together as we all had our own lives now and rarely got the chance to all meet up as one. I usually find weddings a slog and a bit of a bore if I'm honest, but this genuinely was a perfect day. I was honoured to be a part of it. I will never forget that day and it will forever hold a special place in my heart.

The wedding passed and I didn't see Deano for a while, I guess he was doing married life stuff! I was just so happy he had this fresh start and kept thinking that he deserved his new state of health due to his attitude. I knew that Dean had also begun his training to run a marathon. I detested running, so he was on his own for that one! My new job was also going well and I was making real progress with the students. I was spending all of my spare time with Louise and just loved walking Bella, she drew such contentment out of me.

Deano was always in and out of hospital for check-ups and it became the norm. We never worried though, this was indestructible Deano and we had all accepted that this was part of his life, even after the transplant. The doctors just had to make sure his body was functioning properly with the new lungs. Five months after the wedding, Dean had a prolonged period in hospital where he had picked up an infection. I saw him every week and I decided to get the bus up this time so as not to impose myself upon Gemma. The journeys were so long and tedious, but he was like a brother to me and I would have done anything for him.

Dean and I would laugh and giggle in the hospital about stupid topics from our past. I would tell him that he needed to hurry up and get back home so we could start going out again. Dean said he would do his best and be out soon, now that was optimism. After about seven weeks of Deano being in hospital, he was finally released. I was so relieved that he was home and now I could stop worrying as it seemed like he was in hospital for longer than usual. Gemma was so happy to have her husband back where he belonged.

Two days later on the Monday morning Deano was readmitted back to the Queen Elizabeth hospital. He had a serious infection that needed to be monitored. I was shocked to be honest; he had only been back home for the blink of an eye. I would text him every morning to see how he was feeling and he was still positive and said he would be out again soon. I just wanted to go down the pub with him again for our little chats that we would have. There was no judgement with Dean and I could talk to him about anything. We would call it *meat* time as we would meet and eat meat, how witty! I missed these times and wanted them back. I could drink water all night and think nothing of it when with Dean. Some people may perceive you as being a bit dull for drinking the good old H2O and encourage you into having a *real* drink. Hell, I used to be that very same person!

That Friday evening of the very same week Dean had gone back to hospital, Gemma called me out of the blue. She said that the doctors claimed Deano would not make it through the weekend and that Saturday would be his last day on Earth. Gemma suggested that if I wanted to, I could see him before he passed. Was this even real? My brain couldn't quite comprehend the information it was being told.

After the call ended, I thought it was a sick joke; I had spoken to Deano just three days prior and was due to travel up on the bus to see him! This was Dean, the man who taught me not to fear, not to be down, how to get over things even when they seemed bad, the man who taught me to love everyone. *They* said Dean would die when he was twenty and he defied those odds. *They* said a lot of things and Dean always proved *them* wrong and this time was no different! I refused to believe it and knew this would not happen, surely the doctors had made some sort of mistake or Gemma was confused?

23

STARS IN THEIR EYES

I woke up that Saturday morning unsure of what to expect. How do you prepare for the day ahead where you know you have to go and say goodbye to your brother? There wasn't exactly a handbook available to deal with this everyday scenario. It was a really trippy experience to be fair and I'd had enough of those over the years. I just kept thinking it couldn't be real. I ate as normal and believe it or not, I went to the gym in the morning. The gym had helped me through so much over the years and I saw it as a chance to clear my mind for the events that were about to follow. I did some deadlifts and focused purely on the weights.

With the gym session finished, Louise then drove me to the hospital and dropped me off at the main entrance of the familiar, imposing building. I said bye to Louise and I wondered what would transpire the next time I saw her. In retrospect, going up the gym was so selfish that day but I guess it was my only way of taking control of a day that was completely out of my hands. A futile attempt of keeping some kind of normality maybe.

As I walked through the corridors of the hospital, I felt disoriented, slightly woozy to be honest and I recall my heart beating so fast. What was I going to witness? That all too familiar smell of the sterile hospital halls made me feel sick. I will never forget that clinical aroma. The atmosphere felt so flat as people passed me by, like a blur, all merged into one. I finally found the ward that Dean was on after getting lost and not being able to make sense of the signs that were dotted around the hospital. I was wasting time on this merry-go-round but my adrenaline was pumping. I rang the buzzer and walked through the ominous double doors as they opened. As soon as I walked in, I could sense that it was a ward where people came to die. The morose atmosphere was stifling. All I could see in the private rooms as I walked by were sad, lost, desperate faces. I could feel the sorrow and pain in that environment. I didn't like it.

I finally got to Deano's room after taking a wrong turn, and Gemma's mum was standing outside of it. I hadn't seen her since the wedding and now that day seemed a distant memory. She gave me one of those half-hearted smiles that suggested the end was near. I slowly entered the first room to make sure I didn't make too much noise and washed my hands. There was one final door to proceed through which led me to Dean. As I opened the last door to Dean's room, I thought that he would be weak but still conscious and able to talk, how wrong I was.

As I walked fully into the room, I saw that Dean's mum, his brother and his sisters were sitting around the bed. Alongside them all was Gemma and Dean's good friend Matt and in the middle of it all, Dean. The last time that we were all together was for such a momentous and beautiful occasion. This time though, we had all been united in quite different and painful circumstances. I'm not afraid to say that as soon as I processed the room and laid eyes upon Dean, I started to shake uncontrollably. I hadn't really grasped the magnitude of the situation I was stepping into. I tried to compose myself as I gazed at Dean's fading body. His breaths were short and sporadic and he was hooked up to a machine that was assisting his breathing. I sat down next to him and held his arm. Gemma told me to say hello to Deano. I tried but the words wouldn't exit my mouth properly, I just whimpered. I just held his arm and stared intently at his tattooed sleeve to occupy my mind.

Dean had an entire sleeve tattoo up his left arm to honour his family. Each picture was a part of what his nephews and nieces loved. It ranged from bears to dinosaurs to football and Crayola crayons. I will never forget gazing hypnotically at the orange Crayola crayon on his arm, it comforted me in a strange way. If I ever come across an orange crayon ever again, I will instantly be transported back to that powerful moment.

I continued to stare intently at this crayon on his arm while his breaths became shorter and squeezed his hand tightly. The pauses between each of Deano's breaths were becoming longer and more laboured. Everyone in the room was silent. All that could be heard was the perpetual cycle of the mechanics omitted from the machine that was wired up to Dean, coupled with an occasional beep. Gemma leaned over and embraced Dean, kissed him and told him it was time to go. A few minutes after the words had left her mouth, Deano took his last breath and left the earth at 14:16pm.

The nurse came over and delivered the same type of smile that Gemma's mum had given me earlier; she then turned off the machine that was hooked up to Dean and the room fell even quieter. That was it, Dean had gone. I cry even as I write this as the pain is still with me and reliving that ambivalent moment is still so surreal. I will never forget that day and will take it to my grave. I loved Dean but now he was gone.

We all left the room as the nurses wanted to make Dean more presentable. We actually laughed outside the room about Dean, even in that sombre moment. We laughed about how he had a very selective diet and would only eat limited things. He really was fussy, even picky and it was funny that his diet of all things was the subject that arose to alleviate the heavy atmosphere. The nurses exited the private room and said we could re-enter if we chose to. I asked the family if I could have five minutes alone with Deano. They said yes to which I was so grateful for as they had more right than myself to be in there at that time.

As I re-entered the side room, I saw that the nurses had sat Dean up. He looked so peaceful and his glorious beard, which I was so envious of, shone in all its ginger glory! I looked at him and it was clear that life had left him. He looked like a mannequin, a rubber dummy almost. I had shared so many good times with this guy but couldn't help thinking, as I stared at him, that this shell he had left wasn't actually him. Where had that spark of life gone that had once animated that lifeless body? I couldn't make sense of it; I was in a dream-like state.

I then proceeded to open up to him about my life, everything. I thanked him profusely for the lessons that he'd taught me and I apologised for when I told him to get lost when we were kids when all he was trying to do was help me. I held his clammy body that had no colour next to me and hugged him tightly. I was so thankful that I had the opportunity of knowing this stoic, young man. Had Dean been awake at this time, he would have probably cut me a disconcerting glance but you know what, all I felt was love for him.

I kissed Dean on the cheek and felt the most bizarre feeling of warmth consume my body. An indescribable feeling, a feeling that made me want to cry but not out of sadness, out of pure euphoria even though I had just lost my best friend. What was this feeling of warmth and sincerity? It came from within but surrounded me at the same time. A genuine, beautiful glow of truth consumed me; it was an experience that I had not really felt before with such vividness. I sobbed and sobbed and realised that this feeling was love, true love. I had finally experienced true love after all of these years and it connected my best friend and I. I finally realised what it was to have unconditional love for someone regardless of what gender they were. This love differed from the interpersonal biological love between a man and a woman, this was raw and true. All I could do was tell Dean that I loved him and the loving energy that I was experiencing simply swallowed me up. That feeling awoke something deep within that day, the feeling of who I truly was.

I chose to call this chapter *stars in their eyes* because do you remember that god awful T.V show on a Saturday night with Matthew Kelly? Well, if not, here's a quick recap. Public guests would appear on the show and impersonate a famous singer of their choice. They would enter the curtain as themselves and then reappear from a cloud of smoke, looking completely different and made up to look like their idols!

Well, it may be a lame comparison, but I entered that tiny hospital room that afternoon as what I thought was myself but exited a totally different person. The whole event sparked something deep within me. This radical change in me didn't happen overnight but it was the catalyst for a new beginning for me. Dean's death had awoken something in me that was unexplainable. This awakening that had happened to me was caused by his death and it even inspired the title of this book, *The Awakening of Death*.

Gemma drove me back home from the hospital that night. I can't remember what we spoke about to be honest as I was so exhausted. God knows how she must have felt. She dropped me home and we spoke briefly on the driveway. I attempted to say the right words to her, but how could I console her? She had just lost her husband. The pain that I was experiencing was bad enough so how must she have been feeling? I kissed Gemma, exited the car and waved to her as she drove off in Dean's car. I entered the house, walked up to Louise and held her tighter than I ever had before. She held me tenderly in her arms and all I could say was, "He's gone."

Gemma phoned Lee to let him know the tragic news the next day. Lee then phoned me and was shaken. He couldn't believe it. I felt for him. The three of us had such wonderful, magical times growing up together. We were like brothers; the three amigos. I phoned all our friends the following night to let them know what had happened to take some of the pressure off Gemma. It wasn't the most pleasant thing I've ever done, listening to people's reactions over the phone, but it was the least I could do for Gemma. Those awkward phone calls seemed to last forever and I felt drained after all of them!

It snowed that winter and Dean's funeral came around in the middle of it all. I have always loved the snow as there is something that I find so tranquil and peaceful about it all. Walking in the woods while it snowed with Bella was simply magical. It helped me to process what had happened and was so calming.

The day of the funeral arrived and the floor was still covered with a white blanket. I got to the funeral later than I would have liked as traffic was terrible due to the weather. I was panicking in the car and thinking, *oh my God, I can't be late for my best friend's funeral.* Luckily, we arrived in time at the crematorium and as we approached the car park, I saw over a hundred people all lined up in black. It was a huge turnout for the little guy but it just showed how loved he was.

Louise and I made our way to the front of the long queue. I had agreed to wheel the coffin into the crematorium, after Gemma had so kindly asked me. I was honoured. I saw so many old faces there from my past, it was just a shame it had to be through this occasion. I greeted everyone and then waited in silence; it was such a strange atmosphere that I will never forget.

The hearse pulled up silently and the coffin was taken from the back of the vehicle. The coffin was then put onto what can only be described as a trolley and I helped wheel it into the chapel. Dean's dad, brother and Matt each had their own corner and we all pushed. As I pushed the coffin, I couldn't help but think, *what if I stumble and knock the coffin over and Dean falls out?* This thought actually made me imagine a really bad sketch from a satirical comedy show and it provided me with a moment of dark humour that helped occupy my mind, is that weird?

Needless to say, we pushed the coffin to the front of the chapel with no catastrophic events occurring, despite what I had previously envisioned in my mind! The service began and we were all seated. I sat next to Lee and was happy that he was sitting next to me. We had grown up together and were always there for one another. Deano had left us but our bond ran strong. A lot of people were forced to stand as there was simply not enough room in the chapel. The service was perfect for Dean. Gemma spoke about what Dean had meant to her in a heartfelt message and Gemma's sister also read a poem that was fitting for the little guy.

I had requested prior to say a few words as I had to let the world know the impact that Dean's existence had on my own life. I wrote a poem called *What is a friend?* and read it aloud. I thought this was the best option as I didn't want to waffle on and was adamant to convey my message, so a poem summed up perfectly how I felt. I have included it in the back of this book if you would like to read it later on.

Gemma chose *Jay-Z - Encore* to be played halfway through the ceremony as Dean really did come and conquer life. The song is about the career of Jay-Z and tells of how the rapper had accomplished what he set out to do while he was in the rap game and more. This is exactly what Deano did with his short time here, he lived his life fully and inspired people; so, the metaphorical comparison between Jay-Z's successful career and Dean's life were appropriate to him. Dean and I loved Jay-Z's music growing up and went to many of his concerts.

I read my poem and was happy with the way I delivered it. I wanted to be as slow and concise as possible, so that my message wouldn't be lost. I sat back down after the reading and it all seemed like a passing dream. The rest of the service concluded and everyone exited the chapel to the glorious sounds of *Will Smith - The Fresh Prince of Bel Air*. Of course, this made everyone laugh. Dean was ever the comedian, even in death! Dean was such a geek when it came to Will Smith; he literally idolised him!

Everybody congregated outside and talked amongst themselves with mixed emotions. We all then departed and went to the wake which was hosted at the health club where Dean used to work. We all shared stories of what Deano meant to us all, laughed about the old times and all agreed that he was one hell of a guy! I didn't get drunk as those days were long gone and I felt Dean was entitled to more than me just drowning my sorrows. Instead, I was just so proud to have known him and that he was a part of my life! That was enough for me. Gemma held up so well throughout the day, even though the whole experience must have been shattering for her in more ways than one.

24

LIFE GOES ON

The show must go on, as they say. I went through the motions and went about my life the same as I always had, going to work and the gym, but something didn't feel right. Not the fact that my best friend was gone, but life just felt wrong now. I just couldn't help but think, "Is this it?" Did we go to heaven or hell? This is what I had been raised to believe when growing up. I did dismiss it all in my adolescent youth, but now it got me thinking again. Either way, whatever happened in the Bible was not relevant in this day and age. It ignored the fact that we are born in a structured society, work a 9-5, pay into a system that is run by others and then die. Jesus spoke nothing about that! Deano was much more than those formalities that we all face in life. He didn't obsess over money or power. Instead he taught love, selflessness and positivity. I didn't know what to think anymore. But after careful thought, all I knew was that the concept of heaven and hell seemed so whimsical to me. Was it possible that what I had been taught over the years was one big lie?

I Googled one night "what is the meaning of life?" It threw up some funny answers; mainly religious ones. I had been dragged to church and knew that wasn't the way things were meant to be, I knew it deep down. I remember how I had witnessed at church, the seedy affairs and furtive activities that used to happen. I remember the gossip I used to hear each Sunday, even as a child. I remember the fear that was instilled into people. Deano had no fear, only love.

I recall thinking to myself as a child that people at church still did things they weren't supposed to but worshipped God, so would they go to heaven? Who made the rules? It all confused me to be honest, it seemed like they were just keeping up appearances, playing into the facade that society had created by portraying something that they weren't. There were a few sincere characters at church that I felt genuine warmth from, the rest made me feel uneasy and this was from a child's perspective.

There was definitely more to the world than religion, heaven and hell. Did we just die? What about children born into this word with crippling diseases? It made no sense! All I kept thinking about was how much Dean had taught me; it couldn't have all been for nothing, could it? Much like this paragraph, my mind looped in a perpetual cycle of confusing questions.

Would all of the lessons that Dean had instilled into my being one day erode, rot and turn to dust when it was my time to pass? What's the point of learning if this is the case? Come on, I argued with myself, that's mindless to think it's all for nothing. The fact I had witnessed that Dean was with me one moment and then gone the next really perplexed me. Where did he go?

His physical body that he had left behind was just a shell of who he actually was. I couldn't shake the image of his lifeless body sitting upwards when we were alone in that hospital room together. How come I hadn't felt like this when my nan passed? I guess it was because, as we grow up, we accept that when people get old, they die. They have had their life and it seems fair, this is what we are conditioned to believe, or at least I was. However, when there is a tragedy, it compromises this conditioning and upsets the apple cart, an injustice if you like. It most definitely did with me. We've all heard the phrase 'they had their whole life ahead of them', or 'they were taken before their time'. This was certainly the case with Deano.

Dean lived into his thirties, which are considered to be our prime years. It really seemed unfair to me and felt wrong that Deano was taken so soon. I was angry, and there seemed to be a huge sense of injustice in the world. In my opinion, his life was just beginning after his lung transplant and the wedding. He had so much life ahead of him. My thoughts began to shift and I started to think more and more about the existence of the human race. My mind began to alter more and more each day. I can only describe it as though someone had lifted a dark veil that was previously covering my vision. I could now see things clearly for the first time in my life, albeit from a different perspective. The blinkers had gone and I had full awareness of the world around me.

I started to see the way society was programmed and how it operated. I looked at the world from a multitude of angles. What was right and what was wrong? I began to see both sides of the coin for once when in disagreement with someone. I realised that my beliefs were pre-conditioned and inherited. I would watch people bicker with one another and see that neither was *right* or *wrong*. In fact, who knew the answers? It was all a facade.

I had witnessed the fine line between living and dying in the blink of an eye; it was sobering. I no longer wanted trivial matters to consume my life. I decided that I would learn something new every day. I had seen how delicate and precious life can be, I didn't want to squander my gift. Who would know when my time was up too? I would find out what this thing called *life* was all about, and honour Dean's memory by living my life to its full potential.

While my search for the truth escalated, I stumbled upon a few spiritual websites which eliminated the religious aspect of things. I discovered that the dogma that was usually attached with religion could actually limit people's consciousness and keep them grounded. This sat true with me as I could see how religion had kept my own family firmly rooted in fear over the years. These spiritual websites spoke of love and growth, which struck a chord deep within me. I suppose that I related to these newfound teachings as they had many similarities to what Deano had taught me and that deep down, I knew the truth. I suddenly developed a thirst for these new websites that had always been there. I'd just never bothered looking because I was too quick to play the PlayStation instead. It turns out there is more to the internet than memes and pornography, for which I sought for so many years!

These spiritual websites that I'd stumbled across offered so much information about life and our purpose as humans. Now, I bet you're thinking, "Oh this poor guy, he has lost his friend and he now believes a few things that he has read on the net in order to find solace and comfort." You are entitled to think this as I have also thought the same, but the plot thickens.

25

WHEN THE STUDENT IS READY, THE TEACHER APPEARS

A new girl at work started, her name was Olivia. She was gentle, warm and had such a lovely energy about her. We clicked immediately. She just wanted to help people, but struggled with the way society operated. I guess I shared her sentiment and this led us to profound conversations. Olivia was a very spiritual person as her family had raised her that way. She began to suggest new paths for me to allow me to obtain my spiritual information. Wayne Dyer was one of the names that she mentioned to me. I went home the same night and watched some of his videos. This guy was cheesy and unappealing to me, but the more I watched, the more I felt drawn to him and his humble presence.

    I began to watch more and more, *why had I not seen this guy before?* Well, as Wayne Dyer would always say, "When the student is ready, the teacher shall appear." Apparently, this is an old zen saying but I'd never heard of it! That was me however, I was now ready to learn and grow. All of these fantastic people were manifesting into my life and prompting me towards what I needed to learn.

    Strangers would start random conversations with me about life, which I never would have attracted before. It really helped me having other people's perspectives on situations and life. In the past, I would know it all and not care for the opinion of another, but now I craved it. Be it right, or wrong, it was something new to consider. Olivia and I would discuss and dissect Wayne's words with intent and passion every day.

Each day, we would attempt to apply Mr Dyer's teachings into our own day to day lives.

I really began to love this guy and started to read his books. This was really something for me as I hated reading and hadn't read a book since my college years. For the majority of those, I was stoned and could barely recall what I had read anyway. By picking up these books and actually reading them, it really did blow some of the old proverbial cobwebs from my mind.

I began to enjoy my new reading regime as it calmed my mind and helped me to concentrate. The more I read, the more other authors and poets would appear. I was turning into quite a bookworm, what was happening!? These philosophers and theorists began to appear more frequently to me, just as Wayne Dyer once had. I was intrigued to hear their messages and what they had to say. Eckhart Tolle, Depak Chopra, Louise Hay, Bruce Lipton, Ram Dass and even Russell Brand were to name a few. I always thought Russell was just a crackhead, apparently this guy had chosen to walk the spiritual path also and was now clean! A complete U-turn. I suppose that's what I was becoming?

With each book that I read, they all had a collective theory that kept cropping up: the fact that we are infinite beings and that we are here to learn. With that said, I quickly became addicted to learning about myself and discovering who I actually was. I thought I had established this in my late twenties, but I now began to learn about my mind and how it operated. I learnt about my identity and that I wasn't who I thought I was. I discovered that our thoughts actually govern the way our bodies operate and that thoughts also create our immediate reality; it truly blew my mind and science even backed up these phenomena. Why was this not mainstream knowledge!? Illness was our responsibility; we have complete free will and choose everything, be it on a conscious or subconscious level.

I had learnt these new theories about our existence and one particular topic just kept cropping up… love! Ha! That was some hippy crap wasn't it? With this being said, I couldn't help but be constantly transported back to the hospital room where Dean had passed. When it was just him and I and how the tears flowed freely from my eyes in that moment. The tears were not because my brother had left his body; they were because I loved him, his soul, who he was. The tears that were from sheer, unconditional love. That feeling was in me all along.

I started to believe in the theory of love deep down and began to see the world for what it was; we were here to love and be loved. My rational, left side of the brain kept telling me that I was mad, and it would sometimes win. It would say, *honestly Dave, you don't really believe all this crap, do you? How can your past teachings be a lie? Think of all you've learnt at school! There is no such thing as the afterlife or spirit world. Material possessions are all that matter and that's that.*

These are genuinely some of the conversations that I would have inside my head, and still do sometimes; the logical mind is a powerful thing. I was confused to say the least! I decided that I needed concrete proof to back up what I had learnt through my studies and findings. How would I achieve this though, what could validate my findings? It's not as if someone could pop up from the other side to say, "Well done, Dave, all that you have found out is correct, have a gold star."

Lisa, Louise's sister, has always been into her spiritual stuff and always went for spiritual readings from a medium. I never really paid much attention to what Lisa said before about her readings, as they all seemed so vague. I thought that she was just clutching at straws to be honest. Lisa suggested that I visit the medium and stop being so cynical. I agreed to go with reluctance and scepticism. On the other hand, maybe it would give the validation I required so desperately to legitimise my research. Was there an afterlife?

Now in the past, whenever I would hear the words medium or physics, it would conjure up mental images of women with long black hair wearing bandanas. They would be sat in the back of an old caravan, gazing into a crystal ball, telling me that I am going on a long journey. In my opinion, mediums were just intelligent people who would pick up on things people say and put words into your mouth. "Oooh, have you lost someone, a great, great grandmother perhaps or did you have a pet when you were little?" These were the types of things they said right, so anyone can relate?

   I would put this woman to the test. I booked an appointment with her from my work phone, so there would be no traceability; my work mobile was registered with the college that I worked for. I would just give my first name and no surname. I wasn't on Facebook anyway; in fact I am a pretty private person so shy away from social media. Plus, my name is one of the most common names in the world, so there is nothing special about Dave Jones if you Googled it!

   This woman had a month-long waiting list so I had to wait a while before I could see her. With a month's waiting list, she must con and trick people pretty well and be very intelligent to do this. Those poor suckers, it's a shame that she would prey on the misery of others and make a living from it, but still, I would go, if just to prove Lisa wrong. The woman seemed quite pleasant over her texts and she said she could sense that I was searching for something. *Well yeah, obviously, that's why I'm texting you. What a genius she was!* I was going to be polite but expose this fraudster when I met her, it was unfair what she did to people. Earning money from people who were in vulnerable positions and searching for solace was just wrong in my eyes.

26

THE FORTUNE TELLER

I parked my car ten minutes away from the shop where the reading was due to happen. I didn't mention, did I? I passed my test! First time with five minors! Anyway, sorry, that was a little off topic wasn't it! So I parked my car and had a gentle stroll in the afternoon sun. It was a lovely walk and I kept thinking how eager I was to prove this fraudster wrong.

I found the shop, entered and asked for Jo. The people at the counter said she would be ready in a minute. It was a little *hippy* shop with incense burning, gentle music playing and angel statues everywhere. I was judging, but tried not to as that was part of my old character and instead, I considered all that I'd learnt over the past months. I was more open-minded to things now, so decided to embrace the environment.

As I waited, I heard people at the till talking about Jo and how she had the *gift*, it seems like they had been brainwashed too! My eyes studied the shop, absorbing all the crystals and fragrances. I'm not going to lie, I liked the ambience of the place, it was really relaxing. I remember thinking to myself as I waited, *if you really had a gift, why would you charge for it? I wouldn't do that; I'd do it for free!*

No sooner than I'd thought that, Jo popped her head from around the back door of the shop and said, "David, do you want to come in?" I proceeded into a dark, cosy little room with just a dim lamp to illuminate it, *oh my God, are we gonna summon the devil?* I exclaimed to myself! *This was precisely what the Bible had taught me to go against,* my rational mind bellowed. Still, that was my childhood conditioning persisting and I was on a new path now, time to be open. The room was quite comforting actually and I felt at peace, it certainly beat the back of a caravan anyway!

Jo looked like a *normal* lady and she didn't have a bandana on, nor did she possess a crystal ball. As I sat down she immediately said, "Oh David, you've had an awakening, you're a very spiritual person." She then said, "I bet you're wondering why I charge for this aren't you?" *Well the thought had just crossed my mind a few minutes prior!*

She then explained how she had left a well-paid job to do these readings for people. She had developed this gift while doing voluntary Reiki healing on cancer patients. She couldn't ignore the voices she heard and quit her job to help people with this gift. Spirits still didn't pay the bills in the physical world and her rate was very cheap when compared to others; so that is why she had to charge people. I accepted this explanation and actually thought what she did was quite noble. Leaving a high-paying job to take a plunge into the unknown definitely takes courage, but if she really had the gift she claimed, she could see that everything would be fine, right!?

She then proceeded to ask me why I had this sudden shift of consciousness and described it as an *awakening*. I had literally said nothing to her, okay she could be guessing? She then asked about my near-death experience, *eeehhh, ewww, wrong!* Just as I thought, she was someone who was trying to make a quick buck by preying on the vulnerable and had quit her other job for an easier life! I told her that I had never had a near-death experience. Jo looked confused. "Why this radical shift of thought though?" she asked. She paused and said, "I have someone here who is very excited to speak to you; maybe he is the reason behind your awakening?" My ears pricked up with curiosity.

Jo then proceeded to say there was a man in our presence who had a cough when he was in his physical body. *Well everyone has a cough at some point in their life* I thought, *but carry on.*

"He passed with problems to the lungs," she explained. Okay, I could feel my body language subconsciously changing now. She continued to describe the person, "He had a tattoo all down his left arm. He passed suddenly and even he didn't expect it." Jo now had my full attention, *go on* I thought.

I will never forget the next part. She pointed at me, clicked her fingers and said, "Deano!"

What the actual fuck!? I thought. *How could she know this? It was impossible. Was I dreaming?* Goosebumps consumed my entire body and I started to cry. Jo handed me some tissues which were at the ready. I guess everyone broke down in her readings!

Jo then proceeded to tell me all about how Dean watched my driving test and laughed when I stalled and panicked. Dean thanked me for the 10k run that I did down on Woolacombe beach; which was to raise money for the Cystic Fibrosis ward in the Queen Elizabeth hospital which helped him so much while he was on Earth. *How the hell could she know this stuff?*

Dean thanked me for being there for him and he said that I was one of the kindest men to walk the Earth. I thought to myself, *that's a bit rich considering that Jesus walked it too*, but I took the compliment nevertheless! I was sobbing throughout all of this, it was so surreal.

In my head I kept thanking Dean for the lessons he had taught me and Jo stopped me to say, "No, Dean thanks you," and that I should stop thanking him as it was all about me this time.

What the hell, she was reading my thoughts now? This was trippier than any substance I had ever tried in my drug addled youth. She then said something that only Dean would say, "I'm not gay but I love you." That was it for me, as if his name hadn't been enough. She had given me a phrase that would come right from Dean's mouth.

Dean and I would often tease each other about how masculine we were. If any sign of affection was shown between men, then it must be construed as homosexual behaviour! Two male friends who were straight men couldn't possibly show genuine affection for each other without another reason behind it!

I mean no offence by the private joke that I share between Dean and myself for we were never homophobic. However, from a blinkered, macho perspective, when a male is participating in activities that are not fuelled by testosterone, your position as an alpha comes under question. If you were to have slightly effeminate mannerisms then your masculinity would be stripped and therefore, one's sexuality must be questioned. This puerile logic and irrational satire had begun in our school days and we had continued through to adult life as a joke! I thought that it was funny that Dean was saying that he *loved* me, but he was merely repeating the words that I said to him moments after he had passed on his deathbed.

Jo continued to defy logic and toy with my analytical mind as she described the little silver car that I drove, which I had parked ten minutes away. Not even all of my friends knew I drove; let alone what car it was! She told me about my varicose vein operation I had three years prior and about a possible hernia I had due to the gym, which I had started to feel at that time. Every piece of information that Jo gave was impossible to guess or get via some internet research.

Dean said I knew someone called Sue who was very close to me and that we would be helping each other. I didn't know anyone called Sue? Maybe Dean had made a mistake? I left it at that and thought nothing of it, I will allow him to make one mistake!

Lights flickered around me as Jo continued to read for me, it was the most bizarre, surreal experience ever! It was similar to events that I had seen in horror movies when an entity is near and all the lights flicker. Jo explained that we are all energy and it was simply spirits sharing the experience with us.

As Deano drew back due to his energy getting weaker, Jo informed me that someone else was here to see me. She informed me that behind my left shoulder was where people from my maternal side would appear. She asked if my mum had passed, to which I replied, "No." Again, Jo looked confused, as she told me that the spirit that was there with her was claiming that she was my mum. Jo then confirmed that it was actually my nan but the love that she was displaying and projecting onto Jo was like a mother's love for a child. I explained that my nan was my mum in a way and that she had raised me to some degree. Jo then proceeded to tell me how proud my nan was of me and how well I had coped with my tortured childhood. It was really quite emotional.

Jo couldn't make this up, it was all too personal and everything was on point. She told me things about my traumatic past that no one knew, as I had buried them deep within. I have never spoken about some of the issues I faced to anyone, not even in this book, for they are too private and delicate. It was impossible to know these events that Jo spoke about.

Jo knew all about my cooking and how Nan and I would bake cakes together when I was just a child. She informed me that my nan was standing right in front of me at that point but I couldn't see anything, again, it was very surreal. I could feel the air change and a light breeze around me but visually, everything looked normal.

Jo asked me who Louise was and told me that Nan approved! She used the name Louise as if she knew her but had never met her. My nan stated that Louise and I were right for each other as we had the right balance in our relationship, which was perfect for this lifetime.

As the reading came to an end, the lights flickered again and my nan's presence drew back and faded. As Nan left, she was singing. Nan would always sing for me and I would laugh at her for it! Those poxy church hymns she used to listen to were so awful. I will never forget the *church* music, as she would call it. Nan and Dean said their goodbyes and Jo closed the reading with a crazy verse about angels protecting her!

I was Jo's last reading of the day and we chatted for about half an hour after the reading had closed. Jo told me that I had a beautiful soul and that I was on a mission. What she said made sense to me in a way. I have always felt compassion and love for people, even as a child, it just needed to be expanded. I was just too absorbed in my own self-hate and loathing growing up which blocked my true beauty from shining. Growing up, I thought that I had to play a drunk character in order to be accepted by people and to *fit* into the crowd. It's just a shame I had to bury my true magnificence; something that we all possess, but sometimes choose not to show.

I quizzed Jo about what I had been learning; karma, past lives, pre-birth planning and love. She confirmed to the best of her knowledge that all of my research was somewhat accurate. Jo didn't have the magic answer either, for she was on her path. The main thing that she encouraged me to do was to keep exploring and not to rely on what others thought to validate my own experiences, something that I had always done! The human mind is so limited, it's difficult to comprehend the vast complexity of it all and our true purpose in the Universe. We can just do our best while we are here.

Jo is such a beautiful woman. I use that word a lot don't I, beautiful? But beautiful is one of those words that feels like it sounds, do you know what I mean? Either way, her external beauty showed, but radiated from the inside also. Her inner warmth really shone forth to me that day and I felt a calming, tranquil flow of energy shine over me whilst I was in her presence. As I left, I asked Jo for a hug, to which she accepted. That woman had changed my life in an hour. What a gift she had. I thanked her profusely and went on my way.

I exited the quaint, little shop and walked back to my car, floating along in a state of awe. What just happened? Was it all a dream? Speaking of dreams, I had a dream about my nan the night before the reading. In it, she told me that I didn't need to see a medium to know that she was always with me. The dream made perfect sense to me after the reading and I guess it was a visit from my nan who loved me so much and was still with me.

I drove home with a sense of euphoria; it was all real. I hadn't gone mad. This life is only temporary and the soul is eternal. We are here to learn, grow and expand. Earth is just a magnificent school of learning and I am merely visiting for a brief time. I arrived home and told Louise everything. We both read my notes that Jo had written and Louise was just as mesmerised as I was. It was hard to believe, yet easy at the same time. A real tangled mesh of confusing emotions, but deep down it all just felt like the truth.

27

A New Path

So, life was a school was it? I wanted to learn as much as I could and take my game to the next level. I would start by being more selfless. I would practise, with passion, all that I had learnt and I would apply it on a daily basis. I wanted to learn from like-minded people who loved and cared for others unconditionally.

I decided to apply for a voluntary position at a local project that did work with adults living on the outskirts of society. People who the project helped were the homeless, addicts and individuals who struggled with day to day problems in life. These are all people who I used to judge. The irony of it all was those who I once judged were actually me! I had lived in their position, who was I to judge!?

The project also ran a food bank to help those in need. Who knows who I would meet there? As soon as I started, I met some truly wonderful people; full of love and kindness. All of the positions there were voluntary and we were just trying to help the community in any way we could. All I witnessed was true love for anyone who walked through that door, be it a volunteer or someone in need of help.

The guy who ran the project was called Stacey. Stacey had a troubled past that stemmed from gang culture, drugs, and even prison time. You name it, he'd been there! Stacey told me how he had let his ego rule him and that in the past he had a point to prove to everyone, every day. That was until one day when he felt the presence of God consume him while he was alone in his room pleading for answers from a higher force. He got the answer he was after via a spoken message into his ear and a touch on the shoulder, and he vowed never to look back from that point in his life. Stacey told me that anything is possible when you are one with God. He also shared with me that the mind is a powerful tool, if applied correctly.

I'll be honest, the word God scared me and took me back to my Sunday school teachings. I didn't like biblical connotations to things, but you know what, if it worked for Stacey, then I was cool with that. Whatever helps anyone walk a better path can't be bad, can it?

Stacey is literally the happiest person I have ever met and treats everybody the same. He is so inspirational and is an angel sent from above. Anyone who walks through the door of the project is equal to Stacey and I have learnt much from him. Stacey told me that he has no judgement for anyone he meets, for he has done much, much worse than they ever will. He is an omnipresent breath of fresh air in any circumstance and radiates tremendous energy.

For anyone who says, "A leopard never changes its spots," I urge you to dispose of this narrow-minded meme from your thinking. Mistakes are how we evolve and sometimes an individual has to hit rock bottom in order to see the error of their ways. This is how people change, and experiencing harsh consequences are necessary in order for people to see the true purpose of their life.

Helping young, vulnerable adults at the college where I worked, coupled with assisting the homeless at my voluntary job, really gave me a sense of purpose. This sounds very self-righteous doesn't it? As if I were a saint! Was I developing an attachment to being a *good* person? Can good come out of balance too? Bear this in my mind as the book progresses and we discuss what the ego and attachment is.

For the first time in my life, I was actually getting a buzz out of being selfless. I began to meditate as well in order to free my mind from all the clutter. This allowed me to connect with my higher self, all of which we will discuss in the following chapters if this all sounds foreign to you! Life was moving along nicely and I would read and learn something new every day, be it right or wrong. My thirst for knowledge about the human experience really was insatiable and only grew stronger. The more books I read, the more open-minded I became, how had I been asleep for so long!?

Half a year had passed since I first met Jo and I felt a compelling urge to go and see her again. Particularly through meditation, I would feel spirit or something telling me to visit Jo again. I text her telling her how I felt and that I must see her! I may have sounded mad to her, but she said that spirit clearly wanted us to meet and we arranged an appointment.

I made my way to her little shop again and it felt like meeting up with a true friend, she had such warmth about her. I sat down in the small, dimly lit room and instantly felt at ease; it was completely different to my first experience. Being in Jo's presence made me physically tingle, I loved it! Jo told me how we had spoken in her dreams and that our meeting was no coincidence. I explained my feelings and that I had been drawn to her and she laughed. I really only went for a chat, but she began to read for me. The first thing she said was that she could see a beautiful rose quartz crystal. I had literally bought one for Louise the previous evening! Jo then explained how she saw me decorating. I had been decorating with my grandad on the very same morning. How did she know these things? It was truly fascinating.

My dad's dad came through this time and we spoke of the car that I drove and how the sale of his house helped to pay for it. I thanked him for his gift from beyond the grave. My nan came through again, but this time it just felt so natural and it was good to sit there and ask her questions that I had planned. Jo informed me that my nan had officially taken me under her wing now and was always with me; assisting and guarding me. I was so happy to hear that this was now her role in the spirit world.

Jo carefully explained how she saw me with children and getting married. The Monday before my visit, Jo had done a reading for Louise and didn't know that we were together. Half of Louise's reading was about me and babies. Now Jo was on about babies to me as well, so it looked like we were doomed! Jo said three souls had picked us and were just waiting to incarnate. *Jesus, three!* I thought. This was what Louise had been told too. I was just acclimatising to the idea of one but what will be, will be! Maybe babies will appear in the future but I cannot confirm this yet!

My boy, Deano came through to give me a message. He told me to just go for it! Well that's what I have been trying to do and have done with this book you are reading. Dean also had a message for Lee which Jo wrote down. The message was: a bike, a falcon and that Dean would see Lee at a fountain; random indeed! I sent Lee a picture of the notes and he confirmed that he had just acquired a new bike, that he walked by a falcon every day and that he was going to the Dubai Fountains a few days later to meet some friends we both knew. Dean would be there with him! Even Lee couldn't argue with what had been said, and it freaked him out a bit.

As the reading finished, I felt a real sense of euphoria again. Jo closed the reading with her verse about angels protecting her and with that, I said my goodbyes to her. I left that glorious little shop once again feeling enlightened.

28

IS EVERY MEETING JUST A COINCIDENCE?

Now, I would see many customers while working in the college café and chat freely to them all (even the sultry ones) but one little lady, Sue, caught my eye. We began chatting and she said that I had an infectious smile that helped her! What a bizarre thing to say, but every little helps I suppose. So, whenever I saw her, I would always attempt to project my best smile upon her when she entered the café.

Sue had recently lost her husband and was understandably finding life very tough. We spoke deeply whenever she would come to the café and she was so grateful that I was able to give her my time. I personally didn't see it as a big deal as it is what I would do for anyone. After all, my job was to be welcoming! The more time we spent talking together, the more I shared my views on life with her. Sue became accustomed to my way of thinking and said it helped her. I described to her the transition in my own thinking through Dean's passing and how it had helped me to grow as a person.

Sue really was a gentle woman with a big heart but was truly heartbroken over the loss of her husband. Death can be so hard to deal with. I described to Sue that I viewed Dean's passing as though he had caught a train to a destination that we all must return to one day, except he just chose to board it earlier than us. I'm still at the station where he once was, but must wait a little longer as I still have a lot of work to be done. When my train arrives, I will be ready and I will board it knowing

I have done everything possible in my power to make the most of my stay on this planet.

Sue bought my analogy but wanted to get the train to be with John, her husband. I told her that the day would come but not now, she could perhaps get a glimpse into what John was up to though? As the conversation progressed, I suggested that Sue go and pay Jo a visit, as she had really helped me to transform my life. I gave Sue her number and she made an appointment.

A month or so passed and Sue went for her reading. After her visit to Jo, she came into the café to inform me of her eye-opening experience. Sue had a different energy about her and was most upbeat; she was beaming, glowing almost. Sue proceeded to tell me that John, her husband, came through immediately and that Jo couldn't have made anything of what she told her up as it was so accurate. I asked Sue if there was any way that Jo could have tricked her or been vague with her? "Never in a million years," Sue replied. She was adamant that the messages she received were all valid, as names and dates were given.

It was so warming to witness this partial solace that Sue had found from receiving a message from John. I knew that she would still struggle, but now she had some hope. Sue implored me to go and see Jo more frequently, as they had both agreed I had every potential to help people progress on their own individual, spiritual paths. Frequent messages from spirit would help me to understand life in a holistic way.

As Sue told me this information, I felt a strong presence behind me. I thought that it was Gemma, who now worked at the same college with me. Gemma was notorious for sneaking into the kitchen unnoticed, what was she in a former life, a cat burglar!? However, as I turned around, nobody was there. I continued to listen to Sue intently and dismissed the presence behind me as a trick of my own mind. My rational mind still fights with what my heart truly knows, even to this day. The more Sue spoke, the more I felt a presence behind me. I turned, but still no one was there. This conversation was happening over the counter of the café by the way - I don't half have some interesting chats with students and customers from behind that counter!

Sue continued to speak and encouraged me to get advice from Jo on how to develop my intuitive nature more. If I could do what Jo could do, could I help people more? People always seemed to gravitate towards me for one reason or another. The moment those words left Sue's mouth, I felt two firm taps on my right shoulder as if to say, "pay attention." I jumped around instantly but to my surprise and astonishment, no one was there. I know what I felt that day and it has stuck with me. It was spirit telling me that this was the purpose of why I was here; to help others awaken to their true potential while developing my own intuition.

That was it! Sue's words reverberated around my head! I would love to be the person to provide healing for troubled and confused souls. I was once that person who had a perturbed view on life. My perception was indeed murky until Jo had worked her magic and shifted the haze. Jo validated everything that I had learnt up until our meeting. I guess one way of helping people would be through this book for a start!

For those of you who are astute or have a good memory, do you remember what Dean said in my first reading? He said I knew someone called Sue and that we would be helping each other. It made no sense at the time because I didn't know Sue. In Dean's existence there is no time, and energy is just energy, everything happens simultaneously. This is why Dean spoke the message to me in present tense. We will elaborate on this further in the second part of the book. It all made sense to me further down the line as to who Sue was and indeed, we had helped each other in more ways than one.

Now I thought that communicating with spirit and developing my intuition would happen overnight and I could flip a switch; but like everything in life, intuition takes practice. Since that day of speaking with Sue, my intuition has increased significantly over the last year. Events pop into my head seconds before they actually happen. It was spooky at first, but now I have taken it as the norm. I have also had dreams come true, which can be a bit creepy to be honest.

After a while of being around someone, I can see their aura and how they are truly feeling. The colour of someone's aura lets you know their current energetic state. This electromagnetic field, that we all possess, gives off a vibe that we all pick up on at a subconscious level. I can also feel people's emotions when they are in my presence and I can feel a vibrational shift when spirit is near. I often get ringing in my ears before certain situations, telling me to pay attention. These are also downloads of subconscious information from my guides. Guides are something that we will discuss later.

I have witnessed spirit on multiple occasions which appear with flashes and sparkles. They move like waves of neon electricity and are truly beautiful. Often these are of a blue and white colour, as this is said to be the energy that is closely linked to the physical plane. Some have been very poignant experiences and a few have been from my nan who shows her appearance to me while she projects the most overwhelming feeling of love onto me; identical to that which I felt when I was in the hospital room with Dean as he left his body.

I have also manifested new jobs, which are literally perfect for me, and money flows to me freely from bizarre sources. I will discuss how this is done in a manifesting chapter later on. I feel that my awareness of the Universe has certainly grown and I do receive messages from my guides when I am deep in meditation; much like the voice that told me to "write a book" that day. Honestly, I have never considered writing a book, or anything for that matter! At college and school, I found writing a laborious task, so composing a book was never embedded on my *to do* list.

Nevertheless, I have actually enjoyed writing this book for you and the whole experience of reliving my past on paper has actually been a wonderful, emotional purge. Any dark, lingering emotions that were attached to my past have truly been released, and the odd tear has been shed while writing this. If you have problems currently or some issues lurking from the past, try writing them down on paper or in a diary. It may surprise you how the release helps to alleviate your pain, which will have an inevitable impact on your mental state.

Now I do not want to disappoint you but this is where my current story ends, as we have reached the present day. A bit of an anti-climax I know; if I were in your position reading this, I would toss the book across the room in utter disgust. I would have been expecting a fairy-tale ending where I spoke to the spirit world with ease, manipulated objects with my mind and helped millions progress on their paths to true enlightenment, but unfortunately no such ending, not in this book anyway. Maybe I can help you to see things from a different angle in the second half of the book though?

So now you have an idea of my life and my journey up until this point, I would like to examine topics that I have discovered to be the truth. My truths and your truths will be different, but whose truth carries more validity? We shall examine exactly what the truth is to an individual. The book is not over, only just beginning actually, and I will now examine many secrets of life with you that they don't teach you at school. Everything that we talk about from now on, I will relate to situations that I faced in my past and where I went wrong.

Growing up, I behaved the way I did because of how my ego and subconscious mind had been developed. When we have an understanding as to why we behave the way we do, we can manipulate our immediate environment. It all stems from the conditioning that we receive in our early years which shapes our subconscious behaviour. Beliefs from our parents and the structure of society literally mould the blank canvas which comes in the shape of a baby.

The ego that is part of the spacesuit that we occupy for this incarnation governs our animalistic human experience. If we are not aware of the ego and who we truly are, then compulsive behaviour and desires will appear normal to us; much like addictions did to me. When we can identify and observe egoic emotions that drive our behaviour, we can understand that they are not really a part of who we truly are. By doing this, we can be free of torture and see suffering as grace. We can learn to love and remember who we truly are, which is why we are here.

I will show you that everything happens for a reason in our lives and that we have already mapped out our journey to some extent. One of my main purposes of this book is to teach self-love and to convince you that we are all perfect, despite what society has programmed us to think. It is only the ego that berates us and puts us down; the westernised world in which we live in exploits this further.

You may think some of the things that I am about to discuss are utter codswallop. They may torment and even toy with your rational mind, but deep down, truth knows truth. You may think that the passing of my best friend, my deranged childhood and drug fuelled youth have sent me to the verge of insanity. You are entitled to your opinion my friend and I respect that. In fact, if I, myself, had read what you're about to read ten years ago, I would probably be thinking, *what an absolute load of bollocks, this guy has lost the plot*, but back then, I was not ready.

Even if you find the following contents of this book nonsense, I hope it encourages you to do your own research into life and not take everything at face value. There are a lot of lies out there which are easy to see through if you scratch a fraction beneath the artificial surface. Some people have lost the ability to think for themselves and go through life following the crowd. Please try not to be that person like I once was.

I do not claim that my way is the only way because we are all unique. I simply make suggestions with my content. We each have our individual path to honour and walk. Some topics that I write about could be considered callous, from a human perspective, but this book is all about shifting your perspective from that of the finite. We are all the same and truth recognises truth. If you look hard enough, you will see the truth of life is everywhere, it just depends on which angle you view it from.

So, my friend, like I said in the introduction, if I can help to expand one person's perspective on life and shift it to a more positive stance, I am truly content. I just hope that you are that person! What I write about has been written many times over the course of history, for there are only so many ways to document the truth. I am just placing my own little twist on things to make them as accessible as possible for you. Right, enough waffling, let's go!

29

Choosing Your Life Path and Lessons

Consider the concept that we are all eternal energy. Consider that we are all on a quest for wisdom with infinite possibilities. Consider that we are trying to remember who we are while we are on earth. Consider that we long to return to what we already are. Consider that we are a part of a force that creates all. That force has many names attributed to it by man, all of which draw a blank. That force is one of limitless thinking with no confinements to it. That force longs to explore itself from an infinite number of perspectives. That force consists of an incomprehensible myriad of possibilities to our small, fragile, human minds.

Every imaginable realm and dimension has one omnipotent consciousness operating it. This energy is split into multiple fragments in order to experience itself from every angle possible, and evolve at the same time. This happens all at once, while being engulfed in pure, unconditional love and light. Every single one of us is a fragment of that energy divided into individual physical expressions so we can learn about ourselves and what the Universe is at the same time. We are each on a path to gain infinite wisdom to discover what or who we truly are, whether we know it or like it; that is what our soul craves. We already know who we are but have chosen to forget when occupying physical bodies. This is why we choose to enter Earth, so that we can learn to remember who we are.

Think of Earth as a spirit school or even a training simulation for the infinite ever-expanding soul. We learn best through the physical experience; although we never stop learning, even when we are in our natural state of spiritual energy. Our soul's preference, however, is to learn via the physical as learning is excelled that way. The whole forgetting process that happens at birth is like a game to the soul.

When you are attempting to get to a destination, you plan the journey first, don't you? This is what your soul did before you arrived on this planet. It planned to complete unfinished business in the form of karma which had been incurred from previous lifetimes. With each karmic episode, known as birth, the soul hopes to learn from past errors and by doing this, move closer to what it already is.

Alongside these experiences, lessons will be learnt and these will ultimately lead your heart to open and let your natural state pour forth, which is love. If we plan our karmic journey meticulously, our consciousness also has the opportunity to awaken to what it truly is while occupying a human body. What is that? That will come at the end of the book! For now, I will ease you in. With this being said, why would I choose to be born into such a discombobulated situation as I did? I must be one crazy son of a gun to have picked the convoluted scenario that I was born into!

Was choosing two individuals, such as my parents, who were struggling with severe mental issues of their own a wise move? Hell yes it was, it was a stroke of genius! At least that is what my soul would say. My egoic mind might not have been too keen at the prospect of it all!

In the spirit world, there is no physical body, everything is energy. The physical body is a vehicle for your soul while on earth. It can manoeuvre around the world and encounter the events that you are meant to experience in order to shape you. The body is a meat suit, if you like, which enables your soul to interact within the three-dimensional plane and explore this physical world. Is this too much already? If it is, stop me. I mean you can't, but the thought was there.

The physical body comes with magnificence we cannot comprehend. Scientists are beginning to make amazing discoveries as to who we truly are, but in the grand scheme of things we are still in a fairly primitive stage regarding our knowledge of what we are actually capable of.

Think of your body like a spacesuit that encases your soul for this part of your journey. Your spacesuit also comes with a built-in software that will help you to function in this lifetime. This is known as the ego. It will help you to survive while on this planet and provide identity as to who you physically are. When we die and the body perishes, so does the ego. This is why the spirit world is full of love, as there's not an ego in sight! I will have chapters on the ego later on, for now, I will briefly outline what the ego does.

The ego contains a level of rationality that enables us to play our part in society. It is governed by the five senses that help us to explore and perceive the physical world. It helps us to maintain an identity and what we stand for. The ego could be described as a survival tool, as when the body ceases to breathe, the ego dies too. That is why survival is such a priority for the ego, as death really is the final nail in the coffin!

The ego also thrives on what we do, what people think of us. *I*, *me* and *my* are the ego's primary concern. With the notion of *me* and *mine* believed, the ego buys into the illusion that we are all separate from one another. The ego does not like challenges as is simply out for itself and wants to survive. Taking this into account, my linear, rational mind would not have picked such a seemingly complex scenario to be born into as I was. It would have chosen to be born into royalty possibly, so that it could lounge around all day, spending its future days on a private exotic beach somewhere!

The idea of being born into a family that consisted of two people who were diagnosed with manic depression, schizophrenia and multiple mental health problems probably wouldn't appeal to the ego. It would appear daunting, if anything, to such a fragile composition as the ego. Luckily, my soul was doing the choosing and only when I arrived in my physical body, did I then inherit my ego or earth guide, if you like.

The soul's desire is to learn, progress, expand, evolve, grow and become what it is. Before choosing an incarnation, my higher self would examine my karmic path from parallel lifetimes. I say parallel lifetimes as time is a man-made construct, but more on that later. Think of the higher self as the real you who is omnipotent, eternal, and resides in pure love. It has extreme wisdom and can project itself into many dimensions, lifetimes and planes of consciousness simultaneously.

What lessons had I learnt and experienced in parallel lifetimes? What did I need to perfect? Was I still selfish? Did I still judge? What lessons did I need to transcend further? What events could I experience in this lifetime that would help to advance my soul even further? How would I change the world with the domino effect of my actions? What impact would my smallest actions and thoughts have on the world? There are so many reasons for wanting to visit this planet. Each lifetime edges us closer to what we are and expands our consciousness just a fraction more.

Karma would be involved in our birth choice, but karma will be addressed in its own chapter later on. Choices that I made in past lifetimes will have to be amended through karma; not as punishment, but just to enlighten us further. In fact, we can truly learn the extent of our actions towards others through karma. I have zero recollection of any of my previous lifetimes and I have no desire to know any either, as it is only now that matters. However, I feel I must have abandoned someone in the past and this is why my mother left me. The pain I experienced growing up was unfathomable, but I have learnt from it all, beautifully in fact.

I often find it humorous in films or dramas when moody, angst-ridden teenagers scream at their parents in arguments, "I didn't ask to be born," well actually you did! Life is not unfair, we planned it, we create every second with our thoughts and actions. We have complete free will and can choose the circumstances we want depending on how we want to develop.

The global destination of your birth will play a huge factor in your soul's choice when planning its arrival here on planet Earth. How can I have the same perspective on life in my comfortable little western bubble, compared to a starving child many miles away? My soul needs to experience both sides of the coin in order to gain the full picture. By having parallel lives in many different cultures and locations, the soul can gain a broader perspective on human existence.

Race could be another factor. In this particular incarnation, I have chosen to be born a white male and have rarely suffered any racial hate or prejudice towards the colour of my skin. I am aware, however, that other races and cultures can be targeted and abused every day based solely on their physical appearance. If I were going through that on a daily basis, my take on life would be totally different to what it is now.

This is why our pre-birth planning is so vital to the lessons that we can pick up from that particular visit. The lessons we are here to learn are not that complicated from a spiritual point of view, however the ego will make this into a much trickier task than it needs to be! We are here to be loved and to love as that is all we fundamentally are. When we realise this, the world can evolve back to its natural state. We have complete free will to achieve this.

We are all born physically *perfect* regardless of what our appearance is, unless the eyes of society deems otherwise! Much like Dean chose his health for this lifetime, it was perfect for his journey. With that being said, society may have seen Dean's condition as unfair and not perfect, but who are we to deem that an imperfection or abnormality is not perfect anyway? Again, this is the work of the ego.

We choose life-shaping events and we each have a profound purpose and mission to fulfil. We play our part in a play that we have created for ourselves to help us remember who we are. We choose our family, schools, and the partners we will marry. You may well be thinking, "What's the point of all this if you already know these events are going to happen?"

In order to grow, you need to experience events first-hand, the good and the bad. If I were to tell you about a fabulous holiday that I had just been on and described it vividly to you, you would have a vague idea of what I meant. However, only if you were to visit the actual location for yourself, could you share the true beauty of it and understand what I was saying. Also, your interpretation of the holiday would be totally different to mine and you may end up hating it! That's why we must each live through seemingly challenging times in order to develop. We learn through pain. Without pain, joy would not exist, it's all in balance. The soul sees pain as nothing, a mere fleeting event in the grand scheme of eternity. The soul welcomes the sea of suffering, for it is all part of the beautiful dichotomy.

Would you be willing to receive a splinter in exchange for extreme wisdom? A lifetime is a blink of an eye compared to the vast complexity and mystery that the Universe holds. The lifetime of a mere 80 years would appear as a flash to the soul in comparison to infinity. I often recall my nan saying how fast life can go, and I now realise this as I grow older.

We have been given complete free will with this psychedelic thing called life. We are the architects and plan grand events while we are in spirit, but we can choose to travel any path we wish using our free will when on Earth to arrive at these life-shaping events. It's like approaching a crossroad and choosing which way to go; ultimately the two roads will lead to your main objective, but you can't help but think, *what would have happened if I had taken the other road?*

Not to worry though. Like I said, you will eventually end up at your planned destination. Sometimes, we all take a little detour in life. Have you ever felt like something was just meant to happen or you were just meant to meet someone? Chances are, you had already planned it and the situations that led to it needed to be experienced by your soul in order to make the meeting with that person more understandable. You were guided to that particular moment, event or person, by your higher self.

I chose my nan to show me the beauty of unconditional love and absolutely no judgement. I chose Dean to be my friend to spark this deep awakening in me with his passing. His behaviour and attitude to life helped to shape who I am now. I am no longer unconscious, drifting through life with a wandering persona. I'm no longer watching the news and believing everything that I hear, more often than not saying that the world is a terrible place; I owe this all to Dean.

You are probably thinking, "Okay then, why would Dean choose a lifetime of pain and discomfort by being born with cystic fibrosis?" Each path is unique, beautiful and perfect for what an individual needs to experience in order to grow, and even inspire others. Dean's lifetime was perfect for him but his selfless behaviour inspired me.

I have also spoken to Jo about this topic and I will never forget the first time Dean came through in her reading. She said, "Dean is with God." I asked what was meant by the term *God* during our second meeting, as she never explained the first time. Jo explained that Dean was on a very high level in the spiritual world and would have experienced many earthly incarnations. He had experienced what it was to *be* God and his soul had transcended to higher realms. This makes complete sense to me with the way he was and how he behaved. Dean was Godlike: positive, loving, non-judgemental, patient, kind, inspiring and he never once moaned about his cystic fibrosis. He did all this while being a little bit cheeky too! All of these are Godlike qualities in my eyes.

With the knowledge that life is but a blink of an eye and that we are all infinite energy, death is nothing more than an illusion. No one ever really dies, for it is impossible. With the soul armed with this truth, anything can be chosen in a lifetime to learn from. Dean chose to live a life that, to the human mind, would seem like a life of suffering. However, Dean appeared to have little attachment to his *condition* and never once conveyed his illness to me or anyone as a problem. Dean did not moan to anyone about the condition that his spacesuit had installed in it and lived his best life. His spacesuit had a ticking clock built into it, the same as anyone's, but his was much shorter for his needs in this lifetime. Dean was a true teacher; look at the profound impact that his passing has had on me.

Jo spoke of how sometimes advanced souls will think, "What the hell, I will have one more roll of the dice," and elect themselves to come back to Earth in order to shift the consciousness of certain individuals and the planet. They do not need a lot of time on earth, which is why Dean will have opted to be incarnated with cystic fibrosis. This condition was a fail-safe option for him so that he could return home as soon as his work was done. It was all perfect.

He needed little time on Earth this time round in order to fulfil his goals. We choose to bring our conditions into the world, nothing is evil or punishing about this universal creation that we made. It is all for a divine, incomprehensible reason that will become clear to us one day and one that you already know the answer to because you are it. Do you really think our tiny human mind in comparison to infinity, could grasp the true complexity of what the galaxies and Universe hide? Our minds are just a speck compared to the wonders of the Milky Way and that's giving it boundaries!

Wow, that's quite an introduction to the second half of the book, isn't it? I guess you have an idea about the content of this book now! I hope that it hasn't deterred you from reading any further. I hope that it's made you wonder what we truly are and why we choose our parents? What have you learnt from them?

Some of what I say may appear completely contradictory at times, but I will do my best to justify it to you. You may think I have gone completely bat shit crazy from losing my best friend and that's fine also! I have often thought *Oh my God, am I actually losing my mind?* It's not as though what I examine in this book is a topic that is frequently talked about in our society or something you see on the news every night. Why is that? Either way, I'm just happy that you are still reading! You are, aren't you? Go on, keep going...

30

Soul Mates, Karma and Reincarnation

Soul mates and karma are quite commercial terms these days, aren't they? Media has adopted these concepts and even provided little memes for them. 'Karma's a bitch', 'True love is being with your soulmate.' The list goes on and these are all examples of how the westernised world has adopted these fundamental, spiritual principles into our everyday lives.

By becoming commercialised, I feel these terms have become stripped of their spiritual roots and true meaning. People readily accept these terms without actually understanding the principles of how they work and govern our human experience. The fact is that karma is not a punishment, but more of a blessing. The word karma means *to learn* or *action*. When you think of it like that, it doesn't seem like a punishment, more of an enlightenment.

As stated before, when you are planning your arrival on earth, karma, which is the law of learning, will govern the people that you meet and the experiences that you will have. If you did some unjust things to another or others in past lifetimes, you will walk a path that will greet you as the same experiences that you put others through. From experiencing the situations that you put others through first-hand, it will help your soul to understand the consequences of your actions.

These can be in the form of good or bad experiences, hence there is good karma and bad karma. All choices come with an action and consequence in every lifetime and you do, in fact, reap what you sow, as the old adage goes. Cause and effect are in action before your very eyes! Your choices and behaviour will return to you in order to help you learn. Thoughts, actions and deep-rooted beliefs shape your karmic path.

For instance, if you were to cheat on a partner in this lifetime and did not see the full effect of the pain that your selfish actions caused others, then the lesson must be repeated until grasped. When you can objectively see and understand what you did and why you did it, you can learn from it. The insatiable, self-centred ego yearned for the flesh of another with total disregard for anyone else; only concerned with gratifying its own selfish egoic pursuits. If you were to allow the ego to continue this loop of selfish behaviour, then you too will experience the pain of being cheated on in this lifetime or the next. You will see how many lives one person's actions can affect from a first-hand perspective.

We need to experience the emotions that we have caused others to feel in order to understand the true domino effect of the choices that we made. When we experience these feelings for ourselves, our souls can learn from the result of our actions. Unless you've been through it, you can't understand, can you? I could say to you, "You've hurt me more than you will ever know," but you would never grasp the true extent of what I meant. That's why karma is there to enlighten us, not punish.

You can end up incurring more karma in each lifetime by missing the lessons which are sometimes right before you. When you are constantly experiencing the same cycles and patterns in your life, know that karma is simply spinning its web to catch you and is trying to say, "wake up!" You are not learning from your current lesson so the same experiences continue until you do. This can sometimes last lifetimes.

If you go from bad relationship to bad relationship, why is that? Karma. Not to say these bad relationships are a failure, far from it as they will eventually lead you to break the cycle, but until then failed relationships will come your way. You will only ever attract people into your life that you feel you deserve and are worthy of on a subconscious level. Until you learn about yourself and who you truly are, people of the same ilk will continue to enter your life.

Of course, people who are on your karmic path can come into your life to shake things up and show you that you are worthy of love. But you may still feel unworthy on a base level and sabotage the whole experience. Looking back at my relationships, I did this many, many times.

Alcohol and drugs can do tremendous damage, not just to your physical body, but to your karmic path. When under the influence, you are stating to the Universe that you do not want to be responsible for your actions and want to *take a break.* By doing this you can attract all sorts of negative events and energies to you when you are on a *holiday* from the mind. You can often wake up after going on a bender feeling a lot worse than you did before. In the absence of your conscious mind in those *vacant* times, you will have possibly made poor decisions that are led by negative energies. By doing this, you have incurred more karma to learn from. Had you just stayed sober; things that would have appeared bad would have passed, but your choice to go on a *holiday* ultimately made things worse.

I had to learn this lesson many times with my drug and alcohol use. I used the two to mask my problems and pain, but in effect, ended up creating more harm and hurt for everyone else, including myself. All of the truly negative things that happened in my life stemmed from being under the influence. I broke my ankle which affected the lives of others. I would often lose possessions, causing others to watch my back. I would get into scuffles causing others to again help me. I would vandalise other people's possessions through mindless acts of drunkenness, just to impress peers.

When I was out with female friends who had obvious feelings for me, I would end up getting drunk and sleeping with them. Prior to this I had no intention of pursuing a relationship with them. I would avoid talking to them again, for it was easier to ignore the awkward conversations. Some women would see our night together as the beginning of a possible relationship. However, my drunken choice to sleep with them was just a selfish act on my behalf, I essentially manipulated their feelings towards me. When under the influence, I never considered the other person's emotions in the whole situation. I now understand, in hindsight, how my actions made others feel.

I, too, was once besotted with a girl who I was head over heels for. We shared a night of drunken passion together on one occasion. She then dismissed me and avoided my calls. Her behaviour really hurt me, but this is karma in full effect. The pain I was experiencing was what I had subjected others to for my own personal gratification. It is actually a beauty to witness how events unfold in hindsight in order to enlighten you. Through these experiences, you can gain compassion for the people that you abused previously. When you have experienced the emotions that you subjected others to, first-hand, then you can experience compassion. Compassion can ultimately lead to love, which is what we are all here to do.

The term *soul mates* has also been hijacked by the westernised world. When we hear the term soul mate, we automatically think of romantic films, perfect partners that live happily ever after in eternal bliss. I am not saying this cannot be the case, but the term soul mate simply implies someone who can help you learn and grow on a soul level. This can range from a lover to an enemy or simply a stranger.

Think of someone who really presses your buttons, we all have one! Someone who really ticks you off. Got them in mind? Well, this is a soul mate: someone who triggers emotions in you that you didn't know existed. If they are a lover, it could range from venomous arguments to wild, passionate sex. If they are an enemy in this lifetime, you could hate them like no other and even want them dead! Soul mates could even be siblings or parents with roles reversed in this lifetime. The possibilities are endless! All in all, they are there to help you learn and overcome those animalistic emotions.

Soul mates have been with you for many lifetimes, in many different roles. Only through hindsight may you realise who a true soulmate was now that they have gone. When the lesson is done, the person often leaves abruptly. Cast your mind back and think of any extreme relationships that you may have had with another? What did you learn from the whole experience of having that person in your life? Was it positive and did you grow from it or the opposite? Maybe you could learn the intended lesson from that individual now that you are viewing the person in a different light? The truth is that we are all soul mates, but some people hold a more poignant role than others.

So what happens if you fail to grasp your intended specific lesson in this lifetime? This brings us onto reincarnation. You may think we have one life and that's that. I did for most of my life, so I respect and empathise with your belief. However, how can we experience all of life's lessons in one brief sitting?

One life, live it. This is a common term fuelled by the media. Why do you think that term is pushed upon us in this meme obsessed world of ours? When I used to hear the term *one life, live it*, I would have visions of wild parties, jumping off boats into the water, bungeeing, flamboyant gatherings in nightclubs, cocaine buffets, you name it! This is how I used to live my life. Not balling it up in fancy night clubs and eating caviar, but taking my behaviour to the extreme, after all, each moment could be your last.

Drinking a bottle of vodka and having a couple of grams of cocaine in one night was no big deal to me as I could die at any moment. In my eyes, I was living it up. Now my idea of living it up is sitting on my own with some herbal tea reading a book, how times change! I feel that the term *one life, live it* was possibly coined by the omnipotent driving forces of this world. It was designed to make you part with all of your hard-earned money and feed into the capitalistic system as much as possible, because after all, life is short so spend! I am digressing and getting ahead of myself as I have a chapter dedicated to this later on in the book.

The fact is, we need multiple lifetimes to experience all of life's lessons. We also need different perspectives of the world to gain true wisdom. How can I view life the same as a woman, when fundamentally we are different from the get-go? I am aware that now even to label someone as male or female is negating to some extent. It is refreshing that the world is choosing to acknowledge how labels can define an individual. When we label people, it can be coupled with a generalisation or a stereotype. I am still guilty of this.

If I have a boy, then they must like football, blue things and have short hair. If I have a girl, they must like pink dresses, dolls and have long hair. These are some of the preconceived ideas that I grew up with as a child and were conditioned with. Why can't a boy play with dolls or wear a dress? Why can't girls like football? If these narrow-minded ways of thinking that I grew up with are finally abolished, our children can grow up accepting everyone as equals. After all, in the world of love, all is equal. On a side note, centuries ago men had long hair and wore tights, and this was considered the epitome of masculinity. What changed?

The soul has no gender, it is androgynous. The soul has no race, only for earthly incarnations does this take place, in the design of your spacesuit, and is appropriate for how you want to express yourself in that lifetime. For the sake of my example though, and from a biological point of view, I will use the terms male or female to demonstrate the differences and the challenges that we have to face just through our bodily functions and anatomy.

In each lifetime, we will choose a sex to suit the learning curve and experience for that earthly visit. I can remember thinking as a teenager how lucky I was that I was born a man and not a woman. I mean, we men have it easy, don't we? From a biological point of view, no menstrual cycle and we get the easy part of childbirth; we just put our seed there (which is the fun part) and away we go! That is just for this lifetime though, I have had multiple lifetimes as a woman, thousands in fact. My soul will have experienced the excruciating pain of labour which bonds mother and child. I just can't remember it during this lifetime!

If you were particularly prejudiced or racist in one lifetime, your soul may choose to incarnate into the race or culture to which you once held such blinkered, fearful and ignorant views towards. The physical shell of someone is ultimately an illusion swallowed up by our senses but can perpetuate so much fascism and divide from the ego. If you were to grow up being abused purely for the colour of the shell that you chose to show up in, how would you feel? How would that shape your life? Would that make you bitter and conform to the social stereotypes that you were subjected to? Only through experience would you actually know.

There are just so many different aspects of physical life to experience and it can't happen all at once. How can I have the same view of life as a starving child? That soul would learn far greater lessons in my opinion than my cushty little life in the western bubble. Earth is a spirit school; we are here to learn. You didn't study one subject at school, did you? So how can one sitting on this earthly realm quench your soul's thirst for knowledge?

Through each incarnation, our soul mates follow us and have many different roles. They may also be a part of our karmic baggage that we carry too. They may shed light on a lesson that we just kept missing or ignored. A prime example of this for me is Leanne. Leanne helped me to learn so much about myself and I hope that through my actions, she learned something about herself too. I truly believe Leanne and I are soul mates and we have been told this also on many occasions.

Leanne and I still speak to this day, we parted amicably after the initial drama settled. I recall that when I first met Leanne, she stirred such passion and infatuation within me, it was mesmerising. This is the power of two soul mates meeting for the first time on earth. Compare it to a complex chemical reaction happening in front of your very eyes. To view Leanne as just a lesson is quite unfair as we shared some perfect times together that are simply unforgettable. At the same time however, she definitely taught me things that I needed to realise in order to grow, particularly about how I had treated people in the past.

As our relationship progressed, Leanne did the things any twenty-one-year-old would and went out partying. I felt neglected and hurt because of her actions, but it's only what I did when I was her age. Now I deliberately didn't mention this lesson earlier in the book, but those of you astute enough to notice must have recognised a pattern?

My selfish ways which consisted of drinking and taking drugs were detrimental, not only to myself, but to those who loved me. The amount of times Dean and Lee had to look after me were uncountable; I was a burden. My nan also caught the brunt of my poor choices and constantly had to pick up the pieces. I broke her heart the day I walked through the door covered in cuts and blood with no recollection of how it had happened.

I vividly recall the night that Leanne strolled in with her top covered in blood. She had cut her lip after getting involved in a fight trying to protect someone. I loved her so much but was so scared of her getting hurt or something more severe; she was so vulnerable in those states but was oblivious to it all. To see her that way struck fear and terror into my heart. This must have been exactly how my nan felt about me when I was out until the early hours with not a care in the world. I now understand the results of my actions as I have experienced them first-hand.

I had to experience the pain and worry of what Leanne did for myself in order to know what I had put others through. When I realised that lesson in hindsight, it was truly nauseating. The penny dropped and it all made sense. I was appalled that I had been so selfish. My nan, my friends, Stacey, Sophie, Laura, all of these people had been affected by my selfish ways.

Leanne had had a tough life, coming from a broken home; she drank to blot out the cold reality of life, does that sound familiar as well? I must make you aware that Leanne no longer drinks and has been consulted in the writing of this book! Leanne is now a mum, and after the birth of her beautiful child, Laurence, it paved the way for her own awakening as to who she is. Leanne now views life totally differently to how she did before. Her mind is open to all possibilities; see awakenings can happen in many different ways, not just through death. Just for the record, Leanne was not a screaming, brawling alcoholic, she was just like me, trying to find her way in the world. Leanne is now happy and content with life, after learning from her own unique experiences.

Do you recall Becky from the earlier chapters as well? She came into my life for a fleeting moment with such intensity to stir up a whirlwind of emotions within me. I craved to be with her every moment. She was a soul mate. She entered my life for only a few months and was then gone. She left me with the parting message that I was emotionally unstable. At the time, I thought that she was spiteful, but she was only saying the truth. Becky came to show me the way and highlight that my life and emotions really were out of control. She was right with what she said; the beauty of it all.

Dharma can link with karma and rhymes nicely! By writing this book, I am expressing my dharma. Dharma is living the life that you intended for yourself before you arrived here. Karma and dharma can affect how you live this lifetime, regardless of how you are raised. There are just some experiences that you came to have. I feel that for this lifetime I came here to discover the truth and help people discover what is true for them as well. We all have our own, beautiful uniqueness. What is your dharma? What have you come here to do? Work a 9-5? Or is it to help? Is it to heal an old wound? Is it to learn? Maybe you too have just arrived to teach others about themselves? Whatever it is, know that it is perfect.

All that is written in this book is my relative truth and the way the Universe operates for me, but by no means should it be gospel for you. You should follow your own truth as there are infinite paths. Nevertheless, there are interesting concepts in this book, if I say so myself. Hmmm, that previous comment was incredibly cocksure, wasn't it? Claiming that I have interesting concepts makes me sound like I have such a high opinion of myself, doesn't it!? You may be far from impressed with the book up until this point. However, I am going to think that this book is awesome, as I'm writing it! This whole line of thought is just an example of my own illusionary mind though. This self-righteous thinking dwells firmly in the ego plane. This leads us nicely onto our next little chapter, the Ego...

31

THE EGO

Here it is: the ego. I have been flirting with this topic throughout the book and here it is! I'm genuinely excited, is that sad? I don't really care because it is only the ego that cares what others think, for it is separate to everyone else! You will find out why you operate like you do throughout the following chapters.

Before all this crazy spiritual stuff happened to me, I used to hear the word ego or egotistical and think of vanity or narcissism. In fact, I didn't realise the complexity of the ego and it's what makes us tick as animals. It is far more than taking a selfie or flexing in the gym mirror.

The ego is software that is installed into our spacesuit that we possess for this lifetime. It is there to help us interact with the physical world. The ego allows us to build a mental construct about us and the world of separation that we find ourselves in. The ego helps us to cope with the pain of being separated from our natural loving source. The ego is ultimately there as a survival tool, which can lead us to many mischievous things.

We all have two voices in us, don't we? Or is that just me!? Hear me out; we have a voice that is impulsive and drives us forward in the spur of the moment. We also have a quieter voice deep down that tells us the right thing to do. I feel this voice emanate from my chest, from my heart if you will. The old analogy of the devil and the angel sitting on our shoulder is also a fair representation of these two voices.

The righteous, inner voice that shines from our chest can be known as a conscience, but I prefer the term higher self. It tells us what to do in all situations and can offer us the best possible outcome for each situation that we encounter. We each have the power to make our own choices and can choose to ignore that do-gooding voice if we please! After all, a gift that every human possesses, is free will.

Sometimes in spontaneous situations, we need to act fast and may need to make a quick decision. In the event of this, we often choose to use our logical, egoic brains which are based on self-preservation. Doing this may offer a temporary solution to the problem, but may not always produce the best-case scenario for us. This is the voice of the ego.

In caveman times, the ego served the human race as an exceptional tool of survival and navigation. Imagine yourself walking along and encountering a rival huntsman or animal in the wild who is fearful and hostile. They are full of animosity, threatening your very existence and want what you have. You're going to have to make a life-altering decision on the spot there and then, what are you going to do?

The decision that you make will undoubtedly be based on your own survival and that of your tribe. Or you could pause, listen to your heart and attempt to understand as to why this fellow human is behaving the way they are? He or she is operating out of fear, much like you are due to the fact that they feel threatened. This volatile foe could snap at any second, out of sheer anxiety, and threaten your existence at any moment. What do you do?

Chances are you are going to use your quick-witted, logical survival instincts that are installed into your DNA. Your animal instinct will govern your choice and will subconsciously cause your brain to react by triggering messages of fight or flight to the body. Adrenaline will begin to pump out of survival, thus clouding any loving reaction that is inside of your true self. You can either run or deliver the first blow to your enemy/threat. The sense of animosity and uncertainty that consumes the immediate moment is overwhelming, thus prompting you to make the first move.

The option of love and understanding in caveman days was not prevalent because of the fear that permeated the three-dimensional air.

It was literally a case of survival of the fittest. This is an example of how the ego is embedded in our DNA from the beginning of time; simply a tool of survival that helps us identify with society. So you could say that the ego has literally been a lifesaver, and still is to this day. But does it still have such an important role to play in our lives now? After all, the western part of the world has evolved away from those primitive times that man once experienced.

How does the ego fit in to today's society if it is no longer needed as a survival tool? The ego gives us identity. It tells us who we are in society and what we stand for. It holds, protects and clings to the mental constructs that we have built in order to protect ourselves. If we were to engage in an argument with someone in this day and age, what do we choose to do now? What happens when we choose to listen to that prehistoric voice that rumbles on deep within us? The one that says *I feel threatened*. When we do this, we verbally or physically attack the fellow human that we are arguing with who is challenging our beliefs. We will defend the reality that we have created in our heads by any means necessary, because these mental constructs have helped us to advance through life.

People often choose to listen to the mind that resides in the ego plane of consciousness, and this can be frequently seen in our society. How often do we witness individuals trying to convert another's point of view because the ego is feeling threatened? If someone challenges what we stand for, our integrity is lost, is it not? From the perspective of the ego, this is indeed true; therefore, the ego must defend its stance by manipulating and converting the thinking of others so it feels safe and in control.

The egoic thinking of any person is to make another believe that their viewpoint holds more validity than any other theory. The ego's point of view is superior to anyone else's. Politicians are a prime example of this. Politicians will appear on TV, in public or attend council meetings publicising the same agenda; they know what is best for everyone.

Politicians who bicker in cabinet about how the world should be run, are participating in egoic futility. They try to alter another's thinking with their *superior* perspective. They are adamant that their opinions are more validated, in some illusory way, and that they have all the answers. Neither side in politics will ever back down as they are choosing to use their logical, egoic minds rather than open up their hearts and become tolerant to the other person's view. In a sense, they are still using the mind that helped to shape the world so many years ago; the one of fear and safety.

Now I haven't written a book to slate politicians, for they are just different versions of me, but politics is a prime example of the ego at work. I'm sure there are countless politicians who genuinely want to make a difference in the world, and their ideologies come from the heart. But imagine if everyone worked together and cast aside their dogmatic views? Imagine what state the world would be in if the most harmonious concepts were thrown together in one big pot.

The governing bodies that are heavily in the limelight everyday would be leading by example. They could show the world that tolerance and acceptance can work when applied in a constructive manner. Instead, they choose to squabble like children in a playground which is then broadcast all around the globe. Leaders of many countries today still operate from a position of fear and portray the message that is "us against them".

Some have described the ego as the devil but I feel that's a harsh term to give to something that has helped us to survive and advance through time. The ego has helped to shape and evolve the current day that we are blessed to live in. If you believe in the theory of evolution, you will see how animalistic traits run through all of us. When you study the behaviour of animals, you can learn a lot from them.

I love to observe Bella when I walk her, she offers so many clues as to where I have come from and what is in my DNA. She is territorial; she likes exploring and if she comes across another animal's scent, she has to *mark* it with her own scent. She doesn't think about this consciously, it's just something she has been programmed with. She will scratch and dig at the floor as if to say, "I have been here." Again, she does this without thought, an instinct that she has built in her. This is her way of saying this territory is mine now.

Politicians often like to draw a line in the sand to keep other nationalities out and to distinguish where *their* land begins and others end. Does this behaviour not sound like that of Bella's? This is a great facade though and to think as any other nationality as different from yourself is all illusion. Sure, there are different customs and traditions, but that is just relative to those people; they are not an alien species that need segregating because they breathe different air.

I live in England, but what makes it England? The fact that we have a red and white flag? The fact that we have a queen? The fact that we like fish and chips? The fact that it is always raining? What is it that actually characterises who we are as a distinct, separate race? You could say that imaginary customs were started by a group of people in history gaining vast momentum which eventually defined the land. The identity of a country is then born because no one ever challenged them!

The fact is though, that nothing defines a country apart from the ego. The ego loves to compartmentalise things and give them identities so it knows where it stands. It does this out of fear because it sees itself as a separate entity.

England is derived from the old English name Englaland which means "land of the Angles." The Angles were one of the Germanic tribes that settled in Great Britain during the middle ages. This name was then used to identify the piece of land where the tribe resided and labelled it. People then accepted that part of the soil in the world to be known as the label of England. Upon that label, a set of values, customs and traditions were built that defined individuals who settled in that part of the world. That collective set of values were then adhered to by all who inhabited the land. A national egoic identity was then formed on a collective basis.

With that, the rest of the world would then hear about certain parts of the globe from travellers and how others lived. "England did this and

England did that" would then define what *England* was! Each label that was given to each country then defined the inhabitants of that piece of land. Fear, which is created by the ego, thrives on these labels that define others, for it then knows what to expect in its imaginary reality. Other *nations* are then seen as different and even a threat by these labels of separation. Fear is what creates segregation and division amongst the world.

Fundamentally, England is no different to Brazil, Italy or France, for it is all part of the same planet that is created with the same molecular structure. The ego has carved and divided things into separate sources because it buys the illusion of separateness that is dictated by the five senses. *My* country is a statement of the ego, for nothing physical is ever really ours. We don't hold ownership over anything physical simply because it is part of a finite reality that will forever be temporary. Nothing belongs to us, only the ego. "I was born in England," many will say, "therefore I am English." Can you now see how illusory this statement is? Only an imaginary set of customs and beliefs over the years has shaped this part of the world and led us to the point where we have chosen to label it England.

England shares a border with Wales and Scotland, but where does that border start? Who decided that imaginary line? "Right, England starts here and Scotland starts here. When you step over this line you are now in Scotland. You will know this because we have put a flag and signpost to let you know!" Are you now seeing how powerful the ego can be? Creating superficial realities! Don't get me wrong, labelling parts of the world is useful for when you are planning a trip, but do not see those labelled countries as separate parts of a different globe, we are all one.

There is no need to think that Italian's differ from American's or Argentinian's. It is only imaginary customs, traditions and stereotypes that have been passed down through generations that has given a country its reputation and label. We were each born on a particular part of the globe with individual space suits that best express who we are for this lifetime.

The ego likes possessions and separation, so land is a major contributory factor to wars and disputes in the world. The sad thing is, it isn't even real. Speaking of war, when two sides go head-to-head against one another and fight to the death, who are the *goodies* and who are the *baddies*? Well, if *my* country is going to war then we must be the goodies, the liberators, the ones of truth! By granting ourselves this illusory title of the *goodies,* we can justify ending the tyranny inflicted by others, even if that means taking life too; we do it for a righteous cause. If this is the case, then what do the opposing country label themselves as? Do they think, "Right, the good guys are coming to get us, we must be the bad guys and deserve to be punished, let's fight to protect our bad status." Or do they think, "Right, these evil bastards are coming to take what is ours and interfere with our country, let's send this scum packing."

By viewing the whole scenario of war from a neutral perspective, the whole concept of battle as to who is good and bad is purely subjective and futile. For one set of people to think that they are different from another group because of their moral objective is insanity. The ego is justifying its need to go and kill enemies by giving itself a superior title to those who it is at war with, thus perpetuating the problem that they are seeking to avoid in the first place; the irony. When two opposing forces clash, there is only one outcome: more turmoil, despite whatever label has been given to either side by their righteous people. When you fight what you are against, you only create more of the same.

As stated earlier, the ego has evolved throughout the history of this planet and can be linked to animalistic behaviour. When Bella feels threatened by a dog that she sees to be on *her* turf, she will sometimes become hostile towards it. Why is this? Because the opposing dog had posed a threat to Bella's immediate land and her survival that she had just *marked*. Bella is programmed to defend what's hers, it's in her DNA. But it isn't really hers, she is just following the survival instincts that she has been programmed with.

Now Bella doesn't always go for every dog she meets, in fact she is very placid and loving, but she does go for the occasional dog. Why is this?

When Bella was a puppy, on more than one occasion she was bitten by a dog when out walking in the park. Bella has never forgotten this and uses it as a survival tool to seek out immediate threats on her journey. Whenever Bella meets a dog that is the same breed as the ones who bit her all those years ago, her brain associates that breed with danger. Survival kicks in and Bella becomes hostile. Once bitten, twice shy!

Can you see how animalistic behaviour has helped us as a species to evolve over the years? The ego will seek out threats in order to survive. Bella has to be the dominant one in a confrontation when she feels threatened and will never back down. Isn't this behaviour mimicked by some humans in today's society?

I touched on this earlier, how wars can stem from imaginary arguments surrounding land and who it actually belongs to. Although, you could say that half the wars in the world stem from the political choices that are made by figures of authority, but that is another book entirely! When you take into account that animalistic tendencies are still embedded deep within our psyches or DNA, maybe you can begin to understand why wars occur.

How do most wars start? A division of opinion between two groups of people. One group of individuals may choose to believe one theory, whereas another group may choose to believe the opposite. After all, everything in life always has an opposite, this is the beautiful dichotomy that we live in. Who is actually right or wrong? This is a concept that I will address many times in this book.

What happens when the two differences of opinion meet? Neither side is willing to back down due to their blinkered, narrow-minded ways that are run by the ego. These conflicts can stem from religious affairs, money or generally over territory and who is considered to be the rightful owner of it. With no side willing to back down, the inevitable ensues, a futile war.

The two groups of humans, ruled by different dogmatic perspectives, then collide with one another and proceed to attack or kill as many as possible. When one group finally backs down and admits defeat, the war is over. After all the bloodshed which has stemmed from the ego has finished, the side that has lost will begrudgingly admit, "Okay, we surrender, you're right." This is all the ego wanted in the first place. It wanted to be acknowledged for holding the domineering and conquering solution to everything. And yes, that land is now ours and we can now rightfully claim it by drawing an invisible line that will create a border.

To be right for that brief moment in time is the crowning glory for the ego, but rest assured, it's appetite will not be satisfied, much like that of a wild animal. Bella will devour everything when on a walk and at home, for she is a big dog, and she is never sure when and how her next meal will arrive. This is similar to the ego, and the ego will soon become hungry again and demand more stimulation.

I compare the ego to the behaviour of Bella because I see that she behaves the same way when she is on a walk. If she is threatened by another who is a similar size, she refuses to back down. She must win, because this is what her survival instincts govern her to do! You see, the animal runs deep within all of us and can still show its teeth if we feel threatened by an immediate threat. This survival trait has evolved over time and been ingrained into our DNA to protect our species. Territory and the insatiable need to dominate others are all the natural mechanics of our ancestral minds.

32

THE EGO AND OTHERS

We live in a blame game culture, fuelled by the media. Finger-pointing makes us feel better about ourselves and superior to that of the perpetrator. Front page articles on papers usually berate the behaviour of others. They portray the alleged individual as a failure for making a mistake. Instead of offering help, the writer of the news article generally condemns the person or event. The media uses such language about the alleged atrocity to suggest that they themselves have never made a mistake. Nine times out of ten, the headline is usually judging the behaviour of another. The supposed victim or situation in question has not complied with the opinion of the writer's ego. The writer's wording suggests that they have all the answers to all the world's problems. This is the ego at work.

At first glance of a negative headline, the words used are usually suggestive and misleading. What does this prompt us to think about the person or persons involved? Usually the reader immediately thinks, *I would never behave that way!* I have been guilty of this, and still am sometimes. When we judge, we project a vision that we are better than someone which makes us separate from everything and everyone. However, this way of egoic thinking is taking events on face value and not seeing the bigger picture.

As the reader, I can make an assumption on something that I haven't actually got a clue about and deem my thoughts to be that of actual reality. This is my egoic mind taking charge and leading the way. When we do this, the reader of the headline has already fallen into the writer's trap. The reader and writer are in unison with their way of thinking without actually knowing all of the facts. A whole auspicious picture has been created based purely on assumption, which the ego thrives on. I urge you to read a poem called *The Cookie Thief by Valarie Cox* which perfectly depicts the difference between what you believe you know and what you actually know. Unless you have made conscious contact first-hand with something, then you will never actually know the truth. Anything else is purely an assumption created by the egoic mind which keeps us separated from others.

Next time you read a negative headline, observe how your mind will make a knee-jerk reaction to quickly formulate an opinion of the situation. By recognising these spontaneous thoughts that occur, you are the witness to the workings of your thoughts. Believe it or not, your thoughts are not always who you truly are. They are concepts that have been allowed to drift into your subconscious mind over the years, which are not necessarily true.

Let's condemn the human on the front page that made the alleged mistake! I have never been so appalled! With this mode of thinking activated, the ego can have a brief moment of pretentious superiority and is separate from all beneath it. You can now see how a few well-chosen words on a front page can convey egoic morality which can sway millions and exploit the workings of the animalistic mind; clever really!

There are always two sides to every story, despite what the media or people tell us. Regardless of what is the truth, the ego will demand justice based on what it believes. It will want to see punishment and retribution for all involved. It does all of this while being oblivious to the fact there are spiritual laws in place that do not fail. Man's moral law, however, is full of loopholes and contradictions, it can never know the truth. It is based on judgement that can become distorted and skewed. I have already provided you with examples of how the ego can work but let's delve deeper into the powerful force of the ego and what it does.

One of the first primary characteristics of the ego is that it must be right! To admit that you are wrong is simply a sign of weakness and you will experience a great delusional loss if you do this. The delusional loss will come at the price of what others think who are separate from you.

Another main characteristic of the ego is that it will never be satisfied. When you truly learn this, your life can change for the better. You will no longer become attached to chasing materialistic desires in the pursuit of happiness, for you know that the ego's hunger can never be fulfilled. In the eyes of the ego, power, money, jobs, sex, clothes, parties, houses, cars, food, are all there to be chased. There is always room for more in the world of the ego.

I can recall that buzz I used to get as a youth when I was buying new clothes or new possessions, it was a great feeling, but it would quickly fade. So, what did I do? Buy more new things to chase the high! The same would happen when I drank alcohol or took drugs. "I'll just go for one beer," or "one more line won't hurt." That one beer turned into ten as I felt a compelling urge to just keep drinking until I couldn't walk. The ego told me it was good to drink more as it was blotting out my painful and meagre existence.

Cocaine gave me that initial buzz but then more was needed to chase the short-lived euphoria and replicate it. The ego says, "Let's do more." He is an oppressive little fellow if you allow him to be! I fell into the trap of placing stipulations to my happiness. I used to think, *if this happens, I'll be happy*, or *if I have that, I'll be happy*. While all of this was happening, I was missing the beauty of what could have been obtained in the current moment.

I went from woman to woman, thinking the same thoughts when I would first get with them. I would allow myself to be overcome with infatuation and consider my new partner to be perfect (which of course we all are but not in an egoic sense). I would treat my new ladies like a trophy and loved the feelings that arose through having sex with someone new. I needed that special someone in order to have love in my life and feel fulfilled. Why couldn't that love be there without the need of an eternal body?

After a few months or years, the once perfect companion that I had sought after for so long was no longer perfect in my mind and I was quick to find faults with them. Where had that love gone? I would then feel the urge to move on to someone new. Someone with more potential to unlock that magic feeling of happiness within me. The ego would convince me that I needed a new partner every few years and that I could always do better; where would it draw the line? *If my partner had this,* or *if my partner was that I would be happier,* were the constant thoughts that went through my head. Can you see how quick the ego is to torment you if you allow it?

I can vividly recall one time lying in the bath at my old flat with a new partner, looking at her thinking to myself, *she is absolutely beautiful, she's perfect.* The ironic thing is that, just a few years later, I was lying in the very same bath with yet another woman, thinking the exact same thing as I had just a couple years before. Where would the cycle end for my insatiable lust for women?

One night stands never quenched my thirst because I had to be attached to the woman in question to unlock my happiness. Can you understand this now that you have read about my past? I got into the relationships that I so desperately craved but was quick to subconsciously sabotage them in one way or another in order to find something better. Plus, my egoic pain body, that was so familiar with turmoil from my childhood, secretly enjoyed all the drama, a sick stimulant if you like.

When you realise that the ego cannot be satisfied, you can look at life differently. I can now accept and be grateful for the many things that I have in my life. I don't actually need anything external to predetermine my levels of happiness, but I just couldn't see this way back then.

The ego will also berate you and make you feel that you are never good enough. I have that little voice in me that I hear whenever I mess up, "Stupid Dave", I say to myself when I burn something or drop something. Who is that little voice that is quick to rebuke us? The fact is, we all make mistakes, it's how we learn. Even a mistake produces a result, so is it really a mistake? You can simply learn and create a different result the next time you revisit the activity. However, the ego will have you believe that you are pathetic and that nobody else ever makes mistakes! The ego will then become fearful of making another mistake in case of ridicule from others.

All those years ago, I allowed my ego to continually oppress me and as a result of this, I believed that I wasn't good enough. I would constantly tell myself that it was all my fault that my mother left me and that I deserved it. The truth was that I was perfect, and so was my mother. At that time in her life, she was a very confused and a mentally ill woman due to her own complex past. You see, we are all just victims of behaviour that can be replicated in a karmic way if we do not consciously observe matters. The brain is a complex thing and if we do not allow ourselves to process events correctly, it can cause our mental health to suffer down the line.

Problems with our mental health begin to occur when the subconscious mind plays out old traumas at a later date. The conscious mind will not comprehend why the subconscious mind is playing out these old events and the two minds will literally do battle with one another. Until we learn how to reprogram the subconscious mind, it will always run the show; much to the dismay of the conscious mind. I will have a chapter later on explaining how to reprogram the subconscious mind.

I am in no position to judge my mother for her actions all those years ago, as she was only doing what she thought was best at that time in her life. She was simply doing what her mind was allowing her to do. If I allowed my superficial self to have a say in the matter, which I have done in the past, what do you think it would say? *How dare she leave me, how could she, I would never do that!?* This is the same part of the ego that, whenever a labelled *atrocity* happens in the world, we are so quick to judge. "I would never have done that, therefore I am a better person!" This stems back to my example of the front-page articles earlier in the chapter. The same way of thinking could be applied for my mother's actions and her abandoning me, without seeing the full picture.

The ego has to defend its actions. Notice the next time someone accuses you of doing something, even if it isn't true, what do you do? If you choose to defend yourself, you have allowed the ego to enter and run the show and know that it is working well; after all it is a survival tool. If, however, you choose simply to acknowledge the person instead of defending yourself, you are consciously acting. You know the real truth deep down, so therefore it is irrelevant what others think of you. I am not saying allow people to walk all over you, but when a false accusation is thrown around and you know the truth, does it matter what others think? This is where the ego falters majorly, it cares what others think! A lot...

There have been multiple times when I have chosen to defend my reality in this book and as you can see, the ego is still alive and well within myself!

The ego will identify who you are, by what possessions you have accumulated. By doing this, others will hopefully hold a high opinion of me. Whenever I got a new job or acquired a new possession within an organisation, I would brag and boast to my peers and colleagues in order to gain recognition. The ego needs constant reassurance and stimulation from others.

I would be so eager to show off my accomplishments to others, as it defined who I was and that I was successful. The reality of it all was that it just masked my true beauty that was deep within and that can never be purchased or measured.

I would often dress things up to be better than they were, in fact this is something that I still do which I am trying to reign in! Due to this structured, westernised culture that we find ourselves in, this is how success is merited in the real world. It is gauged by possessions, numbers and through grades on a piece of paper. On a side note, who knows what I could have achieved in my school years if I had tried harder with my studies instead of trying to impress everyone! Lord knows I would have done better in my exams as well if I hadn't had been stoned all the while!

Do you care what others think of you? Are they right? It defines who you are doesn't it, what people think of you? Your reputation through word of mouth is so important, but how can you please everyone? I began smoking at school just to fit in with my peers. Smoking was my way of trying to gain acceptance from my peers. Further rejection in my life from others could risk triggering painful feelings of being unworthy again. My ego came up with a coping strategy in order to avoid that pain again.

I would strive for the affirmation of others; through my actions and behaviour. If they approved of my actions, I was happy. I had little thought about the consequences, for in that moment all that mattered was approval. Remember my story of how I would steal earlier in the book? I did this solely to impress my peers and in the hope that I portrayed the image of a *bad man*. The same came from any female I encountered. I would try to impress them with my best lines, deliver them with extra vigour and watch in anticipation for the desired effect. In my mind, my flirty ways gave me extra credibility and acceptance from females, who I would latch on to at the drop of a hat.

Another trait of the ego is making us believe that we are separate from one another. "I am an individual, it's me against the world." Have you ever thought like this or do you see us all as one? What will you allow your mind to believe? In the society that we live in, we attend school and are all raised as individuals with different levels of knowledge and skills.

At school we are graded and put in classes according to the level of our intellect. I remember how this felt and I would feel the need to progress and out-do others in order to be viewed as worthy. In the eyes of the ego, intellect is power and puts you above others. The reality is that intellect is a prison.

If someone knew more than me or was seen to be doing better than I was, then my ego would be bruised and hurt. The ego will often look for ways to even out the playing field in order to gain the upper hand when it is threatened. This is the world we have been born and nurtured into. The westernised society exploits the natural workings of the ego. It is a system that does work, but I want people to be aware of the complex social construct that we all participate in. I will address this topic in a more comprehensive manner in a later chapter.

In order to feel fulfilled and successful in life, we must be seen to be accomplishing more than our peers or at least keeping up with them. This is how we have enabled our happiness levels to be affected by others, through social conditioning.

The following example is something that I have been guilty of and it demonstrates beautifully how the programmed egoic mind works. You know that conversation that we all have when we bump into an old acquaintance who we haven't seen for a while? You know, the awkward ones that we all have! "How are you doing mate? What are you up to now?"

Now, I don't know about you, but in the past and still currently, I have always felt compelled to immediately start listing all of my current successes. Is this just me? Read on and see what you think?

In these conversations, I would also state a list of imaginary things that I intended to do in the near future (but never actually would). I would also feel the need to paint a picture that my current job was far more glamorous than it actually was. I would do this in order to make myself sound like I was a success and that I wasn't a complete and total loser (by our ego's definition of course). Can you relate to this example? I'll be honest, I still do it now from time to time!

Now, imagine if I were to approach those conversations that I had with old friends from the perspective of my own personal spiritual growth and not that of my ego.

"Yeah I'm doing amazing thanks mate, I feel that recently I have really started to judge people less and that I am starting to develop unconditional love for everyone."

They would look at me as though I'd gone barmy, wouldn't they? That is not how success is measured in this part of the world! Instead, society has conditioned us to believe that we need to talk about all the holidays that we have been on, or the new car that we have just bought - now that would impress!

One final thing that the ego absolutely loves when others are concerned are illusory titles of grandeur. "I'm head of a global company, we deal with millions of pounds each day." This statement commands that of power and respect from subordinates and people looking in from the outside. Status is so important to the ego, for status is like a badge of honour and defines who wears it. Being a leader or part of an institution that has *recognised* success is quite symbolic to the individuals involved. They are symbols of societal success and have made it. When someone obtains a recognised position, they can say with belief, "I am a somebody!"

Will participants of a successful company ever reach that blissful feeling of contentment though? Will they ever tick that magic box one day where the answers to life appear to them in a single moment? Or will they do what the ego loves and knows, which is to chase the adrenaline of big deals and making more money? He's a hungry little fellow isn't he!?

33

YOUR BODY IS NOT WHO YOU THINK YOU ARE

Judging is a huge part of the ego; I still do it to this day. Judgement of myself and judgment towards others. Each morning, I set myself the task to try and not be so judgmental towards my fellow brothers and sisters and to myself. I just try to notice things without having an opinion on them. It is hard, but you can train the mind like you would a muscle; the more you do it, it expands.

When I do judge, I then counter that knee-jerk reaction by asking myself, "What has that person been through?" or "who am I to judge them?" They may have reasons for the way they behave. Their appearance is just a way of expressing themselves and I remind myself, I am no better than them and they are free to look or act as they please. I am not perfect, and I try to write this entire book as free of ego as possible, but it is so difficult!

Why do we judge though? It stems back to our survival mechanism as an animal. If we make a judgement about something, we label it and put it in a box, the ego loves this. By labelling something or someone, our minds give the object or person a certain level of attributes and characteristics that will define their behaviour. By doing this, we will then know what to expect from that immediate threat which will inevitably enable our own personal survival. It relates back to fear and a feeling of being superior. When this type of fearful analysis is allowed to happen in our minds, we create separation from those who we are judging. We are no longer *one*.

Maybe this is why we don't like certain people. We label them and believe that our label defines them. We don't like them because they should be more like we are. If they were to conform to how we thought they should behave, then we would like them more, simple! This all stems back to judging.

The ego will acknowledge the superficial appearance of others and view that as who we actually are. In fact, who we look at in the mirror every day can appear so real, but it isn't. How can it, for it is constantly changing, isn't it just an illusion? Everything in this finite world is temporary.

According to science, we get a new body every two years. "How is this possible?" you may think, "I am still here; my body has gone nowhere." Our body is composed of atoms of hydrogen, carbon, nitrogen and oxygen. The atoms and molecules in our body are constantly changing and are constantly replacing each other, therefore we get a brand-new body each year! Each current moment our body is built and restructured purely by how we think and feel.

Quantum Healing written by *Deepak Chopra* explains all this in far more detail than I ever could. The example Deepak uses to demonstrate the concept of a regenerating body is to imagine the house that you live in being rebuilt brick by brick each year, but staying exactly the same. It doesn't actually move but is a new-build. Deepak's book is a fascinating read if you are interested and would like to learn more on this topic.

All that dust that accumulates in your house and drives you mad is just your old skin consisting of fine particles that have left your body. 80% of dust is in fact your old skin and that is why it gets everywhere! Did you know that we get a new stomach lining every 72 hours? That is phenomenal! Our body is constantly repairing itself!

With these two little facts in mind, can you see how your body is not solid matter, so therefore is it who you truly are? When Dean's lifeless body was lying on the hospital bed, was that really him? His body would soon begin to decompose, just another example of how matter is constantly changing. Is it possible that he could have just inhibited that body for a short while in order to use it as a vehicle? Dean used that vehicle as a way to express his true self and interact with the physical world around him in a positive way.

Can you recall your baby body or your toddler body? If yes, did they seem real at the time? They have now gone though and are never coming back. Do you recall your teenage body? Did that feel real? All those internal hormones raging and those visible changes rapidly happening? That has now gone and will never return.

The body that you had when you began reading this book has now also gone! Its molecular structure had been replaced, although it still feels so real. Considering that our bodies are constantly changing, and we only occupy them for a small amount of time, surely, they can't be the real us? With the acceptance that what we see in the mirror is not really who we are, you can really start to believe that the soul or energy inside of you is the real you. The ego will not compute with this however as it is part of your perishable body. It will attempt to convince you that you have gone mad and that your body is you because you are currently occupying and manning your earthly meat suit!

Armed with this knowledge that appearance is all illusion, you can tame your ego and listen to your true, loving inner voice or higher self. You can begin to live spiritually on Earth and begin to make decisions in line with your true loving source. I will talk more about how you can do that later on in the book. Just acknowledging what our bodies truly are for the time being can tame our egos.

Start to believe that who you see in the mirror is just 1% of who you truly are. You are an eternal soul with a very short existence on earth. You are visiting Earth to learn, grow, burn off karma and help to shape the planet; not much to do really!? You will one day return to the source which you can call home.

If this is all too much for you and just comes across as nonsense, you are right to feel like this. Just try to pick out the main bits of the message that I am offering from it all, which is to act from the heart and not the ego! Love yourself, allow yourself to be loved and have love for others; all of which the ego can sometimes deny! It doesn't mean that you have to interact with some far-fetched intergalactic beliefs!

34

Possessions and Pack Mentality

The ego can only relate to *I*, *me* and *mine*. What I have or own is who I am. I have a car, a house, a large salary. All of these acquisitions are separate from others and provide you with an identity. If these acquisitions were to be taken away from you, who would you be? This is what your reputation has been built on in the eyes of societal success. Would a businesswoman who owned a company still be a success if her company folded? Social conditioning would suggest that she was now a failure.

When I watched Deano pass that day, he left all of *his* material possessions here, behind him. They were now rendered useless to some degree as *he* could no longer use them. If you were to pass today, what would happen to all of those material possessions that you had worked so hard to acquire in this life? They would appear quite futile in hindsight, wouldn't they?

The day I moved out of my house that I had previously had with Leanne, I lost a lot of the household possessions. I split the possessions with Leanne, and I felt like all my work over the years had vanished; I now had nothing to show for all my hard work! I allowed my material possessions to gauge who I was and the level of success that I had reached. It all went in an instant and I can't lie, I felt like a failure.

I am not suggesting that we give up our jobs and go live in the woods, but how much attachment do you have to what you have acquired? If you measure your success in life based on the sole perspective of what you have is what you are, something along the line has become distorted.

You are missing your true purpose. Surely Dean's story demonstrates that we are here to learn and grow from the situations that we experience, not from what we have purchased. All that we can take with us are the lessons that we have learned and apply these to our spiritual resume.

We cannot take our physical body with us when we depart either! Does that sometimes define who we are as well? If I asked random strangers, who is Arnold Schwarzenegger? What answers would I receive? Probably ones about his career and his bodybuilding back in the day. Everyone remembers his muscles! These are probably the forefront of what defines who he is at face value, but that isn't really who he is, is it?

Our ego will have us believe that we are our body and that is what defines us. The amount of time we spend grooming and modifying our bodies to show them off to others appears futile in the reality of death. All that our soul can take with it, is the wisdom it has experienced and thus transcends in its return to the spirit world.

I use the word *taming* when talking about the ego in this chapter and the next carefully. Animalistic evolution exists in all of us. It is embedded into our DNA; it is where we have come from. In mans' early years on this planet, it really was a case of survival of the fittest. If man were not *fit* enough for whatever challenges he faced, death would prevail. Armed with only the five senses, mans' reality was truly finite, and survival was everything. Survival is still our sole goal in the present day, but those primitive times of constant threats from living the wild days have now passed in the westernised culture that we live in.

Mans' evolutionary progress has led us to the present day and created the system that we now live in. In the western world we have food, water and shelter readily available for those who play their part in the system. Some can even choose not to work and are supported by the government. This reality poses little threat to the existence of man now as there are systems in place to meet our basic needs. In this part of the world, bears are no longer roaming the roads that we choose to walk. The threat of being eaten has been contained because of mans' evolving ways. Taking all of these factors into account, we now have an opportunity to acknowledge the ego, but not be ruled by it.

In today's society, a primitive mentality still exists due to the ego. Individuals who join gangs are still searching for validity, respect and solidarity, which are all governed by their egoic, competitive nature. They are victims to their ego and past events from their life. This may seem that I am judging these groups of people, far from it. I do not condemn them but, instead, try to understand them. What has happened in that person's life which has caused them to feel that gang life is the only option?

Individuals who seek recognition from peers remind me of myself as I grew up striving for the very same thing. I was a hurt little boy, eager to cover up what I thought were flaws and weaknesses, so I chose the preconceived egoic notion of what masculinity was in order to camouflage my scars. I was attempting to appear like an alpha male to others so that I wouldn't be messed with. My ego told me that this was the right way to behave in order to get respect from others, but in truth it was out of fear. Being my true self, which was a loving caring person, would be viewed as a weakness. Gang mentality is ego-driven and appearing *soft* in a gang situation will get you eaten alive; much like our caveman times!

I always loved that feeling of acceptance and belonging when hanging out with friends and groups. At school, our gang was called the Addiction Crew. We felt superior to everyone else, as we had our own ethos and, in our eyes, were *cooler* than others. Of course, looking back on this is hilarious to say the least, as all we did was get drunk, smoke weed and get into scuffles. We thought that we were truly gangsters, in our little privileged suburban lifestyle, it makes me smile!

When I would go to the football, I felt a real sense of identity also. I was trying to establish who I was, so standing in a pub before the game with everyone wearing the same colours was truly appealing to me. It made me feel part of a collective unit. I would have fought for my football team if anyone were to say anything bad about them and people would back me up, pretty sad huh!?

I now see that these external groups didn't help in the long run to make me feel better about myself. At the time, I thought they did, and I look back on them with fond memories, but objectively, they never filled that chasm of yearning for completeness that I was searching for. I was adamant the answer could be obtained through external measures. This point links back to the tribe survival mentality that I speak about and *taming* the animal that is deep in all of us, which can be connected to our pack mentality.

There was still a hurt little boy deep inside of me that had buried a grudge that I carried around for my mother. Until I accepted that it wasn't my fault, or my mothers, I wasn't able to tame my ego. For so long my ego had run the show and led me to believe I was evil and deserved all that I got. I sought solace in the groups that I joined, but eventually drew a blank after the novelty had worn off. My ego thought that it had the answer to my problems.

I had to *tame* the egoic pack mentality that existed within me to truly get to the root of my problems. I had to become the observer of my own thinking and be aware of the pre-programmed behaviour that I was demonstrating. To make the shift, I essentially tamed my human mind. In Zen practice, they call the egoic human mind the monkey mind, for it never shuts off and can behave like an animal if you allow it to. The monkey mind thinks all solutions lay externally to it.

Notice that I still use the word *tame* to link it with taming a wild beast. The ego can never be defeated, but we can observe our own behaviour and loosen the grasp it has upon us. It is a slippery little character and has a hold of me in a different way now. The concept that I am some sort of spiritual guru is what my ego has evolved into now and can often produce aloof thinking. The fact is this: my heart knows that this is nonsense, and I am no different to anyone, but my ego will milk that concept of a guru until the cows come home.

I also allowed my ego to believe I had to follow a certain path after my awakening, in order to become enlightened. The fact is that there is no way and clinging to the concept of enlightenment demonstrates that the ego had adapted to its new role very well!

Cast your mind back to when I started to do voluntary work. I was working a full-time job and helping people in my spare time; what a saint I was. This is what the ego thinks and can manipulate even good circumstances and twist them for a mini power trip. This line of thinking ultimately detracts from the acts of good that I was doing because of my label as a *good* person that I had placed upon myself.

If we cannot tame the ego, what ensues? Well from the past behaviour and thoughts that I have demonstrated, hell can quite literally become a reality. The ego can adopt a set of beliefs that it deems to be valid. Remember, a belief is only a thought that has been thought numerous times, until it registers a certain level of validity with the owner. These beliefs can then be projected out into the world and can shape the world in negative or positive ways. When you begin to adopt a belief of how this world should be operating and reality doesn't match to this; a hellish, torturous state can occur in the eyes of the ego.

My perception of what a *normal* family should be was created out of the comparison to others. With the image of how a family should be not being met, life became a living nightmare for me, one which I attempted to nullify and block out. If I knew back then what I know now, life would have been much easier, but this is part of the beautiful but difficult journey.

Acceptance of any situation and going with the flow is how life should be in my opinion. When we adopt an approach to life where we can be acceptant to all situations that come our way, then torturous egoic thinking cannot occur. When we label a particular event or situation as good or bad, the ego becomes involved. When the event does not pan out according to our preconceived thoughts, it can then be perceived as a terrible experience. It is easy to choose anger when this happens, which is the emptiest of all the emotions at our disposal and we only torment ourselves with it. When we no longer place labels on events, we have tamed our minds and the ego. This is, of course, easier said than done.

35

Taming the Ego and Unconscious Behaviour with Observation

The practice of being the observer can pave the way for a calm mind and help to tame the egoic mind greatly. Let's examine how observing our own behaviour can help tame our busy minds. The observer is a tactic that can be used to stay conscious when the ego chooses to take over! We will talk more about how to cultivate the observer through meditation in the following chapter.

The observer is that plane of consciousness within that notices everything that goes on objectively. It just sits there happily in the background noticing. Taming the ego comes with the challenge of curbing our desires and behaviour. The observer is on another plane to that of the ego consciousness.

I will use the example of sex to demonstrate the powerful needs of the ego. We are wired to reproduce, after all, procreation keeps our species thriving! With this animalistic characteristic part of who we are, do you allow this to fuel your motives in life? Do you view sex as the ultimate goal? When you finally get what you want, where do you go from there? Start the cycle again? This is something I have struggled with since my adolescent years! Let me explain.

The opposite sex was something that I have always yearned for since puberty. Before those thoughts of lust had crept into my psyche, I always desired the attention and company of women because of the absence of a maternal influence in my immediate life.

Following on from that, in my early teens the sight of a beautiful woman would force me to stare uncontrollably. Walking down the street was torture for my young mind. I would think about how wonderful it would be for me to have sex with them. As soon as that woman had passed, I would find myself looking at an entirely different woman having exactly the same thoughts about her, and so the patterns of my behaviour continued. Within a couple of minutes, I would have visualised half of the women that I had randomly passed naked, without them even realising, creepy huh!? What were these lecherous urges that drove me!?

They were unconscious desires, similar to that of any other animal. These urges didn't stop in my teens either and followed me into my adult life. I was, of course, identifying with the egoic programming of my body and that of the evolution of the species that was embedded into my DNA. I was identifying with my ego as if it were real.

Pornography has become readily available over the last few decades and now with the click of a button, the digital image of a naked body is instantly available to anyone. This temptation created by the wonders of modern technology used to perpetuate the objectification of women in my egoic mind. The notion that the female body was only there to serve my own desires and needs was one that I used to lose myself in.

At one stage of my life, pornography dominated a lot of my spare time and only fed my lust for women. It is socially acceptable to watch pornography in today's society, but people do not understand the damage that it can do to real life relationships. It can desensitize the brain and provide false concepts as to what sex actually is. When we allow our egoic urges of desire to consume us, we are allowing a path of permanent torture to ensue. Things can fall out of balance and become unhealthy when the ego chases a high.

I still find myself noticing the opposite sex, but now I can choose to be conscious of my primal traits. No longer do I identify with the unconscious behaviour of the ego. This is where observing our own behaviour comes in. I can now observe the urges that enter my psyche and challenge what I am actually doing. My higher self will quickly tell me that the woman I am choosing to ogle has a soul, which happens to be encased in a meat suit, just like myself. They too have chosen to visit this planet, just as I have and didn't come here to be lust after by a neanderthal male. They too have emotions, thoughts and feelings and are on the same journey as I.

When I buy into the illusion of lust, I am allowing myself to be consumed by the thinking of the ego and seeing myself as a separate being. It sees another and believes that the body is what defines an individual. Of course, this is simply not true, we are so much more than our physical shells. Women were not placed on this earth to satisfy my personal needs, contrary to what my ego may believe. When I can get past this way of thinking, I can connect with them on a spiritual level, not just a physical one which is based on attraction.

I use the example of sex and lust as it is something we can all relate to. The powerful urges that propel two people together can be for different reasons. Sex is by no means bad. Despite the Victorian views that still exist, it is a beautiful act of oneness that brings about new life, but it can often become distorted.

When two people come together out of love and unity for one another, the ego is removed. When two people come together to satisfy their own selfish physical needs, the beauty of sex is lost, and ego has entered the room! Although the flesh may be one, the energies that merge are remaining separate and lost in translation due to absence of love. They are using sex as an external measure to block out some internal pain that lingers deep down. Identifying the difference between lust and love is a way of taming the ego. This is just an example of how to become conscious of one of the strongest of desires that we have been programmed with as humans.

Another example of egoic behaviour that can be tamed by observation is arguing. Take a step back and observe how your ego responds to people if they challenge you. If someone attacked what you believed, how would you immediately respond? Would you defend yourself with aggression? Would you respond with love? Of course, the ego has to justify itself but by taming it, you'd simply allow the other person to have their opinion of you without trying to defend yourself. It doesn't matter what they think, for you know your truth. You can do this with practice over time and by simply being aware of your animalistic programming. Let's examine those emotions that occur in detail when an argument begins.

The next time that you are in a heated, trivial debate, try to acknowledge that burning desire that bubbles deep within you. That desire to convert the person who you are disagreeing with and make them see that your way of thinking is superior. Recognise that it isn't actually who you are and only a part of your spacesuit programming to defend your identity. That feeling that wants to erupt within you is not part of who you truly are. That rage you experience when someone doesn't agree with your point of view, is just another example of the ego's survival mechanism kicking in.

Acknowledge that feeling of molten rage within you. It is happening because someone is attacking what you stand for. Observe the feeling and let the feeling subside, for it has only occurred due to your thoughts of vulnerability and insecurity. I promise you that those emotions will eventually dissipate after a short time when choosing calming, loving thoughts. A volatile situation can go one way or another depending on your response.

Flip it on its head and acknowledge why you feel like you do. A knowing and a belief are two different things. If you truly know what is true to you, why impose it upon another? When you impose your will or thoughts upon another, it is the work of the insecure ego. It will attempt to gain validity and momentum to its belief as if it were in a popularity contest. By acting from a place of love, you will no longer attempt to force someone to conform with your way of thinking. The argument will burn itself out if there are not two willing parties involved.

Even if you don't agree with their point of view, you are not going to win the argument, as the ego hates backing down. Their ego needs just as much validation as yours does and all they want for that split second is to feel like their illusion of what is right is superior to yours. The initial sting you will experience will be horrid but will quickly subside. You can then walk away happy, knowing that you didn't bite back, which in the past, you may have. You can actually feel better for this, knowing that you have ignored your own egoic programming. You have also pleased someone at the same time, by acknowledging their point; whether it be it right or not. This takes practice and I still defend myself from time to time! If you are discussing a life-changing matter, then you may want to stand your ground and compromise but if the topic is simply about subjective matters such as politics, religion or films, is it really worth it!?

Who actually decides what's right anyway? Everything in life has a perfect opposite and there are multiple outcomes to various situations. Who are we to deem that the outcome we perceive as being valid is actually the best-case scenario for the planet, or person involved? It is all a paradox to say the least.

All I can say is that a loving and empathetic response is always the best choice. Just think of my dog Bella and her futile, aggressive attitude when meeting another dog she feels threatened by. Nothing good will come from it and all she wants is to be the dominant one for that split moment. You are fortunate enough to have evolved past the point of Bella's little outbursts and possess a plane of consciousness that can simply observe your own emotions. It's up to you whether you act upon them.

Allow your ego to be an assistant and not a hindrance. Without the ego, my awakening would not have been possible, but as I have mentioned, it can even use awakenings to its advantage and gain the upper hand on people! The ego gives us our identity in our western society and does enable us to function, but life has evolved so much, do we still need to compete for everything and be ruled by it? By acknowledging what the ego is, we can tame it and have balance in our lives. If we choose to identify with the ego, we will forever be climbing an insurmountable, insatiable mountain. Let love be our new guide, instead of the prehistoric ego!

We will now examine the power of meditation and how to develop that level of awareness further.

36

MEDITATION AND AWARENESS

Initially I found the concept of meditation very off-putting. I would often come across how important meditation was in various books and articles. I honestly couldn't accept it. My egoic thinking back then allowed me to believe that I could still lead a gloriously enlightened life. I would just leave the meditation out, as that was just too hippy for me. Various sources suggested that I should practise meditation twice a day; how the hell was I going to find time for that?

I mean, I was so busy: a job, the gym and well, that's it really. When we stop and say we have no time, stop and actually think about how you spend each waking second? How many times do you scroll through social media sites aimlessly? Or watch mindless TV that offers little for your soul?

For me, that was most of the time, and still can be to some extent. When I asked myself this question, I was honest and objective. I observed what I actually did when I got home from the gym most nights. I would shower, then eat, and prepare food for the next day but what was I doing after that? I came to the conclusion that I was frivolous with my time in the evenings. I watched football, played the PlayStation or scrolled through random articles that stimulated my ego for that moment in time. The whole process wasn't really adding any benefit to my life! Surely, I could find a spare twenty minutes in my day?

So, I eventually succumbed to the pressure and attempted meditation for the first time ever and to be honest, it all felt ridiculous! Imagine the wannabe, football hooligan Dave Jones, fast forwarding ten years and witnessing his future self meditating saying, "Ahhhhhhhhh," and "Ommmmmmmm"; he would have been in hysterics. He would have torn him to shreds for participating in this absurd practice. Well this is how my mind treated the whole experience the first time I actually attempted to meditate. It was as though I had been transported backwards and the old Dave had crept back in. *You look ridiculous* and *this is absurd!* Were all thoughts that popped into my head when I first started out. I was actually judging myself the entire time and we have covered the topic of judgment heavily.

My first meditation experience didn't last very long, my mind was wandering all over the place! I left it for a few days and thought, *well at least I tried it, but it wasn't for me.* A few weeks later, I returned and decided to give it another bash, this time with headphones and with an audio guide to help me. It was a bit more engrossing than the first time, but I still felt stupid due to previous conditioning and beliefs! Are you beginning to see now how our thoughts aren't really who we are? They are just models from society that we have grown accustomed to over time. Our current beliefs are just thoughts that have been thought many times.

Now knowing this, it makes it easier to change a belief. It is the ego that creates rigid belief systems so that it has a firm identity in society, but these can quickly become prisons for the individual. These mental constructs can easily be rebuilt though with patience. Meditation can help with this process. As we empty out the old clutter of our minds, meditation can help us to observe the thoughts that wander into our minds on a daily basis. We must try to ignore the preprogrammed thoughts that crop up and listen to our hearts.

When we just lie down, close our eyes, and focus on our breathing, we realise that our body functions subconsciously, without needing any of our thoughts. When our breath is all there is, thoughts become absent and we realise that our body is just a tool to observe the Universe with. The problems of life only appear when we allow our thoughts to enter the show. If we focus solely on each breath while being present in the moment, then problems that appear so real to the waking mind literally vanish. Nothingness consumes us and we can truly observe the stillness and inner peace that has always been within. It is only a busy mind that creates a busy and chaotic life. We will examine, later on, how thoughts really do create our physical reality.

My second time of meditating lasted longer than my first attempt, but my mind was still very active. The headphones helped to stop outside distractions but still, my mind was like a merry-go-round. This proves how our thoughts really can rule our lives; if we allow them to. I completed the second session and again, left it for a few days before I tried again. I felt uninspired with the whole meditation thing to be honest and didn't want to persist with all the nonsense.

A few days passed and I had another crack at it, still feeling stupid about the whole thing deep down. I began to quieten my mind on the third attempt for brief moments. I was focusing on my breathing and nothing else. It started to become easier and thoughts would occasionally pop into my head but would soon be brushed aside. Watching the thoughts come and go was quite surreal, it was as though I was outside my body peering in at it. This is the plane of consciousness that observes everything that we spoke about in the previous chapter. I would reign each stray thought back in like a wild animal and then proceed back to clarity. Again, like training a muscle, I began to train my thought patterns and started to switch off my mind. The more I practised with my meditations, the easier they became; much like anything in life.

It took me about four months to get into a proper routine, but I began getting up twenty minutes earlier in the mornings to meditate first thing. I would lay my intentions for the day and send love to all who I would be encountering on that present day, easy or challenging! We all have that one person that we know will irritate us on an upcoming day!

With the power of meditation, we are disconnected from the physical world for a few moments, which makes it all the more easier to send love to others, as no judgement is involved. The ego is laid to rest for a short while and we can be our true selves. I try to send people who irritate me love in the present moment, but it is much easier in meditation! I have been surprised by the way these people treat me now, they are far more pleasant to me! Who changed, them or me?

With the illusion of separateness that is created by the physical world no longer running rife before our eyes, anything can be accomplished through meditation. You can either enjoy the silence and peace that being free from the thinking mind can bring, or create a new reality. Affirmations, manifesting, dreams can become reality in this new dimension.

During meditation, pictures can be seen within the mind's eye when one is absorbed in a trance that is absent from the physical world. When you close your eyes, what do you see? Do you see any colours? What are they? The more that you practice, the more colours you will see. I see gorgeous rainbow colours projected upon me, similar to a kaleidoscope. Beams of white, warm, glowing light wash through my mind's eye on other occasions, it is truly magnificent. I also see images and brief pictures like a snapshot of reality within my mind's eye. This could be another piece of evidence to suggest that the soul is eternal and that we can see without one of the senses; which we deem as being reality. We have been taught to believe in what we can see, hear and feel, but science suggests that this is only 1% of what is actually going on around us.

It is the same with the words you are reading now on this page. You are reading them silently, but you can still hear the words. How is this possible though? You are not using your sense of hearing, but you can still hear the words your soul speaks? The voice that you can hear is omnipresent and will forever be your being, this is the true you. This is the voice that will continue when the physical vehicle that is your body has perished.

As well as the voice you can hear when you read these words, there is a level of awareness that observes it all. We have now spoken several times about this observing energy, but let's try a little test now if you are still unsure as to what I mean. Read these words now and watch as another level of your awareness observes the action as your human mind reads the words. Notice the voice within that reads this sentence and then notice the level of awareness that observes that voice and the whole action. It's there, yes? A bit spooky perhaps? This is the part of you that is eternal, the part of you that operates from loving awareness and can guide you through tricky scenarios if you allow it to.

This is the observer who you should use to tame the ego, as we discussed in the earlier chapters. This is the part of you that is truly conscious and detached from your physical actions. This is the awareness that grows the more you meditate. If you remain in this constant observational state of yourself and your actions, you can see where you become trapped in the world.

When you stop noticing your actions, that is when you become unconscious. Notice your actions and what causes you to become attached to what you do. Is it conflict? Is it lust? Is it gossip? Is it pain? Is it the vibration or notification on a phone? All of these traps which cause our minds to identify with the body and the physical world are so very easy to get caught in, but they are all part of the physical illusion that we must overcome in order to evolve.

I still get caught up in my actions, often in fact. Food gets me! I find it very easy to become unconscious when I am staring at a screen shovelling food into my mouth. Am I truly tasting it? Am I truly thankful for it? My air of self-righteousness can often trap me too. If I ever see or hear of others doing actions that I deem to be mindless, I can still make a judgement, oh the irony of it! These are all examples of our human minds running the show for us. When our human minds take control, we are not always operating out of pure love.

When we unconsciously identify with our physical actions and words, we create more karma for ourselves in this and future lifetimes. When we allow ourselves to be consumed with lust for instance, we have identified with our animalistic emotions that we think to be the real us, we become trapped into the illusion of *maya*. Maya is the illusion of separateness; a term used in Hinduism. When we see ourselves as one with everything and everyone, we are identifying with our higher self.

Use that level of awareness, which is the observer, as a daily exercise to see where you become tangled in the physical world. It sounds a bit creepy doesn't it, the observer? But watch how certain conversations and your actions allow you to lose that witness that we all possess. If we are permanently in this state, we can have a conscious solution to every problem that our mind creates. What is it that forces you to no longer be the observer and become the doer?

Meditation is the foundation for which you can build the observer upon. You can really get to know your own mind and see what thoughts permeate your mind without you realising. Do you identify with them as being reality? Make this a daily practice and you can become conscious of what comes into your head in your waking life and in your meditations. Don't beat yourself up if you find this difficult as these are only more thoughts which are all a product of your egoic mind. By beating yourself up, you are essentially becoming unconscious again, which is a product of self-hate. Love who you are and the whole process of it all. Rome wasn't built in a day and neither are you, that is why we have eternity to work on ourselves.

My meditation experiences can be quite trippy at times. If I find the right piece of soothing music and fall deep enough into a trance, I can raise my vibration which helps me to connect with my guides. What are guides you ask? We all have guides alongside us at every moment while we walk this short path on Earth. In fact, if you could see who walks alongside you at all times, you would never worry again. Guides are assigned to us at birth, but we can acquire new ones as our paths and consciousness alter. Guides can be souls from other lifetimes attached to you and want to assist you with your work in this lifetime. They may also be loved ones who pass on and want to help you progress on your journey. Deano has continued to be with Gemma, even though he has traded in his human body! Many mediums have told her that he is constantly with her and supporting her.

My guides, Rosemary and Theodore, are the ones who I believe gave me the message that day to write this book. It was as clear as day when the words, "Write a book," were whispered into my mind. Now I can obtain regular messages from my guides when deep in meditation. I do occasionally pick up on help from them in my waking life, but it is rare as I am often consumed by my five senses and the environment around me. I would say that I am only fully conscious around 5% of each day, but it is an improvement on how I used to be! The more that you progress with your meditation practice, the more you will be able to control your mind.

The deeper you fall into relaxation, the more open you are to inviting your guides in and getting to know them. Allow them in and ask them questions. Observe how the answers appear to you from your blank canvas of the mind, we are all capable of this. Communicating with my guides is so surreal, but far more exciting than any of my hallucinogenic days! Who would have pictured me staying in on a Friday night? The incense burning, the herbal tea brewing and the meditation music ready to go. So decadent, so rock'n'roll!

If you find life a little too frantic or hectic sometimes, try meditation. It may offer you the much-needed release of energy that you could be bottling up. You may be allowing some of your buried emotions to spill over into your waking life, causing trivial situations to be worse than they actually are. With a calm mind, situations that bothered you in the past may now be swept aside. Troubling events may still cross your path from time to time but now, it's simply a breeze to you because you are able to observe them. This is because your mind now has more room to function, it's no longer cluttered. When events no longer affect you like they used to, that is progress. Observe your progress and love yourself for it. Meditation helps you to live in the now.

Try not to be disturbed when meditating, as this just takes you away from the moment and may add to current frustrations (if you allow it to!) There are loads of apps and YouTube channels on this topic, so find one which suits you. I use a meditation app called *Insight Timer* which is wonderful. There are many guided meditations on there that can help you, regardless of what level you are at. It took me a while to appreciate this activity that in my mind, only monks did, but now I'm hooked! Is that my ego that's hooked though, I wonder? Happy meditating!

37

Lessons of life

Balance is so important. Following on from the previous chapters, we have to learn to balance the ego. Everything in the Universe is in perfect balance. When we chose to have our human experience on this planet, we came to experience the duality of human life, that everything has an opposite and can be opposed. It is our job to find out what is true for us. We do not question night or day or the seasons, they just happen. The sun rises, the sun sets. The moon operates on a lunar cycle, which, in turn, helps the tides to move in sync. Everything is a perfect dichotomy. Hot, cold, good, bad, happy, sad, male, female, night, day, joy, pain, everything has a polar opposite. All of these opposites meet in perfect harmony to create a balanced perpetual beauty; they merge seamlessly into one. Life is one huge dichotomy. It is our job to be balanced, like the Chinese philosophy of yin and yang.

In my football days, I had no balance. I was obsessed with becoming an alpha male, being a man's man, as I thought this was what was needed to prove who I was to others. If I was a *lad*, people would respect me, possibly fear me, but sometimes this would just land me in difficult situations. As I stated at the beginning of the book, Danny Dyer was the kind of guy I aspired to be, so you can imagine the way I behaved. I couldn't appear soft and caring in a pub full of men, who had testosterone oozing from every pore.

Becoming a balanced person is so important to our development. Diet and lifestyle are so important. Do you get enough sleep each night? Or maybe too much? - which can sometimes be the case! We don't actually need that much sleep; I get by quite happily with just six and a half hours each night. If you are waking up exhausted or are fatigued during the day, it could mean you are resistant to something on a subconscious level. Tiredness can simply mean you are not embracing your current path. I recall that I would often wake up feeling exhausted regardless of how much sleep I got. In hindsight, I was tired because I hated my job and life!

If you are happy with where you are in life, then your diet could be your problem if you are tired. Eating a balanced, natural diet is part of mental happiness and well-being. If the body is not cared for, how can the mind and soul fall into place? Healthy actually means balanced, not just a plate of salad, which is far from balanced. A meal must consist of proteins, fats and carbohydrates in order to be healthy. These are all the components that the body needs in order to function correctly.

Keep work and play balanced. Try to have some fun in life, that's why we are here, to have fun along the way and remember, there is no harm in being childlike sometimes. Notice I said childlike and not childish, there is a difference. Have some fun, do something that you truly want to do but can sometimes be put off by that adult voice in you which says, "You're too old to do that!" Ignore that voice and have some fun, that is one of the reasons we are here. Uptight people are the ones who let life pass them by as they are too focused on conforming with their imaginary belief structure. Many will simply believe they haven't got time to be enjoying themselves.

I wasn't happy with life and used to be so uptight. I convinced myself that happiness could only be achieved down the pub. I started applying subtle little changes into my lifestyle which made me enjoy life more. As I slowly applied the principles of balance to my physical body, I began to notice a change. I started sleeping at regular times, eating fresh food, drinking fresh water, exercising and reducing alcohol intake. I started to build a steady, healthy platform for which my lessons of this lifetime could truly be absorbed. With a balanced body, I can truly live my life. Give it a try, it worked for me and if you want to go back to your old, familiar ways, that's fine. At least you attempted it and you can say that Dave and his ego can stick their self-righteous advice where the sun doesn't shine!

Always tell the truth, for deceiving others is as good as deceiving yourself. If you go around bending the truth to suit your own needs, people will be out to deceive you. You attract like-minded people. You will never find the truth if you spread lies. This is the basic law of karma in action and will only perpetuate if you feed it. Every so often I am still guilty of stretching the truth when I tell a story. I will often add one extra number to the tale to make it sound more intriguing than it actually was, it's the classic case of a fisherman's tale! Why do I lie? You know by now, the ego! I care how others perceive me. People to whom I am retelling the tale don't know the initial story, so maybe the initial truth would interest them without the added extras. It all comes back to me only cheating myself again.

The next piece of advice I offer to you is the concept of unconditional love. I feel that this is the main reason why we have come to this planet, to learn how to love without judgement. I know a beautiful little girl named Grace who is aged 11 and she has severe physical difficulties and complex needs. She cannot walk and her only independent means of mobility is by the use of her arms, which she uses to move her body around. She struggles with her speech, and sentences can be a real challenge for her. Grace can only use small phrases and minimal syllabic words.

I tell the story of Grace as you may think, as I did initially, that this would be an awful way to live. But this pure, gentle, little ray of sunshine has no judgement whatsoever, she is innocence personified. Grace views everyone as equal; she has no prejudice towards anyone and even on Halloween, sees no difference when people are dressed up, she treats everyone the same. Imagine being able to view life through eyes like that? You would certainly accelerate the evolution of your soul! It is truly humbling in my opinion and I aspire to be like this beautiful little girl who always calls me *Sir*.

I feel such warmth when around Grace. I know that her mother, Mandy, struggles with Grace as she sleeps very little and requires constant attention. I believe that Mandy and Grace chose to experience this temporary time on earth together in order to help each other grow and experience unconditional love. Whenever I see them both, I am filled with such pleasure to be in their presence and have pure admiration for them both, as they are both very brave. I wish that I had an ounce of what they have in their souls: pure, unconditional love for each other and for everyone. It can be easy to have love for a family member, but could you have love for an enemy? I will discuss this topic in a much later chapter.

Forgiveness is a lesson we must also master. To be held captive in your own mind from a past event that someone subjected you to is only your torture, not theirs, just let it go. You only hurt yourself and your health from holding a grudge. I once read that forgiveness is the greatest spiritual tool we possess.

My forgiveness for my mother leaving me didn't happen overnight; I was held captive in my own mental prison for many years. Resentment, self-loathing, hate and misunderstanding were the guards to my mental captivity. Over the years though, I slowly saw that staying in this imaginary cell was only causing myself harm. My stay there was hampering the growth of my soul. I eventually managed to befriend the guards that had held me captive and convinced them to hand over the keys. I can appreciate that this metaphorical comparison is cheesy as hell, but you know what, I kinda like it!

The liberation was a gradual process though. But one day it just happened, it clicked, who am I to judge this woman? She was doing the best with what she knew in that period of her life. My mother struggled with mental health issues all through her younger years which plagued her into motherhood. I am just grateful I picked her as my mum to learn such a beautiful lesson. I can now say I love her unconditionally and would do anything for her.

When I forgave, it was like the weight of the world had been lifted, literally. All those questions of why, and thoughts of not being good enough simply disintegrated. All the heavy baggage that I had been lugging around with me had finally been discarded. I realised that it was optional and simply not needed on this special journey that I am on. I felt free. I can't pinpoint the day it happened, but it was in my late twenties. As alcohol lost its grip on my life, I started respecting my body and looking after myself. I finally had clarity. My thinking was no longer clouded or murky and I feel this helped me to see the bigger picture.

I love my mum and although I forgive her, I also love the choice that she made that day when she chose to leave me. It has shaped me to become a strong person and I love what I have become. I will always be there for my mother and respect her. This may make me sound like either a superhero or a pretentious arsehole, but I assure you, my words are sincere. I choose my words with genuine integrity and assure you that forgiveness is liberating. My mother is my greatest teacher and I thank her for this as she has helped me to truly learn about myself.

So please, if you carry resentment for someone, just let it go. The only person you are actually hurting by holding a grudge or clinging onto resentment is yourself! Life really is too short, and you will experience the most glorious sense of alleviation in the fibres of your body when you let go of hate. Just send them love! This is what your higher self would want for you. If you were to take a grudge to the physical grave, you would only be cheating yourself.

Think of it like this: as soon as the two of you were to rendezvous in the spirit world, your soul would have immediate forgiveness for the person in question. The so-called wrong doings that they put you through on Earth would be seen for what they are; a learning curve. All the hate that you chose to feel because of their actions towards you would simply vanish. With this alternative perspective, why not make an evolutionary step? We are now in a position to do just that and forgive them. With these actions, we could create harmony and heaven on earth.

The next hard lesson is patience or self-restraint. Patience is a virtue *they* say, but who are *they*? I often wonder this. Either way, if you have an abundance of patience, life will be a breeze for nothing can phase you! Afterall, time is illusionary and all we have is the present, so what's the rush? Patience can apply to the perception of time or to self-restraint regarding behaviour control. As regards to waiting for something to arrive, do you really have to have it here and now!?

If it's a case of patience being tested by someone else, consider this: if I were to give you a gift and you didn't accept it, where would it go? It would stay with me, wouldn't it? The same applies to patience. If someone is testing you or trying to antagonise you and you don't accept it, where does it go? It stays with that person and their futile actions are wasted on you. Your patience with the person's behaviour and entire situation is an indication that you have indeed tamed your ego and no longer feel the need to control any event or person.

When a student calls me every name under the sun or berates my personal appearance at college, I simply don't take it personally, it doesn't affect me. Do I choose to meet them on their level and retaliate? Well, no, I would lose my job for one but from the perspective of humanity, I would never match someone's base behaviour. If I chose to mimic aggressive behaviour that was being directed at myself, I would simply accelerate the problem and add fuel to the egoic fire. If I choose not to bite back and operate from a place of compassion, the insult simply stays with its owner. I set an example and rise above it. This may sound like a real hippy philosophy, but it's true.

With no patience to a situation, we can let anything get under our skin! How many people choose to get angry in traffic jams or long queues? "I'm so angry with all this traffic," or, "look at the size of that queue!" Have you ever thought that you are in that queue and are part of the problem by adding to it? What right do you have to complain? None, but your ego does! For in that one moment, your ego will create an air of superiority and apply it to the situation. Therefore, it will make you believe that you should not have to wait or queue like anyone else, for you are better than them! This is why there is always a way around losing your patience, just see the bigger picture! Everything is as it should be without you trying to control it. As regards to time, you will arrive at your destination when you are meant to.

Being humble and full of humility is another excellent skill to learn in life. To boast and brag would make you an elite individual and separate from everyone else. It is a product of the ego. Are you sick of that word yet, ego? Just be thankful and express gratitude when something good happens to you. When you have done a good deed, do you need to advertise it? There is no need to brag and shout about it, doing so detracts from the initial good deed. If you do a good deed and then broadcast it, was it coming from the right place in the beginning?

Sometimes, just sometimes, it's okay to do nothing! As westerners we have been conditioned to believe that more is better and that we must be doing something. While doing a current activity like eating or working, we are already planning the next activity and the next after that, like seriously, it's truly exhausting. Can you just sit down and do nothing? Silence is the ego's worst enemy, so that is why the ego has to continually occupy itself to avoid that awkward moment when, God forbid, boredom occurs. Boredom is what the ego fears for it will bring silence, the fear of being left alone to listen to one's inner peace and discover who we truly are. If we are busy, the ego stays in control, which it loves.

Gratitude is something that we all can practice every day. I often feel like I could be doing more or deserve more. I often forget what I do have and have had. I have a beautiful best friend that is my wife-to-be, the sweetest dog that you could ever wish to meet, my health, wealth, a job I love, beautiful people the Universe has placed into my life at the right time to help, the list goes on. Sometimes it is easy to remain focused on what we don't have and lose our true appreciation of all that is present. In the past I was always guilty of this and occasionally, I still am, but I can now acknowledge the ego at work and snap out of it. I am thankful for all that I have, as it could all be gone in the blink of an eye. What are you thankful for today?

Learn to think for yourself and be more open-minded. My world has changed since I have removed my stubborn, blinkered ways of thinking that were conditioned into me. I no longer choose to believe anything that is told to me by a person that is in an imaginary superior role to myself. The teacher at school plays this role, but how does the teacher know what they teach is the truth? Were they there? They are repeating what they were once told and delivering a curriculum that they have been told which is dictated by others.

A prime example of this was what I saw the other night on *Hell's Kitchen*. If you are not familiar with this show, it is a cooking competition hosted by Gordon Ramsey. On this TV show, Gordon has chefs that cook in the kitchen of his reality restaurant. The chef who is deemed the best by Gordon can run one of Gordon's restaurants for him as the grand prize. I love Gordon Ramsey and I have always admired his passion for food. Throughout my culinary career, he is someone that I would always relate to. Gordon will occasionally train the chefs how to cook and will show them his cooking techniques as well.

On the particular episode that I watched, Gordon made two dishes for all of the contestants to taste. He told them that beef and scallops were the main ingredients in the two meals and asked for their opinions on both dishes. Each contestant was in awe of what had been prepared for them and stated that each dish was perfect. Some preferred the scallop dish, and some preferred the beef dish. "Oh chef, the beef is out of this world," and "Chef, the scallops are perfect," were just some of the comments made by the other chefs.

The truth was that Gordon had lied to them, and the actual ingredients were tuna and seabass. Each contestant was in shock and disbelief. They couldn't believe that their taste buds had betrayed them on such a grand scale! The chefs had allowed their perception to be manipulated from the actual truth, simply by what they had been told by their omniscient idol.

This example shows how easy it is to believe anything that we are told by anyone in a position of authority. Even if what we are being told goes against everything that our own senses tell us. We can often end up believing the words of someone who we believe to be a source of truth. Sometimes people we trust can lie or be mistaken themselves. That's why it is so important to find the truth for yourself. I could have lied in this book or have been mistaken; I mean, I haven't, but that's not the point!

I also welcome the diverse opinion and unique thinking of others. By having a mind that is open to everything and attached to nothing, the truth can be achieved. This lesson is invaluable. With this attitude, you can shed your old skin of tired beliefs that were holding you back in life. The memes that you have allowed to define who you are keep you in a labelled box. They may define who you think you are but may also hinder you from finding the truth.

Fixed, rigid things snap and break eventually, don't be this person. Try to be flexible with your thinking, be like water and allow new concepts to flow to you without blocking them. Have you ever heard anyone say, "You can't do that, that's not how it is supposed to be done?" There are multiple ways to do things in life and if we do not evolve our thinking, what is the point of life? Old beliefs can hold you back and can keep you trapped in the past, while life passes you by.

Fixed, dogmatic beliefs about certain aspects of life always held me back. I was raised with a religious background and held the teachings of the Bible close to my heart, even if they felt off. I would often view people, even friends, in a condescending manner if their opinion did not match my viewpoint on God, or the Bible for that matter. They were going to burn in hell for not believing in the scriptures and I did not want that for them, how could I help them if they would not listen? I knew all the answers, so why didn't they?

If individuals presented information contradicting the Bible, I would just tell them they were narrow minded and naysayers. The ironic thing was, it was myself who was the one with blinkered vision and in the wrong for thinking that my beliefs were superior.

I now view everything differently. If someone has an interesting point to make, I will take it on board and say, "Wow, why didn't I think of that?" I actually encourage new opinions from people now, as it helps to broaden my horizons. It doesn't mean I have to believe everything I hear, but I can at least take it on board. I have now been able to meet so many new, exciting people with this limitless attitude. We are all teachers and can learn so much off one another, if we allow it.

If I wanted to, I could allow my ego to be concerned with other people's issues and criticise them for their choices, but I have reached the point in my life where I no longer find this necessary. Who I am to predetermine a path that a certain individual should walk? How can I possibly relate to their journey and know what is best for another? It is actually crazy if you tear it apart. People have to walk their own path and learn at their own pace; they have chosen to live like this. If they ask for help, that's different but don't steamroller in, condemning the way someone is living. How is that in any way helpful to that person?

That is why conveying my message to the world via a book is the best way to do it. Books are not in your face and you have control over them. The beauty of a book is that if you think it's naff, you can stop reading it. A book can be a beautiful way to deliver a message, as the person reading it has complete autonomy. I am not forcing you at gunpoint to read my book, you chose to pick it up. What I write about works for me, but it may not work for you and that is absolutely fine. You are on your own path. Just know that you were meant to read this book at this particular moment in your life…

I am now secure and happy enough in myself not to criticise others; this critical behaviour no longer stimulates me. People are simply doing what they know in the moment because that is their current capacity at that time. We could find a thousand things wrong with the world each day if we wanted to. I could find offence through anything that I encounter but does it really matter? Just let people go about their business. If it doesn't affect you personally, who cares what people do? If someone wants to dress in a particular way, admire them for having the courage to express themselves. If someone wants to identify as a specific label, just let them. I used to criticise people for dressing a certain way. The truth is my ego was jealous. I would have loved to have the tenacity to truly express who I was through my choice of clothes, instead my fashion mimicked others.

Just let it be. These magic words can really help you. You can watch your life transform when you stop getting offended by what others do and focus on yourself. Do not waste another moment in your life sending negative energy to others. Focus your energy inwards and start changing your own self-limiting beliefs, by doing this you can create your best life.

Become selfless wherever possible. This one is pretty easy to follow but harder to put into action. I try to do the opposite of anything that my selfish ways want. The child in me still has to get his own way every now and then. I like to dictate what films Louise and I are going to watch, where we are going to walk or what gym workout we are going to do. This is a work in practice for me, for I think I know what is best! Being selfless can also relate not just to material possessions but for time as well. Giving time away to others is just as important as giving anything away. If you can spare someone your time, that is invaluable.

I recall once reading a passage that was written by Mother Teresa that described the three hardest things to do in life, they are: including the excluded, admitting when you are in the wrong and returning love to someone when they are demonstrating hate towards you. I was always guilty of not involving the goofy kid at school because they were not deemed cool enough by my peers. This was so wrong of me and I have learnt from my early, callous behaviour.

I now view everyone as equal and do my best to involve all in conversation and activities. I have found that the quietest people are sometimes the most interesting of people. Imagine if I were to discard the validity of a person's opinions based solely on their street credentials. I could potentially miss out on a life-changing conversation with that person. I was the fool.

Admitting when you are wrong goes against everything that the ego stands for. We all make mistakes, but this is how we learn. So the next time you make a mistake, admit it and own it. When we play the blame game or act a victim, we give our power away. If you are willing to part with your power, what else are you willing to part with? Be proud that you made the mistake for it showed you a path of error and try to learn from it.

I want to really focus on the next lesson, as I feel it is so hard to ignore our natural defence mechanisms. When a person is hurling aggression and hate at you, how do you respond? Respond with what you are being given which is ultimately pain? Why is the person behaving so aggressively to you? Anger is the cousin of pain and pain only exists in the absence of love. We are all love and that is all we will ever be. When we are not receiving what we are fundamentally made of as humans, pain enters and all sorts of negative emotions stem from this. When someone is screaming at you, it is a cry from within for you to help them and ease the suffering of their pain. As humans, we just do things a bit backwards sometimes as emotions are funny things! What will you do? You could be the one to demonstrate a different response to what they are used to. You could be the one to ease their suffering with love? Teachers appear in abstract ways, let that person in pain teach you about yourself.

If the idea of being nice to someone who is horrible to your face is too much for you, try this: send them love through your thoughts instead. If you practice this technique enough mentally, maybe one day a situation may arise when you would have nothing but love for a venomous person. You could end up helping the person instead of attacking them. Give it a go, send them love via the mind and see what happens. Remember, hating someone and holding a grudge hurts you more than it hurts them.

Embrace your struggles and hardships; for these are all methods that will eventually open your heart. Each loss can aid your unique discovery as to what unconditional love truly is. These challenges come to you through your own unique karma and you will have chosen them on a subconscious level in order to grow. These karmic struggles are all beautiful for they burn up old actions while creating new possibilities. All karmic teachings are opportunities that lead you to an awakening of who you truly are.

My father would often tell me a story as a child and still does to this day. He would ask me what I wanted to be and give me two options. A beautiful flower in the meadow? Or a weathered, battered old tree on the edge of a cliff? I would always reply to my dad that I wanted to be a beautiful flower in the meadow. He would then respond by saying, "What if there was a storm in that meadow one day, how would you cope?" The reality is that the flower would be swept away and probably perish, for the blue skies had long gone.

In comparison, the old, hardened bark of a tree on a cliff face has weathered many storms. Visually, it may not be the prettiest, but it has withstood the test of time. The tree endured all that life could throw at it and learned to love it all and just *be*. The tree's environment was all part of the necessary process to shape it.

The path that I have walked in life has helped me to realise that I have become that old tree who just exists, regardless of what is happening in the external circumstances. The loss, the gain, I know deep within my core that I can withstand anything life has to offer me. With this strength behind me, I can approach future challenges with pure love and welcoming arms.

There is also an element of perception to all challenges that we face, which will be focused on later. For this chapter, I simply wanted to convey my understanding of my father's teachings in that lovely little story he would tell me. I often tell it to people who ask me about my life, and I think it explains why I am like I am.

Sometimes the easy path isn't always the best option, sure it could be scenic and easy to navigate, but it's no challenge. The rocky, uphill terrain may not provide the best views while you are walking along it, but when you reach the summit and complete the planned journey, it all seems worthwhile. When you are on the top, then you can appreciate that the views are magnificent as you gaze at them from a higher vantage point.

Another little story to reiterate how we must embrace any challenge that comes our way is the caterpillar. The caterpillar, when ready to transform, will form a chrysalis; a protective cocoon while it undergoes its wondrous metamorphosis into a butterfly. A caterpillar will toss, turn and struggle to break free from its new encasing, desperate to get free. It is unaware of the beautiful final product that it will grow into. If you were to disturb or tamper with this process before the caterpillar was ready to be released, it would die.

I love this metaphor for life. Like the caterpillar, if we try to escape the pain and discomfort of the present situation, instead of viewing it for what it is, we could miss the beauty of it all. We may not flourish and if we hide, it may hinder the beauty of the final product that we can become. When we prevail from our challenges, we can fly free and show off our beautiful colours that we have earned. We can be proud of our accomplishments and the struggles that we encountered.

No matter how hopeless and desperate some situations can seem sometimes, know that there is a reason for it all. Even when I was suicidal and held what I thought was a loaded gun to my head, it was all part of the process. All of the anguish that you experience is all part of the master plan. Be optimistic through it all. Dance in the storm and know that eventually, the process will help you to grow into an omniscient soul. Know that nothing but good can come from problems. I am truly thankful to the Universe for my early challenges in life because without them, I would not be the person that I am today. All of this is easy to say in hindsight, but I wouldn't dream of telling someone who is suffering that it is all meant to be. In the heat of the moment, all people need is love and compassion. I would weep with them and share their pain for I know what it is like to be rock bottom and see no way out.

I could write another twenty books on the lessons of life and have only touched on just a few really. Maybe that is a book for the future, who knows? I feel that I can write authentically about how blessings can be disguised as struggles. If you share my belief and apply the mantra that nothing but good can come from problems, then life can be a joyful experience for you. Life is there so you can grow and learn from it! You chose to have this experience so embrace it!

38

LIVING IN THE MOMENT; THE HERE AND NOW

I had to write a separate chapter on time as it is so lengthy (not a deliberate joke), but time could be deemed as another lesson of life that we have to fathom. Apparently, there is no time in the spirit world; it is irrelevant. How do I know this? Well, I don't personally, as I cannot remember what home is like! In the book *Dying to be Me*, based on a near-death experience, written by Anita Moorjani, the author graphically depicts that time is merely an illusion and that everything happens all at once in the now.

Spirit world events such as past, present and future all run simultaneously, as do different lifetimes. This is what the Buddhists call *void*; everything blends into one to the point of a paradoxical non-existence. Ultimately, everything is nothing, therefore time is nothing too. We experience all our lifetimes at once as timelines run parallel to one another. With our limited, human minds, we can only put things together in rational, linear terms. This idea perplexes me to be honest but also makes sense to me in a convoluted way.

The soul is such a powerful force that it can project itself into many experiences at once. Think of the soul as a lamp, the lamp casts beams of light that can go in many directions. The rays of light are still part of the lamp and always will be, they just experience different aspects of reality in unique ways. If you have ever seen the movie *The Matrix*, it isn't too far off from the truth actually. Think of the soul as something that resides in the true reality of love that has the power to experience layered dimensions, planes of consciousness and multiple lifetimes all at once. This human lifetime that feels so real to us now is just a projection of the soul or higher self, yearning to learn and experience what it already is. By having experiences, it continues to grow. Our five senses that feel so real to us are just an illusion and a projection cast from the mind of the Universe that craves expansion. With this notion that the soul just *is* and resides in spirit, time is not relative to it and it can experience many paths of learning at once.

The concept of multiple lifetimes occurring at once is mind-boggling and a bit of a juxtaposition, but all we have is the now. When I first heard the theory of parallel lives, I thought, "Well that doesn't make any sense, how can we plan our future lives if we haven't experienced a previous one to learn from!?" I now accept it for what it is, and I have chosen to focus purely on the now, which is as close to any parallel, multi-dimensional timeline I will ever understand!

All we know from our human existence is linear and cohesive time, but when you actually contemplate deeply about the mind-bending paradox of time, all that you actually ever have is the present moment. Albert Einstein said that time is just relative to one's mind and actions. Einstein stated time slows down or speeds up depending on how fast one moves relative to something else. Therefore, time is a mental construct that governs our own individual existence and is relative to one's existence. I will experience time much differently to you and vice versa. If we feel short on time, we are constantly rushing and don't actually achieve anything any faster than what we imagine. People who live their life like this are more prone to health problems, for they simply run out of time and the body says slow down.

Time is strange. This moment that you experience as you read this book is just a continuum of the now. You will have this moment forever but never again. The past has gone but that was once a present moment. The words that you are reading now are part of that special present moment, however they will soon pass and drift into the past which is still the now.

We are always in the present moment, but those words from above you have just read have now passed. The future doesn't sneak up on you and say "Surprise, I'm here." All we have is the now. When you can accept this, life doesn't have to be so hectic and chaotic from the perspective that our minds create!

Our minds can create any passage of time that they want to. Anxiety is caused by imaginary scenarios and outcomes of future events, most of which never actually transpire into reality. All the stress that comes with anxiety is self-inflicted out of illusion. When you actually think about it, it sounds insane, doesn't it? You sit there and subject yourself to constant mental punishment. Will they? Won't they? What if? What will they think of me? It's exhausting and we create it all! This type of behaviour should have you locked away really, shouldn't it? 97% of the things we worry about never happen and the other 3%, we have no control over, so just let it be. We are all guilty of thinking imaginary scenarios about the future though.

I, myself, can be included in some anxious ways of thinking. I will give you an example of this in a few paragraphs.

So, what about living in the past? The past is like an aeroplane trail that we can see in the sky. The plane has left its vapour trail behind it as it travels but is still focused on flying in the current moment, to its destination. The plane will eventually arrive at its chosen destination but all that matters is the journey of the present; this is a lot like life.

We leave a trail of choices behind us but what's done is done. To worry about the past would simply be insanity. It would be the equivalent of the plane doing a U-turn and flying over the old vapour trails to scrub them out, while making more chaos in the process. Actions like this would be totally destructive to the plane's current objective. With this type of behaviour and thinking, living in the past can create a personal hell, as past events cannot be altered. We have all been there - what if I had, I wish I had, I should have. To live in the past is an exercise of ultimate futility, which eventually leads to depression.

Being present in every moment is so important, as that is all we will ever have. I'm not saying stop making plans all together, as nothing would ever get done. Your mind is a tool to be used as a planner, not to be used as a device to live in false realities. All I am suggesting is to stop worrying about the past and the future. All you are affecting is your own health and wellbeing. Who knows what Dean thought on his final day on Earth, but whatever he was thinking, doesn't it all seem so minute? The fact is nobody knows when their last day on Earth is. If today was your last day, you'd feel pretty gutted that you wasted so much time thinking frivolous thoughts.

I will keep reminding you though that I am not perfect, not by a long shot. I am certainly by no means some wise sage; I'm just trying to share what I have learnt and what is working for me! With this said, I do feel that I have mastered the art of letting go of the past. I no longer let the past dictate my present mood, which is what I allowed it to do so much while growing up. I no longer use my childhood as an excuse or relive old memories. In fact, I view that confused, lost little boy as part of who I was, and I send him love.

Now then, not so much can be said about my perception of the future! "Hold on Dave, you just told me to focus on the present moment and not to listen to the mind?" This is probably what you are thinking, but like I said, I am a work in progress. I think about the future with excitement and nothing bothers me, apart from one little thing. Here is the example that I said I would mention a few paragraphs ago and it is… driving! I am willing to try anything in life but when it comes to driving, I am greeted with sheer panic! I mean, I choose to panic; it is my choice but indeed, I choose it! Where do these irrational fears come from? Our parents and peers while growing up. I will delve much deeper into this in a later chapter about parenting and the subconscious mind, but for NOW, let's just focus on my fear of driving.

I actually enjoy driving places that I know, I put a lecture on about some esoteric topic and listen with delight. However, if you were to say to me, "I need you to drive to a foreign location an hour away," my gut would simply do a somersault! It's crazy, I know. If you told me that I had a new job, I would be excited or that I had to meet new people, great, but driving to a new location scares me! What is that fear?

I am a safe and courteous driver and have no ego when I am on the road, which I feel is responsible for most of the accidents out there. There's just something that terrifies me about new roads I have not yet ventured. When I am on them, it's not so bad but the illusory thought itself just makes me feel yuck! I have gotten better as time has progressed, much better in fact. Driving is my one and only fear and I will conquer it by using the now (just like I did by picking up big spiders)!

For when I am not in the now, my mind can run rampant and create any illusion that I allow it to about future events. *What if I get lost? What if I have an accident? How will I know which way to go?* None of these actually happen though and when I do get lost, I eventually find my way to where I am meant to be. If an event that I deemed bad were to happen, it isn't the end of the world really, for it too shall pass. I should just let go, live in the current moment and have trust in the Universe, as it has never wronged me.

The next statement that I make is very hypocritical, I mean I have just admitted that I don't always apply what I preach, but here it is: To live in the future will create anxiety and stress. To wallow in the past creates depression and your own personal hell. Heaven can be achieved by admiring the beauty of every present moment and accepting the now. The mind is like a muscle, the more you train it, the stronger it becomes. One day, I will reach my potential and drive everywhere without having dramatic thinking such as, "What if?!"

If I allow my doubts to creep in, I just stop in the moment and ask myself, "Do I actually have a problem at this very moment in time?" Nine times out of ten, I will say no, to which I'm sure you can agree if you try this exercise for yourself. Do you have a problem right now while you are reading this book? No, you don't, but if you allow your mind to drift and start thinking about who wronged you last week or about money for the coming week, problems magically appear and snowball. Before you know it, an imaginary calamity has happened, and you are ready to be sectioned!

Living and savouring each moment of time can help us to realise that mental problems are actually an illusion. With applying this technique to life, it has helped me a lot. *Eckhart Tolle* has a very interesting book called *The Power of Now*. For those of you who struggle with psychological problems, I highly recommend this book. He depicts far more advanced exercises to try than I have suggested in the last few paragraphs. It is a really useful book for curbing anxiety and staying calm in the beauty and stillness of every moment.

A classic tale of how I once obsessed about the future and lived in it was when I worked in the café at college. I was constantly questioning when the Universe would provide a new role for me and fulfil my wishes. My thoughts at that time were absent of the present and all that I have been blessed with; I was yearning for the future and new challenges, ignoring the beauty of what I currently possessed.

I recall that I had negative thought patterns for days on end and became ungrateful for what I had. In that time period I had someone reverse into my car and I burnt the entire palm of my hand horrifically. It was the worst burn that I had ever experienced in my life, which is saying something, considering that I worked in kitchens for so many years! That burn stopped me from going to the gym, as I simply couldn't pick anything up.

Now I wasn't concerned about my hand or car before these events happened, but wish that I would have been more grateful and focused on my current level of health before things changed. What's that old phrase? You don't know what you've got until it's gone! You can say though, that these are just accidents and they happen. Nothing is an accident in this perfect Universe. How can anything be an accident when everything works in harmony and balance? We are here in the training simulator known as *earth*, to help us grow! These events happen as wake up calls to remind us to be thankful for what we have in the present moment and bring us back to the now.

My car was perfect, but that changed when someone reversed into it, denting the front, minorly, but still a dent. This also came as a lesson for me in the shape of attachment. Did it actually matter about the dent? Why was I so attached to the appearance of my car? When I was sitting inside of it driving, I couldn't see the outside and I loved driving it. Or, was I worried about the dent because of how other people would perceive me driving an old, dented car!? That is the real reality.

I was also negative about going to the gym up until that point; I felt lacklustre and couldn't be bothered. I sometimes see the gym as a chore, I go through phases like this. With the burning of my hand, I was peeved to say the least that I couldn't attend the gym, even though I didn't want to go in the first place! The mind is a funny thing if you allow it to be. One day, the option of not being able to attend the gym may be a permanent thing; therefore, I am thankful for the now, as I am in perfect health. I practise living in the now every waking moment, for that is all there is.

Are you living in the now as you read these words? Or are you planning what to do next or thinking about what someone said to you earlier? It really is tiring when you observe how the mind can take you on a merry dance. Where will it take you next? At least with the now, you know what to expect.

39

RELIGION

This is a very, very delicate chapter for me. I have many friends with religious beliefs, including my own family, but I feel compelled to write about the effect religion has had on my life and how I have chosen to feel because of it. I have seen much beauty from people who do good acts in the name of religion, so this is not to discredit them.

This chapter is written from my perspective and experiences with religion. It is truthful to me and I write what I have learnt from it all to inform you, not to offend you. It will show you how the truth of the Universe has been twisted by the ego of man and formed what is known as religion. You may read something in this chapter that your soul feels a level of truth towards; after all, we all know the truth and who we are deep down.

On the other hand, your egoic mind that has been pre-programmed with memes that have served you to this day may feel threatened. What your truth is about religion may be totally different to mine, which is fine. What I write may challenge your mind and you may again feel the need to protect your mental construct, this too is fine. Feel free to disagree with my following statements, I mean no harm, just be aware that I am not right and that I am just presenting my illusional truth to you. If you can, really use this chapter to become and practice being the observer towards your emotions. Notice when your ego is getting triggered and stay on that plane of awareness. Okay, disclaimer out of the way, let's go.

If you are hugely religious, ask yourself why? Is it inherited beliefs? Is it something that you found for yourself? Do you feel a sense of solidarity from sharing the same belief as others? Has God changed you? What does religion do for you? Religion brings about so much good in the world and can help many, but as anything, it can be used in a negative way as well. If religion has helped you to advance in your life in a positive way and become more open-minded, keep doing what you're doing. But, if you have rigid, dogmatic beliefs that stem from fear, use the following chapter to learn why fear should never enter the truth of love.

From a young age, going to church just felt... odd. I just couldn't put my finger on it. In the beginning of the book, I stated how I would loathe the songs that were sung and the lectures that were delivered from the preachers. I was a perceptive little child, as all children are, because they are pure and remember what is true. It is only as we grow older that we forget what is true. We create mental constructs or walls as to who we are to protect ourselves from the pain that is created by our individual separateness.

From that young age, I knew when something wasn't right because I wasn't seeing love in church. Sure, people spoke about love but I didn't see it, all I saw was fear. Couples who were part of the congregation would split up and get divorced. I remember asking my dad why this was, as I was puzzled. He didn't really have an answer which frustrated me, as children crave answers! I thought that marriage and love was for life and that the absence of my mother was just an anomaly because I was naughty.

My dad would tell me tales of how babies in the congregation were born outside of wedlock, but it was just an *accident* and they would be let off. I was confused as I thought all people who followed *God* stuck to his rules and didn't deviate, as that was the way things were meant to be!? I soon learnt of all the affairs that were going on right under God's roof!

Every Sunday I would blend into the background and pretend to be preoccupied with my toys. While I would play with my Batman figures, I would inadvertently overhear all sorts of juicy gossip. This all happened after the bread and wine communion had finished! Most people would gather and talk amongst themselves, generally about other people's business. From a young age this just felt wrong and I was truly confused.

Then there was the whole message of Jesus and God and that just confused me even more! It seemed like each story delivered a totally different message to what the previous one did. I became very suspicious of the whole church environment and it felt corrupt to me. Why did it feel like this to me? Was my childlike purity still in touch with the truth, as I had not long come from heaven? Was it my mission to find the truth on earth?

Whatever the truth was, something deep down in me knew that what I was seeing and hearing was not righteous behaviour. Other people outside of the church spoke so negatively about it all. I truly felt like a black sheep when I was in the company of others who didn't go to church. I would always feel ashamed to tell my friends at nursery, then primary school, that I went to church. What was this creation known as religion and why did it exist? I remember as a small child thinking that I would burn in hell for eternity if I didn't conform to what the good book said, it used to terrify me.

Now, there are spiritual truths in the Bible and a lot are metaphorical content that was relevant to the time when they were written; but truth is truth. Man, however, has added his own little interjections along the way and has tainted what was once that of purity and absolute truth. Fear is the total opposite to what is true, for love is all that is real. Anything that consists of fear is part of the physical illusion that we found ourselves submerged in and is not valid.

When I was growing up, I accepted everything that I was told from the good book, even if it involved fear. Why would people want to lie to me as a child? That's what I thought anyway. Even though some stories did scare me for fear that I would burn in hell, I knew no different so just went along with it. To me, the Bible is full of contradictions, loopholes and fear. You will hear this word a lot as the book draws on: fear. For fear is something that we have created in the illusion which is maya.

It is clear to me where man has interjected fear and his egocentric opinion into the Bible. There are many examples like hell and punishment, but the one that sits with me is Noah's ark. I realise that most parables are metaphors or allegories and are not meant to be taken at face value, but as a child, I did. I am sure that many of the stories in the Bible have also been misconstrued and become ambiguous as time and society has progressed. Not all of the teachings of the Bible are bad and again, it's all about balance. From a loving point of view though, Noah's ark just didn't feel right.

There are people that claim this was a real story though and link it to the story of Atlantis. Others claim that the ark landed on the remote and inaccessible heights of Mount Ararat, which is located in Turkey. For me though, this story shows how man has perverted the true meaning of the word *God* and exploited it for his own benefit.

The message I was always taught from the Bible was to love thy neighbour and to have unconditional love for everyone (unless they are homosexual, from another religion or don't acknowledge God's word, but that's another story). In Noah's ark, God instructed Noah to build an ark as God was going to flood the world and destroy everything. God was simply fed up with the way things were going and he didn't like what he had created, his children were getting out of control. You can imagine how this made me feel as a child. I used to get scared that God would just wipe me out one day and erase me as I was a bad seed. After all, he had already taken my mum away from me because I was evil, so destroying me seemed inevitably on his agenda.

All of this unconditional love and turning the other cheek stuff that I was told was just confusing to me. I was told to love unconditionally in one sentence, then in a heartbeat I was being told that God killed everyone one day as he wasn't happy. Our loving, forgiving God, who we must worship, had simply had enough of it all and scrapped the world so he could start again. Doesn't this sound like someone who had a hard day at work!?

Those emotions that were demonstrated by God sound very human, even egoic-like behaviour, don't they? Certainly not the actions of pure, divine love and source energy? Either way, Noah obeyed and built the ark. Presumably, he hired many folk to help him build the imposing wooden structure, as it had to hold every animal in the world. When the gargantuan construct was complete, Noah had to thank his pals for all their work but bid them farewell, as they didn't make the cut. They then consequently died, as he couldn't take them all with him. God had, however, given Noah strict instructions as who to take with him, so surely those poor folk who helped would have understood?

As I stated earlier, many stories in the Bible could be construed as metaphors and were not literal. Metaphor or not, I do not see how this story can be a wise teaching from a perfect God. Let's take this story literally and imagine that it was real. We will discuss the moral ambiguity of the situation in a while. For now, we will look at the logistics of the story and overlook the fact that God deemed it necessary to destroy all that he was.

Noah rounded up two penguins, two polar bears and two of every species going for that matter and managed to get them on board his wondrous ark. Noah had enough food for all the animals and passengers on board for he was doing God's work. After all the commotion had subsided and the floods dispersed, Noah and his crew arrived in Turkey, where all the animals adapted just fine to their new conditions. When it was all done, Noah then sent all the animals back to their natural habitats and the penguins began to waddle happily back to the North Pole.

For the people who argue that this story is true, I respect their findings and beliefs, but this could simply be a tale of natural evolution exploited by the morbid views of man. No *God* interfered with the flooding of the world to scrap all of his failed work; it was simply the work of a natural progression that we know as the Universe. Man, then added the tale of fear into his religious teachings to stop people from hurting themselves too much with what is really true.

Whether it be from a literal or allegorical point of view, the kind of God that is portrayed in this story feels corrupt to me. After all of the destruction passed, God felt bad and promised not to do it again; much like a naughty child when they have done something wrong. He even sent a rainbow to show that he did love everyone after all and wouldn't break his promise. Not many were there to see the rainbow though because everyone was dead.

I chose the story of Noah's ark to demonstrate why I no longer believe in the man-made written texts that depict the God that exists in the Bible. Fear is prevalent throughout the book and as we will discover later on, fear is not real. As I stated earlier, this is my take on things and not necessarily true to everybody. If you are an avid believer in the Bible and read it with absolute love and no fear whatsoever, that is great, but I don't see it like that.

The Bible has helped many and there are wonderful, wise stories in there that translate via beautiful metaphors and allegories. From my perspective though, I want to learn how to love, not how to punish. I do not want to do it by believing in a vengeful, tyrannical, God. A God who will punish us if we belittle him and don't conform to his rigid laws of worship. A God who makes little children scared that they are going to burn in hell if they are not *good*; I was once that child. I now see that the God I grew up believing in is a God created by the ego, a man-made scaremongering fest!

All those traits that God possesses that are depicted in the Bible are traits of the ego, which is the very thing we are trying to transcend. It is clear that man has had an active input into the Bible over the years. Our westernised God has many egoic qualities. The God of the Bible will love us, but only if we do certain favours for him. That is the stamp of an egoic love trait right there, placing conditions on things.

As I have and will state throughout this book, anything can be used for good or bad; anything can be abused. Religion has helped people out of dark, dark places and that is wonderful. Why though must we place a particular label on ourselves? Labels create more division in the world and perpetuate the illusion of separateness created by the ego. When you state what you are with a label, you also state everything that you are not at the same time. You are implying you are different to others on a fundamental level. Religion therefore is a man-made construct designed to keep us in our place and constantly squabbling amongst each other. For one group to identify with a set of beliefs and define themselves with a label, they are creating a constant divide from others. "Come and join our way, for it is the truth," is often a message that is heard within religious groups, suggesting that everyone else's way is just a path of error. This is not love.

Whenever I go on a *spiritual* channel on YouTube and view some truly beautiful material, there are always individuals bickering amongst themselves about religion in the comments section. As soon as the word God enters the equation, that's it. The comments will often consist of religious dogma stating that non-believers will burn in hell and only the Bible and Jesus will save them, why do they care so much? Do they say this out of love? Not at all, for anyone who talks about being saved and burning in hell talks out of fear and speaks from their ego.

It is so sad to read the comments and also painfully ironic that their argument is the total opposite to what true love is. The God they argue over is the God of the ego created by man, and they are replicating the exact behaviour of their *God* by pressuring others to live in a certain way. Does this example not show how religion can create division and friction between others? If anything, it fuels their egos as it allows individuals to believe that they have all the answers. They have all the answers because they read it in one book and never sought to look for the truth themselves.

Religion was used as a tool of manipulation centuries ago by kings and queens in order to control the masses. Those who ruled used religion to keep people rooted in fear so that they would conform to the rules. Religion is an excellent method of illusory mind control when dealing with large numbers. All successful control methods usually have fear rooted at their base. In the western world, Christianity became the most popular. The core roots and principles of the Christianity ethos threw away the eastern belief of reincarnation. This approach was taken in order to make people believe that they only had one chance at life and any hope of a second chance was stripped away. You better get it right in this life or else!?

Donations would be required to the kings and queens in the name of God and this kept the status quo going by keeping the oppressed, oppressed. While people walked around shrouded by fear, money was counted by the elite and powerful and the divide continued. I never understood why God needed money, even as a child, I thought, *what does he want with it? Couldn't he just make it if he was so powerful?*

Nevertheless, people have always made donations to the churches and never questioned where the money truly went. Money is a physical thing and cannot be taken into the formless to be used by God!? So where does all the money go in religion? You could argue it goes into promoting the word of God or buildings to worship him, but where do all the leftovers go?

If you believe that religion is truly there to spread love and unity, I respect you. I too have seen this in my immediate life with the work that's done at the food bank where I volunteer. However, I find it hard to digest that religion is there to serve everyone on a mass scale when places like the Vatican exist. Ask yourself, how can there be poverty in the world when such a human marvel exists? The entire city has been funded purely from the constructs of religion. Does this not seem the slightest bit corrupt to you? It really feels uneasy to me.

In 2013 the Vatican issued financial figures that it's holdings of precious metals alone equated to the sum of $50 million dollars. Imagine if that money were to be distributed to the countries around the world who truly needed it, wouldn't God have preferred that? Or would he have rather it go towards another golden throne? I am aware that $50 million dollars in ratio to the world's financial deficit is a drop in the ocean, but it just puts things into context.

So, what about Jesus? Was he the son of God? I truly believe that there once was a man named Jesus who walked the planet, but again, who he truly was has been warped by man. Jesus, on a fundamental level, is no different to you or I. We will discuss this later in the book. I believe that his soul was enlightened to the state that we cannot comprehend. I believe that he chose to come to this planet to shift the vibration of the world. He chose to come here free of any karmic bonds and show us how easy life can be if we have faith, trust and love everything. Through his behaviour, he demonstrated the real reason why we choose to occupy and visit this planet; to love. Jesus showed us that we are here to create a loving and peaceful world. He showed us that through love, we can evolve and transcend our barbaric ways that are created by the ego. Through helping others, we can create heaven on earth for everyone.

Jesus was also able to communicate with spirit and received messages which aided him whilst he was on the planet. Much like my friend Jo, Jesus spoke the language of love which is required to reach that elevated state of communication. He knew he was *in* this world but not *of* this world. With this knowing, his consciousness could communicate with his true self that resided in spirit.

The Bible forbids that we consult so-called mediums or fortune tellers, as it is a form of devil worshipping. All who do attempt to communicate with the *dead* shall be deceived and tricked by the devil who masquerades as deceased loved ones. 'If a person who turns to mediums and necromancers, whoring after them, I will set my face against that person and will cut him off among his people.' That was a verse from Leviticus 20:6. What a harsh sentence to write. How did you feel reading it? For me, it was certainly fear inducing, almost sick with the terminology that was used. God sounds like someone who is not to be trifled with or disrespected for that matter. You can see why people played their position. Again, these man-made egoic traits often crop up with *God* and he doesn't sound very flexible, just like the ego!

Kings and queens wrote the message that mediums were evil into the good book in order to stop people from realising their infinite potential. This was just another way of controlling people to conform through fear. Jesus was able to receive messages from spirit but no one else will be allowed to! The fact is that Jesus was made of the same flesh and blood that we are, and we all have the ability to communicate with the spirit world. Our pineal glands, or third eye as it is commonly known, have become calcified over time and we have become so out of touch with other possibilities due to society and our conditioning. When we choose to reside on the ego plane of consciousness, other dimensions seem a whimsical reality.

I believe that some of Jesus' core teachings remain true in the Bible and that some of the words that he spoke were recorded with relative accuracy. However, the whole idea of Jesus telling us to live a good life so that we will be rewarded is just another egoic trait. The idea of Jesus saying that we will burn in hell if we do not follow and worship God is again another fallacy added in by man.

Jesus was depicted as wearing nothing but sandals and a robe. Did he feel the need to portray himself as a man of wealth? No, he walked amongst the thieves, beggars and prostitutes with no judgement, just love for them. Did he fight back when people were horrible to him? No, he understood why they were like they were and simply loved them for they were a facet of God. For me, these are the true events of that person who walked the same planet as us. All Jesus did was inspire pure love in everything and everyone. When things start to contradict one another and the message of unconditional love gets warped by fear, the truth becomes corrupt.

One thing to consider is that Jesus was indeed, a brown or olive-skinned Middle Eastern Jew, not a white man which is so often portrayed by Christianity. Why is this? If you believe what history suggests, then Jesus was born in the labelled region of Palestine. He was born in the town of Bethlehem, so for egoic purposes, he was a Palestinian. His parents travelled to Bethlehem from Nazareth which is located in Israel. This would make him far from a white man. Not that the colour of his skin was of any great importance, for ultimately all colour is an illusion which we will look at in a chapter about quantum physics later on. The fact that Jesus is often portrayed as a white man is deceptive and once again manipulates what is true for egoic purposes. Why was Jesus whitewashed?

Christianity was started in the 1st century by a sect of Jewish people in Judea soon after Jesus had died. The Romans were quick to witness the power of the words that Jesus Christ had spoken. They saw how his message and teachings had grown over the years and adopted the religion of Christianity into their own empire in 313 AD. They used the words that Jesus had spoken as a tool of manipulation; much like their swords and spears did. A rigid belief system was then created by the name of religion and was coupled with fear. This powerful combination helped to contribute to the ever-expanding Roman empire.

Christianity then became widespread all over the world as the years progressed. Many powerful rulers saw how efficient the word of Christ was to control people. They used their power to make the religion malleable in order to suit their needs. As centuries progressed, rulers adapted the message and image of Christ in order to appeal to the masses. The elite that held the most wealth could employ the best artists to paint any figure of their choosing. Jesus' image was then essentially whitewashed overtime so that it appealed to the people of the western world.

Jesus was depicted as being white for *commercial* reasons due to the black slave trade. Black slaves were considered to genuinely have a lower IQ than white people! This myth was spread overtime, where eventually white and black people considered it to be fact. Slaves were also seen as being a sub-human product; a lesser race. The idea of a black or olive-skinned Jesus wouldn't fit the ideal of a powerful leader, so he had a facelift and was portrayed as a beautiful white man. There were white slaves at the time as well, as were there black slave owners; but on the whole, it was the Africans who were most oppressed by the slave trade.

The earliest painting of Jesus Christ is apparently in the Coptic museum in Cairo, Egypt. In it, he is portrayed as a black man. If slaves would have known that Jesus had a similar skin colour to that of their own, they would not have believed in the lie that they were all worthless. Imagine if this image had been widely received and word spread that Jesus was not white - the slave trade would have crumbled a lot sooner than it did. Instead, using a well-constructed lie, many slaves accepted that they were a lesser race and never rose against the oppression that they experienced. I could devote an entire book to this topic because it is just another example of how the ego of man can rewrite the truth in order to suit his own agenda.

Another option to consider is that numerous people wrote and shared their views in the Bible. For me, it is easy to identify where man has stepped in to rewrite some parts though. As soon as fear steps in, you know the ego has had an influence. The Bible has many different accounts of events from various sources. We all have very different perspectives of things and so the Bible is one big collective book of perspectives that are neither right or wrong. It only becomes invalid when fear dominates a story. The positive events in the Bible could have been documented by an optimist and the negative ones written by a pessimist. Either way, we will never know as we were never there!

A huge contradiction which demonstrates where a separate opinion may have been interjected into the Bible was one of where Jesus went mad! This is where Jesus apparently flipped out and went full-blown rage mode. He flipped tables up and smashed them to pieces, as he wasn't happy that people were selling cattle and other commodities in a temple that was God's house. That sounds like the workings of the ego, doesn't it? The whole planet is God's house, not a designated building with four walls and a placard outside.

Rather than educating the people as to why this was wrong and being dignified about the whole event, Jesus decided that his usual, loving, understanding ways would have to take a back seat for that moment. By behaving like this, wouldn't it detract from the message of his life? There are quite a few examples in the Bible of Jesus behaving with an ego. I have just chosen this one example to demonstrate how messages can be misinterpreted and falsely documented.

This example shows how rage can be justified in the Bible if done in the name of God, after all Jesus did it. The fact that it is okay to behave in such an aggressive or volatile way, doesn't sit well with me. Jesus' behaviour that day demonstrated that it is fine to go along and destroy anything as long as it is in the name of the Lord, after all, isn't that what the God of ego wants?

In my opinion, this event was either falsely documented or a classic case of an event that has been exaggerated by subjective perception. Righteousness can be achieved by any means necessary, as long as it leads to God... This is the mantra of the ego.

Some of the greatest, most heinous atrocities in the world, were and still are committed in the name of God. The series of the western holy wars were known as the crusades, and they lasted nearly two hundred years. Over a million people died because of this. Protestants and Catholics are still, to this day, arguing and divided over whose God is more valid. Homosexuals are still ostracised by some religious organisations for their lifestyle. The *holy* inquisition was set up by the Catholic church to punish heresy throughout Europe in the 12th century. The inquisition is famous for its torture and persecution towards Muslims and Jews. Abortion clinics are also attacked in the name of God. Fascist and racist groups like the KKK revolve around the name of God. The list is endless.

I was fascinated by the Knights Templar growing up, who paraded the famous red cross around as their coat of arms and did their work in the name of God. They were nothing more than the equivalent to our modern day money launderers. They sold protection to the rich and powerful and were just glorified muscle. The Knights Templar conducted their business in a self-righteous sense and became a very powerful force. Through murder, exploitation and muscle, they became a powerful foe. As their reputation grew, so did their wealth and power. All of this was achieved while adopting a righteous persona in the name of God. I use the Knights Templar as yet another example of how anyone can twist the truth of God in order to accomplish anything that their fragile ego demands. With this ideal, anything could have been written in the Bible to justify man's materialistic needs.

If you still find it hard to believe that man would corrupt the message of God for his own benefit, consider one of the most famous examples demonstrated by Henry the VIII. He begged the Pope for his marriage to Catherine of Aragon to be annulled, to which the Pope refused. Henry then broke away from the Vatican and had parliament declare him supreme head of the Church of England. The Archbishop of Canterbury then granted Henry a divorce in 1533. Henry twisted the rules to suit his needs, all in the name of God. Henry essentially created his own branch of religion to which many still follow today. But who's religion was right? The original Roman Catholics, that Henry was first part of, or his new Church of England religion? The answer is that neither are right or wrong. They are both examples of man's illusory thinking. Both religions demonstrate how man can create laws and hide behind them in the name of God.

Throughout this chapter, I have demonstrated how ego has slipped into the Bible and religion in general. Because of this, this is how people who follow religion could perceive God. The God of religion that we are all so familiar with will heal you, but only if you have been good. He will punish you if you have made a mistake. You must worship him and pay him a fee. The God who judges all of us and scrutinises every little thing we do. Do all of these characteristics sound like something that a divine, omnipotent, loving force would do? Or do they sound very much like that of the ego that we have studied in previous chapters?

It is obvious where man has shoehorned his opinions of God into the Bible over time. The tyrannical God, that prevails when he is not happy, is the God that millions still worship to this day. Millions still believe that only a certain few will get into heaven; similar to teachers picking the best students in class at school. The whole message of unconditional love and tolerance for everything has been hugely contradicted because of man's egoic input. The God that people worship out of fear is constructed from the very same traits that we are trying to transcend and evolve away from. This is the whole reason why we chose to come to this planet in the first place; to learn what we already are, which is love.

I recently read a book called *The Bhagavad Gita* which translates to *The song of the Lord*. It is a book about Indian spirituality and was written before the Bible. I will never forget the words in that book that describe the ego. *A poisonous agency* is the terminology that was used to describe the ego and how it affects us. Literally, the ego is the false self and not who we truly are. With this graphic diction in mind, this *poisonous agency* has been allowed to creep into many religions and corrupt the pure and divine message that was once delivered by Jesus. A message of love.

The Bible teaches fear and punishment and that is not a God that I want to be part of or believe in for that matter. The Bible will have you believe that Jesus was God's son and superior to us mere mortals, but nothing could be further from the truth. The fact is that we are all God. This may baffle you and I will leave you to ponder this thought, which we will address in great depth later on in the book.

I am aware that I may have come across very negatively in the last chapter about religion in general. As stated at the beginning of this chapter, religion has helped many people elevate themselves from dark places; this can only be a good thing. My take on religion in this chapter is that anything can be abused and twisted if you allow it. Religion is a product of the ego which encourages separateness, hence why there are so many variations of religion all claiming to hold the truth. Can we not just love one another without placing a label on it or a set of conditions which religions so often do?

Religion will say that it offers a one-way corridor to God. Organisations will claim that the only way to God is through a certain set of beliefs and taught methods. These ideals teach fear and are false. To say that a one size fits all program will work for everyone is naive. There is not one thing on this planet that is identical, we are all unique. Even identical twins have different fingerprints, they have their own uniqueness about them. We each plan and create a very unique journey for ourselves which will ultimately lead us to a path of realisation and awakening as to who and what God is.

You could say that I live in the past to write about religion and that all past is illusion and clinging. And you would be right. We must focus on the present to progress forward in life, but the past can help us to see where we have gone wrong and still do in the present day. Religion still exists today in various forms, so that is why I choose to write about it as it still has a lot of negative and fearful control over people. Religion can still make individuals do radical things in the name of God. Greed and segregation still exist in religious organisations, so that is why I feel it necessary to write about it. Have we learnt from the acts of error that our ancestors once operated from?

I have, at times, allowed my ego to dictate the writings of this chapter in order to give myself an air of self-righteousness and purity. The very fact that I have written about how I feel about religion demonstrates that I still have many attachments to the unjust events of the world. It shows that my ego is very much alive. I have already spoken about having attachments and judgements. They are part of the suffering that the ego creates.

As I stated at the beginning of this chapter, if religion has helped you to discover who you are, then discard this chapter and send love to those who have abused the name of God for selfish gain. They are on their own path and eventually their actions will bring about events in which they will learn the truth.

Anyway, let's move away from the old school religious texts that we know of, and acknowledge a new method of manipulation that we have in today's current society - media. This leads us nicely onto our next chapter, S&S.

40

S&S

I was originally going to call this chapter the media and structure, but I liked the S&S ring to it, so I chose that instead; it makes it sound a bit snazzier, yeah? S&S simply means screens and structure in my little mind! We have studied the power of religion in the previous chapter and its unquestionable influence to control individuals on a mass level. Now it is time to study a new kind of manipulation.

I am not into conspiracy theories as things just simply are as they are, but this chapter has come about from me looking at the world objectively since my awakening and seeing it for what it really is. As stated at the beginning of the previous chapter, anything can be used for good or bad in life. Anything can be abused if we allow it to. I constantly speak of balance, as I am such a firm believer in it. It's one of the main things that I teach students at college.

Media can be used productively in many ways. I have watched so many YouTube videos that have helped to broaden my thinking and challenge my analytical thinking. Some videos I have discarded, others I have found useful, either way, all have helped me to develop.

I have read so many articles online as well; again, some good, some bad. Some articles have helped to reshape my own perspective on the world. Some have even touched the core of who I am and allowed me to develop into a more loving individual. Social media has even helped to promote this very book through the beauty of Instagram. I am extremely grateful that platforms like that exist so people can promote their message and get their voice heard by the world; it's amazing really, when you consider it like that. The following will demonstrate how I feel about the media when the balance has gone and we spend all of our waking time staring at a screen, as it can become unhealthy.

The majority of society are now happy to share everything online and social media has slowly crept up on us and has begun to swamp our lives. I write this chapter simply because of what I observe on a daily basis. Just take a look for yourself the next time you venture out somewhere and observe how many people are actually living in the moment around them or looking at a screen.

I studied *1984* in my college years, a book written by George Orwell. I didn't think much of it at the time as I was too stoned to comprehend most of it, to be frank! In hindsight though, this book predicts the world that we are now living in. "Big brother is watching you!" was one of the main lines I remember from the book.

Social media now captures our every thought, like, family tree, location, our everything, all in one handy little profile. Big brother can most definitely see all that we do in an overt way! If you have never read the book *1984*, I encourage you to. I do remember it being quite interesting, even with my apathetic stance back then. I may even read it again myself to see what I initially missed, but nevertheless, it left an impression upon me even if I was too *cool* for it. So here we go, controversy time! The following is my opinion and nothing more. Read it objectively and see what you think.

I believe that 1% of the global population are responsible for controlling 99% of the population. Call *them* whatever you want, but *they* have had a foolproof system in place that has worked for thousands of years and keeps evolving. I'm talking about an elite power that is above the government as we know it, and the politicians that we see on TV. The people that we see on TV believe they have power but are only playing their role in the environment that has been created for them by the elite.

I am not saying that these tools of control are a bad thing, they simply are, for we all need a system or else there would be chaos in the world of the ego. Capitalism is a system that works and keeps everyone in check,

I have no problem with that. However, there are more extreme forms of control and manipulation developing as we evolve.

Media has been around for decades and has only gained more power and momentum over the years. Fear has always been projected from the television screen, but now it can be projected from a screen in our hands wherever we are. The media is there to fuel current fires, control us and divide us. The media always has an agenda that can easily create tension amongst everyone. Everything that we see on a screen is what we are intended to see; we see it for a reason. The only events that make the news are ones that can manipulate us and create division through fear.

Media has always had a strong rhetoric that can easily push and toy with our self-righteous emotions. The media can activate our ego at the flick of a switch. We argue about current topics amongst ourselves whilst being controlled by the system. Sometimes emotions can spill over when people have had enough, causing spontaneous knee-jerk reactions without much thought. The media perpetuates current events and adds subliminal hate into every situation, while appearing to care about our wellbeing. The media can make any innocent person or event look bad with a subliminal narrative. The media can paint a superficial picture of anything or anyone.

People who choose to take everything on face value, without doing their own research, can be easily swept away with it all; I was once that person. When events reach a watershed, rioting can even reach the streets to convey how people feel. When we riot and rebel, we create more fear and division amongst ourselves. As a result, we then bring stricter controlling measures upon ourselves from the domineering forces. When riots happen, millions of pounds of damage are caused which inevitably lead to the taxpayer's money being called upon to pay for the repairs. People are literally digging their own hole through their egoic actions.

Crowds follow crowds, as this is how the ego behaves - it doesn't want to be left behind. The matrix that we live in encourages a crowd-like mentality. With this structure and herd mentality in place, we would be fools to fight against it, for it protects us. However, what if we could bypass the system and create our own realities via our thoughts? What I have just stated may sound like nonsense, but you are creating your reality as we speak with your subconscious thinking.

If we don't know and realise that we have the power to create our dream life, we will allow others to control our thoughts and life for us out of fear. The natural workings of the ego that we have all been programmed with in our human spacesuits can be easily exploited. This is prevalent in the western part of the globe by what we watch on our little screens.

When numbers of a group rise above 100 or so, verbal means of communication on a personal level are no longer effective, as the numbers are too high. When the numbers of groups start to expand, Chinese whispers start to happen, and the message of the leader can be lost in translation. In order to control an expanding group in an effective way, a method of control must be installed. Illusion, division and fear are some of the greatest control methods known to man. When applied effectively, the majority of people fall in line. After all, we are all animals, and no one wants to be left out, so we follow the masses. Self-preservation is what we are programmed to do as a species.

Take politics for instance, which we have already discussed. There are numerous viewpoints that we can choose to listen to and adopt into our beliefs if they appear valid to us. This doesn't mean that what we believe in is right, but it is true to us. Much like time, the truth is always subjective to an individual. Individuals will then behave in a certain way in order to match that of their adopted illusory stance.

Considering the above paragraph, you can see how easy it is to control people with illusory beliefs while keeping everyone divided at the same time. When we are prevented from becoming one, our egos have all the power they need. If citizens are forever squabbling amongst themselves about egoic matters that hold no actual validity, then the governing forces can go about their daily business as the mayhem unfolds. Illusions such as social hierarchy, religion, money and politics create much division within the world and perpetuate social structure and the status quo. The media helps to reinforce these illusions so that they appear as reality.

As I write this chapter, the Coronavirus is rife in the media. Countries have gone into lockdown to prevent any further spread of the virus. Individuals are isolating and the media portrays mass negativity, and that people are arguing over toilet rolls!

We have been forced to spend much time with ourselves while in isolation. By the time you read this the lockdown will have passed and as a race of humans, I feel that we will have evolved even further as a result of it all. Remember that we are all eternal, infinite spirit. With this notion in place, *problems* on Earth that our human egoic minds encounter can be seen as opportunities to grow from the soul's perspective.

When individuals forget who they really are and buy into the fear-based, media-driven system that shapes society, they will become part of the problem. If you perceive everything in the media to be true, then you are choosing to lower your vibration and become a match to events that are being portrayed. You are essentially creating your own reality via the law of attraction and will attract scenarios along your path that match that of your expectations. I will discuss perception and the law of attraction in much more detail later in the book. I keep saying it and always will, there are always two sides to the coin, if you refuse to see the other side, then you are choosing to fall victim to your ego.

Our western society has rigid thinking due to how we have been conditioned to think from an early age. Only what we have learnt at school, college or university can be considered true and if it is not in the *curriculum*, then it must be false. If you want to be rich and powerful then you must succeed in the matrix that has been designed for us to live and compete in.

The only way we can achieve anything in this life is to work hard and consistently right? Long hours and gruelling stress are the only ways you make a mark for yourself. Well, if that's what you believe, then it will be the truth. All of this conditioning stems from our school years: do well in school, work hard, get a good job and be a good citizen.

When we first go to nursery, we embrace our own individual uniqueness. If a child has been in a healthy, loving environment for the first three years of their life, then they will be full of self-belief. If you were to ask all happy children at nursery who was the best, each would usually say that they are! After a few years in school, when the ego has developed around the age of six or seven, a child's answer to who is the best will have changed. They will then point to someone who has been labelled as the *intelligent* or *successful* one; why is this?

The school environment forces children to compete with each other. They are then labelled and put into the category of high achievers and underachievers. Come on, everyone remembers the *yellow table* at school? It was the table where teachers thought they were being subtle by naming the table after colours or animals. However, we all knew what it meant to sit at that table; whoever sat there was effectively an underachiever. But why have we labelled children who sit on *that* table as underachievers? Because those children didn't conform to the expectations of the system that we are all nurtured into. Maybe the classroom environment wasn't suited to that unique nature of the child in question and they were meant to flourish in other ways, but never got the chance to. We, therefore, labelled them as failures from the age of five! It is so sad, and I too was guilty of labelling fellow classmates.

Albert Einstein once summed up what I am trying to say about the system that we live in in a more eloquent way! He said, "Everybody is a genius. But if you judge a fish by its ability to climb a tree, it will live its whole life believing that it is stupid." We are all unique souls who arrive on this planet ready to serve our unique purpose. We are not all meant to follow a rigid path that determines what a *success* is. The criteria that we have to achieve in order to be considered a success by others, is one that fits in with the working mechanics of the western world.

If we do not get the grades we are expected to at school, we will amount to nothing. School puts a subtle competitive emphasis on everything that children do. You are graded, put into sets and classes. This implies from an early age that we are different and separate; something the ego really identifies with. We then strive to outdo our fellow man in sport and exams. This then spills over and continues into our working lives. For some, this means working a monotonous 9-5 job, while chasing promotions and climbing the corporate ladder.

While all of this is happening, we are constantly paying into the system that has been created for us with absolutely no argument. It is something that has been conditioned into us and it's just something that you do. As I have mentioned earlier in the book, when I would bump into old school friends, the topic of conversation would quickly switch to jobs and my current status. I felt that if I hadn't achieved a particular something by a particular age, I would be labelled as a failure or an outcast. I would fear that I wasn't where I needed to be at that point in my life and allow my ego to oppress me.

The only way that you will be happy in life is to chase the American dream. This is the house, the car, the job, the kids and don't forget the dog too! All of these criteria consist of external factors that the ego feeds off. Materialistic possessions are the only way to happiness; thus, you end up paying more money into the system with all your hard-earned cash. You will always need a bigger house, a better car, you must have that promotion and your children must succeed. When you feel like you have made it to a certain degree, what do you do? Keep going and make more, which is all the ego knows, or be content with what you have? If we are happy and content with what we have, we may feel the need to show how well we have done to others.

We can choose to post our lives all over social media, and paint the perfect picture if we want to, but what is the real reason we do this? The ego is secretly seeking the approval of others. Why do we think this way? Again, it links back to our conditioning at school and the system that we have grown to know. While we post our achievements on social media, new and comparative measures of success are being fed to us via the news and other media profiles.

Growing up with Dean and Lee, we had bricks to communicate with, otherwise known as extremely heavy and oversized mobile phones. You had a short battery life and credit seemed to vanish as soon as you had topped up. No contracts for us kids back then! If we arranged to meet up, you would have to place real trust in the other person. You would have to believe that they would show up when and where they said they would. Rarely would we have credit on our portable bricks, so there was no way of communicating with people until they actually arrived. There were no apps and you could only store ten text messages at a time in your memory. You couldn't receive any more messages until you deleted some of the old ones!

As time progressed, so has technology - at a rapid rate. The internet has also evolved and has every piece of information on it that you could ever wish to access at the click of a button. Technology now makes the internet accessible from almost anywhere and no longer do you need to wait for a dial tone just to access it!

Camera phones came out around the mid 2000s and then Facebook arose as a social media giant. Facebook was mainly accessed through your computer back then, but now it's all conveniently in the palm of your hand. Videos then became accessible on your phones and we now carry these little androids with us wherever we go.

On a lighter note, younger people reading this will never understand the torment of having to carry around a portable CD player. This clumsy device was carted down the streets about your person. It would usually be held because it wouldn't fit in your pocket. I used to watch out for every bump on the pavement to avoid the repercussions of having the CD skip if you were unfortunate enough to knock it. It's amazing that we can now have thousands of songs at our disposal, without having to lug around a CD player that had about 20 songs on each disk. Like I mentioned in the beginning of this chapter, everything can have its pros and cons. Technology really is amazing, but it all depends on how you use it.

Media and technology have now created an insatiable society. Everything is spontaneous and can happen at the click of a button. I can now purchase anything in a split second or have the latest song in a heartbeat. Attention spans have now become minimal, as we wait for the next notification. What does this do for our relationships? If we are being conditioned to believe everything should be instantaneous, surely our relationships and life should be the same? If our relationships are not going the way we believe they should be going, how will the conditioning of our insatiable culture prompt us to respond to this? Surely we will want immediate results in our relationship too!?

Surveys are online to make you feel inferior about yourself via national averages. How will this affect your relationships? If you aren't matching up to the national statistics of the average Joe, then you are behind the times. The ego does not want to be left behind and will therefore do anything to obtain a new thrill.

I can relate to this with my behaviour in my own personal relationships, past and present. Had this level of technology been around when I was growing up, I am sure that it would have contributed to my already discombobulated state surrounding what a relationship should be. Plus, I am so thankful to the fact that having a camera on my phone was not available in my youth, as this could have led to irreversible damage!

The news has always been around and is a form of gossip; the ego loves gossip! The news is mainly filled with doom and gloom which the ego can relate to and can depress us, if we allow it to. *What an evil world we live in,* the ego thinks! Media and the news work in tandem with pharmaceutical companies who have a solution to all our problems if we need it.

With the beauty of these little handheld devices that we all now possess, our subconscious minds can permanently be infiltrated. We no longer have to wait for specific times of the day to do it either, unlike the old days of scheduled bulletins on the TV. Breaking news is now sent to your phone to alter your mood at any given moment. We are also contactable 24/7 which can make us feel like there is no escape from it all. Of course, we could just turn off our phone, but the ego will not allow that as we must be up to date with everything that is going on. Fear of missing out is the ego's worst nightmare!

Do people wonder why depression in our society is at an all-time high? America statistically has the highest rate of depression in the world. Why is this? Is it because media is everywhere, and the statistics are slowly allowed to filter into the subconscious minds? One in ten adults will get depression! Scientific research and studies are released that confirm that depression is caused by a chemical imbalance in the brain; it's unavoidable.

All of these facts and statistics are being absorbed by the mind. They can then be manifested into our own realities if we are not conscious of our thoughts and what we allow to penetrate our minds. People do not realise the power of the mind. What you think about will ultimately determine your reality and the health of your body.

With all of these statistics and figures floating around, is it any surprise that more and more people are being diagnosed with ailments that are prominent in the news? People are then sent to the doctors, who prescribe them a magic pill, which encases a holistic solution to every human problem known to man. Karl Marx once described religion as the *opium of the people* with the sense that it could cure or numb all fears. Now the new religion is in the shape of a pill.

People now have a new *opium* in the form of a convenient capsule that can be obtained easily. These drugs are proven to help and are all supported by studies released to us through the media. Can you see what a vicious cycle has been created? The majority of the media portray most events as negative in order to depress and scare us. At the same time, it can suggest a subliminal solution to all of our problems by visiting our GP. Our doctor can prescribe us the magic pill to cure all of our problems, which the pharmaceutical companies ultimately profit from.

This is why I feel that the media is our new modern religion. A constant feed of depression and fear to make us feel depressed with the world. The only way that you will ever find happiness is to be better than everyone else or via a pill. Consumerism doesn't do any harm to those pushing it. You must have all the latest, shiniest possessions. If you still feel at a loss, there is always a pill that is readily available to make you feel better. Depression is good for the economy.

If you have suffered from depression as I once did, why is this? In my experience I just didn't feel good enough in myself; I hated who I was. The world was against me and I was a victim. This was because I was constantly comparing myself to others and believing that I was living in an evil world which was being portrayed by the media. I hated my own existence due to childhood issues. The only time I was happy was when I was drinking, but alcohol is a depressant and only increased my worries the next day. I would then escape these feelings by having another drink; and so the cycle continued.

If you are currently on antidepressants, there is no shame in this, but they are masking the real problem. Would you like to get to the bottom of why you truly feel like you do? What are you burying deep inside of you? We will explore this in a few chapters time.

We are not meant to spend our short time on this planet depressed, we are meant to rejoice in our existence. Maybe you have forgotten how truly unique and amazing you are? You have a mission while you are here, and it is not to be depressed. Are you addicted to anything which is perpetuating your depression? All addictions arise from combatting some form of deep subconscious pain. Could your addiction be in the media?

Just the other night, I watched a program about how addictive apps and social media can be. Could this exacerbate depression? These very apps stimulate parts of the brain in the same way that gambling would to an addict. People can become dependent on the affirmation and approval of others via the little *like* button. If that post isn't getting the required number of likes that the individual wants or needs, then the individual could be forced to post something else to make up for shortcomings. I have known people like this that post numerous times in a day. It is an addiction, all simulated by the ego. This fuels a constant need for approval from others for the individual. They are not content with just *being* and people can end up valuing the opinions of others more than their own.

I really feel for the youth of today growing up in this dense, media-saturated culture. What the youth see on screen may be seen as real to them, but I think if it is on a screen, chances are, it is far from real. I am fortunate enough at my age to have seen both sides of the coin. The youth know no different and if you are not on social media, you will be seen as an outcast by peers.

Media has contributed to perpetuating narcissism amongst our society. It happens in general, but especially for teens. Selfies and vanity are rife. A filter can be added to any picture in order to make it appear *better* than it is. So much pressure is put onto the youth to look a certain way. Photoshop can create the *perfect* image, but what is perfect? The sense of separateness is being encouraged by these trends. I experienced the same in my days growing up but at least I could escape the media, now it is omnipresent. Bullying can even happen online causing youngsters to feel unsafe even when at home. Home is no longer a safe haven, for the pressures to be someone who society accepts is constantly following youth.

Most social media platforms encourage unity and connection, but the ego always creeps in. Competition can then become the norm online, which we have already addressed with the ego previously. It strips away the sense of a collective consciousness and that we are all one. On the surface, social media platforms appear to solidify our bonds but can sometimes create more of a wedge between us all. I do feel very harsh and cynical saying all of this, so much good can, and has, come from social media, but these statements have come from what I witness on a daily basis.

41

MEDIA AND SUGAR

Media can drive what is acceptable in our society and what isn't. Alcohol is deemed as being a perfect way to unwind. It is totally acceptable online and on the TV. Wild pictures of last night's antics can be posted online, only to be met with approval and likes from peers. Drunken activity can be viewed as humorous, even when someone is vomiting or causing damage to property. Believe me, I've been there!

Nights out can hardly be recalled because of the copious amounts of alcohol that were consumed, but this doesn't matter as long as it makes for entertaining reading the next day. Through the media, alcohol has become socially acceptable and the norm of society. If the glamour and social norms were taken away from alcohol, what would we have? We would just be consuming a poisonous substance that has no glamour about it. I was once that person who conformed to these social norms and thrived off it, never questioning our real purpose as to why we are here. I enjoyed it all and wouldn't change a thing, but looking back it all seems a bit empty.

Medical research and scientific studies have been done to show that when alcohol is consumed in moderation, it is good for you, or at least that's what the media says. With this information at the forefront of our minds, we do not feel so guilty about our choices because it's good for us. Therefore, we are going to pay into the alcohol industry as they do us a great service. The only problem is we can't always be sure that what we read is true or legitimate.

The studies that were conducted on alcohol consumption and its effects on the body could be true. The only puzzling aspect of it all is that the alcohol industry paid the government to fund the research, what does that suggest? The alcohol industry in the UK alone was worth £46 billion to the economy in 2014. Compare that with the average $90 billion made in the US each year and you're gaining a pretty clear picture as to why the alcohol industry wants you to believe that a few glasses each day is good for you. Hangover cures are even offered online and on the TV, as if to suggest that drinking too much is an unavoidable occurrence sometimes!

When I now see a drunk person, which is a rarity as I am in bed at 10 o'clock at the latest, all I see is a deep cry for help. What has caused that person to act with such confusion? What has driven them to feel that getting absolutely trolleyed is their only viable option for that moment in time? Why did they want to relinquish responsibility for their life at that particular point? Maybe I am being boring again and they are just having fun, but I can't help but wonder what pain lurks deep within that person?

You could be thinking that I am being oversensitive due to the problems that I suffered with in the past? I truly believe that if an individual has discovered happiness from within, any external lure such as alcohol isn't even considered. When situations in my life would not pan out the way I wanted, I would seek to have time off from reality via intoxication. No self-loving person who respects themselves and truly knows who they are would want to willingly put toxic and poison into their perfect body.

I have always found it fascinating that posting pictures of drinking online is acceptable, but alcohol is a poison and a drug. It statistically affects more people than narcotics. Broken homes, criminal damage, strain on the NHS, police time, violence, the list is endless. All of these problems stem from people's pain and unhappiness that are blocked out by alcohol.

Now, I don't want alcohol to get a bad reputation because I deem it so, as anything in life can be abused, but the media makes this drug socially acceptable and the social norm for dealing with problems in a crafty overt way.

Now, what if I were to stroll into work one day and say, "Oh my goodness, I feel rough, I snorted way too much coke last night." It would be met with immediate horror and concern because of social stigmas, legalities, and conditioning. People would sit me down, possibly encourage me to seek help and advise me to have counselling. However, had I rolled in with a hangover, it would be viewed as funny and the norm. The reality is that I chose to deliberately poison and abuse my body, isn't that a problem and a cry for help?

There's a stark difference in the legality between drugs and alcohol, but I, myself, do not see any difference between the two; both can be abused. Anything can be abused for that matter, including food, exercise, screen time, prescription drugs, literally anything! My point is simply to show what a powerful force the media is, for they can make us believe that anything is acceptable, even if it's not in line with our body or soul. Fast food and alcohol offer no nutritious goodness for the body, yet some of us persist to indulge in these past times frequently.

What if the media suddenly started promoting heroin, what would happen? Fancy adverts with trendy, hipster people in clubs shooting up. Gone are our preconceived images of homeless people, sat in the back alleys with needles hanging out of their arms. These images are now replaced with cool, contemporary people injecting *diesel* into their veins, while in a trendy ambience.

Imagine a scene in the coolest night club, but substitute the champagne for heroin, does this paint a more appealing picture than the one of addicts now? How long would it be before we decided to try it for ourselves? Would the youth want to replicate the cool image that was being portrayed by the celebrities? Designer needles could also be purchased in order to maximise your high. I am aware that this current example is extreme and can be met with many arguments, but it is just a satirical example of the power of the media. We need to realise the power of the media and the effect that it can have on the mind: positive or negative.

At this stage of my life, social media plays a small part in my life. I have Instagram and a few meditation apps, how times change!? In the past it would have probably been porn or dating apps trying to get women to send me photos! I used to be on Facebook, but it just doesn't do it for me. I tried it and I didn't see the point, but that's just me. I have always been a private person in a way, hence why I chose to write a book about my dark past aimed to be read by millions.

You may be thinking that this is nonsense that I am spouting and that social media is good. Like I have said, anything can be good or bad, it is just a case of how you look at it. I will say this though, be aware of what is filtering into your subconsciousness, especially before bed. This will stay in your mind and will eventually reside in your subconsciousness while you sleep. Looking at negative material before bed will marinate your mind with a fusion of negativity. You will sleep and awaken in the morning full of doom and gloom if that is what you were viewing the prior night.

When I was younger, numerous people in my family would watch the news at ten o'clock. What a way to end the day, watch all the calamities happening in the world and then dwell on them for the rest of the evening. Why does the news portray the world as such a terribly awful place? It can be depressing to say the least. When you have watched the late-night news, that will be at the back of your mind as you drift off to sleep. Now we have handheld devices to program our last thoughts before we hit the reset button for the day. If you ever wake up feeling like death, could the previous two paragraphs be the cause of it?

I enjoy watching the Walking Dead and people often ask me what I would do in the event of an apocalypse? Some could say that we are already in one! Simply look at any train platform or on a bus. People's eyes are focused firmly on their hand-held robots and unaware of their current surroundings. Add another substance to the mix and you have a recipe for disaster when it comes to people's moods - sugar.

Sugar is a drug. It is addictive and cheap. I once attended a food and nutrition course where I met a very wise gentleman by the name of Henk. He told me that the brain is the greediest of all the organs and the most selfish. It has no regard for the nutrition of any of its fellow organs. It does not care how well the other organs function either. The brain craves all the ingredients to produce the feel-good chemicals, such as dopamine and serotonin. These can be found in abundance in sugar, salt and fat. The brain will trigger messages and thoughts which appear through cravings. The brain is oblivious to obesity and diabetes; it couldn't care less about any of these health issues. As long as the brain is being stimulated, the rest of the body can self-destruct for all it cares.

Why is it that most processed foods taste amazing but are usually bad for us!? Why do you think that when you visit a supermarket checkout, there are copious amounts of tempting treats placed all around you? The manufacturers aren't stupid, just look at the ingredients on the label, it's the brain's dream supply of ingredients, it's what it craves.

With that sugary, chocolatey treat firmly in our grasp, those moments of short-lived happiness can be quickly produced by the brain. What happens when that high wears off though? I need more sugar! We must then chase that easily accessible high which can be found in another bar. It is similar to when I used to snort cocaine, the principle behind it is exactly the same. Many cravings of sugar also stem from a blood sugar imbalance. When sugar is ingested, your blood sugar spikes and your body releases insulin to lower it to a safe level. Insulin can reduce our blood sugar levels to combat the sugar spike. When this happens our bodies then crave the foods that will raise our sugar and energy levels again. So the cycle continues.

Is it any wonder that obesity is becoming a crisis in westernised countries? Recent scientific research has shown that obesity is now becoming one of the leading causes of major cancers. Sugar is cheap to market, manufacture and can deliver us that short-lived high that we will keep returning to. It can temporarily suspend the pain of everyday life, while we indulge in that sweet, moreish treat.

Mixed with the media, sugar can control us. Serotonin is released when we obtain the multiple likes for our posts on social media. The approval of others is what the ego craves. By putting a chocolate biscuit in one hand and a phone in the other, it's a match made in heaven.

Now what happens when trends on social media change and no longer conform to what we usually post? What happens when the likes no longer flood in like they used to? Is it possible that the happiness levels of an individual can become dependent on certain criteria surrounding their social media profiles? If an individual posts a photo or status that they think should warrant 100 likes, what happens when they only receive 50? Would this cause an individual to feel a sense of worthlessness? If an individual is truly dependent on specific criteria, they may even suffer mild depression. What if they have a poor sleep cycle because of this as well?

Each night, people stay up late, staring at their little screens, which emits that warm, familiar blue light. That light can keep people entertained for hours until they realise that they must go to sleep. It is proven that the blue light that is given off from our phones can interfere with our natural sleep patterns. The blue light disturbs the body's natural ability to prepare for sleep. It blocks a hormone called melatonin that makes you sleepy and can disrupt your nights rest.

So, what can we do to combat that drowsy feeling when we wake up feeling exhausted? We can purchase one of those marvellous energy drinks that contain caffeine, chemicals and sugar. The brain is in total awe of your purchase. It adores how you chose to saturate it with all those glorious chemicals in such a short space of time that will uplift its weary state. The body on the other hand is crying out, "How the hell did you manage to get this much sugar into me at one time!?" It's beyond comprehension. The only option your body has to cope with this is to instantly spike your insulin levels, as we discussed earlier. Your body will then store as much of the sugar as it can for future energy as it simply cannot be processed, unless you are an extreme athlete.

After this process has taken place, the short, temporary boost of energy that is experienced will be met with a severe crash and just hours later, life is a grim grind again. The late night that you had has caught up with you and this can cause some people to feel irritable and miserable. While people are in this spent state, it's easy to check social media profiles as they require no physical exertion. Checking to see what our friends have been doing can also affect our mood. Couple that with a notification describing some horrendous event that has just happened in the world and life just seems a dismal existence to say the least. Imagine if this cycle is repeated and becomes a daily way of life, something would have to give.

I touched on mental health earlier. Mental health is everywhere now and it's rife in the media. It is good that people are being made aware of these topics and that it is no longer taboo to talk about them. Emotions and thoughts are being discussed and people are being encouraged to open up, particularly men. This is a real positive step forward and mental health is being globally recognised as a real problem.

Now this is a delicate topic, so I approach it carefully, but does the media add to our current depression levels? I have just stated that it is good that people are being encouraged to open up and talk about things because of public exposure, but can this be a double-edged sword? On the flip side of the coin, if the sugar and media phenomenon continues, will the depression and anxiety epidemic only exacerbate? Why are depression statistics on the rise?

Talking about our emotions is good, but the whole depression topic is everywhere. Are the media adding to the whole problem by stating subliminally that depression is the norm these days? It's kind of a self-fulfilling prophecy sold by the media to manipulate us. While we go about our daily lives, all the background media noise slowly filters into our subconscious minds without us realising. Our minds can then psychosomatically induce symptoms of depression upon us as it is now normal in our society.

What may just be a down day, which we all have from time to time, can suddenly become a much bigger problem. That down day that you had then turned into two and because of mass exposure regarding depression, you make a link between the two and self-diagnose yourself with depression. By acknowledging the rising statistics and giving them our attention, could we then believe that we are depressed when we haven't actually got anything to be depressed about? Where do we go from here? A visit to the doctor who is not going to belittle you and say pull yourself together, he is going to help you. How will he help you? By prescribing a magic pill which fixes all of the world's wrongs.

Reading this back does make me sound very negative and isn't very spiritual at all is it? All I want to do is to encourage people to think for themselves and see a bigger picture with how society and media is run. So many people just follow the crowd. It isn't a personal attack upon the structure of society that keeps us safe, I just feel that there could be a more positive outlook in the media which would help the masses, rather than depressing them.

Depression is good for the economy though, as it forces us to spend money. If we were all happy and content, we wouldn't feel the urge to pump the economy full of our money. This all stems back to the programming that we received in school where we were led to believe that box-ticking external criteria will guarantee happiness. Out do your fellow man, buy a house, a car and get married; when all of these have been achieved, happiness is a dead certainty.

Can you see the purpose of these two chapters and my thinking? That S&S is there to manipulate us and even depress us if we allow it to fall out of balance? We have been conditioned from an early age to believe that happiness is found in external sources separate from ourselves. School bred this ethos into us by encouraging us to become a success; this was done by getting good grades so that you could one day get a good job which would lead to materialistic pleasures.

Nobody wants to be left behind, especially children, as the ego is just beginning to form. If everyone is doing the same thing, then it must be right? It would seem logical to follow the crowd. Social media then continues the cycle as we can see what others have. If we fall behind, we can become depressed and it all boils down to comparison. If we had no comparison, would we become depressed? Social media profiles flaunt success and offer a perfect vision as to what the perfect life should look like. It doesn't matter what anyone else thinks, happiness comes from within, not from the *like* button. You will see that your life is already perfect when you take away the social milestones that we conform to. When you stop comparing and living for the approval of others, you can focus on the state of being, which is in yourself, and consider who you are.

Balance is the key, there are a few dog words that I have, and balance is one of them! If you enjoy a chocolate biscuit, go for it. If you enjoy social media, go for it. If you like buying new things, then do that as well. Take the news with a pinch of salt. When you are able to view it objectively, it's like a real-life soap opera and actually quite entertaining! Just be aware of how much time you give to these pleasures in life as they can creep up on you. Do you choose them, or do they choose you? Has your phone gone off while you have read this book? If so, have you immediately checked it to see what the notification was about, without consciously thinking about it? If yes, then the phone chose you. Try this little exercise every time your phone alerts you. Can you control your impulse to check it?

Happiness comes from within and we will focus on this in the following chapters. Happiness comes from knowing who we are. For if we do not understand who we truly are, how can we possibly understand the world? We will focus on who we truly are as the book progresses for so many of us have forgotten; it took me a few years to remember! The first thing to realise is that we are creators and that we make our own realities. The dreaded ego will have you believe otherwise though and that is why it is time to choose a new way of thinking.

42

Time to Exit the Ego Express

I came up with this little metaphorical concept the other day and really love it! Part of my new job involves me working two days in the inner city at another college under the same provision. I choose to catch the train as it makes the journey a lot quicker.

There is always hustle and bustle on the train platform at 7:30 in the morning. The train arrives and I hop onto it for my commute into the city centre. The train is usually packed and most commuters are like sardines; crammed into a little tin can on rails. The train hurtles forward and projects everyone towards their destinations. It seems chaotic but remember, there is order in chaos.

I often read on the train as it is a good way to start the day with some inspiring texts, but my mind does drift from time to time. I am sure yours has too, even as you have read this book. I guess there is still much practice to be done through my meditations. As my mind drifts, I catch myself looking at each person on the train (without trying to be too creepy) and wonder if everyone does this on a daily basis?

There is always little interaction between people on the journey and people's attention is usually glued to their phones or free newspapers. The newspapers are usually filled with mind numbing sensationalist stories, or tragedies that are occurring in a town near you. Most faces are usually glum and morose and nobody ever looks enthralled. Maybe I am the problem and perceive the whole situation in a negative way and, in fact, these people are happy with their lives. Maybe they look at me and think the same? After all, life is a mirror of how we feel. Either way, I always smile at people and send love to fellow passengers.

Now, who knows where everyone on that train is going but we are all part of the same moment for a brief time. Are those people that share the same space as me happy that they are on that train? Is that what they envisioned themselves doing when they chose to come to this planet? I hope so, but some expressions suggest otherwise to me, again, this is just my perception.

Are we fulfilling our true purpose, or do we just drift along with what society has programmed us to do? Sure we planned karmic events in our pre-birth planning stage, but how we choose to fill in the blanks between those events is totally up to us. That is why we have free will throughout everything we do, and we design our own lives. We are the creators of reality and are responsible for our lives, that is why we should never play the victim.

I call this chapter *the ego express*. I find that so many of us are on the ego express train without even realising and have no idea why we are actually on it. I was guilty of this and it is so easy to get swept along by it. Yes, all that happens is perfect and you will still learn from all events that come your way, but do you really want to be doing what you are doing? You are free to live the life of your dreams, you can create anything. The train example that I have chosen to use is a metaphor for our egos and the rails are the journey or paths our lives can take.

We can let our egos take us for a ride if we allow it and it's now time to make our own path. Don't just board the ego express and let the doors slam behind you. Have you planned your journey? Do you have an idea of where the train is actually taking you? Do you know why you're doing what you're doing or are you just doing what society has told you to do? Are we just hurtling along on this train until death approaches? Are we even ready for death when it arrives? Are we conscious of who we are and what we are doing?

The ego express can be overcrowded and filled with individuals glued to their android screens waiting for the next instalment of bad news or next like. The trivial, political matters are washed down with synthetic food and drink. If we allow this satirical example to consume us, we can end up having no idea where the ego is actually taking us. If we continue to sit on the train that is taking us to a destination we do not want to go to, we are not being conscious.

There is little compassion or humility on board the self-centred ego express. Take note of your ego and wake up to the fact that it is not part of who you truly are. The false self needs recognising, it's never too late to push the emergency stop button and exit the train at the next available stop. Are you truly happy with what you do in your life and career? If yes, then ignore this chapter and use it as toilet paper if a global quarantine starts again. If the answer is no, start to shape your own path and refuse to go with the majority. You can achieve anything if you believe it, for you are the creator. You have part of the creative force that made this Universe inside of you, so use it! Create the life that you came to live today, you deserve it my dear friend.

I have had 32 years of conditioning from society installed into me. Most of my school years were spent worrying whether I was good enough or cleverer than my fellow pupils. I would get upset when exam results did not match the expectations of teachers and peers. Worry would consume me, and I feared that I would be left behind.

Now I realise that all of that was wasted energy and that exam results do not matter; they merely allow you to play your part in a conventional world. As part of my journey I know that I didn't come to this planet to work in an office making millions of pounds. I am not saying this is wrong and if that is what you want to do and you aren't, what is stopping you?

My point is to not waste your life doing what society expects you to do and to do what you truly came to do. Do what your heart tells you to do. If you do anything for the approval of others or to comply with someone's preconceived image of you, then you are not being true to yourself. If making millions is your dream, then go for it, stop procrastinating doing a job you loathe! We will discuss how to make this possible in a few chapters time using a couple of methods. One is via the law of attraction and trust me, it is a law of the Universe, as is physics, gravity and karma. The other way is to reprogram the subconscious mind to create any reality that you want.

It can be hard to reprogram all of those years of false beliefs installed by society, but if you start today, it can happen at a steady pace. I am nearly three years into my rebirth and I practice controlling my mind every day. Start conditioning your own thinking via meditation and positive affirmations. Make your own news in your life and try not to be concerned too much with what is going on elsewhere. Direct your energy where it matters. If news does affect you, make a change by changing yourself, change starts within.

I still have some of the old ways of the world installed in me, but slowly and surely, my old way of thinking seems foreign to me now. This is just to give you an indication of how long it can take to retrain your subconscious mind and begin to live the life that spirit intended you too. You are worth so much more than the status quo.

Is it time for you to step off that hectic, egoic train? The train that is hurtling towards a destination that no one actually has any idea about. Understand that the old, rusty egoic train is part of our human experience but it doesn't mean that we have to stay on it forever. The egoic train has gotten us this far, and it is not a bad thing, we must be thankful, but if we are rooted in that comfortable seat on the train for too long though, it can become unhealthy. As part of our evolution, we can now choose to stop the train and walk the rest of the way, which is also a healthier option!

The train will always be there to some extent, waiting at the platform in our mind, but we must learn to live with it being there. We may feel compelled to take a nostalgic journey from time to time, which is fine as it is all part of this physical experience and what we signed up for. We all know of the high-speed thrills that it can provide and they are exciting but not essential to where we are going. The only problem is that these fleeting moments of happiness that we once allowed to consume us, are merely insatiable illusions which are foreign to our true selves.

Do what you truly came to do, shine your unique light and remember who you are. I keep going on about that don't I, remembering who you are!? As we move further throughout the book, each chapter will move us closer to the truth. For now, just know that you can have the life of your dreams by using two simple methods: the first being the law of attraction.

43

Law of Attraction

Like a lot of topics in this book, the old Dave would have laughed it all off as complete nonsense! The law of attraction is a law, just like karma is. If you have a hard time believing in things that you cannot see, you believe in gravity, don't you? That too is a law of the physical Universe. The law of attraction comes forth from what you think about. If you spend mass amounts of time focusing on something and believing in it, it will eventually manifest into your reality, good or bad. How you feel about something will add energy to it.

A common example of the law of attraction is when you have been talking or thinking about someone and they then text or call you. You say, "Oooh, I was just about to call you!" This is the law of attraction in full action, as we are all connected to the same Universal consciousness. We are like individual beacons that send signals to a computer mainframe that we are all wired into. We are all part of the same program and essentially, there is only one mind. By considering this possibility that we are all one, is it then possible to manipulate the reality around us to our advantage? If we are all connected, then our thoughts affect others and can also bring about certain experiences along our way. Our thoughts shape the current world that we are in. With this knowledge, is anything possible?

If the idea that we are all part of one collective consciousness baffles you, consider this: if a pebble were to be crushed into thousands of pieces, then ground to even smaller fragments and then pulverised some more, we would just have dust. If this compound were then to be placed under a microscope, we would be able to see that this mixture is nothing more than atoms and molecules. Those vibrating components are identical to the same matter that our brains and bodies are constructed from! We really are made up of what is all around us. The mineral, the plant and the animal are all part of us. The Universe is literally inside of us.

An atom is composed of particles called protons, electrons and neutrons. When a single atom is on its own, it is simply that, an atom. When there is more than one atom, this is known as a molecule. Molecules are just multiple atoms joined together. When atoms form together, molecules are compiled, and these are the basic building blocks for the world that we see around us. This, in turn, forms everything that we are. Atoms also vibrate and are constantly moving. When heat is added to an atom, it vibrates faster and the space between the molecules increases. When atoms are cold, they contract, that is why when something is cold, it can shrink.

The encasing that carries our soul around, known as the body, is made from the same building blocks as everything else that we see. Beneath all of those vibrating molecules, there is just a raw continuum of ever-present energy to everything. This is on a quantum level and one of our final chapters will examine what that energy is. For now, consider the concept that one energy is responsible for creating those atoms and molecules that animate our bodies. I find this truly astonishing.

When we hurt others or any life form for that matter, we are in essence harming ourselves, as we derive from the same Universal energy. When you consider that we are made from the same material, is it that far-fetched to think that all of our thoughts are all connected too? If we are all made of atoms that constantly vibrate, surely our energy field is a vibrational representation of how we feel inside. Our thoughts create our vibrational state and what energy we project onto others.

If this is the first time that you have heard about vibrations and you are thinking, "What the hell is he on about?" Let me explain. Your vibration is just another way of saying your overall state of being. From a physics point of view, the Universe is constantly vibrating. Even objects that appear to be solid are actually made up of vibrational energy fields that operate at a quantum level. We were taught in school that sound reaches us via vibrations, and we can visibly see this when a subwoofer is vibrating delivering us a base sound.

We, ourselves, vibrate at certain frequencies in our own energy fields, as we are all part of the same collective energy system. Our vibrational energy fields operate at different levels according to the thoughts and feelings that we project. You must have felt it when someone is giving off hateful or toxic vibes?

When we consume junk food, think negative thoughts, drink alcohol, take drugs, or operate out of fear, then our vibrational level is forced to operate at a very low rate. Sending out hate, judgement, anger and jealousy into the world can only lower your vibration. While operating at such a low level, you will attract experiences and people that match that of the same frequency. The longer you stay on this vibrational level, you will attract negativity as you are a match for it. Have you ever wondered why your rubbish day just seems to get worse? Have you ever wondered why it feels like one thing happens after another or bad things come in threes? It's because you attract things that are the same frequency as you.

When someone thinks a thought, they release energy into the world that we are all part of. This energy is then out into the collective mainframe of the Universe that we are all part of. Think of your thoughts like electromagnetic tentacles that extend out into the Universe and grab whatever they are a match to. That thought will have some sort of bearing on the overall human consciousness and can affect the world in a positive or negative way.

By grasping this concept, you can see how we can affect our own future by using just our thoughts. If we are all connected, then we can manipulate the collective energy for our benefit. This is not wrong, it is our birth right to have what we desire in order to facilitate our growth. Odd adages like, 'Money is the root of all evil', are the reason why people do not have the life of their dreams.

You are in the position you are in today as a product of your karmic disposition and your subconscious thoughts, whether you accept it or not. You have literally thought your life to date and manifested the majority of it. You may pooh-pooh this idea and think that external events are thrust upon us regardless, after all, this is what we are taught to believe when growing up. "Well you know, bad things just happen sometimes," is a common phrase that you will hear.

Now, we do choose life altering events long before we get here based on our karma, as we spoke about in pre-birth planning, but what happens in between those events is up to you. We must fill in the gaps so to speak. Those gaps that you choose to fill in the meantime are created by your thoughts which are just energy. The path that you choose to walk and the people that you attract, are all a mirror of your personal beliefs and thoughts.

For some, this may be hard to accept that we are all responsible for events that happen to us by the way we think but we are all creators. When we operate on the same level as another person, we allow them into our energetic field. They are a perfect match for our vibrational rate at that time. Our whole world that we experience operates on a vibrational field. Our emotions which are governed by our thoughts give off vibrational energy that has a frequency attached to it, which then affects our surroundings and experiences. You know when you are happy and full of euphoria, you can get those tingles and as a result, goosebumps can arise; that is your vibrational frequency rising. What if you could stay in that state permanently, imagine what you could attract?

When you focus on a thought for more than seventeen seconds, it will then begin to snowball and link to other thoughts of that frequency. By choosing to spend those seventeen seconds on that thought, you are choosing to give it energy. The law of attraction then begins to operate, which means what you think about will begin to attract to you. If you spend just sixty seconds on a negative thought, think of the size of the snowball that is being created. Before you know it, it's very hard to stop. More of the same will come your way in order to match those thoughts.

This is why it is so important to start your day correctly. If you begin the day by releasing negative energy into the Universe from your thoughts, then what experiences do you think will be brought forth for your day ahead? Those thoughts are creating emotions in your body that also emit to other people. Have you ever walked into a room and felt the atmosphere when there has been an argument in there? That is because emotional energy has been dispersed and lingered in that area. You can literally feel the sorrow at a funeral or joy at a party, for those are all vibrational energies that exist in our environment from the power of our thoughts on a mass level.

We all know someone who can light up a room with their presence. This is because of the energy that they send vibrationally into the world via their thoughts and attitude. The same goes for someone who is negative all of the time. They can be awkward to be around and you can literally feel the toxic vibes they emit vibrationally.

My past consisted of being poor and feeling sorry for myself. I was constantly broke and whatever money I had would go on drink and drugs. I even pawned my 18th and 21st birthday presents, which were gold chains, just so I could have a few nights out and a couple of grams of coke. the world was against me and I was a victim. This spiral of deprivation only excelled in my life and my thoughts of self-loathing and *poor me* simply perpetuated my circumstances.

I was operating at such a low vibrational level because of my thoughts, all I could attract was more of the same. Had I thought that I deserved more in my life and that I was better than my current situation, then my life would have changed. I had no self-belief, no self-love and merely manifested what I deemed fit for me at that current time of my life. My thoughts created my reality. Negative influences ruled my world, so negativity is what I received. Remember, life is like a mirror, what you put out there will come back to you and we reap what we sow; these are so true. If you are at a low level thinking dark thoughts, then people on that same vibrational level will be allowed to enter your aura and create experiences that your thoughts believe are true.

In our westernised lives, we have been conditioned to believe that you have to work hard in order to achieve your goals. With the power of thought, you can manifest anything you want if you truly believe in it enough and it feels natural. Does being a movie star feel natural to you? If yes, then live and believe that you can do this and the right opportunities will come your way in order to fulfil your goals, just be ready to take the cues when they arrive, and act upon them. Live as though it has already happened. I am not saying sit down and think of being in a sports car and it will be dropped in your lap, but if this is what you know you truly deserve and believe in it, opportunities will be presented to you which will lead you to that sports car.

Everything in the physical world once started as a thought. I imagined this very book that you are reading. It had already happened in my mind and I visualised it every day during my meditations. The brain can't distinguish the difference between a thought and reality, so to it, the two may as well be the same. I knew my book would happen and guess what? You are reading it now! I didn't worry about how it was going to happen; I just *knew*.

You know my past, I am no different from you, I am just an average guy who has had his issues like everyone else. But my book felt natural to me and this was my way of reaching out, connecting and trying to help people. I am literally writing this now while sitting on the sofa with Bella next to me. I had no doubt that this vision would materialise. So, believe in your dreams and act as if they have already happened. Einstein once said, "Logic will get you from A to B, but imagination will get you anywhere."

This may sound far-fetched to you, but that is only due to our conditioning. Had we been born in another part of the world, with a more liberal and spiritual outlook on life, we would have no issue believing these concepts. A belief is only a thought which has been repeated numerous times, until you have believed it. When you have read or heard a statement enough times, it will slip into your subconscious mind and become a belief. If you had been fed the information in this book in the first six years of your life, then you would believe all that I have written to be true. The westernised way of living would then appear alien and crazy to you.

Thoughts can be reprogrammed and it's time to deprogram all of those self-limiting beliefs that the system has installed into us. It's like wiping a dirty window clean and starting again, you can finally view what is truly important to you. Fulfil your dharma and live the life you came to live, be who you truly came to be. Fill your mind with limitless possibilities and positive beliefs.

You are a miracle. You are perfect. Just the fact that you can read and understand these words on this page is mind-blowing. Little squiggles and shapes form letters which make words that you can understand. The very fact that you understand these little shapes that are known as letters on this page is amazing. Plus, these squiggles known as letters allow me to convey my thoughts to you. These can then be translated into information that you can process, which can then reach your brain. This is just a tiny example of this wondrous phenomenon that is life.

I will be totally honest with you, I had a hard time accepting that our thoughts create our reality. When I discovered the law of attraction and attempted to manifest things for myself, I drew a blank. The mantra of 'the only way you obtain things in this life, is to work hard and be consistent' rang through my ears. However, once I had done more research into this life hack, the more it made sense. I began to get people to text me just by thinking about them and sending it out to the Universe through love. I then began thinking of money and detaching myself from the outcome of how it would arrive. The logical, rational mind of ours will instantly conjure up images of where your money will come from in a roundabout way. Ignore these thoughts and just concentrate on how it would feel to receive the subject that you were thinking about. Live as though it had already happened and be thankful for the Universe. The Universe will deliver your request in any way possible. 'Ask and you shall receive.' The Universe knows best.

What was really spooky for me and truly made me believe in the law of attraction was when I manifested my perfect job. As you are aware, catering has always been part of my life. I truly believed that I was due to be stuck in catering forever as that was all I was qualified to do. See how the system we have all been raised in can shape our beliefs about jobs and life? If I wasn't qualified to do anything else, what was the point in looking elsewhere?

As I began to discover more about the power of thought, I decided to put into practice the possibilities of a career change. I wrote down that I would like a more active role in helping young people and that I would get paid for it. I then sent this out to the Universe and stated that what I had written is what I was in present tense. I also stated that if the Universe had a better idea for me, I would welcome that also. I sent the letter with love and waited.

This is where faith and hope come into it. I had total faith that what I had sent out to the Universe would eventually arrive in my reality. Hope is completely different. I didn't hope for a new job as that would be the opposite of faith, even though it is still a form of positivity in a way. Hope, however, is a vibration that is lacking in conviction. Faith is a vibration that you just know something will happen when the time is right. When you have faith in a situation, you send a completely different message to the Universe. You are literally stating to the Universe that you believe in it and that it has your back. With this level of thinking in action, it is just a matter of time before what you truly want and are will be delivered. With faith, your vibrational energy is a match to that which you seek. Like attracts like.

So I wrote my letter to the Universe and with that, I let it be. I simply waited for what seemed like an eternity (it was only about nine months to be honest and my patience was tested) and then it appeared. A job was available that required someone to deliver help and life skills to vulnerable young adults. Well, without sounding too egoic, I thought that this was perfect for me, after all, look at what I had experienced growing up, having to support myself. The role was simply perfect for me. I thanked the Universe for this glorious opportunity and applied for the position.

I began living as though the role were already mine. I would say to myself every day, "I am a life skills tutor." I would meditate on the feeling of how it felt to be doing this job and never allowed one drop of doubt to creep into my mind. This was what I came to do, to help others and teach them through the mistakes that I had made. It was simply beautiful how it all came together.

I received an email offering me an interview for the position at 12:12pm. The day of the interview was on 12/11. Now if you keep seeing recurring numbers, they are angel numbers. Angels are trying to communicate with you, do not ignore them. Up until this point, I had all these ones and twos keep being thrown into my path. All I would see in random places were the numbers, 1212. The angel number 1212 means that your thoughts are being heard and that your dreams are manifesting into reality. This was very appropriate for what I had asked.

I accepted the interview with jubilance and it simply solidified my beliefs that this role was mine, even if I didn't have the necessary qualifications written on a piece of paper. I was almost there in manifesting a new beginning for me, but doubt started to creep in. I immediately shot the negative thoughts down, as if it were an invading aircraft making its way through my mind! I did more meditations on the fact that I was already the life skills tutor. As we spoke about earlier, there is no time, everything has already happened in the now. I was already the life skills tutor and living my life as if I was.

The day of the interview arrived and I was just going to confirm what I already knew; the job was mine. I sent the interview panel and interviewees love and wished them well. My interview went smoothly, which I knew it would and within four hours of me leaving the room, I received an email. It said that I had been successful and that they would like to offer me the position. I froze as I read the email, all those years of catering and stress behind me, all gone in an instant. It was amazing. My manifesting had worked. I mean I had seen it work with little things, but this was huge! That was it, I was a believer, our thoughts do shape our reality and future. When you live from the perspective that what you want has already happened and truly believe it, the Universe has no choice but to put that experience into your waking life one way or another. This will only happen when the time is right though.

Remember in the first part of the book, when I initially had an interview at a college after I had thought that I would love to teach catering and it never happened? This was because at the time, I was emotionally unstable from my breakup from Leanne. I had to go to the care home first to meet my friend Jennie in order to gain a new perspective on life. When I had healed, then I received the call offering me the job I dreamed of. The Universe knows what is best for us, even if our human minds don't agree with it!

I can't lie, realising that my thoughts created everything felt spooky, I really had been sold a lie growing up. All of the conditioning that I had allowed into my mind and accepted had grounded me. We can truly do anything we want to but of course, if everyone did that, how would the rich prosper? Remember these words: what you think about, you become! Earl Nightingale exposed this secret to the mainstream world decades ago, yet people still refuse to believe in their own potential. Focus on what you do want rather than what you don't. When you focus on what you don't want, the Universe simply offers you more of that experience, as that is what you are placing your thoughts and energy upon. The vibration you are creating is a negative one, so you will attract things that match that negative vibration. Think in positive terms and watch your life transform.

In this chapter I really wanted to give you an introduction into what is possible with the mind. If I have awoken some curiosity in you as to what you can have in your own life, then I encourage you to do your own research. There are so many manifesting channels and books available, I recommend checking them out. Just do a quick search on the law of attraction and manifestation. Ask the Universe to send the right information your way and it will appear.

I decided to try the money trick following the success of my new job. I practised a gratitude and money meditation on a Sunday. The following Wednesday, I visited my dad's house and he said there was some mail for me. I haven't lived at my dad's for over 14 years, why would I have mail? I opened the letter and it was an old savings account that my dad had opened and forgotten about. The letter contained a cheque. I couldn't believe that this had happened. I immediately thanked the Universe and realised I would never have thought of receiving money in this random, obscure way.

This money trick has happened twice now when visiting my dad's, old accounts rear their beautiful heads! The Universe works in mysterious ways, just let go, believe and receive! Do not think, "Well, the only way for me to receive money is to win the lottery." This places conditions and limitations on what you want. By trying to control the process, rather than letting go and trusting, you will nullify the whole experience. If you truly believe you deserve what you want, the Universe will get it to you one way or another, just have faith.

Now, you could write all of this off by saying the job was a coincidence and that those accounts at my dad's were always there, and I can agree with you. But these random events of money popping up happen monthly now, and they come from the most random, bizarre places. I mean, I used to be broke and get random bills through the post that I had to pay, now the postman brings me money, literally! I had an old store card contact me just the other day saying that there had been a mistake and they owed me money! In the past, this never happened, all I got was debt and wrong tax codes, saying I owed money. Now it is the other way around. What has changed? My thoughts.

I recently renewed my car insurance and saved £650! Crazy loopholes in my policy meant that I now pay less than Louise and I have only been driving two years! She wasn't too impressed! I received an email saying that my phone contract was up a year before it was supposed to be as a good will gesture. I receive money back from old loans, I win random things. My life is the definition of abundance, ever since I started believing in my true potential and the power of thought. I now want for nothing and can even give my possessions away. Who would have thought this just ten years ago, when I was a drunk scraping by from payday to payday? I would pawn goods and starve myself just so I could drink. This all happened due to my mentality and belief in my self-worth.

When a thought occurs, an emotion follows in the body to match that thought. When we first meet someone who we *think* we love, butterflies are produced in our stomachs to match our thoughts. When an event happens that we perceive as upsetting, we think sad thoughts which then create the emotion in our bodies.

Live by the emotions that follow your thoughts if you want to become a master manifestor. How does it feel to be rich? Allow the emotion to be produced into your body from your thoughts and build from this. Your vibrational energy will bring events that match your energy field. You are already a manifester, you just probably don't know it! Your current day position has arisen from your past thoughts. Situations from the past that were unpleasant to you were actually created by you. You focused on what you didn't want, which is as good as saying, "I will have that in my life please." Now you know about this, you can use your thoughts in a more productive way. I didn't want to be broke or ill all the time so that is what happened to me. I could have been thankful for what I already had and what I wanted but I chose not to. Now you know this little life hack, start playing with it!

Do not place any time restrictions on your wishes, as we discussed earlier, the Universe has no concept of time. Everything is in the present tense. Your wish will arrive exactly when it is meant to. My grandad loves to grow fruit and vegetables. When he plants the seeds, he doesn't start ripping up the soil a few days later searching for his vegetables, they appear when they have been nurtured in the right conditions and are ready to. The same goes for manifestation, do not grow impatient and demand that the object of your desire appear immediately, this in turn can block the whole process. Just have faith and know that it is on its way.

Try a little exercise if you don't believe this. Pick something simple, coins are a good one and see if you can bring it into your life. I love skulls, I don't know why but I always have. There is a £2 coin with skulls and roses on it in circulation; I knew this one was rare. I asked the Universe for this and within one day, this coin came into my possession! I had never seen it before; I was so happy. I now use coins and feathers as my symbols from my guides and the Universe. Place your order with emotion and imagination and then forget about it. Carry on with your life as normal. Be happy and grateful when your symbol of choice from the Universe shows up.

Look into the science behind this phenomena if you need rational proof of the whole process. Learn how thoughts release energy into the Universe that we are all part of. If energy is released into the Universe, it has to go somewhere right? Thoughts join the mass database we are all one with which is known as the collective consciousness. These thoughts begin to work with one another and then deliver experiences that match that of our thoughts. I used to think that my thoughts were harmless and simply in my head, how wrong was I!? When I had a bad thought about anyone, I essentially had a bad thought about myself, for we are all one.

Ever heard anyone say, "Bad things always happen to me." With that line of thinking, is it any wonder? They have as good as said, "More of the same please, this is what I feel I deserve!" If what you want doesn't arrive, ask yourself why? Do you honestly believe in what you're doing or that you truly deserve it? Are you judging others? By doing this, you make yourself separate from the Universe and everyone in it. When you are separate, how can you tap into the Universal abundance that we are all part of? Love everything and everyone knowing that we are all one. With this approach, anything is possible, and your future is merely a product of your current thoughts and karma.

Remember, thoughts start the ball rolling, but emotions are the key to manifesting as they amplify your electromagnetic field. Thinking a thought with no emotion ends up becoming a mental exercise, the heart and head need to be as one. When passion, feeling and emotion are added to the thought, momentum is added because the heart, which is the most powerful part of us all, makes your vibration even stronger. Who you truly are in your heart will mirror your reality.

Another way to have the life you desire is to reprogram your subconscious mind. The subconscious mind is an amazing thing and as you learn about its power, it may explain a lot about you as a human.

The next chapter will explain about the subconscious mind and will show you how to reprogram it.

44

THE POWER OF THE SUBCONSCIOUS MIND, SCIENCE AND HEALING

Apparently, 95% of our daily routines are run by our subconscious minds. You wake up, get ready, eat breakfast, get in your car and so on. You don't ever need to think when driving now do you? Have you ever driven to a familiar destination then realised that you don't even remember getting there because your conscious mind was so preoccupied? This is the power of the subconscious mind; it drove you where you needed to be for it knew the route! There are things called synapses which are in your brain. Synapses are found where nerve cells connect with other nerve cells. These are key to the brain's function, especially when it comes to memory. The more and more that you do something, the synapses make connections to other nerve cells that are like little roads. The more that you do a certain activity, the more established that *road* in your brain becomes, until eventually you do the activity without thinking. Practice makes perfect!

There was a point when I entered a car and was petrified! After all, you are aware of my phobia of driving. I remember thinking when I first sat in the driver's seat that there were so many buttons and levers! *There are three pedals and I only have two feet, how the hell am I going to this?* Gradually, over time, my mind began to absorb these once complicated steps and before I knew it, I was driving a car without thinking. This is an example of the subconscious mind in full effect. Apparently, it is the closest thing to our souls or genuine selves.

Another great example of the subconscious mind and how effective it is at running our lives are shoelaces, yes, shoelaces. I was going through the arduous process of putting my shoes on this morning. I don't know why but I always seem to find this a chore. I often wear ankle high Converse which I find clumsy to get on. As I finally got my foot into the shoe, I was planning what I was going to buy from the shops for my evening meal. After I had finished writing an extensive shopping list in my head, I discovered that I had completed the exercise of tying my shoelace.

I stopped for a moment and pondered as to how I achieved this glorious feat without even giving it a thought!? This is the power of the subconscious mind. I then untied the shoelace and decided to study with my conscious mind the process that just happened. I observed how intricate the movements were and the fine motor skills that were demonstrated through my fingers.

Now, I am aware that this story does not do my case for sanity any good, nor does this book, but I found this to be a profound moment and was in complete awe! If my mind could command my fingers to perform such a complex movement without my conscious mind witnessing it, what else could it do? Something as simple as tying a shoelace was once a mystery to my subconscious mind and had to be learnt. With this in mind, what else could it do with the tasks that it had already been programmed into it?

Now that you understand the power of this force that lurks beneath your conscious mind, imagine how you would behave if you were to programme it in a certain way? The brain learns by repetition. Think back to those little synapses, where little roads in the brain are established and connected to other nerve cells. These roads help your memory and are key to the natural functioning of your brain. The more you use those roads, the stronger the memory becomes until it slips into your subconscious mind. What did you learn when you were first programming your subconscious mind as a child? If you were raised in a particular way, those core values will be instilled into you and chances are they are still driving your behaviour to this very day, without you even realising it.

Rudolf Steiner had a seven-year theory to child development, as do many psychologists. In the first seven years of a child's development, if something traumatic happens, this could have severe repercussions mentally for the child later on in its adult life. Take my life for example, my mother left me which was something that I couldn't accept or understand. This event would shape the running of my subconscious mind until I decided to address it late into my twenties. Couple this with teachings such as, "We can't afford that, money is precious," and, "hard work is the key to get what you want in life." You can already see the future that is being created for the child.

We now know that we have evolved from animals, as explained in the chapters about the ego. With animals being known for adopting many ways of survival, what would a child do with the notion that it too is ultimately an animal and separate from everyone. As a new inhabitant to this planet, it would observe exactly what to do to survive in its new environment. Monkey see, monkey do! By witnessing others in day to day life, children can learn the necessary coping strategies that are needed in order to survive the illusion of separateness.

Now, what if that child witnessed violence or abuse? If a child grew up in a hostile environment, they would surely mimic the behaviour of those around them. That way of life would appear normal to the child as they would know no different. The events that they witness are then absorbed by their infant brain which is constantly developing. They would then see this type of behaviour as an appropriate way to live in order to protect one's very survival, it would be their truth.

A coping mechanism is developed for surviving in this hostile world that we find ourselves in and from this, around age six or seven, the ego is formed. Aristotle famously said, "Give me a child until he is seven and I will show you the man." Can you now see how conditioning and observed behaviour will shape a child for their adult years? They are simply doing what they can in order to get by.

Now, the following is something that I only discovered recently after a conversation I had with my mum, but it has always stared me in the face. We were speaking about my irrational fear of driving to new places. As soon as I got onto this topic, my mum said, "Oh you sound just like your father, he would never drive to new places, in fact he hated it!"

That was it, the penny dropped, *Oh my God* I thought, my fear of driving was obtained by witnessing my dad's behaviour growing up. I thought about it and it all made sense. We never drove to new places and always went on the same routes! Every route that my dad took back then I knew like the back of my hand. The fear that I felt was not actually mine, I had inherited it from my dad! Now when I have those thoughts of dread creep into my mind about venturing someone foreign, I shoot the thought down! I know that it isn't actually my thinking, it is a belief that has been downloaded when I was a child into my subconscious mind. I simply copied my dad's behaviour as it worked for him, so surely as a child growing up, it would work for me too. As an adult, I am simply re-enacting my survival programming that I learnt as a child. I was so happy when my mum made that statement about my father. What else had I learned from him and other people that drove my subconscious behaviour. Where had my dad mimicked his behaviour from? Was it just a continuation of irrational fears handed down from one generation to another? It really was a *Eureka* moment for me!

Growing up, I told myself that I would never be rich, that I would always struggle, and I actually accepted this. I accepted this because that is what had been programmed into me. Not to knock my dad for instilling this into me, he was only recreating what he had learnt. We are all just victims of victims, through continuous family karma. I never had money, that was the end of it. My environment was a product of my beliefs and conditioning that stemmed from my childhood. Environment really is everything. Imagine a pebble sat in a stream; it hasn't always been that shape but gradually over time, the persistent conditions have moulded it into the shape it is. The same is with a child's life, it is moulded by its environment.

What if we were programmed differently as children? If I had realised this years ago, my self-destructive ways would have ceased immediately. I would have rewritten my own programming. Instead, I chose to go out and get wasted to block out my subconscious that was full of pain. I would then stumble home and listen to music about negativity and the struggles of life as I dozed off. This whole cycle was just perpetuating my situation. I was basically brainwashing myself all over again with more negativity. I will explain in a few paragraphs why we must be conscious of what we are thinking about or listening to as we drift off to sleep.

I would fall asleep listening to songs about violence, depression and how important it was to be better than anyone else in an egoic sense. Don't get me wrong, some music has helped me to get through some dark times and it has truly helped to alleviate some of the pain too. Jay-Z helped me with truly positive lyrics and taught me never to give up, so it's not all bad.

However, in my experience, the vast majority of rap lyrics are egotistical, misogynistic and glorify the use of drugs and violence. I have always felt a strange connection to this genre, and still do to this day, but I'm careful what I listen to before sleep. I have always felt a deep connection with the samples that artists use and love Motown and soul, which are so heavily used in rap. The original songs soothe my soul and I love them, but I also love the way modern day producers can re-master them and give them a contemporary, modern twist. I grew up listening to 60's and 70's music because that is all my dad would listen to. Is this the reason for my love of soul sampled hip-hop? It resonates with my subconscious mind that was formed as I grew up.

On a side note (which I have a lot of), Rudolf Steiner states that music is the only link that we have to the spiritual world that is used by our five senses. I find there to be a lot of truth in this statement. When I hear a particularly beautiful piece of music, I experience goosebumps and feelings of euphoria, which I imagine exist in the spirit world permanently for it consists of pure love. Music also has the power to immediately transport you to any time or place in your past. The people you were with and what you were doing at that particular period in your life can all be recalled in a nostalgic record. I imagine that you too can relate to what I am saying here when you hear a piece of music that touches your soul on a personal level.

So, music can be used in a positive or negative way, as can anything. Watch how your mood changes when you are driving depending on what type of track you are listening to. When listening to an aggressive song, I find that my driving matches the tone of the music. With this in mind, perhaps choose relaxing music while you are driving!

Now, back to the subconscious mind! Imagine if you could rewrite your subconscious programming in a positive way? Well, the good news is you can! You can literally brainwash (sounds extreme) yourself into a positive state of mind. You can start living the life of your dreams by reprogramming your base brain. I regularly use affirmations to kickstart the process. I think positive affirmations throughout the day, in meditation and before bed. I also listen to positive talks as I sleep and over time, I can honestly say that these have transformed my life and the way I feel about people and myself.

Those first six to seven years of a child's development that we have spoken about are so key when it comes to shaping their adult minds. As a child is in their primary years, their brain is constantly in a *Theta* state. This *Theta* state is the gateway for learning and intuition that programmes a child's subconscious mind for their adult life. Imagine if you could enter that Theta state again to reprogram your adult mind? Well you can.

The brain enters that Theta state just before you doze off to sleep, you know, that groggy semi-conscious period as you're drifting off. So your brain enters the same frequency which it was in while you were in the first six years of your life. With this in mind, we can use this precious window of opportunity that we have, just before drifting off to sleep. We can use it to shape and rebuild our subconscious mind by using affirmations. Say to yourself, "I am well, I am perfect, I am wealthy, I love myself and others." Instead of thinking, "What a crap day, I really hate such and such a person, I am dreading tomorrow, or I have no money." Can you see the difference? Which state would you rather sleep in? One of love and positivity, or fear and negativity?

If you spend your last waking moments of each day replaying what you could or should have done, this is going to affect your mood and health. This will then cause you to worry about the future, it's a vicious cycle. You will then meet the dreamworld in this mental state. When you awake in the morning, the Universe will then greet you with experiences to match that of your subconscious programming and vibrational state. I used to be a vibrational match to negativity and see life as a grind. Now I love every day and greet each morning with a smile and gratitude, it sounds nauseatingly corny doesn't it? But it's true. I love life and it loves me back.

Please beware of the words 'I Am', these are particularly powerful words, as you are making a statement to the Universe. The Universe hears everything and in essence, you are declaring how you feel with the words 'I am' for they are present tense. When you say, "I am", you state everything that you are and everything that you are not at the same time. Remember, everything starts with a thought, the thought then transpires into an emotion created by the body. If the thought persists, it can transpire into reality. "I am annoyed, I am tired, I am angry." "As you think, so shall you be," goes the age-old adage or, "I think, therefore I am," which was the philosophical proposition of René Descartes. Those little thoughts of energy that you have released into the collective consciousness, that we are all part of, will manifest into your reality if you continue to focus on them. By thinking, you are determining the state of your health as well. Thought really is everything. Just change your mindset and you really can alter what you experience and how you feel, including your health.

I say to myself constantly, "I am healthy, I am wealthy, I am in abundance, I am grateful, I am love, I am caring." After 90 days of saying these, they will sink in that obscure part of the subconscious mind that drives your waking days. You will begin to live differently and notice changes. Boycott the news, instead, create your own news and tell yourself that the world is full of beauty. Stick strictly to your positive affirmations and focus on what you would like from your future, while being thankful for the present. Perception really is everything, if you didn't watch the news, how would you view the world, honestly? Would you constantly be witnessing war and murder? Or would you start to see your immediate circle for what it is? You have the chance to alter this and live a glorious life, which is what was intended for you. It all depends on how you programme your subconscious mind.

I used to fear becoming ill as it would stop me going to the gym and halt my progress in life. We were raised to believe in germs and diseases and that getting ill is something that just happens. I would often witness, as a child, how my dad would go into a state of panic when he had a sniffle. He would state that a cold was on the way and after three days he would fall ill. I observed this growing up and continued that behaviour into my adult life. I would constantly obsess about avoiding colds and sneezes, so guess what would happen? I would get ill, just like my father did all those years ago. The subconscious cycle had continued.

I would become anxious about getting ill and I would constantly be living in the future. I was fearful of something that hadn't actually happened and with that, I was not appreciating my current state of health in the present. The Universe would hear that I wasn't content in my current state and arrange a scenario that matched that of my thoughts. This all happened because I believed it could happen.

My subconscious programming allowed me to become ill. When I had a cold, I would then miss a week at the gym which I feared the most because of my loss of progress! My fears manifested into reality as this is what matched my subconscious wishes. I was a vibrational match for it. All the pills and potions that I used to take in order to keep me healthy, failed miserably. All the pills were placebos anyway, that I did not truly believe in. All I really needed to do was to believe in who I actually was, which we are slowly getting to...

Since I have adopted my new way of thinking, the old ways are gone. I no longer get ill; I simply cannot remember the last time I felt under the weather. I am healthy and content to live in the current moment, why would I choose to change my current state? Had I have lived through the Covid-19 pandemic with my old train of thought, I am convinced that I would have become ill.

Think back to when we spoke about atoms and how they vibrate, do you recall that our body is made of atoms and molecules? The vibrational rate in which we operate is governed by what we think about. The thoughts that I projected all through the pandemic were that of a high vibration and frequency. "I am in perfect health," and, "everything is as it should be," were what I thought about daily. When a thought is a positive one, it creates a high state of vibration throughout your body. Only energy that is on the same vibrational frequency can then match up with it. A virus will operate at a low vibrational frequency, so if you are in a constantly elevated vibrational state, the two cannot be a match. My thoughts came about from what I chose to place into my subconscious mind. These in turn activated the law of attraction and I received what I thought about. My health was perfect throughout the pandemic which gave me the opportunity to help those who needed it.

Now, I know what I have just written in the previous paragraph will come across as nonsense to some as we have not been taught this as we grew up. But science can prove many things, even the truth. What I have written is not mainstream knowledge, why is this? If people knew they could be well by consciously choosing their thoughts, we wouldn't need to purchase any pills and potions to make us better! That is why the media is there to manipulate our thoughts to that of a negative, fearful state. Our vibrational rate can then be affected by what we see and believe on the news. Nothing is real unless you give it credibility and believe in it. By believing in something, you activate the great law of attraction and then receive what you think about. The science that we learn at school only serves the capitalist system that we are born into.

That is why science like the law of attraction is not taught on a mainstream level.

When I first met Louise, I was so jealous of her because she never got ill! I quizzed her on this, and she said that she simply didn't believe in it and that she didn't have time for it all. Still to this day, she has never been ill, despite doing a job that is full of pressure. Belief is everything and Louise's analogy of illness proves this. Her positivity towards her health affects how she is. She also states she doesn't have time for illness. What message is Louise's subconscious mind sending out to the Universe? The law of attraction only delivers what it hears and if Louise's subconscious mind only operates from that of pure health, what will she receive?

Louise also has some of the poorest hygiene that I have ever witnessed. I was appalled when I first got to know her. When it came to washing her hands, she just didn't do it and never has. As for the washing of her food, don't even get me started on that! It goes against everything that I was taught in my cooking years. When I prepare and cook food for others, I take extreme care of the ingredients, as that is my responsibility as a cook. I respect that the people who I am cooking for will not share my sentiment of belief! I will be honest though, when I now cook for myself, I eat food that's mouldy, don't wash anything, and have a pretty lax approach to it all! I now welcome dirt and germs to be honest for they are good for me and part of who I am, but that is my belief which I choose to program my subconscious mind with.

Think about it though, there is good and bad with everything in life, we have spoken about this numerous times throughout the book. There are good bacteria and bad bacteria. What did we learn growing up? Bacteria is bad and can make us ill. The fact is that we evolved alongside bacteria for billions of years before we reached our human state of evolution. It is in us, around us and everywhere! It is a part of who we are. Most bacteria are good for us and are needed, especially in our guts. Would it then not be madness to destroy what is essentially a part of us?

What do we see on the TV? Buy this disinfectant that will kill 99.9% of bacteria, including all the good! If we destroy everything, then our immune systems simply have nothing to build with and ultimately, our immunity will suffer because we are out of balance. When we do come into contact with a virus or unfamiliar bacteria, our immune system could become compromised due to such sterile environments that we now live in. Our immune system has had nothing to work with because everything that it can learn about has been killed.

Say we catch the flu for instance, our immune system will fight it off in the best way that it knows how. When we are happy and healthy again, our immunity has been boosted because we now have a copy of that virus stored in our natural immunity library. Our bodies now know how to fend off that same virus in the future. If we were to catch the same virus again, we may feel under the weather one day and not realise that our body has fought off what was once a potentially dangerous virus. That is why it's important to be exposed to the natural world in order to build up our defence systems.

With this knowledge that we need bacteria to help us, I am by no means saying that you should go home and start smearing excrement up the walls, but do you really need to wash your hands ten times a day? This is why Louise is never ill as her subconscious mind doesn't believe in it and she has a great immune system due to her unconventional hygiene practices!

So, is Louise a genetic freak or just proof that positive thinking will activate the law of attraction? A virus can make you ill and they can affect us all, but in order to get ill, a virus needs a variety of things before it can infect. Viruses rely on the cells of other organisms to survive and reproduce. They cannot store energy for themselves, so they cannot function outside a host organism. Now the key word here is *host*. If the host is not willing, much like Louise, then the virus simply cannot live somewhere that it is not welcome. Do you believe we are meant to fall ill? If you do, as I once did, you are a welcome host to the virus. You are openly stating to the Universe that you are willing to become ill. What is that going to do for the law of attraction?

If you still have a hard time believing that belief shapes our immediate reality, then there is an extreme example of the power of belief in America. Radical religious cults will handle venomous snakes in service and drink the poison of the serpent as part of a ritual. Some members of the congregation will often get bit but still live, why is this? Their belief in the power of their *God* is so strong that they believe they are protected from the demons that are in the snake and its poison.

If you or I were to drink the poison or be bitten, we would probably become very unwell and even die, simply because we do not have that level of belief to protect us. I accept that poison can make me critically ill and so does my subconscious mind, therefore that belief creates my reality. Please do not attempt to drink snake poison or get bitten by one after reading this extreme example!

What I learnt while growing up had programmed my subconscious mind to welcome all viruses and infections into my body, which, in turn, made me ill. In other words, I stated to the Universe that I believe I am susceptible to viruses and bacteria making me ill, for they are separate to me. I have to say, my deep-rooted beliefs have now changed who and what I am. I no longer consider viruses as a threat in my life or that they are separate from me.

Have you ever heard anyone say to somebody who is ill, "Oooh, stay away from me, I don't want to catch that!?" There are three things wrong with that statement which will ultimately lead to illness. The first error is that the individual is making themselves separate from others and also separate from the virus. When we state that we don't want to catch something, we are living in a fearful future tense that isn't real. We are therefore not grateful for our current state of health and the law of attraction must assume that we desire a different state. The final error in the original statement is that an individual has acknowledged that they are capable of becoming ill, so they are a willing host.

When we view ourselves as separate entities in the Universe, that is when problems happen. I send love to viruses, but I don't have time to waste with being ill. I am only here for a very short space of time on Earth and I want that time to be lived to the fullest. My attitude towards my health is now that of an optimum level, this is what my subconscious mind now emits into my waking life, without me even thinking about it.

I could write a book on the effect of the subconscious mind, science and placebos, but I encourage you to delve deeper into them and do your own research; find your own truth. The body really is the most readily available drugs cabinet going and we have 24/7 access to it if we choose too. When you are a child and you fall over and cut yourself, you are taught to clean it and leave it be, that it will heal by itself. We grow up believing this and whenever a cut occurs in our adult lives, we don't even give it a second thought, we just let the body do its thing, as this is what our subconscious mind believes.

Our body is a self-healing mechanism that is a marvel. But what if a cut as a child were to be treated differently in our infant years? What would happen if a child heard an overanxious mother scream, "Your leg is going to fall off, oh my God, do you realise what you've done?" How would the child's immunity then develop? Would they grow up with health complications due to their conditioning? Would cuts always become infected? I don't know, I just found it an interesting thought. What do you think?

To recap this chapter, please be aware of the power of the words, 'I am' for what you state, you become. Practice daily affirmations to reshape your subconscious mind. Be deliberate with the words you say and the emotion behind your desires. Before you go to bed, think of all the positive things that happened in your day and tell yourself what you would like from tomorrow. You will then be in a positive trance as you drift off to sleep for the next six hours or so, depending on how much you enjoy your sleep! Give it a go! What have you got to lose?

If your current train of thought has led you to a point in your life that you are not satisfied with, or you feel a lack of fulfilment, what harm can be done by trying something different? If we always do what we have always done, we will always get what we have always got. Einstein said that insanity is doing the same thing over and over expecting different results. If you were to reprogram your subconscious mind with new thoughts, surely you would live a different life.

Sometimes we need to walk down a new path to invoke change and growth into our lives. Do not allow the fear of change to be something that is programmed into your subconscious mind. Fearful expectations can eventually be eliminated from your subconscious mind with practice and repetition. I learnt to acknowledge this when driving to a new location! My fear of this came from my dad's beliefs that I had inherited into my subconscious mind. In my infant years, I learnt that colds and infections were normal by observing my dad and others at school. This all happened while my own immune system and subconscious mind was developing. These then controlled my adult life.

Where did your fears come from that drive your subconscious mind? Your parents? School? Media? Can you now identify with this? If so, spend some time reprogramming your beliefs if you do not like some of your behaviours. If you do love the traits you have learnt from your parents and others as a child, embrace them and use them to your advantage. Find what is true to you and place that into your subconscious mind each day and night. When you do reprogram your subconscious mind and release old ways that no longer serve you, you can watch the miracles unfold.

If you do still find that your reality keeps following a specific pattern, despite thinking differently and changing your subconscious beliefs, it may be that old traumas need addressing directly. Old wounds that carry painful emotions could be weighing your soul down and dominating your unconscious thinking and vibration. Words and affirmations may only be masking the problem, you need to do some real healing and get to the root of the problem. Your inner child may be hurt and screaming for love, or an experience in your teenage years may have been swept under the carpet that needs processing. Whenever trauma has been neglected, know that it needs healing.

Healing is pretty ugly stuff and our human mind does its best to avoid it. Healing means sitting with painful and uncomfortable emotions and befriending them, just as we would with a positive emotion. The mind will see these painful emotions as detrimental to our human shell, as they are not producing the feel good feelings as positive ones do. Your conscious mind is trying to protect you by not allowing these emotions to come to the surface. It will do anything to distract and occupy you from learning and understanding these emotions. This is where as humans, we develop addictions to stop us exploring what lurks beneath in our subconscious. Ultimately all emotions are all equal and part of the human experience, but in our society and culture, we have a tendency to strive for the ones that feel good and block out the ones we label as painful.

I recommend addressing these buried emotions no matter how uncomfortable they are, and when they are confronted, you will heal; manifesting what you want will also become a lot easier too, as nothing is holding you back, allowing your vibration to rise. I recommend seeking professional advice to help you heal severe trauma, but if you feel bold and strong, you can do some work on yourself as well. Remember, it is you that ultimately has the power and does the healing, not some external force. Professionals only guide you to what you already know and nudge you to see things from a different perspective. You have to be willing to accept change which is the first step, and do your own work which leads to the healing.

I mentioned earlier how letting go of old pain and forgiveness is the key to freedom, but that can sometimes be easier said than done. When I forgave my mother, my life shifted; I learnt a karmic lesson. This only happened by becoming sober and finally confronting those buried feelings of pain, shame, not being good enough, and abandonment. The drugs, alcohol, football, and serial monogamy were no longer forefront in my vision, and there was nothing to bury or distract the wounds from my conscious mind.

In a quiet, relaxed place where you feel safe and comfortable, try recalling a past experience that brings profound pain or discomfort. If one arises that you are okay with, you have healed this trauma. If however one event arises that brings feelings of distress and discomfort that you cannot sit with, this is a key sign that you need to heal this in order to let go and move forward.

Observe the emotion or feeling without attachment or judgement; simply notice it. Sit with it, recognise it, and allow it space, do not be afraid of it. Accept it as you would a joyous or happy feeling. Pushing it away will only prolong the pain. Befriend the emotion and know that it is not something to avoid; it is part of your human experience that is trying to teach you and should be embraced, not rejected. If you need to cry, cry. If you need to scream, scream. If you need to grieve, grieve. If you need to forgive yourself, forgive yourself. Allow all to pass through you.

As the emotion burns, continue to notice it and invite your heart and Universal love to heal the wound. Watch as you become comfortable with the emotion and feel love into the whole experience. Eventually, you will just notice the emotion for what it is, and it will not appear so menacing to you, no longer will it scare or control you. If it appears again in the future, simply go back to observing it, and do not push it away, sit with it and it will pass in a healthy way. This may continue to happen for hours, weeks, months or years, but whenever it does arise, be proud you are processing it. Starting a daily journal and writing about how you feel with your current emotions can also help with the whole healing process as well. You could also join a group for people who have experienced similar trauma and emotions. What I write in this book is what has worked for me, but there are many ways to heal; we are all unique.

Know that everything that happens to you is for a healthy reason and is part of your growth. Love that you have the courage to do this, and love everything about yourself, even if that feeling has been buried for many years. Know that somewhere, there is someone who feels exactly like you do. We are all in this together and you are loved unconditionally by the Universe

Most trauma stems from childhood experiences and when we are at a young age, our brains have not yet developed the cognitive ability or capacity to process the event properly. This unprocessed wound then stays with us into our adult life, and as mentioned earlier, this drives our subconscious response to everyday situations that we then encounter. From an adult's perspective, we are able to look back and process the whole experience differently. We then relearn our subconscious behaviour. It is the emotions that make it so uncomfortable to do this though, as they are so painful. This is why many adults shy away from childhood problems and choose to distract themselves instead, just like I did!

My inner child needed help to process its pain, as it couldn't understand it. Now I love that child and view him as someone who needed my adult help. I had to relearn the whole experience from my adult perspective and understand why it all happened. No longer was avoiding the issue and ignoring it doing me any good. I embraced the emotions and lessons over time and released the pain. It was all part of my karmic path that helped me to grow into who I am now.

When you can understand why the event that is related to the painful emotion happened, you release karma and grow from it. You needed that event to happen so that you could ascend; if you keep missing the lesson and the meaning behind it, it keeps repeating itself. You will attract people to you that highlight the emotional wound because it is still an active vibration deep within you.

When you have healed, you can now move forward in life and let go of the past. This is indeed a tough exercise to do, and sitting comfortably with burning, childhood emotions from an adult perspective, is something that I have only recently been able to do myself. Thank your conscious mind for trying to protect you all of this time, but you have grown enough to move forward and embrace all aspects of life, even the difficult spectrum of human emotions. Know that all emotions are energy in motion, and if that energy is not allowed to move freely within your system, it can become trapped in your beautiful body.

The spiritual path isn't all about love, light, and superficial positivity. It's about embracing the ups and downs as one. We have come to learn about emotions and the contrast of life; to reject anything about the physical denies the divinity of it all. It's okay to still feel down some days, this is part of being human, but know that it is all part of the process and do not allow it to consume you. The fact that you are conscious of these feelings is a positive in itself and will help you to move forward. Accepting the dark times for what they are, is true humility. Knowing that the darkness is an opportunity to grow will propel you into the light. It's about loving yourself, healing, getting your hands dirty, and dealing with the pain you do not want to. You are a powerful creation and have the power to heal.

The more you heal, the lighter you will become, and this ultimately raises your overall vibration. When you heal, you can then help others. Until then, helping others who need help when you are still in pain, is like jumping into a river to save someone who is drowning, but forgetting you cannot swim yourself. Make sure you fill your own cup first before fillings others', otherwise you end up feeling drained. I have been guilty of this people pleasing technique for many years and it can be exhausting. I chose this people pleasing technique to avoid triggering those feelings of rejection. I had not healed properly and worried that people would not like me if I did not do what they wanted; this in itself was unhealthy.

If you really find it hard to embrace uncomfortable emotions, and understand why the whole experience linked to them had to happen, the emotion and subconscious thoughts will get your attention in other ways, which is what our next chapter is all about.

45

AILMENTS AND DIS-EASE

We all get ailments from time to time, they are not bad, we just perceive them as bad due to our minds clinging to the reality of how things should be. Ailments are actually our bodies' way of trying to communicate our thought patterns to us. Dis-ease is any deviation from that of our natural functionings. We are supposed to experience perfect health for we are love. Therefore, when we are not experiencing our natural state, which is perfect health, something is out of balance. This can be in our bodies or even the world.

The body is one giant metaphor. Ever had the weight of the world on your shoulders and developed shoulder pain? Or has anyone literally been a pain in the neck, and you wake up with a stiff neck and blame it on the way you have slept? Back pain is also one of the largest problems when it comes to keeping people off work. What does the back do? It supports our entire frame and structure; it is also behind us. If you are feeling unsupported in your life, or have guilt about things that are behind us, it can metaphorically manifest in physical back pain.

We are all born perfect in the vision of whatever force that created us and I believe that any illness we induce is a product of our thoughts or due to our pre-birth karmic planning. The world that we live in has taught us to believe that pain is bad and that it is not normal. We should shut it up quickly by reaching for the medicine cabinet. The pharmaceutical market is worth $934.8 billion, according to recent statistics, (I have chosen to believe these numbers, although who actually knows if they are true?) with this figure predicted to rise to $1170 billion in 2021. This is scary!

Linking back to our S&S topic, is it any wonder that the media's main agenda is to induce fear, paranoia and separation? If we choose to believe all that is portrayed to us through the screens we watch, this could cause people to visit the nearest drugstore to deal with their problems. Profits then rise even more for the pharmaceutical market because of how the world is depicted through the media. The two go hand in hand.

We have spoken about how everything can start with a thought, which is energy and then leads to an emotion being produced by the body. If the emotion that is produced isn't dealt with or addressed, it then resides and lingers in the body, for it is energy and energy has to be released somehow! If it is not released and dealt with, the trapped energy becomes blocked and can manifest into something physical. This process could happen in minutes, take several months, or even years until it rears its *ugly* head, but rest assured, it will arrive. Our bodies are like physical containers and by following the laws of physics, if there is too much activity going on inside a confined space, it has to spill over eventually, one way or another.

My mother has a history of depression and self-persecution. My mother would harm herself when she was younger, which led to her admission into a special hospital; where she sought help. These acts of self-punishment that my mother subjected herself to, were then controlled with medication and various psychological treatments. If we only treat the immediate symptoms and not those deep, harboured issues of the past that lurk deep within, then we are only doing half a job. Had the root of the problem been confronted, which was her past, I am convinced that her self-sabotaging behaviour would have been cured. At the time, the doctors managed to control it and that would have to do. My mother was released from the hospital when everything appeared to be under control, not cured.

My mother was diagnosed with epilepsy shortly after she chose to leave me. I believe this happened as a result of her actions. My mum manifested epilepsy due to her subconscious beliefs that her actions should be punished, which already existed from her previous mental history. The spiritual symptoms of this condition are a sense of self persecution, rejection of life and self-violence. Does this condition sound relatable to the actions of someone who believes that they should be punished?

Still to this day, my mother has the condition. The dis-ease is controlled with medication, rather than exercising the demons that caused the diagnosis to manifest in the first place. I have discussed my philosophy of the situation with my mum and she agrees that medication has only managed the problem and kept it at bay.

Shortly after deciding to leave for London, my mother was also diagnosed with multiple sclerosis. The spiritual manifestation that appears in the body for this crippling condition derives from someone who has a mental hardness, inflexibility, and an iron will. I feel that my mother had to develop these mental constructs in order to protect herself. She had to live with her harsh decision, which was to leave my father and I. In my opinion, her mental toughness was a survival tool that her subconscious mind chose in order to function. My mum had to put up a wall to cope with her choice, she had no other option. What a difficult decision it must have been for her to make when considering her future, but once she had made her choice, she had to stick by it; I actually respect her for that.

Putting up a mental wall and developing this *iron will* is actually a sensible thing to do, in my opinion, in order to cope. Within a year of her leaving me, the condition of multiple sclerosis suddenly arose, with no prior history of the illness being registered anywhere in our family. My mother's epilepsy also awoke too, the need for subconscious self-punishment was rife.

I discovered these metaphysical, spiritual terms of diagnosis in Louise Hay's book, *You can heal your life*. I urge you to read this book if you have any persisting niggles with your body. When you read the symptoms of your condition in Louise Hay's book, you may be surprised with how accurate the diagnosis is. You may be shocked at how easy it is to link your persisting ailments to unaddressed mental thought patterns, that camp out in that subconscious mind of yours.

I sent my mum a copy of Louise Hay's book and she was shocked at how accurate the reasons for her dis-eases were. I am trying to help my mother come to terms with her issues. She is aware that I am writing about her and she is happy for her struggles to be discussed if they can help others. With my help, I know she can become healthy and full of vitality again, instead of being a slave to the medicine cabinet, which has consumed her for the majority of her adult life. She, too, is ready for change and to become independent of supporting medication which only masks the problem.

I have always admired my mum's positivity and her attitude that life must go on. Yes, it must, to a degree, but issues must be dealt with and not swept under the rug. The rug will continue to fill and one day, the contents will spill out to the floor, a lot like life. Let life unfold before you and enjoy it, but make sure that you deal with every passing emotion and situation accordingly. Do not disregard emotions as a sign of being weak, like I used to think. If emotions are ignored, this will cause symptoms in the body to arise for the appropriate emotional state.

"Men don't cry," was a meme that I grew up believing in. I witnessed it in films and on TV. These macho men would save the day but did not show one ounce of emotion whilst doing it. Children in the school playground would berate you if you cried when sustaining an injury or falling over. Crying was deemed a sign of weakness. Dean, Lee and I would say this growing up! If you cried, then you were less of a man and may as well be a girl. I am sure if Dean were here in the physical form today, he would be the first to comfort me if I were crying, and then he would probably have a dig at me for crying later when the situation had calmed down. After all, we need balance right!?

Where does all that emotion go for men who must behave in a certain way? What about men in the army? Imagine crying on the battlefield or in front of the battalion. Would most soldiers be ridiculed and viewed as less of a man? All that emotion, which is trapped energy, has to go somewhere. What about all the horrors that have been witnessed on the battlefield by soldiers? With so much going on in the heat of the moment, processing those emotions which are running rife around the body is going to be difficult. When soldiers then return home, they are isolated and alienated. I feel this is why so many soldiers suffer from post-traumatic stress disorder. Is processing their emotions when serving their country viewed as a sign of weakness? It is so sad, but I think the answer is yes. It is the cycle of the macho man persona which I have fallen victim to in the past, as I was scared to be myself. I understand that I am generalising here, and I have never been in the army but this is my experience from accounts of people who have served.

While I was growing up, and up until recently to be honest, I have always suffered with sore throats. I would always let situations pass and not say how I was truly feeling in the moment. I would always say, "Yes," when I really meant, "no." The pent-up words of what I truly wanted to say, would reside as blocked energy at the back of my throat. I would then awake with a sore throat the next day because of my blocked throat chakra. Chakras are like spinning wheels of energy that reside in the centre of our bodies. We have seven in total which are located in different parts of our body.

The first is the root chakra, located where our genitals are. This is the foundation of our body and gives us the feeling of being secure and grounded. The second is the sacral chakra. This is found near our belly button area and is responsible for how we relate to our own emotions and the emotions of others. The solar plexus is the third chakra and is located just below the rib cage. Its energy flow represents our confidence and how in control we feel about our lives. The heart chakra is located where the heart is and allows the flow of love to others and ourselves. The throat chakra is situated in the throat area. As I have found out in the past, it represents our ability to speak the truth and stand up for ourselves. The third eye chakra is the sixth chakra. If this is blocked, it can affect how intuitive we are about life. Individuals with a particular potency of energy in this area are able to communicate with the divine and the spirit world. My dear friend Jo must have an abundance of energy in this chakra! The seventh and final chakra is the crown chakra which represents how spiritually in tune we are with ourselves and our higher consciousness. If one of these areas are blocked with residue energy from an old thought pattern or out of balance for any reason, ailments can occur.

Sore throats were such a frequent thing for me as I couldn't say what was truly on my mind. However, my mind, that had been conditioned with a western philosophy, would then associate a sore throat with the beginning of an illness or an impending cold. I would then manifest flu-like symptoms and develop a cold because of this. I would have about four to five colds a year as a result of this. I have now learnt how to speak what is on my mind and not to avoid confrontations. I can now fully express who I am. I no longer feel the need to hide behind the image of a geezer or lad, and can now be who I came to be on this planet.

We can all catch viruses if the circumstances are right, as I discussed in the previous chapter, I am not disputing that, but if we do get ill from the virus, it is our body's way of showing us that something is out of balance. If our immunity is low, then we can become prone to catching viruses. We catch the virus for a reason in order to show us that we need a break to rest and recuperate. This could be a mental rest, physical or both. My nan would call this, 'burning the candle at both ends.' I would always party too hard to hide from the worry and shame of who I truly was. I would always become ill because of my beliefs and lifestyle. I just thought that my nan was being boring and over-sensitive, but I guess she saw the bigger picture!

When my body encounters a virus now, I have enough balance in my life to fight that virus and no longer become ill. Plus, with my new mental attitude that I pinched off Louise, I don't have time to get ill! I love the present moment and I love being in perfect health. I tell myself constantly that I am healthy, I am wealthy, I am grateful and I embrace the feelings that these words induce.

I had terrible varicose veins in my mid-twenties, which ran all the way down my right leg. I was told that only pregnant women and elderly people had this condition. If this was the case, why did I have it? Was it genetic, as my dad's mum had them? They were unsightly and caused my legs to go numb. I had an operation five years ago in 2015 to remove the veins, for which I am forever grateful to the NHS. I thought it was just the *luck of the draw* that I had this condition. I now understand that nothing is unlucky or unfair in this perfectly balanced Universe of ours for we create our reality.

It turns out that the meaning of varicose veins from a spiritual perspective is an inability to deal with where you stand in life and can stem from poor relationships with parents and work. Literally, you cannot stand the situation you are in, be it personal or professional. You resent the current moment and joy does not flow easily to your work or relationships with parents.

The right side of our body is the masculine side and the left is our feminine. The legs are a representation of standing and they keep you moving forward in life. Most days, my legs were numb, and this was merely a metaphor my body had created to expose my subconscious beliefs. The fact was that I had become numb with my life at that time of my existence. I resented my past and my relationship with my parents. Oddly enough, it was the right leg that was affected the most, this would be my masculine side, the relationship with my father. I guess I still held deep resentment towards him for he had kicked me out. The joy did not flow.

I enjoyed learning about food and practicing new techniques from my hotel work but deep down, I felt worked to the bone and drained. Working 13-hour shifts in a high-pressure environment did take its toll, I can't lie, sometimes I couldn't stand it.

Although my relationship with my parents had improved, it was nowhere near where I wanted it to be. I felt like I had papered over the cracks. So, all of these true feelings that resided within me, grew within my body and exposed themselves to me via the legs as a sign. The dull ache that I would experience after a long day was a clear representation to my attitudes towards life and family. It really makes perfect sense when you have an open mind and realise that we are all perfect and not meant to get ill. Our body is our servant and is constantly doing its best to serve us. I just didn't read between the lines and wondered why blood wasn't flowing properly around my legs.

Quite simply, joy was not able to circulate throughout me, especially with my dependency on alcohol. Ailments help us identify our current mental state and that we must address the negative emotional states that persist. When we acknowledge that our emotions have stemmed from our thoughts, we can move forward in life and learn.

If you have any persisting niggles, I urge you to look into the spiritual meaning of your ailment and what your body is trying to tell you. Do not just take the doctor's diagnosis as gospel - look deeper. Yes, the doctor may have a qualification and modern-day medical advancements have thrived with research, but consider a holistic approach to your problem. Medication often treats symptoms rather than the root cause. Sometimes what has been prescribed for you may not always be the best solution.

Doctors have studied from textbooks but as we know, research is constantly evolving and contradicting old discoveries. Books that doctors have learnt from have been written by man. Man can sometimes make mistakes and modern-day studies can prove that. Research 100 years from now could completely contradict what we consider to be the truth now when it comes to health and medication. Have an open mind when it comes to healing. Just as I write this book, I too could be completely wrong. Consider all options and do your own research.

I can relate to how my thought patterns caused my illnesses and ailments but that's in my reality, what is yours? The doctors did wonders for me with my operation, but it was I who put myself there in the first place due to my thoughts. I would be constantly ill from colds due to my lifestyle and my mind refusing to believe that my body could cope with any bacteria. I share my health issues with you as I have first-hand experience, and I am no different to you. We are all made from the same atoms and molecules that create everything, so what makes my body any different from yours? The human blueprint is the same for everybody.

My view is that doctors only diagnose us from a superficial, physical viewpoint. They are merely assessing the shell that we walk around in and not from the driving thoughts that command our bodies. We are spiritual beings having a physical incarnation. Doctors understand the functioning of the body perfectly well. They learn how we are put together and how we function biologically. In a doctor's eyes, dis-ease can stem from internal biological issues, genes and external circumstances caused by bacteria. If we diagnosed thoughts on a mainstream level, I feel we could drastically reduce the rate of which patients return to clinics with persisting health issues.

When we pluck a weed from the ground, we make sure that we remove the root while we do it or else it will grow back. The same goes for our ailments. We can treat them on a superficial level but if the root that they are attached to is not removed, they will persist and reappear overtime. Strangely enough, as I reach the completion of this book, my varicose veins in my right leg have returned. The surgeons stripped them out years ago, so why have they returned? Surely the surgeons did their part and all was healed?

The veins in my leg demonstrate that the relationship with my father is still not where I would like it to be. It has improved overtime, but his attitude to life frustrates me because he is stuck in the past. My dad would have made someone a beautiful husband, but he has chosen to live on his own and to root himself firmly in the past for fear of being hurt again. I know what I think is not best for him as it is his life, but I can't help but feel that he has hit the pause button on his life. My thinking has struck a nerve with my body deep down and blocked a flow of subconscious joy towards my dad, as it hurts me to see him live in the past. I love him for who he is and consciously accept his choices, but on a subconscious level, that frustration is obviously still there towards him.

I have long distance Reiki healing which helps the energy flow around my legs and use affirmations to reprogram my subconscious mind. I believe that one day these veins will no longer be constricted and that joy and blood will flow freely. I just need to let go of any old emotions that still linger deep within. The subconscious mind is a convoluted place and needs to be thoroughly explored in order to weed out old feelings. Going back to the surgeon's knife is something that I no longer consider, for what happened before was only a temporary solution and masked the problem rooted deep within.

Our glorious vehicles that are known as our bodies would run more harmoniously and malfunction less if we understood the power of our subconscious thoughts. Look within and be objective about your past or current state. By doing this, you can see what is causing your ailments, what is your body really trying to tell you? What have you programmed into your subconscious mind? You will be surprised what fear can create within the body.

A condition that I have always suffered with to reiterate my point is acne. To a doctor, acne is caused by poor diet, hormonal issues and even stress. This is what I was told when I used to visit my GP complaining about my skin. I was prescribed drugs which didn't work on a long-term basis and would only alleviate the symptoms on a temporary basis. My skin would soon flare up again after my body has adjusted to the medication. My thoughts were the real driving force for this condition.

Teenagers get acne due to hormonal changes in their bodies. I do believe this, to some extent, but do teenagers hate the changes that their bodies are going through on a subconscious level, leaving the safety and innocence of childhood behind? It's a perplexing time watching yourself and everyone around you develop, especially if you are developing the way you do not want to. This can lead to self-hate and feeling ugly which is the metaphysical meaning of acne. Metaphysically, acne can translate like this; not accepting oneself which is associated with negativity. Also, unresolved issues of guilt, anger and self-hate can produce serious acne. Leading an addictive lifestyle can also produce acne. Does this sound like the Dave that was described in the first part of this book? I was angry from my past, had a poor diet, struggled with addictions and hated myself.

I lived with acne on my face in my teens and into my late twenties. I used to see so many adverts which would show the science of how bacteria builds and clogs the pores, eventually developing in the form of a spot. These adverts made me rush out to buy their products. I was constantly reaching for an external solution. I tried every product going for my face and nothing worked. Sure, dirt came off onto the face wipes, but why did my spots persist? My skin was cleaned three times a day! My acne was a permanent feature on my face and would worsen depending on the level of intoxication I was subjecting my body to.

The skin on my face did ease up as I grew older, but it was my back that was the real problem. I would have large lumps that would grow under the skin and would become ever so painful. My back would be covered in these large, septic spots that were so sore and if popped, they would bleed horrendously. I had to be careful in my choice of clothing, as if I caught one, it would bleed through my top, causing extreme embarrassment. My bed sheets would be covered in large patches of dark blood due to them popping in the night as I turned. My partners were able to look past my skin issues and it didn't bother them, but it bothered me. I felt hideous and ashamed.

Holidays were an absolute nightmare. I was so self-conscious of these hideous cysts on my back, I was like a human dot to dot! The very thought of being seen by people on the beach, or around the pool, made me feel like a freak. Sad isn't it, that I let my hang ups spoil the enjoyment of a holiday? I would rarely go in the pool, even though I loved to swim. I cared more about how others would perceive me, instead of focusing on my own enjoyment. Oh, Mr Ego, how I allowed you to hamper my progress in life for so long!

My body was covered in these huge spots and I would want to hide away from the world, due to embarrassment. I would constantly cover my body up and be ashamed of it. In reality, I wanted to hide away from myself and was embarrassed of who I was deep down. The fact that I didn't have a family unit growing up and that I was different from my friends was the real cause of all my symptoms. I know the truth now, but it took me years to realise this. I now love who I am and my back is spot free!

As I write this, as a 35-year-old man, I feel like I am armed to face anything that the world chooses to throw at me, simply because I love myself and know who I truly am. My life has just begun, it's like a second birth! I can have anything I want as a product of thought and belief, including my health. Listen to your body, as it is trying to help you, not hinder you! Please don't abuse it by telling it to shut up with a manufactured placebo!

This chapter may sound somewhat negative towards the wonders of modern science and that is not my point, far from it. Modern science is discovering new wonders about the human body every day. I love reading books on new discoveries and the marvels of what man is achieving through science. With a better understanding and a more holistic approach to our health, we could avoid the intervention of medical help from our doctors. After all, prevention is better than cure. If people can understand how their thoughts determine their health, then the General Practitioners, as we know them, would not be so overrun. The mind is a powerful tool.

What the NHS did for my brother Dean was amazing and incredible. Without the research that scientists had done into Cystic Fibrosis, treating Dean's karmic condition could have not been possible. Dean's life could have been shorter than it was, had it not been for the medical advancements. That is why I praise the staff and scientists that helped to sustain my friend's life for so long. The help that Dean received, coupled with his positive thinking, helped him to lead a relatively normal life, considering his condition. We can all become conscious of our thoughts, so that we live a happy and healthy life, after all, that is what was intended for us. Dean came to this planet with his path already planned, his health was predetermined through his karmic choice. This did not stop him demonstrating the power of positive belief and living well beyond his predicted age.

Your body consists of 50 trillion cells and each one is listening to your every thought. They are eager to serve you and carry out your command of thought, how will you program them? With fear and hate or with love and harmony? How you think will determine the health of your beautiful body, which, in itself, is a miraculous gift.

46

NUTRITION AND EXERCISE

Establishing that our thoughts create our current level of health, what else can influence the wellbeing of our body? Our diet of course! Now we know that everything has a certain vibrational frequency, what vibration is your food? Most processed man-made foods are vibrationally low or even dead. Consuming these foods constantly will ultimately lower your own vibration and affect your health.

Foods that are vibrationally high are those which are alive like you! Vegetables and fruits are alive and carry a high vibration. Putting vegetables into your diet can really alter how you feel. When you do purchase vegetables, try to make sure that you purchase organic vegetables whenever possible. Most supermarket vegetables have been produced in unnatural ways and sprayed with carcinogenic chemicals. Eating a diet that is rich in foods that are alive will leave you feeling alive. You could say that eating just vegetables is healthy, but what is the real definition of healthy?

If you were to do a search on the internet as to what is considered *healthy*, you would get a million different results. My interpretation of *healthy* is balance. I have cooked for many years now and many of those were for the elderly and malnourished. I have attended many nutrition courses over the years, and I have seen what has worked and what hasn't worked, and in my opinion, balance is key.

Everyone wants a quick solution to their weight and there are a lot of fad diets around now. Ketosis is one that consists of just proteins and fats. This diet is a very efficient way of converting fat into energy and you will have terrific weight loss results, but it is not healthy. In the absence of carbohydrates, the protein's sole purpose cannot be met. Protein helps repair cells and contribute to muscular preservation. With protein and fat being used as the primary driving force to create energy, carbohydrates are no longer needed. Sustained and frequent use of this diet can be adapted to suit the body, however, this is not what the body prefers.

Look at all of the natural wonders that grow from this planet like fruit and vegetables. Essentially when they are digested, they convert into sugars, which is all carbohydrates are. We are intended to eat all of these beautiful vegetables and fruits which grow so abundantly on Earth. To eliminate these little delicious wonders from our diets really is unhealthy in my opinion. The body will adapt to anything you throw at it, including these fad, superficial diets, but why do you want to give your best friend such a hard time? Love and pamper the gift of your body. Try to be mindful of what you are putting into it, after all, you are what you eat.

As stated earlier, the body needs proteins which contribute to the maintenance and rebuilding of muscle tissue. Carbohydrates are what provide energy for our bodies. Fats help to contribute towards maintaining hormone levels and they also allow vitamins from vegetables to be absorbed correctly. When these three elements are present in a meal, the body can work in harmony and operate at an optimal level.

It is established that we all need protein in order to function. Where do we get that protein from though? There is a whole book to be written about the ethical implications of eating meat and consuming dairy. I consumed meat and dairy all of my life for it was all I knew. I never questioned if I should be eating it, for it was all I knew and what had been programmed into me as a child.

I now see a divine connection between everything and a level of oneness to it all. That is why meat is no longer for me. I could never inflict such fear onto another creature by leading it to the slaughter for my own egoic needs. Could I cut an animal's head off? No, but my choices in the past only led to the slaughter of thousands of animals. I simply purchased the animal's dead carcass for my own bombastic needs. I essentially paid someone to do my dirty work for me with little regard as to how the animal was treated. If no one ate meat, then the demand for the death of animals would cease. The meat industry that only cares about profit would simply collapse because of supply and demand.

There are numerous health benefits from cutting out meat and dairy from our diets. The hormones that are pumped into animals and the fear that they experience are all part of what we then put into our bodies. Animals are genetically modified to grow at an unnatural rate so that they can produce maximum size in minimum time. Chickens can be fully grown in six weeks forcing limbs to break as their bone structure is not in sync with such forced growth. These genetically engineered birds that are injected with antibiotics are then shipped off to slaughter like inanimate objects. We then fry the genetically engineered birds and consume the chemically raised creature for our own egoic needs. Consider what we are actually ingesting and the impact of our decisions on the welfare of animals.

There are also global repercussions that occur from the consumption of meat. Forests are cut down at an alarming rate in order to create space for the 2-5 acres of land that are used by cows alone. 1-2 acres of rainforest are cleared every second destroying countless wildlife. The methane gas that is produced by the animals even adds to global warming as it is on such a mass level. The water that is consumed by these animals also takes a toll on the world.

The planet is amazing and has been through five ice ages, before humans even evolved. It is constantly rebalancing and knows what to do, but it is finite. Miracles are possible and do happen, but I don't see why I should contribute to the downfall of the planet. I want to leave this planet in the best condition. I can now do this to the best of my knowledge as I have done my own research.

I even had a debate with spirit in my last reading that I had with Jo. I asked my guides, "Are we meant to be eating meat?" Their answer was one that resonated with me. My guides stated that it is everyone's personal choice. We have evolved this way and we are all one, but we must be conscious if we choose to consume meat. The real issue is, are you consuming meat for glutinous purposes with no regard for the animal or how the creature got onto your plate in the first place?

My guides also stated that the real problem with the meat industry is the unethical process that the whole industry incorporates into its methods just to get its products onto the supermarket shelves. The animals live through horrendous conditions and the plastic packaging that they are wrapped in is a real problem for the planet.

So that is spirits take on the whole meat saga. Be your own person and if you continue to eat meat, try to be conscious of how you obtain it and the frequency in which you consume it. Be aware of what chemicals you are putting into your body and the fear and dis-ease that that animal once experienced.

Better options can be eating organic meat, where the animal has actually had a life. Your choice is adding to the quality of life that animals will have. By eating organic grass-fed animals, you know that they will not be slaughtered after just spending a few weeks on the earth. The animals will not have been pumped full of growth hormones; this too is a conscious approach. Of course, you could just stop eating meat altogether if that sits better with you, which is the road that I have chosen. Just be conscious of your choice and the whole domino effect that it has on the world.

Before quitting meat, I read an article on Native Americans. They are extremely spiritual people and nurture their cows in a holistic way. The cows graze the ground and are loved as if they were part of the family. When the cow's spirit leaves its body, the physical that is then left behind is eaten to honour the life that the cows had. No meat is wasted and its carcass nourishes the human body through which blessings and thanks are given. When you think about it like that, it is a beautiful, harmonious process; the cycle of life embodied through an act of love. I found this an interesting way of life.

Protein can be obtained from other sources and not just living animals which I am more aware of now. Nuts, lentils, chickpeas, beans, and pulses all offer generous amounts of natural protein. Complex carbohydrates are important too. Wholegrain rice and sweet potatoes are my favourite carbs to keep me ticking over, whilst avoiding a sugar crash. Root vegetables can provide this too. As far as I'm concerned, any vegetable is game, if it grows from the same earth that we walk on, how can it be bad?

Organic is the way forward, as mass-produced vegetables are sprayed with carcinogens and go through unethical processes towards the earth. The same goes for salads as well, be mindful of how they are produced. A salad does not have to be boring either, as I once thought! An example of a tasty salad that I love is; carrot, beetroot, mixed leaves, pumpkin seeds, roasted asparagus, olive oil, white wine vinegar, balsamic and wholegrain mustard; trust me it is delicious. Experiment with seasonal produce and try to buy organic wherever possible. I had a view as a child that vegetables were so boring and drab, but with a tiny bit of creation, they can be so much fun! They are so beautiful and colourful on your plate too!

I speak with such passion about taking care of this amazing gift that is our body, because I used to abuse mine. I had no regard for the magnitude of the gift that I was in possession of and took it for granted. Constantly, I was pumping it full of junk, the body is much like the Universe reversed. What we put out to the Universe is returned to us, but what we put into our body is what we get out of it. If we fill it with man-made junk, this can be the equivalent of pollution. Our bodies will then give us an experience to match that of what we consume. We will feel lousy, sluggish, constantly irritable and tired.

When we nourish our bodies with fresh, natural, vibrant foods, we are going to radiate vitality. Foods have vibration too and vegetables are alive. What do you think will be higher vibrationally? A carrot or a piece of bread? The choice is yours. Vigour and energy will be prominent in your thoughts and feelings when you choose foods that are alive. We will be able to think with clarity and process information easily. When we eat foods that are made in a factory, how do we think we are going to feel? Is your food from a man-made factory plant or a natural plant? We literally are what we eat.

The word *diet* is just another word for torture in my opinion. Diets do not work and if you are serious about losing weight, a holistic lifestyle change is needed. Diets do not have balance and specific ones like the ketosis diet eliminate components and ingredients that the body needs! As soon as a diet is completed, the individual returns to consuming the foods that they did previously, and the weight reappears. The word *diet* has too many negative connotations attached to it and people are already setting themselves up for failure from the get-go. They view the diet as a challenge and punishment, this will lead to something that is not achievable.

People can associate diets with cutting out foods that they love and depriving themselves of anything fun. Remove the barrier of a diet and change the way you live in general. You can still eat the foods that you enjoy, just in moderation. If I ate pizza every night, I would eventually get bored, plus, I would feel like rubbish all the time. (I am sure that there are many who disagree with that last statement!?)

In the past, I would live off pre-packaged foods and convenience items that offered little nutritional value to my body. Cooking to me consisted of throwing whatever possible into the microwave. I no longer use a microwave as I cannot comprehend the logic of taking a baked potato that has grown out of the earth in natural conditions, and then zapping it with nuclear energy. What goodness will be left in that poor little spud at the end? I really didn't care what I ate in the past or how it was produced! My priorities lay with alcohol and it really didn't matter what I ate when I was pissed! I used to weigh about eleven stone and looked like a bean pole. My weight started to increase in a healthy way when I started going to the gym.

This is where exercise comes into a lifestyle as well. For some, the word exercise can mean different things. If you told me that we were going for a 5-mile run, I would probably faint at the thought of it. Running just isn't for me but like music, different things float different people's boats.

I have a dear friend whose name is Luke. Luke loves competing in triathlons. To me, this is hell incarnate. Luke, however, thinks that I am crazy going to the gym, picking things up and oiling my body up in the mirror, as he puts it (I don't do the latter, just for the record.) Essentially, what I am doing when I go to the gym is just picking heavy things up, so Luke is right there. This sounds ludicrous when you put it like that, but it works for me.

I absolutely love lifting heavy things. I get a twisted satisfaction about squatting heavy weights, even though it makes me feel sick at the time, it lets me know I'm alive and that I can push more weight if my mind allows it, not my body! It is just another example of how powerful the mind is. When attempting a new weight, I begin to feel nervous and think that I may fail. When I shift my thoughts to positive ones, the weight goes up. This is similar to life, when we have belief, we can achieve anything, not just in the gym.

My point is to find what works for you. Luke has found his happy place through running. Exercise doesn't mean going to the gym and running for hours on the treadmill, find out what works for you. There are classes, sports, yoga, even walking, anything that stimulates those feel-good chemicals in your brain. I have recently started yoga myself and find it very challenging, which is surprising as my ego told me that it would be child's play!

If you say that you do not have enough time, then you are making excuses, make time. We could all make a thousand excuses to avoid doing something if we wanted to, but once a routine is established, you will learn to love it! Procrastination is the partner of excuses and when you learn to live in the now, you can start doing!

They say once you do something for more than 21 days, it becomes a habit, bear this in mind when starting your fitness journey. Sounds simple doesn't it? If only! But you may be surprised once you have completed your new regime for a set amount of time. You may fall in love with it and no longer view these activities as chores. The way that you will feel, will make you want to leave your old lifestyle behind. The endorphins will be flowing and it can become addictive, just keep it on balance. Exercise is like life, the harder it is, the stronger you become! Do you like that one? I nicked it off our gym wall, but it is very true and inspiring. Also, another gym saying which can be applied to life is, "If it doesn't challenge you, it won't change you."

The old roads that we walk can be so familiar sometimes. We know the road and what to expect. We know that it may not always be the best choice and it may even annoy us, but we still decide to continue down it anyway. This can be the equivalent to sitting in, drinking alcohol on the sofa and eating junk food. This is the norm for much of society but deep down, that little voice tells us that we are better than that.

To begin a walk down a new road can be daunting to say the least. It is unfamiliar, out of our comfort zone and just intimidating to the ego. But remember, that old comfortable road was once a new road which you had to trundle down, so bear this in mind for your new journey. Embrace this new road, who knows what beautiful scenes you will witness? Of course, this road I am talking about is completely metaphorical, but if you do wish to walk down an actual road that is new to you, be my guest, at least you will be exercising. Once you're halfway down your new road, you will wonder what prevented you from visiting this wonderful place before. The old road will look so dull and grey, you will never look back.

YouTube videos can be a fantastic way to learn new exercises if you are unsure or afraid of what you will look like. I understand it is off putting the first time you walk into a gym or class with little idea of what you're doing. This is only a product of the famous ego and can be squashed immediately. What you are saying is that the fear of disapproval from others is worth more than what you think of yourself. If someone were to judge you, what does that say about them? You are number one and remember that all the people in the gym had to start somewhere; they probably felt the same way that you did. So, go and live a little, try something new.

This leads me onto water, random I know, but for me exercise and water go hand in hand. I drink about half of my daily consumption of water when I am at the gym. You may see all the health and sports drinks advertised which are deemed as healthy but in fact, they are just liquid sugar. They may be a hindrance to your goals if you do not burn it as energy. If you are an athlete, then these drinks are beneficial, as the energy will be converted as intended. But if you are just at the beginning of your fitness journey, refined sugars need to be avoided.

Water is just wonderful in my eyes, without it, where would we be? I drink it all day long and cherish every mouthful. I thank the Universe each time I have a sip. Now I know that all I bang on about is balance and how important it is, but you can actually drown if you drink too much water or induce intoxicating effects upon yourself. So, beware of how much you actually consume!

Interesting studies have been conducted regarding the power of water. Dr Masaru Emoto concluded that when water is stored in containers that are labelled with positive words, it changes its molecular structure completely. Even through speech, water still changes its structure. If water is spoken to negatively or stored in a container that is labelled with negative words, the water takes on a totally different composition.

If you were to freeze water that had been stored in a negative environment until it crystalised and placed it under a microscope, its structure would be random, fragmented and would have no cohesion. When water from a container that has positive words on it is frozen and then placed under a microscope, it has a totally different look about it. Its crystallised structure is symmetrical, has cohesion and is beautiful. Taking this experiment into account, consider that our body is made up of 60 to 70% water. How we treat that water in our body is so important. Ensuring that we are constantly hydrated is paramount.

On another side note, (I do those a lot don't I?) our thoughts shape everything about our bodies. With the water experiment in mind, if we are forever thinking negative thoughts and ones of self-hate, what is that going to do to the water content in our bodies? If spoken words can affect water's structure so dramatically while it's in a container, then surely how we speak to ourselves internally affects our giant container of water which is our body!

If we were able to place the water content of a human body under a microscope, one that was constantly subjected to negative and oppressive thoughts, what would the molecular structure of that body look like when frozen? Surely it would look the same as the container that was full of negativity; embodying qualities that are disjointed, fragmented and have no cohesion. Transform this to our waking lives and what sort of quality of life do you think that we will experience? Probably one that is dogged with ill health, aches and pains. Maybe after reading this, you will have a different approach to the beauty of water and just how powerful it is?

Water can be infused with herbs or citrus fruits if you really find the taste appalling and want to add excitement to it. These can actually help as natural diuretics too and help you to shift water weight. If you have a salty, fatty meal, do not obsess over the scales the next day, or at all for that matter. If you were to pay attention to the scales after a treat meal, they may have gone up but that isn't actually fat, it is just water weight that has been retained, due to the excess sugar and salt from the meal. By going back to your normal diet and drinking water, you can easily flush out the excess water after a meal that is not the healthiest.

The scales can actually lie anyway, the numbers may be going up but you could be losing fat and also building muscle, let your clothes be the true guide as to how you gauge your progress. If you obsess about numbers, they will play mind games and we all know the power of a thought! Tell your body that you are *releasing* weight if that is your goal, rather than *losing*. Losing is a negative emotion and we want to remain in a positive state about our new goals.

Supplements, in my opinion, are just a waste of money and are just processed chemicals that are sold in glamourous bottles. I attended a food and nutrition course once where the gentleman speaking told me the science behind supplements. I was genuinely horrified! I spent so much of my hard-earned money on these magic pills, to prevent me from becoming ill. Of course, they never worked, I was always ill, so I would repeat the cycle by buying more in the hope of curing myself.

The gentleman used the example of a carrot. A carrot contains beta-carotene, this vitamin can be bought in the form of a supplement. Beta-carotene has wonderful properties for the body, so why wouldn't you want the benefits of this vitamin going into your body? Sellers of the supplement can advertise its properties on the label and list the health benefits that it provides. They are not lying either, that vitamin is backed up by science. This is, however, where the supplement becomes useless.

The properties of beta-carotene are absorbed into the body when they are encased in their natural surroundings, a carrot. The beta-carotene works harmoniously with all the other compounds found in the little orange miracle (which were originally purple) that nature has provided and are released into the body. With all these components amalgamating together, the properties of each vitamin and mineral in the carrot can be dispersed around the body, much to nature's intention.

The ingredients are all working in harmony together to do their jobs, providing the total package for the body. When you extract a specific part of that natural compound, the desired component of the harmonious package cannot perform its intended action and function, due to the loss of the surrounding ingredients that support it. It is the equivalent to taking the flour away from a cake recipe and baking the flour separately. Will baking flour on its own help you to obtain that sweet, light, spongy texture and flavour, that is provided by a cake? It simply can't, because it is just flour and missing its other supporting ingredients that react with the flour and cause the cake to rise. There are no eggs, sugar or butter present to complete this chemical reaction. (Yes, baking is a science!)

Can you now see how this example applies to nature? In the absence of a natural environment, individual ingredients cannot perform their specified tasks. To extract something specific from nature is achievable, but you are stripping it bare of its intended surroundings. To state what the extracted vitamin provides to the body is also not a lie, as when it is in its natural state, it will perform its specific role. But, without the natural elements that help to provide the holistic potion, the ingredient in question cannot deliver and is simply a waste of time and money. It is synthetic and unnatural. The supplement market is expected to be worth around $278 billion by 2024. All they are providing in the cold light of day are very expensive placebos. All the hidden nasties that are also in supplements and added extras are not what the body was intended to ingest.

Take the creatine tablets that I used to take, in the hope that I would get big and strong. Creatine is a naturally occurring substance that can be found in eggs, meat and fish. When creatine is in its natural state within these foods, it can be absorbed by the body. When creatine is in a capsule form, it finds itself in unnatural surroundings with gelling agents and all other sorts of goodies. Most of the ingredients in supplements are hardly recognisable.

Of course, people will tell you that supplements work and there are many studies to back this up. I too would agree that supplements do work but not through their intended purposes. I feel that supplements exploit the power of the mind: "As you think, so shall you be."

If I were to give you a pill that came with statistics and a medical explanation from a leading professional in the pharmaceutical world to demonstrate its success ratio, chances are, you would believe that the pill could provide the same results for you. The mind would then create the desired effects that the pill promised. It is no secret to the supplement industry how fantastic the human body is and how powerful the mind can be. The mind can create anything that we believe and desire. This is why I stopped wasting hundreds of pounds on supplements per year. I am now healthier than when I used to take supplements.

When we choose a holistic approach to the mind, body and soul, we can achieve anything. Illness will no longer become an option you consider.

Leading a healthy lifestyle and practising positive affirmations along with meditation can really transform your life. After a few months of living this way, you will wonder what took you so long to discover it!

Let your mind be open to new possibilities and be closed to nothing. I had a 'know it all' attitude for so long and my negative cycle of life would simply persist. You can change the way you think and change your life, it's so easy when you start. Health is so important and you have a right to be happy and healthy. I used to vow never to change, as this was a sign of weakness, and stay true to myself, how wrong was I!?

47

OUR BRIEF HOLIDAY ON PLANET EARTH: WHAT SOUVENIRS WILL YOU TAKE BACK WITH YOU?

We all have a set amount of time on this earth which has already been predetermined by our higher self when we initially planned this wacky trip. When you plan a holiday, you set an amount of time that you will experience the trip for, it is the same with life. Your exit is already predestined, and it will all be perfect. While you are here on your holiday on planet Earth, you may as well make the most of it and leave a positive impression while you are a guest on it. Also consider what you will take home with you from your journey. On what will you choose to spend your currency? Some luggage will not be allowed on your return flight, therefore, you will not want to place too much emphasis on the things you cannot take home. Invest your time in the right things in order to gain the most from your holiday.

While you are here, be conscious with what you learn and who you actually think you are. Do not let your ego and intelligence place limits on who you actually could be. With this ideal, you are only as smart as what you last read. If you become lost in the structure of who you think you are, that is created by your intellect and your ego, you will miss the beauty of the trip. Simone Weil articulates this in a beautiful quote of hers, "The intelligent man who is proud of his intelligence is like the condemned man who is proud of his large cell."

Academic knowledge is just the product of having a good memory and recalling it in certain situations. The mind that generates knowledge will one day be dust, so be wary about the amount of time that you attribute to gaining knowledge about trivial and frivolous matters. Try not to get lost in the analytical side of things because it will cloud those everlasting beautiful holiday snaps that can be taken when using an objective perspective.

Wisdom however can be taken home with you on your return journey. Wisdom will be carried by the soul and has infinite space in which to fit it all in. I am not suggesting that we stop learning light-hearted content completely and retreat to a cave, but we must see knowledge for what it is. If you enjoy learning, go for it but don't let it cloud your trip. It stems back to balance again and again! Sure, I love to learn and I have quite an extensive knowledge of pop music throughout the 90's; I am not entirely sure if that is something I should be proud of though?

I still choose to focus on trivial matters from time to time, but now I mainly focus on wisdom. This is what I want to take back home with me. Imagine if wisdom were a class at school. Imagine if we could acknowledge the power of wisdom from an early age. Imagine if they taught children at school the importance of love in the world. Imagine if we taught our children the power of meditation in order to handle emotions and expand consciousness. Instead, I feel that we place too much emphasis on past events and trivial subjects in school.

The knowledge that we are taught only moulds us to comply with the world that we live in. Mathematics is of great importance to us in order to help us with money matters later in life. English is essential as it has aided me in the writing of this book. Science can also be an invaluable subject to learn as it helps us to understand the world around us. However, the content of what we are taught in these subjects ultimately feeds a carefully constructed system that has been created to preserve order and divide us.

Imagine if what we were taught didn't have an ulterior motive to benefit others and perpetuate the rank and division between people. What if we learnt in a harmonious way and learnt that everyone was equal? The imaginary class system that so many of us buy into would be eradicated. Rich and poor people would be a thing of the past and oneness could be achieved. Imagine if what we taught at school set the platform for our journey and why we are here. A classroom within a giant classroom which is the earth.

The science that is taught at school currently only benefits the system that we live in. Children do not learn about the power of thought and law of attraction. Children do not learn about how we vibrate at certain frequencies and can avoid illness with our vibrational beliefs. Why? Because that would be bad for business. We accept that the laws of physics and gravity are real when we are educated at school, so why isn't the law of karma or law of attraction taught? These are in essence the scientific workings of the world too. They are spiritual laws.

If children were to realise from an early age that we are all composed from the same ingredients that are found in water, the plant, the mineral and the animal, then perhaps they would have an easier time accepting that we are all one and not view themselves as a separate entity. Imagine if that was taught in modern day science classes? The reality of quantum physics and that we are all just one pool of energy. What world could we build upon that knowledge?

History is a wonderful tool and is beneficial in order to help us learn from the past mistakes of others. It can also be used to see what worked in the past and how our ancestors helped pave the way for where we are today. It is good to know where we came from and how we have evolved, but do we need to be tested and graded on it to separate those with a good memory from those who haven't? Or does this ideology just play into the hands of the system? To separate the clever from the unclever at an early age is surely the beginning of the rich and poor divide. What do you think? Do you think that it is imperative that we remember dates and equations in order to advance spiritually? Or does this only serve the system that creates division on Earth? Do you think that we have a pop quiz at heaven's gates in order to enter when we pass? I'm not so sure.

Imagine gently approaching the pearly gates with a sense of apprehension, coupled with sheer awe for the magnitude and celestial beauty of your surroundings. The golden gates slowly open to reveal white light and a paradise of your wildest dreams. A bearded man then approaches and says, "Tell me what you have learnt during your time on Earth?" You then proceed to tell him how forgiveness, unconditional love, oneness and unity are the core lessons that you have brought back with you.

"Rubbish," he replies, "what was the date of the battle of Hastings?" You think and reply, "Ummmm, I always forget that one, give me another!"

The bearded man reluctantly gives you one last chance, "Okay then, an easy one, what is the mathematical equation for Pi?"

You think to yourself, *oh damn it, I was always so awful at maths* and respond, "I forgot, I don't know!"

The robed man looks dumbfounded and bemused as to how you could not know such a simple and elementary part of mathematics. "One last chance," he says, "for I am a saint."

He then asks one final question, "What was the meaning of Brexit?" (Sorry I had to get it in there!) *That's it*, you think to yourself, *I'm done*. "How am I meant to know that!?" you whimper. With that, the gates slam shut and you are cast to hell to suffer for eternity!

Can you see now how all of these trinkets of knowledge only help feed into the man-made system that we have been born into? They have no relevance to the progression of our soul and only exploit our minds and ego. We could teach children how to manage their thoughts and identify emotions. More of an emphasis is now being placed on the well-being of children, which is fantastic; I never really had that support when I was at school.

Well-being sessions in school are becoming increasingly common and are readily available to help children. I believe we are taking huge evolutionary steps by doing this and we can build on this even further. Imagine if mental health was woven and embedded into all parts of the curriculum. A child could then identify the information that they were being taught with their own unique opinion.

Instead of placing so much importance on the past, children could be taught about the importance of the future. How their conscious actions can affect the future of the planet. How important it is to look after the planet while we are here so that it is intact for the next generation of souls that wish to learn when they choose to visit. The whole aspect of oneness could be reiterated from an early age. Children already know this, we did too when we arrived here. The trouble is we are untaught what we already know. We are taught to be separate and to fall in line. If what we already knew when we arrived here was perpetuated and continued into our adult lives, the world would flourish as it would simply be an extension of spirit - our natural source.

I realise that countries need structure and laws in order to function. There is nothing to stop this from still happening, but let's incorporate the power of love and unity into our teachings; not that of the ego and separateness. Let children live what they already know. We are all one, but unique in our own special way. Souls can learn about what they really came to study at school and excel our evolution as a human race. Everyone just wants a happy life, don't they? So, if that is everyone's objective, what is stopping us? The illusion of separateness created by the ego. With global education about recognising the ego, we could make it happen. Everyone would finally be aware that we need the ego to function but that it is the false self.

If an equal world were to be created, how would we manage it? There would still have to be some rules and regulations, or the world would have no balance due to lack of communication. We would still need a hierarchy system as such, but this would no longer be ruled by the megalomaniacs that crave abundance and omnipotence in all aspects of their lives. Rulers would realise that hoarding all the world's wealth for themselves and allowing others to suffer is not contributing to their own personal growth or the planets. It is actually hampering their own transcension and they are only cheating themselves by holding onto such self-centred ways. When love and pure love rules the world, the mass consensus of the globe would then be to look out for one another.

When I go on holiday, I try to take care of the accommodation in which I am staying. I try to leave it in the same state as when I found it, the same could be said for our brief holiday on planet Earth. It is our responsibility to be conscious of how we treat this giant hotel that accommodates our very existence for our current trip.

We are guests on this planet and it doesn't need us, it has already proven that by existing for billions of years before we arrived. The Universe is abundant and can provide sustenance and nourishment for everyone if we look after it. If we replaced what we took, the earth would thrive. This isn't the case with our current position though.

I believe that the earth knows how to adapt and survive just like we do, after all, it looks after everything that lives on it and has done for millions of years. The Earth apparently went through five ice ages before we even evolved into humans. This suggests that the planet is constantly evolving and forever will be, regardless of who is on it. It is constantly rebalancing itself.

The media makes us aware of the current state of the planet by reporting on the effects of global warming. Rainforests are being cut down and the planet is being stripped of all the resources that it has. Natural disasters seem to be occurring more frequently and I feel that the planet is trying to communicate with us. Mother Nature is trying to make us aware of our global attitude towards the planet. In turn, the planet is once again trying the rebalance itself while heeding us with warnings about our behaviour.

Covid-19 could be seen as a warning from the planet. It could be saying, "Stop destroying me and look after me, for I sustain you!" Covid-19 forced us to unite and realise that we must evolve with the planet in order to survive. Pollution rates have dropped extensively due to global travel being restricted. The planet has done what it has always done and rebalanced in a short amount of time when lockdown was active.

There are many theories as to how the virus started and we will actually never know. Unless we were to see actual evidence in our immediate reality of how things were, we are none the wiser. Remember, you will only see on a screen what you are intended to see. One theory as to the origin of the virus stems from *wet markets*. If you are not aware of what these are, I encourage you to do your own research and see what you think. In my opinion, I can see how a virus could mutate from these conditions and be seen as a warning from Mother Nature. Stop killing and eating things unconsciously. Until we learn that we are all part of what we see, global imbalance will continue.

You can change the planet today. You might think that sounds crazy but it's true. If we all do our bit and spread the word, then change can happen! Change happens from within and starts with you. I now recycle everything, whereas before it was far easier for me to just throw it in the bin. What did I care about the planet? It wasn't my problem! I wasn't gonna be around in a hundred years to see the consequences of my actions! How little I knew! If we all adopted the attitude that I used to believe in, then it can only contribute to the downfall of planet Earth.

We can buy products that are produced with sustainable materials and are ethically sourced. Again, if we all followed suit, the people who produce these products would have no market base and would cease to trade. Maybe this would then awaken a change in these people, and it would help them to see that the choices they made were not the most conscious? We cannot criticise people who know no better, so let's show them an alternative way.

You cannot stop world poverty, that is in the hands of the elite. They are in control of the debts that are owed to them by many countries. They could scrap the debts if they really wanted to but that would upset the balance. I sound like I am criticizing these people but again, they know no better. I accept them as they are as they provide me with an opportunity to present new ways of thinking, which is what evolution is about.

We can all do our bit by donating money to charities and giving to the homeless. If we all gave, the world would spin in harmony. If every person in the world donated money, poverty would be eradicated. We would simply be moving money around to its next destination. In essence, that is what money is, a source or energy that is moved between people. How do you treat yours? By giving away what we have to others, we do our bit which contributes to the greater good. Try not to have a defeatist attitude like I once had, instead, do your part and spread the word. Be proud of the planet and the opportunity that you have to be part of this wonderful experience.

If there is something that you do not like in the world, do something about it rather than complaining about it and feeding it with more negativity. Speak up for what you believe in. Spread your truth and be who you came to be. Know and believe that every action you do is having a mass impact on the planet and the global consciousness. For when a butterfly moves its wings, it affects the wind across the other side of the world. Your actions are the same.

I am now considerate of every product that I buy and always look for the most sustainable option. This again takes conscious practice, and I am trying to do the best with the knowledge that I have at this current time in my life. I am a work in progress and human like you, I have my flaws but observe them and try to work on them. Developing a spiritual view can influence the choices that we make when we purchase goods and can be beneficial to the planet and our bodies.

While we are visiting this planet, let's do our best to make it an experience we can look back on and be proud of what we did. We can be happy that we took such care for the planet and our fellow man. Let the brief holiday that we find ourselves on be a productive one. Let us shape a positive future for the planet and for the human race.

When you return home, what memories and spiritual souvenirs will you take back with you? How will you have left your accommodation which was Earth? Will you have truly enjoyed yourself and changed things according to your truth? Or will you long for another return to do the things you wish you would have done?

48

Heaven, Hell, Dying, Souls & Spirit

There is no place or room called hell in the religious sense, as I was once led to believe. I knew this as a child but went along with what I was taught at Sunday school and allowed my purity to be tainted by the tales of the Bible. There are no fiery pits with mass conflagrations or a horned guy armed with a stick, poking you for his own personal amusement. The fact is that heaven and hell are happening right now. We do not have to wait to return to spirit in order to experience either.

Everything in our reality is a product of the mind and thought. If you view Earth as a hellish place which is full of evil, then guess what it will be? Hell. If you pertain to the notion that hell waits for you when you pass, that too is what will greet you. If you view this planet as heaven, then guess what it will be? Heaven. If you think that heaven waits for you when you pass, then you will be met with your preconceived image of what that is, no matter how limited or vast that may be.

While we are on Earth, these realities of heaven and hell are real to what we see, everything is about perception. Everything in our lives is an inner mirror of our consciousness and what we believe. What realms do the people who are consumed by their anger and rage live in? What realms do the people who have peace and love in their hearts live in? Once again, everything is an internal affair.

I view my current life as heaven, in the past it was hell. I used to create hell for myself continually through my karmic choices and thinking, which led to what I would attract. Now, all I see is good in the world and that people are just doing their best. The ones who we deem to do *evil* acts have simply made choices that are dishonest to their true self. Their true self is a place of love.

They have chosen a path of error rather than evil, but our egos like to label their acts as evil so that we feel superior and separate from the *bad* people. They have chosen to walk this path because that is all they know. Where do all the people who have chosen error in their life go when they have left their body? What is the dying process?

When we pass, it is quite a pleasant process actually. How do I know this? I haven't died! Well I have, and so have you, many, many times and we are still here; we are just occupying different vehicles. We have done this multiple times, but the veil of forgetfulness prevents us from remembering past lives. This happens so that we can truly focus on what we came to learn for this lifetime. The density to each person's veil will be relevant to their journey and karmic path. Some come to Earth and never forget who they are, if this is the case, that is what is relevant to their journey.

This is where spirit comes in. Spirit can help to jog our memories if that is what we seek. Spirit can relay messages as to what happens when we do pass and what the process of reincarnation is like. We can learn this through trusted mediums. Now this is where I am asking you to open your mind and to be objective. I mean, it's not as if I have asked you to do any of this already with tales of pre-birth planning and metaphysics, but this is how it is!

When I first made acquaintance with Jo, I had no idea what she would say. I thought that she would be vague and ambiguous. The level of exact accuracy and personal facts that she delivered to me were simply astounding to my analytical mind. Taking this into account, spirit is as real as we are, in fact it is our true source. Jo gained my acceptance and trust within about ten minutes of me meeting her.

So, when you have found a medium that you can trust, would spirit not want to speak to those who are ready to listen? Dean described his passing to me as an instantaneous moment and it just happened, taking him by surprise. With Dean's description of the dying process, it really was quite simple, one to even be enjoyed for it is all part of the perfect cycle of our existence.

Numerous times the process of dying has been described in a pleasant and beautiful manner. These have been through spiritual literature, near-death experiences and messages from spirit. Even my own mother had a near-death experience, where she blacked out on the motorway, and described it as peaceful.

The words *dying* and *pleasant* do not really go hand in hand, do they? Especially in a culture that is heavily influenced and saturated by western ways and propaganda. Violence, pain or suffering are usually what is associated with death. This is because that is what is portrayed in our western society through the media and films. Now this isn't to say this isn't true if that is your belief, for belief creates everything in life and in death. But on the whole, dropping the body and returning to our natural state is like taking off a tight shoe. This expression was coined by a spirit named Emmanuel who was communicated through medium Pat Rodegast.

The Bhagavad Gita compares death to taking off an old coat. Imagine being stood in a hot, noisy, congested room that appears so real to you at the time. You then spy the exit door because you need some fresh air and make your way through the crowd. You approach the door, open it and step outside to reveal tranquil bliss consumed by peace and love. You toss the old coat aside that was once your perfect vehicle of exploration. The reality of the previous stuffy room now seems like a distant memory and the shackles and constraints of the human body no longer there to limit your infinite existence.

This is the reality of dying. As you make your transition, you return to rediscover the truth that you always knew and were a part of. The beauty of oneness. The illusion of separateness created by *maya* is shattered and you see your true divinity for what it has always been. It is our job to realise our true divinity as to what we are on Earth.

Have you ever woken up from a dream that felt so real and immediately felt relieved? The relief is caused by the realisation that you were asleep and back in reality, but what's to say the dream was your true reality and physical life is but a dream? Either way, the realisation that happens when you do wake up from a dream is what dying is like. It is beautiful and should be cherished and honoured. As soon as you make your transition, you will see how life is but a fleeting dream and that all is perfect. You will realise the perfection of it all, even though it appeared so abstract when you were in the thick of it!

Now, there is not a set process for dying that we all follow, for we are all individuals. We will all experience different sensations and experiences based on our mind. Those who have had near-death experiences each have a unique account of what happened to them, but in general, most souls who return to their natural state will go through a similar process. As we are all creators, belief really does shape everything that we will experience when we transition back to love.

If an individual were to have a particularly rigid or dogmatic view of what happens after they pass, then that shall be met, for the mind creates reality. Beliefs that have been learnt on Earth stay with us and once again, I will state that we have complete free will over everything, including the passing process. If an individual were to have a certain fixation with Earth, then the process could become a long-winded one, but there is no rush, for we have forever.

Depending on how the person passes can have a profound effect on the passing experience too. If it was a sudden passing, the soul may be lost and confused and need guidance from their guides. If the soul passes because of suicide, complex karma would be incurred and would cause more pain to the soul in the long run. As stated earlier, this isn't as punishment or that suicide is condemned by spirit, you are loved no matter what and you are the only one that ever judges yourself, but when we take birth on this earth, we enter into a divine contract that is to be cherished; it is a gift to learn.

Remember when I wanted to end it all by putting the gun to my head? Killing myself would have only brought about a temporary solace to a moment that passed. I would have had to come back and face the music sooner or later. My choices would have been selfish and that of the ego. It was only when I thought about the love that my nan had blessed me with that I stopped those desperate thoughts; you see, love always triumphs.

This is not to discredit those who are feeling suicidal. I know what it feels like when suicide is the only feasible option; it's like swimming against a painful current you can't control, you feel helpless. What level of pain is a person in that their only option is to end their human existence? They long for the return to the oneness of love on a subconscious level. They have my heart and sympathy for I too have experienced that feeling of complete torment, emptiness, and hate for life.

If you are reading this and have contemplated suicide, then I urge you, please do not. It is a temporary solution that you will have to live out in the future of your development. The pain will pass, I promise you. I understand that you don't want to hear this when you are in the thick of it, but it is true. Life is a miracle and there are billions of souls who would love to be on Earth, you have a gift. If your level of pain is so unbearable that you have no hope, please speak to someone and contact a helpline. I have enclosed a list of numbers and websites at the back of the book. You are never truly alone.

When an individual who passes is firmly in the moment and content, they are open to all that is around them. As we begin our journey home, old friends, loved ones, guides, and even animals make themselves known to us. Seeing familiar people instantly helps our soul feel at ease in the whole process. The image that a loved one projects will be an accurate representation of how they were remembered by us when they were on Earth. Of course, this image of their shell is not who they actually are, it is just a mental hologram made visible by their thoughts to identify themselves.

When the initial jubilation of our return home has been processed, guides will assist us in conducting a life review. Our guides are always helping us and are constantly by our sides throughout our journey. They are there whether we choose to acknowledge them or not. The life review with our guides helps us to learn, grow and develop even more.

We examine the choices that we have made, good or bad, and the domino effect that they had towards others and the planet. As we already know, the ego is a part of the human experience so we can view our choices objectively with no judgement, for the ego has been left with the body. There is no God to bow before and judge us, we simply assess ourselves. We can learn from the choices that we made due to the absence of the ego. Choices that we made will have karmic ramifications that will influence our future adventures and visits.

Our human thought patterns will also be examined in order to identify how we did indeed create our own health while on Earth. A constant nagging thought that you paid no attention to may have been the reason an individual was dogged with ill health in their three-dimensional existence.

We will experience the emotions that were caused by our actions to every single person that we ever crossed paths with, good or bad. This is so that we learn first-hand what we subjected others to through our choices and behaviour. Bear this in mind the next time that you act selfishly towards someone or wish them harm. By doing this you are buying into the illusion of separateness that is created by maya and essentially harming yourself, for we are all one. You will experience what you put others through, it is spiritual law. I say this not to install fear into you, for fear is part of the illusion of maya, but from a compassionate sense that will ultimately help you to identify with your choices and actions. When you realise that we are all one, your motives towards others may indeed change.

When experiencing the emotions that our actions caused others to feel, our souls may feel confused and have a profound time of contemplation, which will ultimately lead to growth. The soul that chose a path of error may now see why they went down the road they chose because of human conditioning.

The soul may still have attachments to the physical world that also need to be processed and released. They may choose not to proceed into the light because of this. A period of darkness could be manifested by the individual perceptions of that consciousness as a result. So hell can exist, but only in the individual's consciousness, much like on Earth. Our thoughts really do create reality in all planes of our existence. The only truth is that spirit is light, and we are all part of that light. We all eventually enter the light. What is the light? Mull on this but we will address it in much greater detail in the closing chapters.

After processing all of our past lifetime, it will feel as though we are home. We will have returned to our natural state and strive for more growth. We are one again. We can choose to have jobs in spirit, but not like the ones we have on Earth so don't feel disheartened with the prospect of an eternal 9-5! We will choose to do whatever offers our soul the most potential of growth. We could choose to stay with loved ones who are still on Earth and become their guides. I know that Dean has chosen to do this by becoming Gemma's guide.

We may choose to plan another adventure and reincarnate again on Earth. Earth is our greatest teacher. Its dynamic allows our souls to develop through the limitations of another physical experience. Pain is a great teacher to the soul. To the human shell, pain can be daunting, but the soul loves it! The dichotomy of pain and joy is very appealing to our growth.

So, what happens if our consciousness has evolved past that of a human experience? Where will we plan our next adventure? I believe that we can incarnate into any physical plane that is appropriate to the level of our consciousness. I do not have the level of comprehension or knowledge to speak of extraterrestrials, but all I know is that the galaxy, cosmos and Universe is our playground in which to learn. When we have outgrown Earth, surely we would like to experience another dimension?

We can create anything imaginable, so a physical form as an extraterrestrial would be no more complex than a human birth.

Not all dimensions need a physical body to learn from though, we can choose anything that we can imagine to suit our learning needs. Imagine standing in the middle of the cosmic abyss. You don't know who or what you are, but you know you want discover, explore, and learn about yourself. Any course be it physical or non-physical is available to you in order to further your learning and development of self. Your vibrational frequency will determine what course you incarnate into. For something that cannot be perceived, cannot be incarnated into. Metaphorically speaking, you cannot study for a university course when you are still at pre-school level.

Spirit consists of many planes that will host many different soul levels. Those who dwell in the lower astral plane will be drawn to Earth out of impulse and vibrational alignment. The lower astral is the closet to Earth and souls reside there because of their current vibration. Some souls do not incarnate at all and choose to linger around the Earth plane to feed off dense energy. Lower astral beings are the ones who still have extreme attachments to the physical, and wallow in low vibrational events, such as: addictions, extreme hate, violence, rape and murder.

The intermediate and higher level of the astral plane will house souls who want to learn about who they are and release old karma weighing them down from past mistakes, but are not obliged to return to Earth if they do not want to. All souls eventually will though, for they yearn to ascend. The higher Astral could be our concept of what Heaven is. Old emotional wounds, trauma, or regret may prevent a soul from rising higher, so they may choose revisit Earth to release and learn from old errors and karma, but this is through choice.

After the astral plane, there are the mental, causal, and akashic planes which are for souls who no longer need a physical body to progress with their learning. They can learn via their spiritual or light body. Then you move into the realms of unfathomable consciousness where the ascended masters and angels reside; the divine and celestial planes. Don't think that higher means better though, because ultimately everything is one. We will examine in more detail what it means to move higher and higher in chapter 55.

Lives run parallel in spirit and all we have is the now. We have many different experiences all at once projected by our higher self or soul. As we addressed earlier, our logical brains can only comprehend reincarnation through linear terms. If you are only just adjusting to the idea of reincarnation, stick to the basics at first, I don't want to frazzle your brain! It still baffles me to be honest, sometimes my brain hurts!

If the concept of reincarnation still feels like mumbo jumbo to you, consider there are plenty of accounts from children documenting information and events that would be impossible to know from their limited perspective. One of the most famous examples of this is an account from James Leininger of Louisiana. When James was 2, he started to talk about aviation, to which his parents had no knowledge on the subject. As James grew older, he would often have nightmares about being shot down in a plane by another plane with a red sun on it. He frequently spoke of being Lieutenant James McCready Huston, who was a World War II fighter pilot. This man who the boy spoke of had been killed 50 years earlier. According to his mum, James would scream, "Airplane crash, on fire, can't get out, help!"

James later spoke of how he had flown a plane called the *Corsair* from a boat that was named the *Natoma*. James' dad decided to do some research into his son's claims. With his findings, he discovered that there had been a small escort carrier called the Natoma Bay which was in the battle of Iwo Jima. The pilot was called James Huston. His plane was shot at by Japanese fighter pilots and as they hit the engine of his plane it caught fire on March 3rd, 1945. According to a psychologist that worked at the University of Virginia, Huston's plane crashed the very same way that James had described to his parents.

This account still makes me get goosebumps, and there are numerous accounts of tales like these if you want to do your own research. In fact,

I encourage you to seek the truth for yourselves. Our passings in previous incarnations could be responsible for unexplainable phobias that we have in our adult lives. Our return to spirit shows us that the demise of our physical body can never extinguish who we really are. Everything will make sense to us, even what may seem like a traumatic death to the ego.

Love is our natural highest vibration. When we are in this state, we may be able to receive messages with those who have passed, as our vibrations are a match for those in spirit. Thoughts may pop into our heads that we hadn't previously considered, this is usually a message from loved ones.

Most of us may not be able to communicate fully in this lifetime, for it takes many cycles of birth and death to master this. Spirit can however communicate with us in many different ways, if we allow it to. It is very hard for spirit to lower their vibration and match with someone who is in a negative, depressed state as spirit is love and the two simply don't match.

Most people report seeing *ghosts* in the middle of the night. That is because when you wake up, you are in a state of minimal resistance to that of your source energy. Your conscious mind can barely function as you stumble to the bathroom. Therefore, this is when you would be most susceptible to seeing spirit. It is only when we start to think our negative and judgemental thoughts that our vibration is lowered. If you have a wish to see spirit as *proof* of their existence, raise your vibration to that of a loving frequency. With practice, you can easily achieve this.

Just for the record, a *ghost* is a mental projection from someone's mind who is in spirit. A spirit who had a particular fondness for a place on earth when they were incarnate, may often think of that area and because they do this, their thoughts project a pseudo manifestation of their once human form to that place. That image of a person that we may then witness is nothing more than a manifestation of their thoughts into the physical world. Think of it like a hologram of their once human shell relieving old haunts, literally. That hologram has no substance to it and cannot interact with the physical world.

We too project these mental avatars of ourselves when we think longingly about a place or person, but these mental projections are rarely seen by other people for they are on the ego plane of awareness. Gurus have been known to be in a room and appear in other parts of the world all at once. They have also manifested objects before people's very eyes. This is all done with the power of thought.

I have seen my nan in my waking life on a few occasions. I saw her aura and energy appear like electric neon colours, coupled with an overwhelming feeling of love that made me want to cry. I see her too in my dreams and I frequently have visits from Deano in my dreams. Dreams are important, believe it or not we leave our body each night. Sometimes your soul will barely leave the body and hover over your physical shell. This is when our minds piece together the events of the day and week. These will then metaphorically transpire into physical thoughts so that we can interpret them as humans.

We do also visit spirit and meet loved ones in our dreams; this could be classed as astral traveling. These are the dreams that you wake up from where you are left with a vivid impression of a loved one. We can also go and do work in other galaxies that our subconscious mind blocks out when we awake. Have you ever awoken after a long deep sleep feeling exhausted? This is because you were off helping others on another plane of consciousness. The most common dream that we experience is the first one that I listed. This is the most frequent one that will be experienced by those who relate strictly with their physical existence.

Children are not long from the loving source of the Universe and still know the truth. For those of you reading this with children who are interested in learning about spirit, ask them questions about where they came from. Why did they choose you to be their parent? The ego begins to develop around the age of six or seven, so that is when children tend to forget where they came from and start to be fully consumed by the physical world.

Are imaginary friends actually spirit that children can communicate with? This is a possibility. Louise has a friend who has a young son. He is three years old and will often talk all night to people in his room. He stares and says, "Hello," to people, but no one is actually there. His mum says it is slightly spooky, but I have assured her this is natural and that her child is just being a child. He has an open mind which one day may be closed, much like the rest of us. If only we could rediscover that childlike mentality that I have been harping on about. If we were open to anything and attached to nothing, much like a baby, how our lives might change? Communicating with spirit would be much easier then.

Whether we can communicate with spirit or not, loved ones are always watching us and are right by our side, whether we choose to acknowledge them or not. I can often feel my guides' presence near me, and they often get my attention through ringing in my ears. I often feel Dean's presence as well as my guides. He always sends me many physical signs, which could easily be dismissed or written off as coincidence. Dean will often send me visions, feathers, coins and crap music in the shape of Will Smith or Aqua, these would appear in the most obscure of places! Ask your loved ones who have passed to send you signs. It can be very comforting to know that those who passed are watching and supporting our missions.

Spirit has so many ways of sending us little signs to let us know we are loved. Pennies from heaven is always a common one. Always check the dates on any penny that you find as they can often be related too. What were you doing in that year? Feathers are also a common sign and can appear in the most bizarre places.

Synchronicities and coincidences are also signs that cannot be ignored. When you realise that nothing is coincidence in this perfectly balanced Universe, then you will start to see the beauty of life. Number plates on cars and recurring numbers can all be messages from the other side as well. Look into the meaning of a number if it is a regular occurrence in your world.

I will often get a ringing in my ears at certain times, this helps me to pay attention to the current moment and what is happening. This ringing can also be downloads of information. The right ear is information of a spiritual nature. The left is a download about Earth and people's negative natures, it lets me know why people are like they are.

Robins and butterflies often visit me to let me know all is well and that the Universe really does have my back. Butterflies land on me and we just sit there together creating a beautiful moment of oneness.

Have you ever felt like you have walked into a spider's web but there is nothing actually there? That is a passing spirit that just wanted you to know that they are by your side and a reminder that you are never really alone.

Music can be a wonderful communicator and songs that remind us of our deceased loved ones can crop up in the most random of places. I often hear Will Smith songs come on randomly and this always reminds me of Dean; he really did like Will Smith! I personally think Will Smith is an awful rapper, but Dean loved him, each to his own I suppose. So be on the lookout for random songs in specific moments to help guide you.

Next time you find an object in a random location, do not write it off as a chance occurrence, actually consider the complex process that it took in order to cross your path at that exact moment and be thankful. You can practice being more observant to your surroundings and watch how these messages often appear to you. They have always been there, it's just that you will now be accustomed to them.

The following story can be seen as a coincidence or as circumstances too complex to explain. It demonstrates how intricate and multi-dimensional the Universe really is and how it works. It is a story about a sign from Dean that was all too perfect and mind-boggling when you break it down.

An exact year to the day of Dean's passing, I was travelling back from London on the underground. Dean loved poppies and every year he would always wear his to show respect to all who were involved in any war. As I sat on the gloomy, dingy carriage, I was thinking about how quickly a year had gone and what I had learnt from my Dean's passing. I couldn't believe how much I had changed in a year and I recalled that poignant moment where I was in that tiny hospital room where I watched my best friend pass. No sooner as I was thinking about this, the train pulled into a station. The carriage doors abruptly opened, and a huge paper poppy blew in through the door, drifted through the air and made its way halfway down the carriage to land in between my feet where I was sitting. Let's just examine the phenomena of that event.

I was travelling on a train a year to the day when my best friend had passed. I was thinking about my friend who loved poppies. I was sitting in a random location on the train. I could have chosen to sit anywhere but I chose there. As my train pulled into the station, there was a huge paper poppy resting on the concrete platform. It must have been dropped about seven days before, due to remembrance Sunday, which was on the 11th. The day I travelled was the 18th, so a week or so prior to my travelling was when the poppy could have been dropped.

Then consider that the poppy was laid on the exact part of the platform where my train would arrive. On the arrival of my train, enough wind was generated to lift the poopy up so that it flew through the doors as they opened. With enough gusto behind the poppy, it flew through the air, swirled and landed halfway down the carriage at my feet. All of these events occurred at the precise moment while I was thinking about my best friend. When you consider how perfect and balanced that whole event is, it makes you shiver! It could all just be a coincidence though… Again, the analytical part of your mind may choose to interpret this event as a unique coincidence. The real question is though, did *I* choose to sit in that precise seat, or had it already been predestined?

49

THE POWER OF PERCEPTION

From our previous chapters, we have established that there are definitely two sides to every story. Media can report a story in a positive or negative way, it is up to the viewer how they perceive it. Now this is going to come off incredibly ironic, but do not believe anything anybody tells you. This may make you think, "Why the hell have you just written this book then Dave?"

This book is supposed to challenge you and awaken you to the truth in your life. I hope that it encourages you to search for what is real. Don't always believe everything that is written, (apart from in this book, of course) as man has written books and man can lie. Instead, do your own research and discoveries. Try to look at every situation from multiple angles and choose what feels right for you in your heart of hearts. When you find the truth, it will resonate deep within.

I have examined much literature in the short time of my awakening. Not all of what I have read has resonated with me, in fact some of what I have read didn't register at all, for it was not my truth. When you find the truth, you will know it. I have only applied the aspects that have sat true with me in this book.

In the past, I have believed everything that was told to me by my friends, people in a position of power or from textbooks. Looking at the teachings of the Bible and its story regarding Noah's ark, I believed every single aspect of that while growing up. Only for a split second did I contemplate that what I was being taught was false, but went along with it regardless. I would often adopt the opinions of others and parade them as my own, without doing any research into the subject at hand. Make your own mark on this world and do not believe anything you see just because it has more likes or credibility attached to it. Dare to be a loner and follow your own path.

Perception is everything and will shape your reality. What world do you live in? If you immediately think evil, why is this so? What even is evil? Is your opinion formed because of what you have seen on the news? Imagine for a moment that the media and the news didn't exist, what malignant things would you witness truthfully? Without the internet, what would you see in your actual reality? Would you exit your house each day and witness murders? It is all about perception.

These events do occur in life, of course they do, I am not sticking my head in the sand by denying them, but by actively seeking them out, I am only lowering my own vibrational frequency which then leaves me useless to help others. My negative energy towards erroneous events is not something that is going to help to stop them. Therefore, we must invest all of our energy into making the world a better place by changing ourselves first. By focusing our energy on positive events, we are creating more of the same. By choosing a positive flow of energy, you feed the collective consciousness with love not fear.

Life can be beautiful or a dark place, it simply boils down to how you choose to view it. Heaven and hell are all constructs of the mind and our beliefs shape our reality and what we see. I have said earlier: for every bad event that you see on the news, there are a million acts of good happening across the world in the very same second.

Is the news accurately reporting what happened? Without witnessing an event for yourself, do you actually know the truth? Unless you have made conscious contact with the event in question, you will never know the true course of events that actually unfolded. To place belief in someone else's perception of an event is extremely trusting.

I was telling a story the other day to a colleague at work about a past event. The event happened when I worked as a chef with Gemma. It was quite a humorous tale and I told it how I remembered and perceived it.

While I was telling the story to my work colleague Gemma actually walked into the room. She asked what we were talking about and I repeated the tale to her and what it involved. "It never happened like that Dave," she responded. In my mind, I was shocked, I could have sworn that's how it happened? Gemma then proceeded to tell the story based on how she perceived it. Can you see how easy it is to believe another's interpretation of an event when it isn't actually true? An event simply is, it is the ego who processes and interprets the situation for what it is. The ego will then define what actually happened to suit its perception of reality.

What the previous story demonstrates is how easy it is to take another's word or account of an event at face value. Who does this the most? The news. The news is a real-life account of Chinese whispers which are then manipulated and broadcast worldwide. Our egoic minds then add to the tale with a judgement and condemnation. With all of this thrown in, it's easy to see how an event that may have never actually occurred can become real.

Let's take a stabbing for instance. First off, did the stabbing actually happen? The news said it did, so it must be true, I even saw pictures to prove it. Let's assume this stabbing is now real, what do you think when you hear those words? One person thrusting a knife into another. Where are you allowing your mind to now take you? In your mind, you have probably already made a judgement about what happened. You will have either labelled it good or bad. If you have labelled it a tragedy, why is that so? You are not wrong, any act of violence towards a fellow man is a step backwards and a choice of error from the truth, but do you see the whole picture?

Do you choose to view that one person's actions as the world on a decline? Or are you choosing to miss the fact that violence is on a statistical decline as the centuries have progressed? Does one act of violence outweigh the numerous acts of love that follow from people? Do you choose to just see the stabbing and miss the police who attend? Do you then miss the ambulance and hospital workers that are all involved in the act? Do you miss the communities that rally round to encourage others not to choose the same route as that one person? Do you miss the rehabilitation work that will be done in the prisons and community for the offender? See how much good has come from one seemingly negative event?

Do you let that one lost individual, who was acting out of fear, tarnish the whole of the world? That one act of fear from that lost soul is far outweighed by the immeasurable acts of good that followed. Taking all of this into account, how can the world be on a decline? Through falls come great beginnings and out of the darkness comes light. It's the oneness of it all that makes it so beautiful. Each soul has to learn and remember what is true and without their actions, they would not have the opportunity to grow. Through their actions, we can also learn and grow.

To all people who are involved in *tragedies*, is it not just an opportunity to ultimately forgive, love and grow, rather than condemn? Soul contracts are made in the pre-birth stages when planning a lifetime. Karmic paths will determine the murderer and the victim. These contracts are made to honour growth and help us to remember who we are for that unique journey. All concerned will learn from the event. How many times have we seen that tragic events are the catalyst for much-needed change? Crisis precipitates evolution. Labelling any event is just placing a judgement on the situation from the finite limitations of the human mind.

It is our job to help individuals who choose to offend, as they too were once little babies. What has happened for that little baby to grow up into someone who acts spontaneously out of fear? Or are they just evil? Again, this is based on perception and this is everything. If you view the world as a place of evil, where people are selfish and thoughtless, then you will be met with experiences that match your perception. With a perception of love, you will see events differently, I promise you that.

Another example of perception is a bus. I used to catch the bus all the time up until recently and have spent half of my life travelling to and fro on public transport. A bus is a big vehicle that drives on a fixed path taking people to their necessary destinations. Are all people on that bus experiencing the same thing? They must be, mustn't they? For they are in the same moving vehicle that has a predestined route.

This is where perception comes in. The world is unique to you and nothing until you see it or touch it exists, for you are the perceiver. There could be twenty people on a bus and that is twenty different journeys. Is someone hungover on the bus, are they only seeing shops as they drive by as they need sugar and food to feel human again? I was probably that person to be honest for many, many years!

Is someone on that bus angry about an argument they just had with a spouse? Do they see only grumpy faces to match their mood and notice the clouds in the sky? Is there someone on the bus who is in love? Are they seeing smiling faces and the sun creeping out from behind the clouds? Is someone sitting there who is anxious and living in their own headspace, while missing the world around them? Can you see how the world is unique to you and it can be whatever you want it to be? It really is quite a beautiful design.

If you view the world as a happy place where people help one another, that is what you will see. You can accept that people make mistakes, as that's how we learn. Start to see the good in life, rather than the one bad event that happened out of a million acts of good. When acts that we deem as bad occur, make it your mission to help people, rather than condemn and spread more hate into the world; adding to the collective negativity.

When we shift how we operate via our thoughts into a place of love and compassion, we immediately shift our vibration. You've got to have had those euphoric feelings and days where everything just seems to happen perfectly? Cast your mind back to your thought patterns that day and what it is that you did. Usually, it will involve helping others and thoughts of happiness and love. These thoughts vibrate at a high frequency and bring along similar events. When first falling in *love* with someone, those honeymoon feelings are blissful. All is well in our lives and nothing can seem to go wrong when we are in this phase. This happens as we choose to see all the good and operate from a high vibrational frequency which is who we truly are.

When you operate at such high frequencies, it's easy to just let go and trust that the Universe has your back and really wants you to have the best life possible. Granted it is easy to have faith in times like these when everything is going well, the real test is when things are not going so well. Can you remain vibrationally high through the rougher times and have faith?

Louise was having a meltdown yesterday over something trivial, such as household cleaning. I assured her I would help when I had finished my current task but that wasn't enough, she became irate and the air around us physically changed. I watched the events unfold.

She then proceeded, in the space of five minutes, to spill a glass of water everywhere and tread on some crystals that I had left on the floor. Her mood seemingly worsened, and she chipped the fireplace mantle as she slammed my crystals back where they belonged. I simply observed in silence while she had a mini breakdown and thought how perfect it all was to witness what I write about in full effect.

Her thoughts and perception progressively became worse and she only attracted more *chaos* into her immediate vibrational field. I sat there and saw how the tiniest things can come to teach us and thought that it was beautiful. Two people sharing the same space had totally different perceptions of reality. Afterwards we spoke about how perfect it all was and laughed about it, hindsight is indeed a wonderful thing!

The way we perceive things doesn't always make them true. Just because you do not believe in something doesn't mean it doesn't exist. A little story to demonstrate this happened to me the other day. I was looking out of my kitchen window at the beautiful garden. There was a squirrel going mad at something and I thought to myself, *what the hell is he going mad at? There is nothing there!* As I walked out of the kitchen, a magpie appeared from below the steps to the garden which had previously been obscured by the angle in which I was viewing it from the kitchen.

At that moment it then dawned on me as to why the squirrel was going nuts; he could see something that I couldn't and felt threatened by it. I then realised that there are often things that happen in life that we do not always understand due to our current perspective. We can often make a judgement about a situation without seeing the whole picture. Sometimes it takes a shift in how we perceive things to fully understand the matter.

If you view and believe Earth to be an evil place, then that is how it will be for you. I am not saying that you are wrong to feel like this, as it is your unique life, and you can live it however you want. If we all walked the same path, it would be very crowded to say the least! Even if you do view Earth as evil, do you want to change it? If so, this provides you a platform to be the change that you want to see throughout. As already stated, when you hate or condemn something, you are part of the problem and create more of the same. You can then notice how many things go wrong because of your vibrational state, you will begin to see that it is no coincidence.

An angry man lives in an angry world. In my younger days, I would witness violence, see the worst in people and lived in fear. Appliances would break, things would go missing and random bills would arrive through my door. I would write it all off as bad luck and think to myself, *this is just part of life and sometimes it is an evil place.* I was so wrong; it didn't have to be like that but my thoughts created my truth at that time. I was choosing to see one side of the coin and my perception and beliefs were hampering my progress in life. Does your perception about reality impede your progress in life?

50

TEACHERS

What is a teacher? A teacher is someone who helps us to learn about who we actually are. There have been many historical figures over the years that have left wisdom, teachings and priceless information on Earth. Many great teachers have had their messages documented and spread throughout the world. Some teachings are more well-known than others, but the core of all teachings that have left profound impressions on the earth have all stemmed from love.

We can be taught by great sages or by our family and friends, there is no right path to take. I have been taught by Deano, Bella, Louise, my parents and many of my friends. There are names however that just keep cropping up in history. Why is this? It is because their teachings resonated with people as the truth. Teachings of the truth always survive the test of man-made time.

A great teacher who I consider is Jesus. I have already stated my views about religion, so I look at the teachings of Jesus objectively without any religious dogma attached to them. With no religion attached to this being, I often wonder if Jesus was a real person. I believe he was and that he was someone who once walked the same earth that we do. Why would he choose to come here though?

Jesus is an omniscient teacher and has the evolution and advancement of the human species close to his heart. Jesus was a very advanced, enlightened soul that operated at an unimaginable rate of vibrations that we cannot comprehend. This level of vibration helped him to achieve a near *egoless* form in which the true power of unconditional love could be demonstrated.

Jesus or Yeshua, which was his real name, embodied the cosmic energy of Christ into his physical shell in order to shift the level of consciousness for that period of time. Jesus was taught by a group called the Essenes who helped him to apply his teachings to the current period of time. Jesus would use the environment and nature to convey his teachings, so that people of that time period could comprehend the vast complexity of what he was teaching.

When on a beach, Jesus would let people observe how the waves of the tide came in and went out. Each time a new wave came in, it moved seaweed and silt a little further up the beach, but on a miniscule level. This example he used demonstrated the progress that we make in each incarnation. Each wave represented a lifetime that we grow from, but in the grand scheme of eternity, it can appear insignificant. This however does not detract from the beauty and awe of each lifetime and the progress we can make. Each one is precious and something to be cherished, as it provides us an opportunity to work on ourselves to move higher. Ultimately, Jesus taught us how to get off the wheel of karma that our actions keep us upon each lifetime.

Despite what religion tells us, Jesus did teach reincarnation and how to master and manipulate energy to our benefit. He also showed us that we create our own reality from within, despite what governing forces are thrust upon us externally. "The kingdom of God is within you," was a message that had been forgotten, and still has to some extent. Jesus meant this literally in the sense that we are powerful beings, even in the flesh and as an individual. He showed us that we have the power to create our own reality.

The 'I' that is in all of our minds is the illusory separate self. That 'I' is our own unique perception and experience of the world. Each individual experience that we create and deem as being ours, is ultimately part of the Universal consciousness that we are all part of. Everything is constantly being fed back to the source that we are all one with. This is also what Jesus meant when he said, "The kingdom is of God is within you." You are part of that omnipotent force that creates and records everything throughout each lifetime. You don't need to go anywhere, your divine beauty and infinite perfection as an individual is right here inside of you now as you read these words.

As I mentioned earlier in our Religion chapter, the truth of God, Jesus, and reincarnation have become warped and misconstrued over time. The councils of Nicaea, Trent, and Constantinople all played a big role in rewriting Christianity, so that it became a workable model for the Church to maintain power and order. If people knew that Jesus was showing them that they were God and not some subservient, powerless entity, the power structure would be upset. Jesus wanted to show us that he was our brother and friend; he was no different from us, he was us. He wanted us to know that we have the power to rise to his level by choosing love.

Jesus was pure love and accepted that his exit from the physical world would be via the cross. Despite numerous attempts to kill him previously, Jesus had the power, as we all do, to decide when he would depart, and laid down his life when he was ready. His physical body struggled to contain the light and cosmic energy he had aligned with, and even at a young age, his physical shell was weary because of the vast vibrational difference; the cells of the body struggled to contain the light. This is why he was reported to have a glow or aura about him. He was set to leave the physical at a young age because of this. Various accounts suggest he died between the age of 33 and 40.

The cosmic Christ consciousness that Jesus' physical embodied, was also said to pervade the physical bodies of John the Baptist and Saul of Tarsus. This was because the human body's current level of evolution at that time was incompatible with such enlightened, vibrational energy. The molecular structure of the human could not cope with such pure light, and that energy could not be contained or channelled solely into one physical vessel at that time on earth.

On a side note, it is said that Saul of Tarsus will reincarnate sometime this century to correct the mistakes that he made which set Christianity on the wrong course. He will eliminate any fear from the teachings of Christianity that man has added along the way, and create a new system that the world can learn and live by. Because of these truthful teachings that will be taught, religious organisations will view the messages delivered to the extent of blasphemy; even though the messages will be of truth, it will be a clear indication of how distorted religious dogma has become.

On the cross, we can only imagine what Christ went through that day, but even that in itself was a teaching. Jesus showed us that death is simply a natural transition of energy, and regardless of the physical, we are eternal. I believe what he showed us was that fear is not real, and that the power of the mind and love are our infinite truth. I believe he put himself into a deep state of meditation where he was able withdraw from the whole experience to ease his suffering. Of course that was not the only suffering and sacrifice he made; his whole life was a sacrifice.

Some say that Christ wasn't crucified and that the whole event was fictitious or a shared psychic event, but either way, the real sacrifice was made when he chose to leave the unconditional love of spirit when he had no obligation to. His soul was free of karma and only out of love did he come to teach and embody unity consciousness. The animosity and hostility he experienced throughout his life were there so he could teach people a new way; of course, not all were ready to accept what was being taught. The truth is his words were felt in the hearts of many as Jesus travelled, but the paradigm of power was being upset by his work, and fear that the current hierarchy would collapse brought about Jesus' death.

All the great teachers over time have always taught love, compassion, and understanding, just like Jesus. We all know this to be the truth deep down. Whenever a teacher's words gain momentum and threaten to unite people, instead of divide them, an example is always made of them publicly to restore the fear element to the social structure. Martin Luther

King was assassinated because he teachings paved a new potential path for unity, love, and social solidarity. The message he carried held of a vibrational frequency of love and did not try to fight or be in conflict with anything. Unconditional love were also part of the Buddha's teachings, who was born 500 years before Jesus.

Consider what it is to be love and live by it. Imagine the power this would envelop, and how it would affect your reality. Imagine understanding energy, time and space, anything could be achieved. This was Jesus' message and teachings. I read that Neem Karoli Baba, who was a great Indian saint, would cry at just the mention of Jesus, because of his sacrifice, and what he embodied. The Maharajji, as he was known to his followers, would meditate like Christ did, which was to lose himself in love.

A young boy once asked the Maharajji if Jesus did get angry and Maharajji started to cry and said, "Christ never got angry. When he was crucified he felt only love. Christ was never attached to anything; he even gave away his own body." As the Maharajji gave this answer, the boy and the group that were present in the room burst into tears; at that moment they knew the passion of true love. Maharajji then sat up and said, "The mind can travel a million miles in the blink of an eye-Buddha said that." This story shows that the mind and love are indeed powerful things.

The mind is responsible for performing miracles and Maharajji would astound followers by performing miracles of his own out of pure love, much like Jesus did. Maharajji would be known to walk through walls, manifest food from nothing, and be seen in multiple places at once. He was able to do this by being one with everything and understanding the way energy worked. Out of love, which was his energetic vibration, he could then affect the molecular structure of his own body and his immediate environment, because there was no attachment to anything. He did it out of love.

To give you an idea of how powerful love is, have you ever heard the story of Jesus walking on water? To the human mind, it is a laughable tale and one that is physically impossible. But remember what we have learnt about faith, belief, molecules and vibrations. Consider a being who enters this world knowing exactly who they are and that they are one with everything. This being does not allow themselves to become consumed by the illusion of maya, which is exasperated by the five senses.

Now consider a being whose consciousness has evolved to an infinite level because they have had millions of incarnations in many different dimensions. They would vibrate at a frequency that operates above that of dense, physical matter, which is also composed of vibrating molecules. When something vibrates faster than another vibration, it can only rise. Think of frozen water, this matter is vibrating at a slow frequency. Now consider how boiling water operates; it moves vigorously and rises at a rapid pace. This rate of molecular vibration has far more energy than a frozen ice cube. If the boiling water were to be poured onto the ice cube, it would melt. Which of the two is operating at a higher vibrational level? The boiling water is.

Take this simple physics example that I have just used, but substitute the boiling water for Jesus and the ice cube for normal water, are you with me? Jesus as the hot water was above anything that was below him, such as the frozen water. Couple this level of vibration that Jesus was with pure faith (similar to those who walk on hot coals) and I believe that Jesus did in fact walk on water. His vibrational energy was simply above that of the water that vibrated at a much lesser rate. Jesus donned the disguise of a human space suit to show us that he was the same as us and that anything could be achieved if we believe it. He showed us that he was just like us and that faith and belief are everything. Jesus came to teach this.

I often think this of Deano, not that he was Jesus, but why did he choose to come to Earth? As Jo once stated to me, Dean was very high in the spiritual realm and came to Earth to shake things up and teach people through his actions. Dean inspired others by his behaviour, could this be comparable to Jesus? I mean I never saw Dean walk on water, although he did try to convince me that I could once when I was drunk; to which

I tried and fell in! Dean's aura was infectious towards people and he showed people that no matter what was going on, anything was possible with a positive mindset.

He conquered the limitations of the disease that was part of his human shell and rose above it, he evolved from it. The real Dean never stopped shining and that touched me on a personal level. When I attend fundraisers in Dean's name and for cystic fibrosis, I see the domino effect that Dean's message caused; the message that was his life. He affected so many people in a positive way, it really is quite humbling to see.

Recently I attended a fundraiser where one of Dean's friends was running a marathon. This gentleman who was running used to be slightly overweight and Dean inspired him to get into running. Before Dean's lung transplant, he could have never run due to his condition. He even struggled to walk some days without getting out of breath, but this didn't stop him from inspiring others. Oddly enough, the word *inspire* is close to *in spirit*. Does this show that inspiration is one of the closest states that we have to our natural loving source? It is such a wonderful feeling when we are inspired by something or someone. That feeling stems from who we truly are and where we come from.

Before Dean passed, he was beginning to increase his fitness and eventually wanted to run a marathon. However, his sudden decline in health never allowed him to fulfil this dream. Dean's tongue-in-cheek attitude allowed him to bet his friend that he couldn't run a marathon, due to him being lazy. Low and behold, Dean's co-worker is now running marathons, and even enjoys it.

I look at Gemma's life, how she has awakened to the possibility of her own potential and she now lives differently. Dean was her teacher too. I look at my own life and the potential that this book has to teach others and that it may help them. Dean really has started something phenomenal and can be so proud of his short time on Earth. What legacy and teachings will you leave behind? Ones that raised the vibration of the planet or ones that fulfilled your own selfish egoic desires? It's your choice.

Dean taught me so much; he was a teacher. Many teachers have visited planet Earth over the years and have left valuable lessons and messages so that others can see the way of truth. I once read an article that had an interesting concept on teachers and advanced souls. The article spoke about what happens to the soul when all life lessons are learnt. These enlightened souls can return to source energy if they choose to or spread the word of truth.

While on Earth, souls who made their choices in alignment with that of love and emulated the beauty of loving energy only move higher and higher. Much like Deano, enlightened souls elect themselves to return to Earth and shift the consciousness and vibrational frequency of the planet for the better. Their time on Earth can shift the entire vibrational frequency of the planet exponentially and spark evolutionary growth. Teachers like Martin Luther King Jr, Albert Einstein, Charles Darwin, Muhammad, Mahatma Gandhi, Gautama Buddha, Lao Tzu, Confucius are all examples of this, and the list can go on!

Jesus was pure, enlightened energy and his soul's mission was to shift the awareness of the world, much like the people mentioned in the previous paragraph did; they just all chose to do it in different ways. As far as I'm concerned, Deano was a God and I can see comparisons in his behaviour to that of pure love. It is interesting to think what we could achieve if we allow ourselves to be open-minded and operate from love. What revolutions would you start? We all have the power.

One person can change the world. For those of you who doubt this, look at the actions of Rosa Parks that one day on a bus. Her beliefs sparked an awakening into racial equality that has since been built upon. This pivotal event happened in 1955, not that long ago considering; look at how far we have come in such a short amount of time. Rosa spoke her truth that day from a place of love for herself and was a great teacher for humanity.

Children can also be our greatest teachers. I would love to be shown that which I did not already know about myself and the world, through the eyes of a child. Do not assume that we have to play the role of parent just as we are older and know it all, for we know, time is not real. Where has that child that teaches you travelled from? Are they an enlightened soul who has come to be your guru?

Nature can also be a teacher to us. Just yesterday, I was walking Bella and observed how the pollen fell so softly and freely. The wind gently swept it along to its chosen destination. I watched as the bees were going about their business freely, pollinating flowers, while the birds just sang. Everything seemed so effortless, that is how we need to be, effortless. We can learn to just trust the process and allow things to happen naturally, instead of trying to control everything. We can learn so much from nature, after all, it is perfect, harmonious and in balance. Nature does so much while not actually doing anything, it all seems so simple.

Animals are beautiful teachers. They live in the now and give love to their owners, no matter what. They can pick up on emotions and are very intuitive. They comfort you when you are down and are always there to put a smile on your face. Imagine if we could mimic some of those traits and be like that!

Have you ever heard someone say, "Why do bad things only happen to good people?" An explanation for this is down to the current level of individual consciousness that inhabits that body. A karmic contract could have been arranged before birth in order to teach and help the souls involved grow. A more advanced soul out of love may offer to be in that precise place, and that precise time, in order to teach. You see there are no accidents in pivotal events, and each coming together is a karmic teaching on a soul level that is planned in advance.

When something that we deem as bad happens to someone that we view as good, we view the unjust event as a mistake and we say, "Wrong place, wrong time." In reality, the situation has been agreed in advance and two strangers coming together to help each other learn is indeed, "Right place, right time." So next time an accident happens to you out of the blue, or you meet a stranger in the middle of nowhere that provokes a reaction out of you for no reason, consider the cosmic planning and chain events that had to happen in order for that situation to be experienced; mind blowing! We do create the gaps in between karmic events depending on our current level of vibration, but some events happen because of karma, astrological planning, and our constant co-creation with the Universe. Not everything is as black and white as we think and all experiences enhance our learning and teach the soul. There is a lesson in absolutely everything in life.

Everything is a teacher and we are all teachers in our own rights. We are all at different stages of our path. Some are further down the path than others but rest assured, we are all helping one another to navigate that path in a complex way. We are all teachers, but this is sometimes overlooked by our human minds. Who is your teacher? It can be Jesus, Buddha, or a close friend? Rest assured, whoever it is, they have found their way into your life for a reason.

51

IDENTIFYING FEAR AND SUBSTITUTING IT FOR LOVE

We have chosen to have a human experience on this planet at this particular time in history. We have chosen it to remember who we are and to bring love. Fear is all part of the human experience, so we must embrace it but also know that it is erroneous thinking. Fear can dominate our lives so much, if we allow it to, and believe that everything we imagine is real. Fear is a product of the ego that has helped us to evolve and survive, so it is not all bad, but we must recognise it for what it is. Fear is simply an illusion as it deviates from our natural state, which is love. Fear is learnt and babies arrive on this planet fearless.

When there is no balance in life, things become unhealthy. When we are fearful, we think primarily about self-preservation. Fear is a product of the intellect which we think protects and keeps us safe. Fearful people can make rash decisions and mistakes. As I mentioned earlier in the S&S chapter, at the time of writing this book a virus known as COVID-19 is *terrorising* the world. In the initial outbreak of the pandemic, people made decisions based out of fear and chose only to think of themselves. This is what fear will do.

At the beginning of this year, 2020, I said to myself, *people are beginning to wake up.* I saw all the cumulative progress of the last few decades and how people are becoming more acceptant of race, gender and seeing the good in life. I thought to myself in January, *what challenges are going to happen this year to awaken more people?* Of course, I imagined nothing like Covid-

19, proof that there is always something bigger around the corner that we are unaware of. Brexit had been the current topic of fear up until that point, as people were unsure as to what would happen and then it just seemed to vanish due to the next instalment of fear - COVID-19. Brexit became a distant memory as people's minds were preoccupied with something new. Classic egoic behaviour.

Change is inevitable and part of our growth. After all, we are evolving on two fronts. The evolution of our physical species known as the human and the evolving of our consciousness as to who we are when we occupy these physical shells. What if we accepted events of change for what they simply are? Part of life and a prompt for us to evolve with them.

At this current time of writing, the coronavirus is deemed as bad and even evil by some, but everything has a purpose and reason. Is it not a warning from nature to change the way we are living? Is it not a prompt to evolve, after all, viruses are always mutating, shouldn't we? For when things are out of natural balance, dis-ease occurs. Are we the ones who are out of balance? When we are comfortable in our little bubbles, fear keeps us there and the winds of change are not always welcome, for they threaten to pop our little bubble of safety that we all live in from time to time. Fear will immobilise you in your life and keep you in the same familiar lane. The familiar lane is not always balanced.

Our egos are geared and primed to be fearful of any uncertain and unfamiliar situation, this is what got us to where we are. In times of uncertainty, rash responses and spontaneous actions are necessary from the perspective of the ego. As Covid spread, so did the fear. Some people were buying non-perishable foods as though an apocalypse was imminent. I do not blame people for panicking, but this type of behaviour keeps our planet from progressing. When we have patience and act with a calm, loving approach, we can see that there is more than enough for everyone to go around, this includes poverty.

When we panic, we act out of impulse and fear. When fear is dominant, it clouds our judgement. Rather than using the mind as a thinking tool, which is what it was designed for, we sometimes allow it to control us and steer the ship. Fear is False Evidence Appearing Real. Our minds panic and create turmoil and our vibrations feed into the whole environment, creating more frenzy. Now what I have written about is one side of the coin, there is always another.

Amongst all the panic and fear there is always the option to take a step back and observe, you have the tool of love to use instead. After the initial commotion of Covid had passed, people had time to stop and reflect. Could this virus have an ulterior motive? I have read of how the famous canals of Venice became crystal clear. It was stated that CO_2 emissions were significantly reduced. Dolphins were coming closer to the coast and there was a certain level of calmness in the air when I went outside for a walk in nature. Nature was indeed rebalancing in a short amount of time.

If we can view the virus from a perspective of love and appreciation, we can view a so-called tragedy as an opportunity. We can then see how the virus can infect anyone, regardless of race, sex, religion or financial situation. It has reminded us that we are all connected, we are one unit all in the same boat. It has reminded us how material things no longer matter and that the essentials are all that are needed.

The virus has helped to show that life does indeed go on whether you are working or not. The virus has brought to light the real jobs that are needed in life, the ones of help and care. Hospital workers, carers and key workers are roles that have helped us through this challenging time. We are constantly evolving and our race has faced many crises before, to which we have overcome. We must look after our health, each other and the planet. We need to have love for the planet for is it not the planet who looks after us? Cutting trees down and acting unconsciously is a process of fear; without trees, we would cease to exist! They are the lungs of our planet.

From a loving perspective, we can view the virus as a glorious step in our evolution that we were fortunate enough to live through and experience. Global restructure can happen and it moves us one step closer to realising that all things in life are equal. A new world order can be put in place for the better. The virus can be viewed as a huge wake-up call and you will probably have a greater perspective on it as you read these words.

I have seen nothing but good in my experience of the viral events. People in my community have been helping the elderly, leaflets have even been posted through the doors offering help. People have been laughing in the shops I have visited and strangers are talking about something that connects them all.

The shops have been full of fresh beautiful produce and while the dry goods may be low, they are not diminished. Now is the time to be eating fresh vibrant foods to love and nourish our bodies with. There is no problem supplying the shops with food; the supermarkets at the moment are thriving. I send love to all who made this possible. We are so fortunate really when you look at things. Love has been evident to me throughout all of this. I am now a lot more grateful for the food that I receive.

What path do you walk? One rooted in fear or love? Depending on what frequency we operate from, it affects our work and actions. Recently I have realised that I have lived a lot of my life in fear. I used to drive at the speed limit for fear of incurring penalty points rather than driving at the limit with love so that I protect everyone around me. I was so concerned for what others thought about me out of fear, rather than loving everyone for having their own unique opinion.

I used to fear not eating the right foods because I would be ill. Now I love the food I eat and love the nourishment that they provide my body. I used to exercise out of fear for how I would look. Now I exercise because I love my body and want to take care of it. I used to fear losing my hair, but now I love every hair that I have! I used to fear being alone with myself for I didn't like who I was. Now I love who I am, which allows me to love all who I meet. With fear of oneself comes fear of others. No longer do I perceive others with a fearful judgement, for I no longer fear my true self. Fear and love can totally change the way we live depending on which one we apply to a situation.

When you meet anything head on out of fear, you only perpetuate that which you are seeking to avoid. Are you anti-racist or pro unity? Are you anti-hate or pro love? Are you against poverty or do you help those in need? Are you anti-war or pro peace? All of these acts will facilitate change, but each carry different vibrations which will deliver different results. Our state of mind in which we approach a situation is so important. When you condemn something, you actually compound the situation and create more of what you are trying to end. A mindset of fear and hate to end a war will only bring about more of the same. John F. Kennedy once said, "Those who make peaceful revolution impossible will make violent revolution inevitable."

Remember our water experiment that we spoke about. Even spoken words have an effect on the molecular composition of water. If we are using words like anti-hate and anti-racism, what words will our bodies hear? Ones of negativity. We need to be careful with the words we select for they carry subconscious vibrations. Words of fear will exacerbate fear whilst words of love will create love.

When we act out of fear, we are living in the illusion. We have spoken about why people choose the route of fear due to many external factors. When we choose fear, it seems that it is the only logical and rational thing to do because our ego wants us to survive. Can fear make people walk paths that they really don't want to?

Louise and I watched a documentary on white power recently which struck a chord and really appealed to us. We didn't watch it because we were considering a new pastime to combat our current vanilla existence, we watched it because we were interested in what made these extremists tick. I stated before we watched it that these were not bad people, they were people who behaved in an erroneous way. They were merely confused people who had forgotten who they truly are. They were most likely acting out of hate and fear because of some unresolved issues that had occurred in their childhood or past.

After watching it for half an hour, the lady who was presenting the documentary began interviewing members of these so-called white supremacist groups who had all agreed to be filmed. I could see deep down that these people were not evil, in fact they were just scared little children projecting their fear onto others. They sought approval from mixing with like-minded people.

The interviewer was a Muslim and a feminist, a terrific combination if you are a neo-Nazi! She announced this to each person she was interviewing at the beginning of each interview. You could literally see some irk in their skin at the announcement. She then proceeded to read to them all the hateful comments that she had received online, due to her skin colour, religious beliefs and just for being female. The comments were all shocking and said by people who must have been in a lot of pain themselves.

The interviewees were silent and some looked grossly uncomfortable with this composed, dignified lady reading these awful statements aloud. They all agreed that these comments were unacceptable and hurtful. All the participating gang members all got to know this woman over the period of a week. At the end of filming, some even considered her a friend so much that she would be welcome to come back anytime. They'd had the opportunity to get to know her as a fellow human being, rather than a separate entity because of the colour of her skin. The fear of the unknown was no longer prevalent.

The woman making the documentary also attended the marches and rallies that were held by the white supremacists. At these marches, grown men dressed in white robes and wearing white hoods would march around whilst holding placards with racial and homophobic slurs scrawled across them. The passion on some of their faces was so intense and hate literally oozed from their pores. It was so sad to witness this, as all I saw were hurt little children who had found a sense of solidarity with others of the same fearful ilk.

In every interview that the composed presenter conducted, she asked the same question: *what has happened to make you behave in this way?* Most didn't divulge and clammed up, but one man looked close to tears when asked about his past. He said he wanted to stop and wasn't comfortable. There it was, this lost soul had been hurt in the past and had never recovered from it. His actions in the present day were a way of him regaining control of his life, that he never had as a child. Projecting some of the pain he had experienced onto others, through superficial beliefs he had adopted, was his way of fighting back.

The individual had preconceived ideas about an entire race of people who were all individuals and unique. He was fearful about a group of people he knew nothing about. In his mind, he had created a mental construct that defined these *foreigners* out of fear. This all links back to the self-preservation of the ego and how judgements of the unknown quickly descend into fear. It was upsetting to see how lost one individual had become and how he was embracing this dark, fearful path that he was walking down.

One of the men in question was even surprised that this woman was so kind and held no malice towards him, it gave him a new perception on Muslims; that they were not all the same. This man also admitted to having severe issues in his past that had clearly not been addressed.

Now I haven't written this part of the book to tell you that I enjoy watching programmes about racist people and psycho analysing them, nor that I pretend to know the true origin of a virus. I use the virus and the men that were in the documentary as examples of how fear can control things and run rife if we allow it to. What if people chose not to live in fear and believe all that they were told in the media about the *deadly* Coronavirus? What if people didn't make fearful judgments about others who they didn't know? With love and faith, reality can be so different.

When it comes to fear of what will happen next, can we not see that as a race, humanity has overcome far worse? Do people realise they will not leave this planet before they are intended to and with their passing comes a lesson? Have love for the way things are and what will be will be. Like Buddha said, "Relax, nothing is under control." With this mentality and the realisation that we do not actually have any control over any global situations that arise in our lives, we can just let it be and enjoy the trip. A judgement is the only thing that defines an experience and we all know that judging is a product of the ego. Let's live the life that our soul intended for us in order to grow. One surrounded by love and not fear.

The supremacists who I spoke about had not taken their time to do any research of their own about other cultures. Instead, they went with generalisations and stereotypes that are subtly created by the media. Other misled opinions that they have heard have resonated in their minds as if they were their own thoughts. Issues from the past had never been embraced or healed and the tiny child in them was screaming for help, leaving them vulnerable and open to grooming from like-minded people.

Left unaddressed, the fear had been allowed to grow from their childhoods and festered deep within them into their adult lives. This eventually caused them to fear concepts that were foreign to them. On a side note, I always find it ironic when individuals choose any form of condemnation towards another human being. They are totally unaware that in parallel experiences, they have lived multiple lives consisting of race, gender and homosexuality. We are all one, so essentially, they were abusing themselves.

The unknown promotes fear and when we choose this, we operate at a low frequency. When we choose to love, our world changes. I cannot lie, I have already admitted I still act out of fear sometimes with my driving. I am choosing to love driving and not to be so fearful about it. I trust in the process of life and know that my thoughts are sometimes not that of my own and ones that I have observed and learnt.

What happens to our bodies if we are permanently living in fear? If we are permanently rooted in fear, then your adrenal glands make a hormone called cortisol which is then released into the blood supply. Cortisol increases your heart rate and blood pressure. It is responsible for the fight or flight procedure that we are all programmed with in order to help us survive. If cortisol is constantly present in our system, all energy is directed into the self-preservation mode and lessens the flow of energy to other cells of the body. This happens because the body is addressing its primary task given to it from the commander - us! If we are constantly choosing to feel fear, then this is how we are telling our body to respond and operate on a permanent basis.

When the body is in a stressed state, the immune system can become compromised due to the abundance of cortisol that is present in the bloodstream and with this, you are more prone and susceptible to illness. The immune system cannot perform its intended job which is to defend us if there is a lack of energy available in the body. The body is constantly allocating energy to what it deems to be the most important job, which in the presence of fear and cortisol is immediate survival. When acting out of subconscious fear, we are choosing to live in a state of permanent stress which in the long run affects our health; this is because our immune systems are forever compromised. When we choose love, we vibrate at a higher frequency and the Universe will align with the vibrations that we are emitting. Our immunity improves and our body operates at its intended frequency.

If fear is sold by the media 24/7 and examples of love are few and far between, what world will that create by those who watch it and believe it? I have been upset at how some of the media have handled the whole coronavirus situation. The media had exaggerated statistics that have been proven to be fabricated by health officials. Fear sells and keeps us in our place.

I have written this chapter to show how fear is worldwide and can be the only driving force to some people's lives, but it is all illusion. This illusion can create health conditions and rule our lives, but if it is an illusion, what is reality? The only truth is love and we will examine this further.

52

WHAT IS GOD?

"Oh my God, a chapter about God! I knew this book was some giant ruse to try and convert me." If this is what you are thinking, do not worry. I have mentioned the name God a few times throughout the book but I have tried not to make a song and dance about it, just in case you ran away. Now you're maybe thinking, *hold on a minute, didn't you write a chapter saying how much negativity came about as a result of religion?* And yes, you would be right. Religion is a product of the ego that can divide us if we allow it to. So no, the word *God* in this chapter has nothing to do with Religion. So please, do not be put off by the words or talk of God, it is not being used in the traditional sense as we know it.

I want to talk about science and God and discuss how the two can now go hand in hand, which in days gone by was unheard of. In earlier chapters, I described how everything we see and experience are just atoms and molecules vibrating at different rates; science provides the evidence to support this. The very same atoms and molecules that we are comprised of are found in all creatures, plants and just about anything that is on this globe of ours. Apparently, a fruit fly's DNA is 60% identical to that of a human. DNA, which is short for deoxyribonucleic acid, is the molecule that contains the genetic code of organisms. This indicates that we are all made from the same materials as such and interconnected, even when it comes to those pesky little flying things!

When you scratch beneath the surface of an atom, which we have spoken about earlier, you delve into the depths of protons, neutrons and electrons. Quantum physics takes this to the next subatomic level discovering that neutrons and protons are made up of quarks. A quark is a tiny particle that makes up the protons and neutrons. Gluons in simplified terms are the glue that hold the quarks together. Quarks combine to form protons and neutrons which in turn make up your atom's nucleus.

At the time of writing this book, a quark is the smallest thing known to man. No doubt as we evolve even further into our scientific future, we will discover something even smaller. Quantum physics can indicate even now that when you keep breaking down particles you will eventually be left with nothing. All that is left in that nothing is raw energy. Energy is not made of anything.

The first law of thermodynamics states that energy is always conserved and cannot be created or destroyed, it simply is. Energy simply changes from one form to another. Rudolf Clausius stated that by following this law, all energy in the Universe is constant. What is this energy that pervades through everything and animates each quark, atom and molecule? What is this energy that constructs every living thing on this planet?

If the entire planet operates from one universal pool of energy and uses atoms to create everything that we experience, surely there must be some sort of organising intelligence behind this energy? These atoms and molecules that are used to construct everything in our reality must come from somewhere, some omnipotent source. The trees, plants, soil, mountains, animals, water, everything is all in us! Our bodies literally contain grains of sand, a rock, a plant, an animal; the only thing that separates us is that we have an ego. We all share the same land and all need water, sun and nourishment to grow. Does this not suggest a certain oneness to everything?

You could argue that a mountain or rock does not need anything to exist and that it is an inanimate object, but remember, rocks are made of atoms just like we are. Thomas Edison who was famous for inventing the incandescent light bulb made many discoveries in his lifetime. His inventions and findings stemmed from his great scientific mind. Mr

Edison was asked if he believed in God during an interview in 1910 for the New York Times magazine. Thomas answered, "I do not believe in the God of the theologians, but that there is a supreme intelligence I do not doubt. Nature made us, nature did it all, not the Gods of religions."

Keen to explore the depths and limits of nature, Mr Edison conducted an experiment where he placed two chemicals together into a solution. He discovered that some of the atoms from one chemical combined with some of the atoms from the opposite chemical. Mr Edison was puzzled as to why some of the atoms from the separate chemicals had joined together in the solution but not all of them. The answer, he concluded, was that each atom demonstrated a conscious choice as to whether or not it would join with the opposing chemical. Those atoms that chose to match with one another were a vibrational match.

We have spoken about vibrational matches earlier and how you attract certain events and people into your life via the frequency you broadcast. Maybe that is why sometimes no matter how hard you try, you just cannot take to a certain person; for your body at an atomic level is simply not a vibrational match to the other person's frequency, you actually repel one another.

Now with the notion that even the smallest thing such as an atom has consciousness, does this not once again suggest that there is a divine intelligence that permeates everything around us? It may be hard for us to comprehend a rock as having a sentient awareness of internal or external existence about it, but imagine in a million years, which is a dot on the planet's history, how this rock's consciousness could evolve?

All consciousness forms matter, therefore, atoms have consciousness too, just like Thomas Edison proved in his experiment. There is life and consciousness brimming in everything that we see. Energy flows through the rock, the same as you or I; it exists in everything! We are all one giant life force being animated by the same energy that exists in all of creation around us. The Universe is literally inside of us, we are not separate from it which is what our five finite senses would have us believe.

Now you can call this cosmic, invisible source of energy whatever you like. Ram, Jehovah, The Tao, Mother Nature, The Universe, God, the fact is, it doesn't really matter. As soon as you label something that is formless, you bring it into the world of form which is finite and attempt to state its qualities with the name you have labelled it with. As soon as you label something, you have given it boundaries. You have already given a human definition to the driving force of energy that is responsible for the animating of our bodies in our day to day lives.

It is only our egos that simply must categorise everything, or else we cannot accept them out of fear. The fact is that the vast complexity of whatever force that created us is incomprehensible to our finite human minds. Just by writing a chapter about God, it is slightly foolish on my behalf, but my ego thinks otherwise!

We are forever making scientific advancements but still only scratch the surface as to what this energy that is in all of us actually is. To think we actually understand everything that goes on around us is a product again of the famous ego. Socrates, who was an ancient Greek philosopher, said it best, "True wisdom is knowing how little we know." All we can do is just do our best in this current visit to the planet. With an open mind and open heart, we are on the right path.

The term *God* can make people shirk and think of negative images immediately, why is this? In my mind this is because of the westernised, man-made God of the ego that we all know is a tyrannical, vengeful character. *He* is one that we have grown up to know through teachings and films. It is off-putting and this is why some people label themselves as atheists for they refuse to believe in such a monstrosity. People who choose to worship an external God out of fear and not love are also missing the point. Why do people worship someone who will judge them and condemn their every action if it does not fit the celestial narrative? Is it for the fear of being punished if you don't, much like that of an angry parent?

You can make up your own name for this force if it helps you. I personally do not like the term *God*, as it carries such negative connotations that stem from my biblical days at Sunday school, however, that is just me. There is no denying though that there is an invisible source of energy that animates everything and gives us life.

With science reiterating the theory that there is certainty a governing body in this world of ours, why has it created this reality? All this collective energy must surely be part of a bigger picture? But life can seem so callous and cold sometimes, I am sure you will agree? "If there is a God, why do bad things happen in the world?" This is an argument that I have heard so many times and one which I used to use so much myself.

The fact is, our egos are really fragile and quite insecure; the ego is shy of a challenge if you ask me, it shies away from things it doesn't understand in order to fulfil self-preservation. Our egos want an easy life and just want to protect our identity. The ego wants to be void of any hardships or challenges but without these trials and tribulations, how would we learn? We would not be able to experience the good of life if there were no dualities or comparisons.

As mentioned before, life is one big dichotomy full of different perspectives. In *pre-birth planning*, we spoke of how our higher selves will plan a route that is fit for our soul, so that lessons can be learned. These challenges will shape us and help us grow, and they are only a temporary illusion anyway. In the context of eternity, life is but a blink of an eye.

Taking all this into account, we choose to label events as good or bad, or rather, our egos do out of fear. A good event is something that brings us pleasure and happiness. A bad event is something that is detrimental in our pursuit to happiness and well-being. However, have you ever been in a position where something at the time seems so horrendous, but actually worked out for the good in the long run, if not better? The soul will view events such as these objectively and see them for what they are; opportunities to grow and awaken, without placing any subjective judgements on the scenario.

With this in mind, how would you view a child dying after spending less than a week on the planet? A friend of mine had her sister experience this event first-hand. At the moment in time, this was obviously traumatising and incredibly agonising, torturous in fact. This event happened many years ago now and the whole experience can now be perceived differently. My friend can objectively say that before the time of the child's passing, the family was split and in turmoil due to melodrama that families are sometimes consumed with. The passing of the child ultimately galvanised the family and united them. They were more of a unit after the tragedy and now join every year to celebrate the child's passing surrounded by love.

Now I would have thought to myself, *what God could be capable of such extremities?* To take a young life so quickly initially seems so evil to me, but by doing this have I not made an egoic judgement? By doing this, have I not created evil with my own way of thinking? Clearly, I have superior thinking to that of the Universe and I know what is best for the existence of the Milky Way.

However, when you look at the bigger picture, has it not had a positive effect on the family? The brave soul that chose to occupy that physical shell for a brief amount of time was an advanced soul to say the least. That soul opted to come to Earth for a limited existence in order to shift the consciousness of those involved, and you know what, it did. That soul chose to visit Earth out of wisdom and love and graduated early from the classroom which is life; their work was done.

It's still easy to condemn this event as heinous through the eyes of the ego, but if a soul chose this path out of love for themselves, is this not a blessing to all involved? Their arrival demonstrated how fragile life is and that love is the only truth there is. Love can heal and unite everything. This actual event happened and has led to a positive outcome. The child is still deeply missed but his passing serves as a reminder that life can pass us in a flash. The real truth though is that love is eternal and that we are all reunited one day.

Everything that happens to us will pass and is for our own good. Can you now see how there are always multiple perspectives on how to view events in life? Do you not think that it is part of the master plan that we know nothing about? We are all just happening and being animated by an unseen force. When we resist and try to take control, negative events happen to us. When we release attachments to everything and just let it all happen as it should, our pure loving consciousness can really shine through, radiating who we truly are and where we come from.

Now what does God do for us? Again, that question sounds like God is external, but the reality is that God operates in all of us and gives itself everything. The Universe then gives us everything for we are it. The Universe strives to experience every possible aspect of itself through a multitude of scenarios, all happening in a seamless moment of oneness. This Universal energy manifests into the physical world as billions of tiny expressions that walk the planet, known as humans! That is before we even consider that *God* is the trees, the water, the animals, and the mountains. The omnipresent cosmic energy is content with just *being* in everything. That is why we must just *be* and be content with just *being*.

When you cannot just *be*, this is where the ego can kick in. When you feel the need to control everything and everyone in your life, you are operating at a vibrational level of fear. This is where anxiety can creep in, along with other mental health problems. You are not willing to accept things as they are for they do not match your preconceived image of how life should be. If you believe that the world should operate in a certain way in order to match your own individual judgemental criteria, you are setting yourself up for a fall. You are saying you know what is best for you and casting God's master plan aside. All you are actually doing is living from a perspective of the ego where it seeks out moments of pleasure to gratify its needs, the world does not operate like this.

When you let go and let God and have no attachment to how things should be, life will change. The Buddha said that all suffering is caused by the attachment of the mind to how things should be. When we accept everything as it simply is without labelling it, this is living from a perspective of God. This is a hard concept to grasp and I still struggle with it sometimes. I still operate from a place of fear at times, but when I accept that everything happens for the greater good of my soul's development, I find life a lot easier to digest.

I have heard a lot of spiritual speakers say that life is perfect. When I first heard this ludicrous, callous statement, I was offended. What about rape, murder, starvation? Then I remember how our soul plans our karmic path according to our journey. I remember how life is but a blink of an eye and the real truth is that we are eternal beings trying to remember and rediscover the loving source that we originated from. I then remember how people who act off of error are operating from a level of fear and from lack of love that they have experienced in their own lives. So, after years of deliberation and expanding my blinkered, narrow-minded consciousness, I can say that life is perfect. God doesn't make mistakes; this isn't amateur hour!

When I no longer label an event, the oneness of it all is perfect. By no means do I wish to see suffering in the world and I do not cheer when I witness violence or pain, but just accept it as something which is part of the Universal dichotomy. That dichotomy is ultimately one and that is all there is. Each event that happens in the world, regardless of a label, is God happening in disguise.

All painful experiences are opportunities to awaken our soul as to what it is. Turmoil also provides us opportunities to help ease the suffering of others and realise that we all have the same emotions. If we have experienced a life-changing event first-hand, are we not then better equipped to truly express empathy and compassion towards someone who has experienced the same trauma as we once did? Does this not help us to ease the suffering of others and further the notion that we are all just one?

My mother abandoning me caused great distress as a child and as a young adult. This painful experience ultimately helped me to learn the gift of forgiveness and compassion. However, I only arrived at this point of forgiveness after going through my own personal hell; which was engulfed by alcohol, drugs, being kicked out of my home and failed relationships. These painful experiences have helped me to have compassion for any homeless person that I meet, I cannot judge for I am the same as them. Yes, we are all responsible for our lives but when we are only doing the best with what we know, anyone can wind up in an unpleasant situation if they do not know how life works.

I have empathy for anyone who has issues with addictions. I chose them as a coping mechanism and you know what, they provided me with temporary solutions and helped me to survive. For me to judge an alcoholic or drug addict is hypocrisy at its best; if anything, my experiences of pain and addiction have only helped me to love everyone who I meet who has addiction problems for I was once that person.

I have empathy for others when relationships do not work. I know the pain of heartbreak, that sick feeling in the pit of your stomach when two people who once shared an intimate love for one another go their separate ways. For me, the pain of rejection and the ending of a relationship is the greatest pain I have known in life, but that's just my personal perspective. So whenever I meet someone who is experiencing heartbreak, I truly feel their pain. I love them because I know that the feelings they are experiencing at that time are truly nauseating.

My whole life has been a vehicle of awakening as to who I truly am, as is yours. The events I have experienced have stripped away the layers to who I truly am; a compassionate loving soul. That is who we all are, that is who God is. There is grace in suffering and when you can truly be a witness to all events and accept them for what they are, you are truly seeing the bigger picture. The suffering that permeates all aspects of life connects us all. It is all perfect.

When tragedies happen across the world, do we not for a split second come together? Floods, terrorist attacks, viruses and war can all make us stop and think for a brief moment. Even if we approach it from a selfish perspective and we think, "I'm glad that wasn't me!" Is there not a split second of compassion that follows that thought that goes out to the *others?* Do we not experience for a fleeting moment a true sense of empathy for the people that had to live through the turbulence? Does it then not dawn on us that the individuals across the other side of the world are just another version of us? They are experiencing life through a unique perspective to ours, but are ultimately the same. We are all one. We all breath the same air, eat, sleep, defecate, have sex and die. We are one pool of mass Universal energy split into unique individual entities. This source of energy which experiences itself in a myriad of forms and in a multitude of ways can be called God.

The Universe does not know what it is. In order to know oneself, we need others. Therefore, we are simply the Universe longing to experience and explore what it actually is through an infinite number of reflections and projections of itself; by doing this, it expands and evolves. Through continual acts of error, we start to become more aware of our true selves. The truth is that we are one loving awareness rediscovering what it is through the process of elimination.

If we expand our consciousness and think in terms like *God* does, life unfolds its mysteries to you. If God gives everything to us and itself, what can we do? We can give too. When we mimic how Universal source energy behaves, the Universe blesses us. When we operate from a place of love, we are emulating our natural true self which is that of the creator. If we are selfish and steal, what does the Universe hear? That you are separate and that you are clearly lacking in your life. Experiences will then manifest to match those of your actions. If you are lacking, you will forever live in that state.

The Universe is constantly providing experiences to match that of your thoughts and feelings. You know by now; your thoughts and beliefs create your world. If you are constantly putting others first for they are just you in a different package, then you are acting like source energy. Behaving this way and putting others first can help you to live the life that you have dreamed of, plus it feels nice!

Scientists have shown that we are all wired to help each other and when we do it stimulates the reward area of the brain and creates positive feelings. When you act like this because this is who you are, everything happens organically. When you act in a benevolent manner, because you expect something in return, that is not love and only neutralises the whole situation.

As we have established, we are all made of the same *materials*. Bearing this in mind, is it not senseless to fight and argue amongst ourselves if we are not all one? An ancient native American proverb states that: "No tree has branches so foolish as to fight amongst themselves." When you consider the human race as one giant tree, is it not insanity to fight amongst ourselves when we are all part of the same living organism?

The ego will have you believe that you are separate to everyone for it craves survival and longs to protect its identity. As I write this, racial tension floods the world. The notion of separateness based on colour still appears real to the five senses, as that is all we can see and is tangible to us. Do not forget and dismiss the facts of subatomic mass if you still believe in everything you see with the naked eye. When we break things down, we are nothing more than atoms. That is why colour is nothing more than a perception and upsets me when people argue about what they perceive.

There isn't any real objective colour in the world. The spectrum of a rainbow is just a shared illusion which is consistent to everyone. Different light frequencies are interrupted by our individual sight and perceived as colour by our brains. Ultimately, colour is just in our heads! That is why when people argue over the colour of skin and define others because of it, they are in fact arguing over a very complex and elaborate illusion created by the Universe. There are no others! When we simply brush the ego aside, we can realise that we are all one limitless mass of collective Universal energy. We are all experiencing the same thing in different ways, this is God.

According to books, when Jesus was on the cross, he said, "Father forgive them, for they know not what they do." I feel these words were supposed to convey the message that humanity may as well be crucifying itself. When we are destructive towards another, we only harm ourselves, for we are all one. Think how we feel when we have experienced conflict with another. We feel guilty, anxious, worked up and angry; does this not suggest that we have only hurt ourselves and it is our body's way of telling us this with unpleasant feelings?

The Buddha said, "You will not be punished for your anger, you will be punished by your anger." Plus, there is the karma that you have created that will unmistakably be played out at a later date with roles reversed. The oneness of it all is perfect. When we stab someone, we actually thrust the blade into ourselves; be this metaphorically or physically. We are not only hampering our own growth when we sabotage another, but the entire evolution of the planet and loving awareness.

So, what have we established? God is a source of energy that animates every single thing on the planet. God operates at a frequency of divine love and there is nothing else. Only man creates separateness when he is consumed by the illusion of maya and this is a thought of error. God gives and it is pure creation. Nothing is impossible to God, only man's analytical perception creates boundaries. Okay, here comes a crazy statement, and that's saying something considering the entire nature of this book! I have mentioned it a few times throughout the book to sow the seed, but here it is. "I am God."

Now, before you think, "Oh my God, Dave has induced some sort of messiah complex just because he wrote a book!" Hear me out. I am God. You are God. We all are God. I am not talking about the man-made God of the ego, used to control and strike fear into those who don't believe. This is not the God who demands praise and adulation. The God I am talking about is the universal loving energy that animates us all.

From the evidence provided by scientists that we are all made of the same *stuff*, does this not suggest that we are merely individual fragments of God? Each of us has the power to create anything, for we are God. Each of us also has a unique purpose and important part in the giant play that is life. We are not separate from God as the energy that is used to animate us is God. We are Gods amongst men, as Jesus once said. When you can accept this notion, anything can be accomplished as we are God. We are creators, we create reality.

God is capable of miracles, after all, just look at the world we live in! Is it not astounding when you truly contemplate it? Look at the variety in everything, it is unique and perfect. Everything is in harmony and perfect balance. The trick of manifesting does not seem so difficult now, does it? When you grasp the fact that you are made with the same energy that animates the Universe, you are truly realising who you are. Energy cannot be destroyed, it is eternal, you are energy, you are God.

Maybe you can view life from a different angle with the concept that we are all one. God is in everything we see and experience, we are just God happening in the eternal now. When you eat a vegetable, you are experiencing the Universe. The sun, the rain, the soil, the insects that have crawled over the vegetable, they all are part of one complete package that has enabled that vegetable to grow. The vegetable is everything, as are you. You are literally eating and experiencing God from your own unique perspective.

God is not some angry figure of power who sits in the sky all day, getting frustrated and pissed off with how the world is turning out. God is simply energy that animates you as you read these words. That same energy animates me as I write them, that energy was fuelled by unconditional love! If you wanted to slip a little deeper down the rabbit hole, you could say that I have written this book and read it myself, for I am you. You could say that there is only one loving awareness experiencing these words and it is animated in a variety of ways. God is simply experiencing and interpreting my writing from a multifaceted perspective. I use the words perspective and experience a lot, for that is what the Universe craves, a myriad of experiences with an abundance of perspectives.

Now I have realised the truth of unity and oneness, I even look at spiders differently! I used to view them as horrible little creatures who scared me but they clearly have a purpose, as does everything. My judgements were those based on fear and not love. Like my teacher, Wayne Dyer said, "What is the difference between a flower and weed? Nothing, only a judgement."

Our human condition labels both forms of flora separately and gives them a set of attributes due to their superficial appearances and our conditioning. Individuals will argue that weeds have negative properties and are bad for the ground. By saying this, people are basically saying that God made a mistake in the placing of the living organism and we know best as to where it should grow. Weeds and flowers both grow from the earth which are fuelled by the same energy that also sustains us.

A human judgement does not define an object. An object simply is. Why is it acceptable to eat cows and not dogs? A judgement. Fundamentally there is no difference between either, only cultural conditioning. There is no difference between anything in the world, only individual human perception. My life is no more important than a wasp or an ant. Only the level of evolving consciousness that inhabits the shell of each living thing is the difference. God is present in all.

Why does all of this occur? We need answers, don't we? After all, we are humans. If you had the eternity of nothingness and everything in your grasp, what would you do? You would maybe put a film on to occupy yourself? That is what we are. We are part of a divine play put on by God so that it can experience itself. We are the actors and it is our job to remember who we are, divine beings. Some actors do not want to be woken just yet for they are happy *acting* out their roles. After each refreshment break, known as death, we are reminded of what is the real reality and then continue to return to the stage of earth to occupy a new role. Each individual continues acting until they have had enough of the divine play and chooses to awaken. There is no rush for the film to end for we have eternity, but rest assured, eventually each actor will wake up. God just enjoys many different stories and we are all actors. When you finally realise that you have been had and you are not who you think you are, you may laugh aloud!

This has been a bold chapter, I know. If a random stranger had come up to me at the football years ago while I was smashed and told me that I was God, I would have probably laughed at them. I would have told them about my past and that only bad things had happened in my life, so how could God attract that? Due to my conditioning at the time, that is what I believed.

I would have also thought that the person telling me all this mumbo-jumbo was part of some cult. I would have encouraged them to go and talk to some of their like-minded people and leave me alone. The fact that you have made it this far into the book and the fact that it found its way into your hands in the first place is an indicator that it was meant to be. You may not be ready for what you have read but you were definitely meant to read it. A few seeds could have been sown but I believe an awakening can happen through a multiplicity of factors, kind of like the straw that broke the camel's back. Is this book the thing that finally pushed you over the edge? Have you been wondering what's the point of it all for a while now?

I believe that it can sometimes take something radical to shift our consciousness and perspective on reality, but that doesn't necessarily mean something traumatic. My experience of awakening was brought about through a painful event, but maybe a birth could bring about an awakening too? It doesn't have to be a painful event, but I do feel that it is very hard for people to awaken when in their comfort zone. That familiar path which we have spoken about so much in the book keeps us safe but prevents us from growing.

Reading this book may not simulate harrowing events that trigger an awakening, but one day, that event will happen for you as you are life longing to become what you already are. That may happen to you in this lifetime and words that you have read in this book may make more sense when they are relevant to you. But know that deep, deep down, these words resonate as the truth with you, for you already know them, you have just forgotten them along the way. We all must *awaken* at some stage in our evolutionary journey, as that is how we move closer to God and return to our natural source.

It is an oxymoron and unfathomable paradox how we start off as God, longing to explore and forget who we are in the process. All of this happens while we are in fact God! As our consciousness evolves with each birth, we then start to remember who we are and return to our natural loving state, which is God, a one way roundabout trip if you like full of infinite experiences!

The thing is that much like this book, consciousness and God will never stop evolving. The truth is that we will keep exploring on an infinite basis and with the realisation that we are God, we can occupy different vibrational levels of consciousness. These can exist in parallel universes and we can experience more complex physical and non-physical realities with each incarnation.

This book is full of thought-provoking concepts about our existence that you can take or leave, but wouldn't you like to live the life that was truly intended for you? Imagine if every child was taught that they had infinite divinity and possibilities deep within them, what would the world look like?

I am God. We are God. Remember these words and take them forward with you. You are part of a holistic creation and science can reiterate this point if your rational, analytical mind craves proof. Even if you think that we just die and rot, there is no denying that while you are walking the planet, you are part of a whole collective mass of energy, where everyone is equal. Armed with this knowledge, why would you ever want to cause harm or be selfish to any living thing ever again, including Mother Nature?

If you can remember from earlier in the book, I was always searching for that feeling of oneness and social collectivity. I just wanted to be with other like-minded people and longed to be accepted. From my step family to my football family, that feeling of oneness made me feel complete. By realising that God is in everything, that makes me feel all the more complete. I no longer need to look externally for any of this for the Universe exists within me. We are part of one huge cosmic family and we are never really alone, for everything around us is one.

The world around you is a miracle and has been made with pure loving perfection by your imagination, for you are God. You are love, you always have been and always will be. You created this physical world to remember who you are and bring infinite love into the physical reality.

Step by step the world is being shaped into a loving world, exactly the same as spirit. We are just going through the teething process and erroneous thought era but it will pass. Any other train of thought that is not love is error and that of human fear. God is love, you are love, you are God.

53

TELLING OTHERS WHAT TO DO

Even as I have written this book, which has taken me about 18 months in total, my perspective on the world and Universe is constantly evolving. I have had to constantly keep adding to this book as the initial draft was written within 4 months, but I keep learning more each day. Louise kept telling me to release the book and so did many others, but I didn't want to leave anything out that could possibly help you on your journey.

I did what was true to me and what felt right; I released it when it felt complete and guess what!? I did, because you are now reading it! This book is a good example of how consciousness can just keep growing if you allow it to! The evolution of consciousness will never stop growing if we use our minds in the way they were intended. This book is also an example of how we must do what feels right to us and not let others dictate.

One thing that I have learnt, and keeps coming back to me, is that you cannot force anyone to do anything they are not ready for. People will do things in their own time and when they are good and ready. We all have our karmic path to follow and to force anything else would be counterproductive. To expect someone to behave in a certain way and conform to your beliefs is not love. We are all walking down our own unique individual paths at our own pace, there's no rush for we have eternity. The separate paths that we navigate are perfect for our development and will eventually lead us all back to the ultimate destination of where we came from, God.

Like I have stated throughout this book, your journey is your journey and I am not going to please everyone with the contents of this book but for me, they are the truth. I love people and want to make people happy by sharing my truth, but this isn't always what is best for everyone. Louise told me a little story once which I love, you can apply it to the contents of this book. You could also apply it to your own life when others tell you how you should be living. It is an Aesop fable and it demonstrates that no matter what you do, even if it's with your best intentions, there will always be someone there ready to criticise you.

There was a father and his son walking with a donkey on a hot and dusty road. The sun was glaring down upon them and making the walk quite uncomfortable for all involved. The father was low on water but saving it for his son. They still had what seemed an eternity ahead of them until the conclusion of their journey. The man persisted with his path and encouraged his son and the donkey to do the same. The man loved his son and the donkey dearly and even lightened the load off the donkey's back by carrying some of his own possessions.

As the road drew on, the man and his son crossed a fellow traveller. The traveller greeted the man and his son but was perplexed as to why they were not riding on the back of the donkey. "Why are you both not riding on the donkey?" the man asked. "It's a scorching hot day and the road is long, use that donkey for what he is meant for!" With that, the traveller left and continued on his own journey.

The father had heard the traveller's words and thought that he was right. As much as he loved the donkey, he was exhausted and so was his son. With that, he decided to mount the donkey and his son sat on the donkey's back too. They both rode on the donkey's back for the rest of the journey; after all, their needs were greater.

Not too long later, the man and his son, riding on the back of the donkey, met another traveller. "Hello there friend," cried the man from the back of the donkey to the fellow traveller on the road.

"What the hell is wrong with you both?" replied the traveller. "Can't you see that poor donkey can't cope with both of you on it. Son, let your old man ride upon the donkey for you are younger." And with that the traveller passed and went on his way.

The son, feeling guilty, immediately hopped down so that his father could continue the journey. "Maybe that man was right Dad?" stated the son. The father had to agree with the stranger's inclination. To be honest, the donkey couldn't cope with both on its back.

About half an hour passed and the father and son met another stranger on the road. "Hi Mister," said the father to the stranger.

"Have you no love for your son?" asked the traveller to the father. "Of course I do," replied the father, "why would you ask that?"

"If you loved your son, then you would have him riding on the donkey's back, not you!" exclaimed the irritated traveller and with that, he left.

"Son, I didn't think of it like that, I am so sorry, I do love you. Come and sit on the donkey and I will walk the rest of the way. I could use the exercise anyway!" As soon as the father said this, the son and him swapped places.

Approaching the end of their journey, the father and son crossed a frail old lady who was sitting on the side of the road with her head in her hands. As she heard the couple approaching, she looked up.

"What kind of a man are you?" said the old lady aiming her question at the father. "Can't you see that the donkey cannot cope in this heat with the boy on its back, get him off immediately!"

The father stuttered and tried to apologise to the old lady for he hadn't thought of it like that, he was just taking the previous person's advice. With that, the son hopped off the back of the donkey and walked alongside his father. The old lady scowled with disapproval at them both, ushered them both to leave and sunk her head back into her hands.

The father and son eventually reached their destination after a long and tiring journey. They both walked into town as the sun was setting. The trip had taken its toll on the father and son who were both beaten.

As they walked through the town and made their way to the inn to rest for the night, a man sat outside the local store shouted to them.

"Hey, you two, you look pretty tired, have you travelled far?"

"Indeed," replied the father, "we have travelled from the nearest town, which is 20 miles away, we are so tired, the heat has finished us. We have travelled here to stock up on supplies, that is why we have our donkey."

The man who was sitting outside of the store began to laugh, "You mean to tell me that you have travelled all of this way and you didn't once think to sit on the back of the donkey? Your journey would have been a lot easier had you both ridden the way. The donkey would have coped; they are resilient creatures."

With that the father looked at his son and said, "Son, let's just do what we want in the future."

This story demonstrates that you will always have people in your life who will know what is best for you and try to run it for you. You will meet people who take offence to everything and criticise your every move. Use your knowledge and what you have learnt in this book to view these people differently. Those who insist they know what is best for you may mean well, but it doesn't mean that you have to listen to them. Understand that their past has made them this way and do what is true to you. Send them love at the same time and hope that one day they will understand why they behave like they do; for they are acting out of how they have been programmed. You are now conscious enough to know otherwise. Follow your own heart and it will lead you to greatness.

Awakening to who you truly are can push you forward on your own path and let you focus on you. The cynical voices of the past that came from others will no longer hold any credibility with your soul. When you awaken to your truth of who you truly are and do what you came to do, it will be beautiful and scary at the same time. Beautiful for the fact that you finally remember your divinity, and scary for the fact that most of what you have learnt from others up until that point has been a lie! Until that day arrives, keep exploring and living your life without fear.

54

Enlightenment

It's a paradoxical irony that we have to discover what we already know deep down; we are all one. As humans, we have finite concepts about situations, even enlightenment. After all, we are born and die. This is all we know as humans, so there must be some sort of finish line in sight to reach our goal of enlightenment. The fact is though, as our consciousness continues to evolve, God does too and the path we walk continues to unravel; there is no finish line for we are infinite.

Enlightenment is truly knowing who you are and living by it, while having no attachment to it at the same time. There is no end. God is everything in the present moment, God is the *now*. God is everything and nothing. There was no beginning and no ending in spirit, as difficult as that is for us to understand. You cannot label God; like I have just foolishly done! Everything is just happening at once and we will continue to evolve with no set line to cross to say, "We've done it!" For this lifetime, make the most of this precious physical incarnation and expand your consciousness, but rest assured, all is perfect and meant to be.

If I had read this book just five years ago, when I was beginning to get my life together, I would have not been ready for the content. Yes, the information would have sat true with my higher self, but my egoic mind would have rationalised things and dismissed it all. My mind would have squashed the content of this book as nonsense, for my intellect was a prison and only hindered me.

An awakening is a genuine thing that happens when the ego has been shattered. Seeing Dean's lifeless corpse beside me when I was alone with him was a surreal thing. All the laughs we had shared, the childish behaviour and wrestling games we used to indulge in had gone, were they even real? These were the thoughts that spun through my head that day as I sat next to him on his deathbed. This bizarre event was enough to shatter my ego and crush the perception of reality that I had set about for myself and believed from others. For me, something truly dramatic had to happen in order to shift the dynamic of how I thought. The 18th of November 2017 was that day for me. That day allowed me to evolve.

I had been thinking differently about reality ever since the night I arrived home from the hospital where Dean had left his body. My mind was slowly shifting from day to day about what our purpose was. One day, while I was setting up a room for a function at college, probably about five months after Dean's passing, it happened, it just clicked. I thought to myself, "Oh my God, I've been asleep."

In that very moment, all experiences from past lives came flooding back to me in a rush, it was like all the knowledge that my soul had previously pooled was active again. I actually felt in that moment that I could pick up the pace of where I had left off in my previous lives. I felt like I was ready to continue to help myself and others to grow. It was all perfect the way it had all happened, all the abuse I had suffered at the hands of myself, all the heartache I had put myself through, it was all necessary.

The whole moment was very trippy and far-out to say the least but from that moment, it was like I knew my true self again and I was no longer afraid to hide behind this costume I had been wearing. I use this radical example in order to convey the extreme shift of consciousness that my mind went through that day.

If you still find it hard to believe that we have the power to shape our future and are doubtful, then think back to the *God* chapter and realise that God is within all of us. What does God do? Create. That infinite, omnipotent, celestial force dwells in each and every living thing on this planet, including you! If the left sided part of your brain refuses to believe this and needs tangible evidence, which I did too, delve more into science and do you own research. I keep encouraging you to find your own truth! Do not believe all that is seen on a screen.

When you realise that you have the power to create anything, why can't your dreams be achieved? We are made of exactly the same atoms and molecules as the people who we view as *successful*, it is all down to conditioning and how we apply our thinking.

I used to play the victim all the time and used it to justify so many failures in my life. I also used it as an excuse to feel low and drink. My mother left me, I am an only child, I got kicked out of my house, I have no money! These were all things I was responsible for. My soul planned my destination on earth as an only child. I chose my parents and the situation I would face. My father kicked me out because of my appalling behaviour and I would have to agree with him, it was what I needed. I never had any money because I wasted it on drugs and alcohol; yet I chose to blame my employers for not paying me what I was worth. My thoughts were that of negative energy, so that's what I attracted. Like attracts like. Take control of your life and use your power, you are God!

We can send out what we desire into the universal collective consciousness that we are all part of, and experiences to match that of our wishes will be returned to fulfil our desires. "Ask and you shall receive," but believe at the same time. Be very careful with your thoughts, as what you think about you will become. To the Universe, your dreams are merely a drop in an abundant ocean that everyone is entitled to.

There is enough to go around, as we are all one and the Universe wants us to experience life to its fullest potential. It's only conditioned beliefs from society and others that have led you to believe the myth that resources are limited. Let your birthright shine forth. You are a body of light and deserve all that is good to unfold in your life. You are perfect and so is the Universe.

You may think that I have written this book while wearing rose tinted glasses. "But Dave, what about poverty and war?" As I have spoken about, life is one huge dichotomy, without opposites how could we know love? Do not mistake these opposites as separate though, they are all one.

The pain leads to love and without one, the other would not exist, everything is part of the holistic package. There are no polar opposites in the grand scheme of things, everything is one. Belief of separate forces or energies is one of error. All is God. Learn to look at life from the soul's perspective, in reality you have left the world of spirit to be in this body for what is a few seconds in the scheme of eternity.

Events that we label as bad in the moment are what help us learn. It is how we choose to label them that creates torture and suffering or happiness and joy. Humanity is on a learning curve of ups and downs, embrace them all and think, "What can I learn from this experience?" I am not suggesting that you become an emotionless drone to everything, after all emotions help us. Be sure to process your emotions because they stem from your thoughts and ask yourself, what are they trying to teach me? Emotions are like waves, they come and they go.

I have recently started to read the books of a gentleman called Ram Dass who recently left his body. His teachings say that we should live from a place where we should act as if we have personally chosen every event that happens to us in life, be it *good* or *bad*. If you can live from this perspective that every experience that happens to you in life is as though you chose it, you are becoming the master of your egoic mind. The mind is meant to be the servant, not the master, you can control how you react to every situation with meditation and practice.

We automatically assume that we know what is best for ourselves, even though our minds are just specks in comparison to the Universe and Galaxies. It makes the egoic mind seem very insignificant when measured in comparison to the size of the Universe, doesn't it? Have you ever tried to grasp how big eternity is? There is a Chinese idiom that demonstrates how limited our thinking minds actually are. The story is about a frog in a well.

There is a frog down a well. He is happy there and thinks that all is wonderful, his well is huge! One day, another frog pops his head over the top of the well and looks down to see the other frog.

"Hey, why don't you come up here?" shouts the frog to the one in the well.

"I have all I need down here," replies the frog, "the well is huge and the water goes on forever."

The frog up top says, "Nonsense, you should come up here, there is an ocean nearby that is infinitely vast, it would make you so happy."

The frog in the well replied with astonishment, "You mean to tell me that there are waters bigger than my well? Impossible."

"I promise you," answered the frog up top.

The frog in the well sat and thought to himself, *how could anything be bigger than this well? Maybe it is 100 times bigger, that would be amazing but surely nothing is that big.*

After thinking the frog replied, "Okay, I will see your vast ocean, but I guarantee it is nothing like down here, for I have all the space I could ever need, there possibly couldn't be more than this in reality."

With that, the frog at the top of the well threw a vine down so the other frog could come up and survey the new scenery. The frog climbed up the vine and made his way to the top of the well. He hopped over the top and gazed out at the ocean in front of him to which his head exploded!

I love this story because it demonstrates the true working of the egoic mind. All we have ever known in our tiny circle of life is that which is true to us, there couldn't possibly be more. We think we know it all. Our mind can attempt to imagine what God and eternity is and define both, but the grim reality is that the human mind is nowhere near. When we compare our problems to the size of the Universe, they suddenly become very miniscule. Suddenly the worry of what tomorrow will bring or if Aston Villa will stay up seem very trivial indeed. The frivolity of it all can even bring a smile to your face!

While we are talking about the vastness of the Universe and time, the same could be said about the whole reincarnation cycle that we are a part of to return to God. When you truly grasp how long you have been doing this cycle of birth and death for, it will astound you, even scare you. An example to put into context of how long you have been doing the whole reincarnation process for comes from an old sage.

His description was this, "Imagine a mountain three miles wide, three miles long and three miles high. Once every hundred years, a dove flies up, over, and around the mountain with a silk scarf in its beak and brushes the surface of the mountain. The time it would take for the scarf to wear down and corrode the mountain away is how long we have been doing this!"

This example puts into comparison the vast complexity of the cycles between birth and death that we go through in order to expand our consciousness and remember what we are. The example still is not an accurate representation, but gives our human minds something to work with.

With this outlook applied to the sheer existence of our being, I realise that I actually know nothing in the grand scheme of things and simply relinquish control over everything. I simply let God do its work through me. I am resistant to nothing that is thrown in my path and just let it happen. It simply is what it is. I just be, I just am. This is the closest I can come to enlightenment in this lifetime!

55

DEAN'S DESCRIPTION OF THE DIVINE

In a very recent reading from Jo, Dean came through for the majority of it. It was like chatting to him as if he were in the physical. He said, "Do you have any questions for me?" *Right*, I thought, *I've got you this time.* I always ask him what he does when we meet up in my dreams and he always leaves before answering, doesn't he want me to know!? I always wake up feeling perplexed as to why he doesn't answer me. Was I not ready for what he does in the dimension of love and energy? Either way, I thought there was no way he could escape me now and I asked him, "What do you do?"

Dean answered and gave me a mind-blowing description of what he is actually up to. He also elaborated greatly on what my original question was. Dean described how he is spirit and one with all, he is not floating about in the clouds. Dean's chosen diction was specific so he could relay what he actually is and does. You can appreciate that spirit does not use language and the true beauty of God does not have or need any words. Dean's answer was distorted but made sense to my human mind, in a warped way.

He described how he is just 'AM'. He just 'IS' with everything. Now I realise how important the words 'I AM' actually are. The AMness of it all is just God. I can understand that this may come across as poor English, but I grasp the fact that describing the indescribable is a great feat, even for Deano.

Dean stated that he can do whatever he wants. His thoughts create his reality in an instant. Anything that is perceivable is achievable. He can think of anything that is appropriate to his level of consciousness and it becomes a reality. Dean can be in any galaxy or dimension at once - all via thought. Although there is no physical reality where Dean is, if he wanted to relive a part of the physical world, his thoughts would create a sort of three-dimensional hologram. By creating this, Dean could then relive memories or experiences of his choice. His energy could even choose to relive the moment with great intensity. Again, is this another example of why we experience déjà vu, because time is not real?

Dean stated that he is one with everything and just dips in and around the Universe helping others in this realm and other dimensions that are indescribable. Dean said that he may just pop a thought into a person's head on earth one day who he sees is struggling. Have you ever had an amazing thought that has seemingly come from nowhere? Chances are, that could be a gentle nudge from spirit to push you in the right direction.

Dean stated that everything in every reality is based on vibration, much like what we have discussed in our earlier chapters about our earthly realm. Dean stated that even speech and thoughts are vibration and can affect reality. We are creators in the physical existence and when in spirit. Anything we think and believe will become our reality, even if it deviates from the actual truth of love.

Thoughts and beliefs are a reality for an individual. Dean's insight again concluded that we are all creators, for we are all God. If you believe in a God and the devil, or good and evil, then that is what shall greet you when you pass. However, to think of such polarities are thoughts of error because you are acknowledging that there are two different forces and again pertaining to the notion of separateness. The reality is that there is only God, nothing else.

If I were to attack and criticise your beliefs on earth, that would make me foolish because A) I would be operating from an invalid frequency which wasn't love, and B) you are a creator; even if your beliefs are that of error, they are still real to you and your truth. For me to convince you of anything different would be insanity on my behalf.

Can you now see how everything in our lives is true to us, for we are all creators, and beliefs shape reality? We have come to create anything we want on earth, much as we would in spirit. Our physical reality makes things slightly longer to materialise, but rest assured they eventually do if enough energy is put into the thought. This is different to spirit where Dean said that everything is instantaneous.

I also asked Dean if he now believed in God, for we never spoke of anything like that on earth. His answer started with, "God is not what people think," and, "while we are human, we will never truly understand." Dean then went on to say, "God is space that fills everything." God wants to fill all infinite space with love, for that is all it knows. A three-dimensional reality based on illusory separation was created so it could eventually be filled with love. God fills all space with love to expand everything; while at the same time, everything has already been filled, because there is no time. There is no rush for we have eternity but it's already been done. Wrap your head around that one!

Dean tried to explain how he is just like an orb of energy that can be part of everything in an instant via his thoughts. Spirit does not see like we do in our physical reality, they see everything as waves of energy displaying different colours of light. Dean used the example of a car crash to describe this in human terms. Whereas we would see twisted metal and feel distress, spirit sees it as waves of energy giving off colours that portray the current situation and emotions.

Does Dean's description match that of Albert Einstein's? That everything is energy and that's all there is to it. We are infinite energy, constantly occupying different bodies. The bodies that we inhabit are forever changing, the only truth that never changes is that of loving energy. It always has and always will be. Dean said it was impossible to describe what he truly was now, but there was even a kind of moisture to his existence of energy.

Dean then explained how each lifetime moves your awareness one step closer to what you already are, which is God. He used the term *brownie points* which are appropriate to each lifetime; not as a reward, but to describe the elevation of the consciousness that each lifetime can bring. You create heaven for yourself but have to earn it through experience. This is why we choose to visit Earth, or the complex training simulator which I have now come to see it as. We build our reality based around the wisdom that we gain from experiencing many different existences.

Dean's term *brownie points* got me thinking. Jesus said a similar thing when he said, "In my father's place there are many mansions." Whatever level of brownie points we have collected through our multiple incarnations will then determine what level we exist on our return to spirit. The appropriate plane or mansion will host our level of consciousness depending on the soul's growth.

There are a multitude of levels in which our consciousness will exist when in spirit, all are a fitting match for our vibration and awareness. These mansions or planes of consciousness in spirit are manifold to say the least. We have complete free will, whatever path the soul chooses to walk on earth, then so be it, that's the soul's choice. When an individual passes and returns to oneness, its current level of awareness will only be able to create an appropriate reality to that of its expectations. If an individual believed in hate, darkness and evil on earth, what reality will that level of awareness be able to create when they return to spirit?

The closer the soul is to the truth of God, will determine the level of the mansion in which they will reside in. The soul will simply be a match for whatever level of consciousness they host. If an individual's imagination has a certain boundary attached to it, how can it advance through the different levels of consciousness? For that is all it knows, so that is all it can perceive and create. When the soul in question longs to move closer to what it already is, which is God, it then plans its next journey in order to grow and expand. Whatever karma the soul has attached to it will determine where it next chooses to learn.

If you are lost at my description, think of a Russian nesting doll as God. That is all there is, the doll is a representation of infinity. As the tiny dolls within begin to expand via each incarnation, they grow bigger. They are always God but continue to get larger as they obtain wisdom as to what they truly are. The dolls never stop growing but they can never leave the main largest doll for they are a part of it. This is a practical example to define the potential in which our consciousness can develop and grow. No matter how small or large the consciousness is though, it is always God. When the soul realises what it truly is, it expands creation and creates more love. Now imagine an infinite variety of dolls and you have a minute glimpse into how we are forever expanding in loving awareness.

The Buddha said, "You go higher and higher until you are lost." The Buddha was referring to your journey back to God. I like to imagine the path back to God is like climbing an endless multidimensional ladder, sounds exhausting doesn't it? But don't worry, that's only your ego thinking! Each lifetime allows us to climb a certain rung of the ladder, depending on our actions and understanding. Some lifetimes may even allow us to climb a few rungs at a time or move sidewards, the possibilities are endless.

I think this is why I have always liked role-playing computer games. The premise of these games is to explore and level up. The more experiences and battles that you go through in these computer games, the higher your level goes. You can acquire better perks the further you advance in the game; the same is with the path back to God. The nearer you get to the truth of God, the more you become lost and forget who you actually thought you were. All ambition to become enlightened is lost and all that matters is to become consumed by love; everything else is illusion. You are no one, you simply are God, you are AM. You slip into the void of nothingness, which is God, yet you are everything at the same time.

I was left astounded by Dean's description that day of what he does and what God is, but it made sense to me. There are certain laws between spirit and Earth and Dean was only able to divulge what I was ready to hear. When we are ready, the truth will unfold to us. Imagine being told all of what I have just written about 15 years earlier!? My primary concern back then was about my next pint of Stella and where the next line of coke was going to come from.

Throughout our transition back to spirit, we do not lose our unique sense of humour or our traits. Dean wanted everyone to know that he takes full credit in writing this book, for without him dying it would not have happened. Even in spirit he is a cheeky chappy! Each memory and aspect of our personality in each lifetime is taken home with us.

With the notion that we are all infinite energy, occupying multiple forms to enhance our learning experience, provides a most interesting platform in which to view life. Each experience or lifetime moves us one step closer to what we already are. Each physical experience is temporary and will pass. Each physical reality is forever changing. Each challenging event that comes our way in the physical plane expands our consciousness, and while we may not see it at the time, hindsight can show us that there is indeed profound wisdom in suffering. Crisis precipitates our evolution. Without an event that we label as a *crisis*, we would not evolve. No one ever evolves in their comfort zone, we need challenges to move us into a state of love, something that we always have been.

Just like nature, everything is in balance. We could even label nature as a beautiful crisis but we don't. The leaves fall and die each year, is this a sad process? No, because we know that in spring, new life will bloom and flourish. The states of our reality are the same and are forever changing. Nature is simply a series of ups and downs as well, depending on how you label it. To me, nature works in cycles; just like humanity does. The world we are experiencing at the moment is on a definite shift. The year of 2020 has brought much crisis to the human mind, but people are waking up and using these *crises* as a path for change. To arrive at this current point in humanity has taken many, many downs but it has all been worthwhile. The ups and the downs are not separate but are all one.

Slowly and surely, we are evolving into a more loving physical reality. Love is prevalent across the world if you look in the right places. I hope that by reading this book it has helped you to expand your thinking. There are no good and bad, there is just one, which is God; how's that for a paradox! God is loving energy; nothing more, nothing less.

56

Conclusion

The truth of what we are and what God is brings me joy each day, it sounds cheesy but it's true. Stella and cocaine are no longer needed and not even considered. The very thought of those toxic substances makes me feel nauseous. It is so surreal to think that the person who abused themselves for so many years was even me. Even if you paid me to get wasted for one last time, it wouldn't tempt me. I have one drink every so often but subjectively speaking, it tastes fowl and I just don't see the point. It leaves me feeling drained, why would I want to drain my light? It's not for the fear that if I have more than one drink, I will be on the slippery slope to ten and end up lying in the gutter again! It's the fact that artificial happiness no longer satisfies me compared to true spiritual nourishment. I now feel complete in knowing my true purpose as a human and that feeling is unmatchable.

By knowing who I am, I have learnt to accept people's differences and embrace them all. If everyone was the same, it would be a boring world. No two things are the same on this planet. We don't judge animals or trees for all being different, do we? Why do we feel the need to judge other humans, it is strange when you think of it like that, isn't it?

Focus on making the best version of yourself. If everyone were more concerned with their own development and helping, rather than trying to interfere with other people's business because they know best, there would be little room for politics or war. Instead, we could support each other and focus on making the world a better place to live.

Remember, that which divides us, weakens us. Yes, we need structure, but if we ignore the superficial illusions of religion, politics, social class, gender and worked in harmony, imagine the world we could create. It would be a wonderful experience for all who walked it. For the cynics out there who still think this is impossible, you are right because this is what you believe and change starts with yourself and no one else. If you don't change, the world doesn't change. You are a creator and you create reality.

If this book has made you question reality and sparked an awakening within, try to stay grounded, for the ego will take you on a merry dance. With the change that happens through an awakening, try to keep everything in balance. When something is out of balance, it needs addressing. My thinking has dramatically altered and yes, I see things from an infinite perspective, but I am still here on planet Earth. I am firmly part of this experience as that is what I signed up to do. To have my head in the clouds would be just as unhealthy as being glued to base reality by consuming twelve pints every day and eating processed food.

I still enjoy watching Aston Villa play scintillating football each week, (hmmmm) however, I no longer have an attachment to the result and will not sink into depression if we lose a game; which believe me, can happen a lot! I still enjoy going to the gym and picking *heavy* things up, but I no longer feel the need to eat three chickens and two steaks a day to grow big and strong. For that was simply unconscious behaviour feeding my ego.

While I was living that way, yes, I was doing it for myself, but I was more concerned with the opinion of others and if they would comment on my size. Little regard was placed upon how those animals arrived on my plate when I was living that way. Now, while I live in the physical, I am conscious of my choices and the impact that they have on the world. I still love my food, but I simply enjoy meals and don't let them consume me, like I have done in the past.

I have also learnt the importance of yoga to balance what I do at the gym. For to be rigid and inflexible is just as unhealthy as doing nothing.

Yoga helps the energy to flow through all the chakras and to be nimble, whereas building huge muscles brings about a very fixed and unhealthy posture.

The previous paragraphs show how I have learnt to balance the physical and spiritual as one. I accept the physical world for what it is and don't push it away. In fact, the gym is where I do most of my work on myself, spiritually and physically. If I see someone who I deem to have a better body than me, I automatically assume they are on steroids and my insecure self has kicked in! I also know that human judgement has then entered and for that moment, I have left unity consciousness. If I see a woman in the gym who I immediately lust over, I just observe and accept my human emotions but know that she is just another expression of the divine and one with me. I can then appreciate who she truly is and not objectify her.

Religion, politicians, and the power structure that I wrote about earlier in the book are all part of the oneness of God; nothing is outside of that energy. They are all part of the physical world I chose to incarnate into, and offer me the opportunity to learn about myself. I chose to write about how religion, politics, and society is structured to show how easy it is to manipulate and divide people. Structure and fear can prevent individuals from following their dreams if they are not conscious of it. I have seen this with myself and it left a bitter taste in my mouth, but the system created by these fellow souls is part of my human experience.

I can't lie, when I wrote those chapters, I did feel like I had fallen into the good vs evil trap. In my mind, I was the good one, and they were bad for perpetuating the divide in society, but without negative, positive cannot exist, again showing me the oneness of it all. This is my karmic predicament for this lifetime. The truth was that it was I who had created the divide in that moment by viewing them as separate. We do not see the world as it is, but as we are. My consciousness is now at the point where I no longer view it as me against them, but choose to change what doesn't sit well with me, and teach people a more empowering, positive, and loving alternative. I try to keep my heart open to all the events that happen in the world. I know that I also create my reality and see what I want to see. Everything is one. When I reject anything, I reject the one at the centre of it all.

To reject anything good or bad is the workings of the human mind. Even illness, which can be karmic or induced upon ourselves, has a lesson attached to it and shouldn't be rejected. Some spiritual communities shame those who are ill and say that they do not love themselves because of their condition; this is toxic, and is actually the furthest thing away from love, it is actually creating more fear and separation. By doing this, they actually reject God, and therefore themselves.

People who do this are not yet secure in walking their own path and must ridicule others. The same goes for shaming those who are not 'awake'. I was guilty of this in the beginning of my awakening. As I have said throughout though, we all have our own path to walk, which is no better or worse than anyone else's, as they all lead to the same place. Not everything is always clear to the human mind when it comes to the soul's curriculum for each lifetime. Those who think they know what is best for others show that they still have much work to do on themselves, as they still live in fear.

I have written about how thought patterns and emotions create our reality to empower you, not to make you feel guilty about what you create. Yes we do create our day to day health with our thoughts, emotions, and lifestyle; but nothing is always black and white when it comes to the soul's path. You never know what the soul has planned for you in your karmic journey, and there may be a crucial lesson to learn from a karmic illness, even when you are vibrationally high, fit and healthy. As always, it boils down to looking at everything with an open mind and thinking: *What can I learn about myself from this situation? What is it trying to teach me?*

You may be a stubborn soul who has trouble asking for help and speaking your mind; an illness may force you to learn this lesson so that you have no choice but to ask for help. A particular condition may even inspire others to look at life differently by the way an individual handles it all. A soul may choose a specific illness to raise awareness around the concerning area, and how it can be healed. Their path may help the collective evolve with new holistic ideas and medical advancements.

My mum's health is something that we have both discussed extensively. I do believe that my mum's health will improve when she forgives herself, as her symptoms did come about after she had left me. I feel her dis-ease is to do with subconscious thoughts and emotions that have not been confronted; she still beats herself up for what she did. However, it could also be a soul choice, and we have both learnt so much from it all. Had she not chose to leave me, I would not be writing this now; the perfection of it all. We both continue to work together by talking about how we feel, which makes our love for one another even stronger. I believe that one day, she will let go of her pain and see that she was just doing what she thought was best at the present time.

Dean's condition that he chose before he arrived here was used as a tool to inspire others and show that darkness can be transformed into light; this is the true meaning of a karmic illness. Dean used this illness to shine his light and overcome any limitations that the physical provides. He showed others what the power of positivity could truly do, and that you can live whatever life you truly want despite your physical condition.

Even great Saint's have become ill; Ramana Maharshi had cancer and knew that he could heal himself, but saw that his current body had served its purpose for that current incarnation and accepted it was time for his transition. His devotees couldn't understand why he became ill, but he saw it from the soul's perspective and acknowledged that it was his way of exiting the physical world for that lifetime, because his work was done. Through his passing, he taught that there was nothing to fear and that being in the moment was the only reality there is. Ramana stated that self-realisation is the greatest gift that you can offer to the world.

This is why when Jesus performed healing miracles, he only performed them on people who he could see had inflicted dis-ease upon themselves due to their thoughts and emotions. He saw the unique karma of each individual, and would not heal those who had chosen a particular illness for that lifetime, because they were learning specific lessons from it. He did this not through lack of love, actually the opposite; he respected the individual's path and offered compassion because of their brave choice. By performing these healings, Jesus wanted to show us that we have the power to do this too. By seeing ourselves in perfect health and using the power of love, we can overcome anything.

My beautiful teacher Wayne Dyer also had cancer, but accepted it as part of his soul's path and didn't reject it; in fact, he said he owned it, and wondered what could he learn from it. He did not let the condition control him, and frequently stated, "I am well." Wayne believed that you had to focus on the solution to the problem, rather than the problem, otherwise you perpetuate the issue. Wayne was eventually healed from his cancer via spiritual healing. He made his transition a few years later from a heart attack at the age of 75.

Ram Dass, who made a profound impact on my life even had a severe stroke; it was extremely debilitating for him. Doctors said that he wouldn't live long, but he proved them wrong by displaying the true power of the mind, and living for a further 22 years. From his perspective, he described it as "fierce grace," because it took him closer to his soul and God. It offered him a new opportunity to learn new lessons, and become even more present in the moment. He just viewed it as a new chapter in his life, or likened it to a new incarnation. He stated that only comparison to his previous state of health was that which caused the suffering; comparison often causes suffering in all walks of life.

Jerry Hicks, who was the husband of Esther Hicks, died of cancer. He received a lot of criticism from particular communities after his passing. Esther, who channels a consciousness known as 'Abraham', promotes the message that we create our own reality via thoughts and emotions. People could not understand why Jerry would have cancer if he was so vibrationally high and practised what his wife preached. Do people forget that he was 84? We all have to go one way or another! Death is as natural as birth. Illness can provide a perfect exit for a particular soul; even through leaving the physical, a lesson can still be learnt for the individual and those surrounding them.

Illness also offers an opportunity for compassion to be cultivated amongst all of those who are affected, even towards medical staff who are only human and doing their best. Even when our thought patterns and emotions are in line, our soul could have planned a particular illness to help us grow and learn a specific lesson. Dean would often allow new treatments and drugs to be used on him to see if they could work, and offered himself to Cystic Fibrosis research. This is just another example of brave souls who choose their path to help the world evolve. The medical treatment that we receive is still part of our physical experience that we chose, and should be embraced holistically, just as much as embracing the power of the mind.

I recently had a friend who died for 40 minutes and was pronounced dead after a cardiac arrest. The doctor tried a new technique of resuscitation on my friend that had not been tried before, ever, and it worked. That split second decision that the doctor made, has now forced the medical books to be rewritten because of this event, and this new technique can potentially save millions of lives in the future because of my friend's soul path. His cardiac arrest has now helped the medical field to rethink its methods and practices when it comes to this condition.

My friend is now a medical anomaly and he has helped to pave a new way forward. He has made a full recovery and now thinks differently about life because of this Earth shattering event. My friend has always worked in caring and educational roles trying to help others who have chosen a challenging path; whenever you meet him, he always radiates sincerity and positive energy. This is just another example of the beauty of his soul. The fact that he experienced all of this trauma in this lifetime reiterates how brave his soul actually is.

I have already touched on this topic earlier, but think about children who choose to come to this planet with illness already installed into their physical shell; what have they come to teach and learn? These brave advanced souls who choose suffering so that others can learn and evolve from them are indeed love personified. Some children can help medical knowledge advance even further and provide answers that were not previously known. Many children who raise money and awareness for the condition they are suffering with spark inspiration and compassion from others; it can make you cry when you truly think of the path they chose to inspire and teach others out of love.

This was always a major gripe of mine growing up, and I couldn't understand why God would inflict suffering upon innocence. The fact is, as we now know, God is just the loving energy that animates everything and makes all things possible; it has given itself to us so that we can discover who we truly are. God isn't doing anything to us, we do it all to ourselves because we are God. We choose everything, and create everything, by using our free will to further the expansion of our consciousness. All paths lead back to source energy and each unique experience helps us rediscover and awaken our true power; contrast and duality is there to make this all possible. So a child choosing to visit this planet with illness is a true inspiration and has chosen a bold path out of love.

That is why it is so wrong to shame someone who is ill and say they are not 'spiritual' because of it; when really, what does the human mind actually know about how the Universe works? So don't go beating yourself up if you become ill, or cannot manifest what you want in a set amount of time; you never know the real reason behind anything and this is where faith comes in. Again, when you release attachment to things, watch how they clear up and manifestations happen a lot quicker, because you are no longer feeding them with negative energy. This is all part of the journey of contrast in which we can learn from.

I wrote that last paragraph because recently I have been very guilty of putting myself down. I can often feel less 'spiritual' because I don't wake up one day feeling my usual high vibrational self, and immediately think *what have I done wrong?* This causes another subsequent vibrational dip, and can leave me feeling run down. You know by now who is responsible for berating ourselves and others, and this time, we will just call him Mr. E! Self-awareness of when your thoughts are slipping into that of a negative, or self-critical nature is key; this is where you regain your power by acknowledging your pattern of thought, and switching them to a more positive state.

When you do notice a vibrational dip, throw on some music that gives you goosebumps to lift your mood, call a friend who makes you laugh, meditate, go for a walk, or exercise; all of these will switch your feel good feelings back on, which then loop back to your thoughts. Otherwise it's a slippery slope to self-loathing, and your external reality will then reflect back to you how you feel. Don't allow Mr. E to put you down or control you out of guilt, you are simply doing your best; why do we need to be so hard on ourselves!?

All events that we label as good and bad are one, and are all part of the process to help you remember how perfect you already are, despite what is happening in the present moment. There really is no good or bad, just creation. When you fall, it's just another opportunity to pick yourself up. Light cannot exist without darkness, reminding us that we must sit in the middle of duality peacefully, and watch it all happen around us without judgement. When we are able to do this, we are balanced, free from the attachments of the mind, and free from our prison cells.

Remember, love is really all there is, and you are perfect as you are learning how to be a human. You are powerful, and your thoughts are powerful things and do create the future, but know that you are not a bad person when you do get ill; even if it is in your 90's! It's just another opportunity to learn something new and move those thoughts to a more loving state for everything that unfolds in your unique experience. Each situation that comes your way is a reflection of your inner state and offering you an opportunity to learn more about yourself. You are quite literally here to know thyself in all your glory, and all the contrast that life brings; be one with it, have fun, and love it all.

I feel so passionately about what I have written about in this book and tried to include a holistic package for you. Love really is the answer and I think that we can all agree that sometimes, it's just nice to be nice, after all, we are all in the same boat. I have always been a great admirer of

Martin Luther King and we can all make his dream a reality if we choose to operate from the frequency of love.

To me, success is coming to this earth and doing what you truly love. If you love sweeping the streets and you feel that it is your true purpose as to why you are here, then you are a success. If you own a company worth billions and it feels natural and you love it, then you are a success. If you work in an office and love every moment, then you are a success. If you own a huge global franchise but are unhappy with what you do, then in the eyes of society you are a success, but to your soul, you are cheating yourself.

If you do not LOVE what you do, ask yourself what it is you do love and start living life from that frequency. The Universe will support you if you do what you love, I promise. If you truly feel that you are fulfilling your dharma and are happy, then you my friend have made it. Of course, my definition of success may be totally different to yours and that is fine, for it is up to you to find your truth.

I have typed most of this book from the comfort of my lounge and garden most nights. You could easily do this too if you have a story to share perhaps? Throughout the journey of my book, Bella was snuggled by my side for most of it; she helped me to stay focused. Towards the end of the book though Bella was diagnosed with cancer. The news came as a complete shock and I cried for a whole night solid when I found out. I then thought, *Dave, you have just written a book promoting the power of living in the moment and you are already speeding ahead to Bella's passing!*

I took a step back and re-examined everything. I am not perfect and yes, I still have to apply what I write about to myself from time to time. I then cherished every second with that animal and loved her more than ever, but within a month of her being diagnosed, Bella left her little teddy bear suit.

I found her passing more difficult than Dean's and my nan's in a way. I used to think that all dogs were just stupid little mutts, how wrong was I? Bella and all creatures are love personified and she taught me so much. She passed at home with us in front of the fire; she was so poorly, it was her time to go. As she left, I felt her energy leave her furry body and felt indescribable sadness but then I thought, *where could she go?*

The very first night of her passing she came to visit me in my sleep, she was healthy and happy! She was so full of life and was like a supercharged version of her! You could say this was just a dream but I have now learnt the difference between our brain's processing experiences that have occurred in the day and actual visits from spirit. I awoke feeling peace and joy knowing that Bella was well and happy.

We have heard her paws in the kitchen several times now and it is becoming more and more common. I also leave my lounging about clothes by the side of the bed where she used to sleep. When I arrive home from work, they smell just like her! It seems like she still likes to rest there. I feel her presence when I meditate and experience her warmth. I know that she is one with all I see because she is God too.

I thank the Universe for making such a perfect creature and putting her in my life. She taught me more about love and life than I could ever know and for that, I am eternally thankful. The comparative examples that I have used in this book to describe her animalistic behaviour and the ego will stay on the planet forever in this book. I hope that her life helps people to understand what we have evolved from as much as she has helped me.

I have really tried to convey my passion to you about the truth I have found. There is only love, everything else is just illusion, so just let it be! Consider what love is for a minute? I am not speaking about the biological attraction between humans; that's superficial. I am speaking about what we are, what it is to be love.

I have experienced true love and what it actually means on a handful of occasions in this lifetime. One time was with Dean when he passed, and the other was when my nan visited me that day at my grandad's. The only way to describe it is through tears, humbling tears as to the true power of what loving energy we are made from. Have you experienced this feeling? I hear that the birth of a child can spark this feeling, as they are a gift from the divine.

Taking what we are to a universal stage, could you love a complete stranger with the same level of compassion that you have towards your spouse? What is the difference between a stranger and your spouse? Sure, you know your spouse and love them, but were they not once a stranger? Does that not suggest that the love you have for your significant other was always there? When your loved one stopped becoming a stranger, did that love miraculously appear? Yes and no. They awoke those feelings in you but they didn't magically place the love there, it was always there because you are love. You just felt comfortable enough to loosen the armouring that was wrapped around your heart and allowed them to awaken what was already inside of you. That person that entered your life was just a mirror to show you what you were; we are all capable of love for that is who we are.

If that special someone were to die, that love doesn't actually go anywhere. They wouldn't take it with them, it is always there, for that is who you are. Yes, you will grieve and this is all part of the process: cry, scream, for the pain of separateness is upon you once more, but there will come a day where you realise that the love you have for that person is who you are. Love is always inside of you for that is what you are made of. Can you now see how love is universal and links us to everything? You will see loved ones again because love survives everything.

With love now in mind, could you love a stranger who behaves and lives in a way that is the total opposite to what you believe? Could you love them, even if it went against every fibre of your moral beliefs? That love for them is there deep down and you recognise who they are on a subconscious level, for they are God. What is it that stops us from reaching out and helping? Fear.

Fear keeps you anchored and unable to love that stranger because you don't want to get hurt. Could you allow the shackles of fear, which guard your heart, to shatter? Could you love a complete stranger without casting judgement on the way they live? Anyone you have ever loved was once this stranger. Could you put this stranger first and help them in any way possible? Could you detach from your ego completely and see that the stranger is no different to yourself? Can you see that they have the same feelings as you and that love is inside of them too? Could you do all of these things expecting nothing in return? Could you see that every person you have ever loved was once a stranger? Could you allow what is naturally inside of you to shine forth for that split second without fear? Can you now see that every stranger is God in disguise and just another version of you?

When you are in love with another, do you want them to be happy? The common answer is yes, but what if that person's happiness lay with another? What if they wanted to leave you in order to be happy with someone else? Would you still love them and bless them in their new walk of life? You love them, don't you? And true love never tires of being selfless. Or would you discover that the love you thought you had for that person was in fact that of the ego? Egoic love only recognises *others* as separate entities who are simply there to stimulate personnel needs and make us feel complete. This is where I have fallen many, many times in my life.

The term *unconditional love* is a convoluted one, to say the least. Pure, unconditional love to our human minds is quite complex when you actually consider the term unconditional. The moment you place a condition or boundary on love, you have given it human characteristics and allowed the ego to get involved. This is not to say you are a bad person, far from it. I still do this unconsciously from time to time, quite frequently in fact. It is hard to offer ourselves to a complete stranger because of social conditioning and that one little word again, fear. Fear is the natural mechanic which aids self-preservation. You are eternal though, so what is there to fear?

The next time that you experience a fearful situation, watch how you react? Do you allow your mind to take you on a ride or become the master and observe the moment? The more meditation and practice you do to control your mind, the more you allow yourself to cultivate a beautiful path for love to parade through. The more you understand what love actually is and allow it to flow, the closer you move towards the truth of what source energy is. There will be a day when the love just oozes from us because that's all we have to give and that is who we are. When that day does happen, and we release all attachment to it, that is what true *God* realisation is.

By choosing to come to this earth, we have done a brave thing and have shown much courage. Do not worry about making mistakes and not being perfect; you have chosen to learn by being a human, this in itself is already perfect and respected by the Universe. You are a brave soul because you have chosen to leave the loving perfection of oneness that we are all part of. Your natural home is love, so to come to a world where love is not yet a perceived reality is indeed a brave thing to do.

With a child's arrival on this planet, physical separation is a new thing. It is not what a child is used to because they have arrived from the oneness of love. The first time a child experiences something that is different to love, it is perceived as a painful experience because it is foreign to their natural state. This painful experience is then remembered by the child and they wrap armour around their heart in order to protect it from further pain. Pain is a natural occurrence in the absence of love. Adults who then choose a dark path are simply children who did not receive love; they are creating all they know and have forgotten where they came from.

We then spend our whole lives trying to avoid painful experiences for they are unnatural to what we actually are. These painful experiences will eventually bring us back to our natural state if we allow them to. The pain eventually brings an awakening as to who we actually are and that love is all there is. In a way, we become children again and rediscover our purity. As you have read this book, you know that it was pain that pushed me to question who we truly are. My quest for the truth came about from the awakening of death...

57

MY BOOK IN 30 POINTS!

Here are 30 key points I would like to leave you with, a kind of summary if you like. I originally started off with 5 points then 10, then 15, but there are so many, I could go on and on, but I've done enough of that……

1) Love is all there is. It is what we are made from and can conquer anything thrown in its path. Unconditional love is the way forward. Love for yourself, others, and all of creation transcends any element of illusory fear. Love is another word for God. That one source of energy is God, which is love.

2) All we have is the now. You will have this moment forever but never again, how will you spend it? This present moment can be whatever you want it to be. By savouring each waking moment, the past and future are simply illusory. You can use your mind as a tool to plan future events but that is all it is, a tool; do not allow it to plan you! The author, Robin Sharma said, "The mind makes a wonderful servant but a lousy master." When we worry about the future, anxiety occurs. When we live in the past, depression prevails.

3) Learn to understand the ego and its natural mechanics. When we can identify with the false self that is the ego, we can begin to understand life. Be conscious of the behaviour that isn't actually who you are or where you came from. This space suit that your soul travels in has an ego fitted in it to help navigate the world, but it shouldn't rule you. When we operate from a place of fear or judgement, the ego is probably running the show.

4) Know that you are a perfect creation and unique. You created yourself and have infinite power. You created yourself because you longed to fill every corner of the infinite Universe with love. Don't mimic anyone else and be your unique self. Learn to share the talents that you chose to bring to the world. Being who you came to be makes you a success. You can fulfil your dharma living this way. Self-love and acceptance are so important, after all, it's only ever ourselves that we are truly alone with. We will forever be our own companion, so start loving who you are!

5) We are all infinite souls with temporary bodies, not a body with a soul. We are all on a spiritual path whether we choose to acknowledge it or not. We are all on the same mission to return to where we came from. We have many lifetimes and we are all constantly learning at different levels.

Respect everyone's path, for it is unique to them. Everyone has planned their journey which will all lead back to the same destination. We have multiple incarnations and we are constantly changing form. Birth is a doorway into the physical realm where our souls come to learn and while we do this, we inherit an ego! Death is the exit from the physical plane, with this, we leave the ego experience that is our body behind.

6) Everything is perfect as it is. Everything is in balance and is exactly where it is supposed to be. To think anything less is a product of the ego and you are viewing your existence from a finite perspective. Our minds are a wondrous phenomenon but still cannot comprehend the vast, limitless chasms of the Universe. Earth is spinning a thousand miles an hour and all of the planets are perfectly aligned while working in harmony with one another. Then there's us, worrying about what tomorrow may bring… Everything is in order.

If events that happen in the world upset you, view them from a soul perspective but let it spark the change within you. When you change, the world changes. Let the unjust events be the catalyst that propel you forward to change the world yourself. Events that happen in the world that you view as wrong are perfect opportunities for your transformation. Let them inspire you to become the change and inspire others to change too; you see how perfect it all is?

7) We are all one. I am God, you are God, we are God. God is consciousness and consciousness creates matter. Even if you still feel that we just wither and die when our time is up, that is fine. But we can't deny that all living things on this planet are all made up from the same matter as one another. With this in mind, the next time you are destructive towards someone or something, you are essentially

harming a tiny fragment of yourself. Know that all of creation is inside of you. Worship God by acknowledging the divine presence in yourself, all who you meet and all that you see, for that is God. To worship a man in the sky who will burn you if you do not comply with what he wants is fear-based, to say the least.

8) Try to lead by your actions and not words. By demonstrating behaviour without justifying it, you can teach someone a lot more than a well-chosen rant, which is ironic as I rant a lot in this book!

9) Be thankful for what you have. Gratitude is the great multiplier and only brings more of the same.

10) Learn to be happy and enjoy life. If life throws waves at you, learn to surf and enjoy it! We are only here for a tiny amount of time, so have fun! Learn to embrace the good and the bad as one. When we operate from a frequency of love, our worlds mirror our unique perception of the world.

11) Embrace your struggles, for they help to provide the platform which helps to shape who you are. Your struggles will eventually help you to remember who you actually are. Ever heard the story of the straw that broke the camel's back? That moment when it all becomes too much or you have been through it all could be the final piece to the puzzle. That final moment of trauma or pain that you experience may be the catalyst for your awakening.

All pain is a possible vehicle for an awakening as to who you truly are. When you have finally had enough and let go of it all, you let God shine through you because you have finally surrendered.

Remember the story of the caterpillar, it has to undergo great darkness and struggle in order to reveal its true beauty; the same is for you. Act as if you chose every situation for yourself, what can you learn from every experience? For it is simply another opportunity to move you closer to God.

Think of the heart like a coconut. The Persian poet, Rumi, who lived in the 13th century compares the heart to a nut and says: "You have to keep breaking your heart until it opens." I don't know if you have ever tried to crack a coconut open. But it's damn hard work! The pain we experience in life forces us to place an armour around our heart in order to protect it from feeling that level of pain again. Pain after pain forces that armour to constrict and become even harder over time, until one day, something gives. The shell cracks and all that pours out is coconut milk or in this instance love; you have finally surrendered.

12) Meditation can expand your mind and awareness. It can truly help to alleviate issues that are created by the mind. You can witness thoughts come and go while in meditation, while in waking life, they may appear real. Notice that thoughts are not part of who you truly are. Know that they are just recycled information from various sources in your life.

You will realise that the mind is where your reality lies and you can change that reality. To be blunt, our lives are nothing more than mental constructs and they can be easily realtered. The only truth in between all of our beliefs is that we are a loving Universe experiencing itself.

Meditation can create new awareness, allowing space for new concepts and possibilities. With a clear mind, you can also stay in the moment and observe what actually gets you caught in the game. What causes you to be consumed by the illusion?

13) What you think about, you become. If you approach everything with negativity, doom and gloom, guess what your life will be full of? If you want a new job, don't hate the current one you are in, imagine a new perfect job! Imagine how it feels to have what you desire, it feels good, yeah? Act as if it has already happened and the Universe will have no option but to send an experience your way that matches that of your thinking and feeling.

One of the hardest things for me to accept was that we are responsible for our lives. Our thoughts create reality, you are the creator. Any events that happen are karmic and have been planned by your soul. Do not be a victim for then you choose to relinquish your power. You are a creator!

Nikola Tesla said, "If you want to find the secrets of the Universe, think in terms of energy, frequency, and vibration." Everything is energy and vibrating at specific frequencies, even your thoughts. Each thought produces a electromagnetic wave that has a unique vibration attached to it. You then attract events into your life that are align with your vibrational frequency.

14) Being true to what you believe and acting out of love because of it is true dharma. The truth for an individual is relative and can change from day to day. As long as you honour what you believe to be true, then you are fulfilling your incarnation.

15) How do you want to be remembered at your funeral? Someone who acquired much wealth and power but did little for humanity and looked out for themselves? Or someone who was positive, selfless, compassionate and inspired others?

16) Perception is everything. How you perceive something doesn't actually define what it is. Neem Karoli Baba, who was a great Indian saint, clarifies the notion that perception is everything with this one beautiful line: "When a pickpocket meets a saint, all he sees are his pockets." If you think that we live in hell, then that is what will greet you. If you see the beauty of all life, then that is what will shine through. The idea of an eternal hell after life is man's morbid creation. Heaven can be right here now if you choose to see life that way.

Taking this theory of perception to the next level was Max Planck. Mr Planck was a German physicist and is known for his work regarding quantum physics. Mr Planck's work demonstrated that when an individual looks at an object, the characteristics of the object actually change on a molecular level according to that of the observer, how amazing is that!?

This is why scientists over the years have contradicted one another and cannot agree on one objective truth. This is because our subjective mind affects our objective world; this phenomenon can be linked to the observer effect. If you wanted to prove anything, you really can, as you always have a subconscious influence over the variable that you are studying and observing; your consciousness interacts with it on a quantum level. Even when an individual thinks they are being neutral or objective, they still hold a certain level of bias towards something on a subconscious level.

'Reality' has an ever-shifting structure which is almost dreamlike. Most scientists who study quantum physics, neuroscience, behavioural genetics, and evolutionary biology are starting to reiterate the theory that how we think affects the world around us, and what we experience. Ancient teachings and philosophies have always spoken of this and known the true nature of our 'reality'. Ultimately, our perception around something dictates our vibration about the thing in question, and that determines our reality.

Another amazing fact is that the molecular level of a vegetable is also altered depending on who plants it. If you were to plant your own vegetables, its nutritional content would alter depending on your specific needs. For instance, if you had an undiagnosed illness and planted a vegetable, it would grow knowing exactly what your body needs. The more you nurtured it, the more it would know about you. As the vegetable grows, it will tune into all of your problems, even the spiritual ones, and provide all that you need. You literally create everything in your world, even your food!

17) We are here to learn, grow, develop, evolve, expand and to realise that we are God. Earth is a spirit school and we are all studying a difficult curriculum. We are all here to work on ourselves. We are all travelling towards the same destination, which is to return to the source from which we originated but we have each chosen a unique path to get there.

Nothing is permanent and everything is constantly evolving. As we have evolved from animals, we have animalistic traits which are in our DNA. As animals, we hate change because that poses a threat to our safety and our bubble, but that is how we learn. We have to overcome our DNA programming in order to grow. By choosing courage, you crush the illusion of fear and allow love to shine forth, which helps your consciousness to expand.

Anything can be your own personal guru to help you learn and grow. I frequently leave glasses of water on the floor next to the sofa and Louise frequently kicks them over! She will go ballistic and accuse me of being reckless. At first, I felt bad but then I realised that Louise's guru comes in the form of a glass of water! For each time she knocks it over, it offers her an opportunity to lessen her attachment as to how things should be; so now I leave it there deliberately to help her work on herself! You could say that I am the sick one for doing this, but I do it out of love. One day she will knock the glass over and not a flicker of emotion will consume her, for it just is. That is freedom from one's mind.

18) Thought patterns, beliefs and lifestyles create your future health. Deep, unresolved mental issues will eventually manifest into some sort of physical ailment or dis-ease. Thoughts create emotions that are energy, if you do not allow that energy to be released, it will become trapped in the body. It will show up as a metaphorical problem in a certain part of the body. It is as if the energy is saying, "Get me out of here!" If you have back problems, chances are that you feel unsupported by people or the process of life. Contrary to social interpretation, dis-ease is not bad, it is trying to help us by showing that we are out of balance in one way or another.

19) Karma is an actual law, such as physics and gravity are. Karma or quantum physics are not taught at school for the simple fact that they are bad for business. We are taught mainstream science that feeds the society in which we live.

Karma means to learn or action. Know that every time you make an action or choice, it has a global effect. Cause and effect are always active when making decisions, even through our thoughts. We are doomed to make choices, it's part of how we learn. The way someone behaves towards you is their choice and their karma. How you choose to react is yours.

20) Everyone is a teacher. If you think that you can only teach people things, then you have a lot to learn. An open mind is a beautiful canvas to be in possession of.

21) The earth has been around for about four and a half billion years. Our ancestors were on the planet around six million years ago but the most modern form of human that we can relate to are the Homo sapiens which walked the blue planet around 200,000 years ago.

When man's history is put in comparison with the existence of the planet, we are but a mere blip on it. All of our ancestors' work and progression has happened in a relatively short amount of time. Their work has enabled us to be in the position that we are in today. We have evolved to the point where we can consciously focus on operating from a frequency of love, instead of fear. If you want the world to change, it will not happen with you feeding it with negative energy. Change starts with you for you are the Universe.

22) So many people argue about what we should call God but does it really matter? How can we label such an unimaginable, invisible, formless, omniscient beauty? After all, as the Austrian philosopher Søren Kierkegaard said: "As soon as you label something, you negate it."

When we have a preconceived vision as to what God is, it already doesn't do it justice. Man has such a warped perspective as to what God is. For most in the western world, the term *God* will denote a white guy with a beard sitting in the clouds judging every move that we make.

If you were to strip away the physical illusion of separateness that we are all submerged in, you would see that everything operates in waves of energy and light from one source only. A cushion has energy, a brick has energy, it just operates at a different frequency. This indestructible pool of infinite energy has one source and one source only. This energy translates to love and love is what fills all aspects of the Universe, even the physical worlds. Every Universe and dimension are essentially one.

If you want to label this source of energy as a certain something, to give it egoic recognition, then that is fine. Understand by labelling this force you have already drawn a blank as to what it is. You have tried to define it and by doing that you have given it boundaries. You have given the formless a form, which is impossible to do and leads us once again down the paradoxical rabbit hole; this quite frankly hurts my brain if I think too much about it. I only use the term God or Universe to convey my point in this book, which is in itself a bold claim.

23) Balance, balance, balance! Everything in the Universe is in balance and we must learn from this. When our lifestyles are out of tune and not in balance, our experiences will follow a similar pattern. Make time for yourself and have productive time alone. Eat nourishing foods that are vibrationally high, get enough rest and drink water instead of sugary drinks. All of this, in the long run, will affect your mood for the better. Look after the body first and then the mind and soul will follow. You will know when you are out of balance, as you will probably become ill or have those lengthy periods of lethargy that we all suffer with from time to time, myself included.

24) When you live to serve others with no expectation of return, watch your work return to you in ways that you didn't expect. Now, if you give all your money away and say, "Okay Dave, I did that and now I'm broke, thanks a bunch," you're doing it for the wrong reasons. In the beginning of my journey, I would give money away and receive nothing back, but I was doing it for the wrong reasons. I was giving with the expectation to receive. When you can truly give from a place that expects nothing in return, then the Universe will hear you because that is pure love and that is what the Universe is. Basically, it stems back to that guy again - the dreaded ego! When you do help others or give something away, who is that person who acts out of impulse? Is it your calculated egoic mind or do you give from the goodness of your heart, which is out of love?

Try not to boast about your good deeds either for they detract from the actual good that you have done. It's better to give pennies in private than pounds in public.

25) Try to become independent of the opinions of others, when you see yourself as separate from everyone, that is when the problems begin! We are raised in a society where what others think is paramount. From an early age, we see how important it is to fit in at school and achieve. Failure in an academic sense could lead others to label us as a failure or an outcast. If they do, so be it, who's right or wrong anyway? Surely people who think that you should conform or live in a certain way are indeed the lost ones, for they never sought to make their own path in life and question what the truth was. Following the crowd is a trait of the ego.

What you think about yourself is the most important. When you become upset over what another has said, you are basically saying that you value that person's definition of you more than your own. You know who you are deep down, don't allow others to define you.

We are all one, so someone's definition of you is in fact their own illusion; their definition isn't right and it isn't wrong. Their definition is just a unique perception as to who you are. If you consider this then that means there are 7.53 billion versions of you existing out there because everyone has their own opinion.

Once again, these opinions do not define you and it is only you that truly knows what is inside. Everyone's definitions and opinions are animated by the same universal energy. There are no others, just multiple perspectives in which the Universe chooses to learn and experience itself.

26) Water is so important to our bodies. We are water, we came from water. When we are groggy, it is probably due to our hydration levels, just drink more! And no, alcohol does not count! Bless your water before it enters your body and love the feeling it provides for you. Water has intelligence, think back to Masaru Emoto's water experiment that I spoke about in our health chapter. Water's molecular structure is shaped by words and labels; how will you treat

yours? Thinking negatively towards your own body, which is a vessel of water, will affect your own molecular composition.

27) There is a difference to what you believe and what you know. What you know is what you have made conscious contact with yourself. What you believe is an illusory idea that you have heard or seen from elsewhere. You may say that this book is just a book of beliefs that have arisen from my head. However, I have witnessed unexplainable things, felt God's presence in my life and have always had constant reassurance from spirit and my guides. I have made contact with these phenomena, I challenge you to find your own knowing and truth.

28) You chose to come to Earth at this precise moment in history to learn, you may have just forgotten it! The earth is going through a huge vibrational shift at the present moment and the age of Aquarius is upon us. This is where individual consciousness expands and global awakening is happening as to who and what we are. We have chosen to live through this huge period of evolution in order to awaken us. That is why there are more souls on the planet than there have ever been; everyone wants to learn! Your soul is always learning, regardless of your habits and lifestyle but what if you became conscious of who you were and why you came here? You could then excel the learning process.

29) Death is not the end. The brain cannot compute this statement as yes, the body will one day decay and return to the earth. Your thinking brain is part of the finite vehicle that will one day perish, so how can it comprehend life after death?

This is where our soul comes in. Our soul is the driver of this vehicle that we currently occupy, but one day, our soul will drop our current body and occupy another form, after all, energy permeates everything. With this in mind, death seems impossible for we are simply infinite masses of loving energy, occupying temporary physical forms. We are spiritual beings choosing to have a human experience which will bring us closer and closer to source energy after each lifetime.

For those of you still in doubt that we are eternal, why is that? Fear perhaps? If we do indeed just die, then nothingness would occur as this is the absence of all life; but nothingness is still something even if it's a black, blank space. Dean said to me that God is space and just is, does his description suggest nothingness as well? Dean's illustration of space suggests that even nothingness needs consciousness in order for it to be conceived and experienced. You could say that it is impossible to become conscious of the unconscious and that nothingness or a void are still an experience. Both statements substantiate that death is a clever illusion made possible by the physical world.

I will be honest, my head hurt after writing that last paragraph. I had to have a tea break to clear my mind, so good luck trying to decipher that paradoxical definition! There are a lot of those in this book, but it's the only way to try and understand this force of energy that beats our hearts. It is something that our human minds will never truly understand and, once again, reinforces that I know nothing in the grand scheme of things!

30) My final point is that I would like to apologise for the use of the word ego. I have used the word ego four hundred and twelve times throughout the book! If there is a world record that exists for the number of times that a word has been written in text, then surely, I should hold this accolade and receive some sort of award! I am truly deserving of this, wouldn't you agree? Or is that just my ego speaking again…

58

SIGNING OFF

Well that's it, my first book written. Who knows if I will write another but I have learnt to never say never. If concepts have appeared too abstract for you in this book, that is fine. In this book, there may be things that you completely disagree with and others you do, either way, thank you for finishing the book. Consider that just because you do not understand something or believe in it doesn't mean that it doesn't exist. When you arrived on this planet you had no concept of physics or food, but they still existed. Gradually you learnt to accept these truths as you grew, the same are with the topics in this book.

I have said this throughout the book, but everything that I have written is my truth and my reality. The truth is the truth and there are only so many ways in which you can write it. What I have written in this book has been written centuries ago by many people, I have just tried to give it my own personal twist and hopefully my backstory could help you relate.

I believe that when you view life from the perspective of the soul and think, *what can I learn?* The present moment makes much more sense. I have poured my heart and soul into this book. I have tried to compile all that I have learnt in two and a half years into one book so that it is all there for you; your spiritual handbook if you like!?

If you were to examine this book and compare chapters, you will see how my consciousness has developed throughout my writing; some points may even seem contradictory. I spoke about how we have been conditioned by society to seek external pleasures, and stated that this will not make us happy. Then in our law of attraction chapter, I encourage you to manifest the life you of your dreams. The Universe offers you contrast out of unconditional love so that you can create whatever life you desire. The real question at hand is your level of attachment to things. Attachment towards material objects creates karma and keeps the reincarnation cycle going. Enjoy the abundance that life has to offer, it's nice to have nice things, but that's where it stops. True happiness comes from within. The truth is that the spiritual path is one of paradox and delicate balance.

Living in the here and now is all we have, but again, there is a paradox. Do not confuse healing and accepting the past with living in it. As mentioned in our healing chapter, processing and accepting the past liberates the subconscious mind. Accepting the past releases karma and allows us to become centred and comfortable in the present moment. Healing the past, which was once the now and still is, allows us to enjoy and savour the present moment.

Another spiritual paradox is to have compassion and love for those who are suffering, but to do it without attachment. I often feel compelled to help people, as I cannot bear to see the suffering of others. At the same time, I can acknowledge the perfection of it all and know that suffering will help that soul to grow. With this realisation, you can become centred and just share the current moment with that fellow soul out of love. This will make you a more effective healer, despite all the noise going on around you. Acceptance of all that is, is true love and humility. As Christ said, "I am in the world, but not of the world." Everything is a fine balancing act, treat the spiritual, and the physical, as one.

Thank you for finishing the extensive book. When I see a large book, it initially puts me off, so I can appreciate that at times it may have been a slog for you. Please understand though that I was trying to cram the secrets of the Universe into text, and this can be pretty heavy work!

If you have been struggling in life or are not happy, I hope that this book can lead you to discover a new path. I hope that I have helped you to see that love really is the answer to everything. Even when I was down and out, the love from others kept me going and kept teaching me. Nan, Deano, Lee, Bella, Sophie, Nicky, Stacey, Becky, Laura, Leanne and Louise all kept me going with their love. I included all of these people in my story because they helped to shape me. Love for others helped me quit my cocaine addiction; love for my body also helped me stop drinking. Love for who I actually am helps me to live each day to the fullest.

I hope that I have encouraged you to think for yourself, if you didn't already, and consider what love is. I say this to you because I was asleep for so long and stumbled through life believing all that I heard from others and the media. Sometimes love is so hard to see on a screen or hear in gossip, but if you scratch beneath the surface, you will see that the perfection of love permeates everything in a cryptic way.

We are all equal and the idea of anyone living a life of misery upsets me, you are worth so much more and then some! I now encourage you to find your own truth and live the life that you truly deserve. Know that love for anything you do will make your dreams a reality. What's stopping you from taking that plunge into the unknown? The ego?

The words 'Write a book' have now manifested into the physical world. By reading this book you have helped to make those words, that I once received during my meditation, become a reality. I wish you nothing but happiness and would like to leave you with a phrase I have been saving for the whole book, my little signing off piece if you will!

The next time that you are about to participate in an event that has the potential to shape the Universe, (all events do) think, does what I'm about to do stimulate my ego or nourish my soul?

So, from a former self-hating, coke-sniffing, stella-swigging, self-sabotaging football lout, to a self-loving, morning-meditating, crystal-collecting, sage-burning, spiritual kinda guy, I bid you farewell.

Namaste.

This simply means that I acknowledge the infinite divinity in you, that I am also a part of, and for that, I bow to you.

I send you love and light, have fun on your journey my friend, Dave.
xxx

Poems

The following are poems that I wrote and read aloud at the funerals of my Nan and Deano.

My Light

A light is something that emits a warm glow,
It can illuminate a room or show a path we did not know.
To me, both of these definitions describe my nan,
For when times were dark for me, she would understand.
She would always offer a solution when I felt lost,
And the warmth she provided for me, alleviated the frost.
Foolishly I would sometimes ignore her advice,
Causing me to stumble in life, and to realise that she was right.
No matter what I did, she never judged,
Instead she would just open her arms and tell me I was loved.
One particular part of you that I will remember were your marvellous cookery skills,
Even to this day, I am inspired by your wholesome, loving meals.
To have known you was truly a gift in my life,
I thank God for putting you there as my happiness, my nan but most of all, my light.

What Is a Friend?

A friend is someone who makes you smile even when you are low,
a friend is someone who can teach you lessons and help you grow.

A friend is someone who is selfless and is always there,
a friend is someone who is generous and will always care.

A friend is someone who makes fun of you and questions your tight clothes,
a friend is someone who makes a joke wherever he goes.

A friend is someone who is always positive and will never grumble,
a friend is someone who teaches you to have strength and always stay humble.

A friend is someone who puts problems into perspective,
a friend is someone who wherever they go are respected.

A friend is someone who makes the worst jokes,
a friend is someone who goes through it all, yet still copes.

A friend is someone that will do a good deed for anybody,
a friend is someone who shows interest in your boring hobby.

A friend is someone who will never hold a grudge,
a friend is someone that no matter what you do will never judge.

A friend is someone who helps you to realise your dreams,
the friend I am talking about is my friend called Dean.

Suggested Reading

The Bhagavad Gita
Three Magic Words by Uell S. Andersen
The Biology of Belief by Bruce Lipton
Quantum Healing by Deepak Chopra
Be Here Now by Ram Dass
Paths to God by Ram Dass
Polishing the Mirror by Ram Dass
Miracle of Love by Ram Dass
Emmanuel's Book Compiled by Pat Rodegast and Judith Stanton
Emmanuel's Book II: The Choice for Love Compiled by Pat Rodegast and Judith Stanton
The Erroneous Zones by Wayne Dyer
There's a Spiritual Solution to Every Problem by Wayne Dyer
Co-Creating at Its Best: A Conversation Between Master Teachers by Wayne Dyer and Esther Hicks
Recovery: Freedom From Our Addictions by Russell Brand
The Power of Now by Eckhart Tolle
A New Earth by Eckhart Tolle
Dying to Be Me by Anita Moorjani
Return to Love by Marianne Williamson
Seth Speaks by Jane Roberts
Tao Te Ching by Lau Tzu
The Little Book of IKIGAI by Ken Mogi
You Can Heal Your Life by Louise Hay
Sapiens: A Brief History of Humankind by Yuval Noah Harari
The Masters of Limitation by Darryl Anka & Bashar

Suicide Helplines

Worldwide
www.befrienders.org

United Kingdom/Ireland
The Samaritans: 116 123
www.samaritans.org

United States
National Suicide Prevention Lifeline: 1 800 273 8255 TALK
www.suicidepreventionlifeline.org

Australia
Lifeline Australia: 13 11 14
www.lifeline.org.au

Printed in Great Britain
by Amazon